MOMENT OF EARTH

Jeremy Hooker

CELTIC STUDIES PUBLICATIONS XIV

Moment of Earth

Poems & Essays in Honour of Jeremy Hooker

Edited by
Christopher Meredith

CELTIC STUDIES PUBLICATIONS

ABERYSTWYTH

2007

First published 2007

Typeset in the Cynrhan type family by CSP-Cymru Cyf

Cover design by CSP-Cymru Cyf

A Catalogue record for this book is available from the British Library.

ISBN-13 978–1–891271–16–8
ISBN-10 1–891271–16–4

Celtic Studies Publications

for customers in North America:

Celtic Studies Publications
c/o The David Brown Book Co.
P. O. Box 511, 28 Main Street
Oakville, CT 06779
USA

editorial correspondence:

CSP-Cymru Cyf
Centre for Advanced Welsh and Celtic Studies
National Library of Wales
Aberystwyth, Ceredigion SY23 3HH
Wales

Contents

List of Illustrations

Cover illustration: an original artwork by Lee Grandjean, who has said of it,

> I wanted to create a design that was not illustrative. Rather my intention was to shape a dynamic fluid pattern; a network that had an obviously intended formal composition, but was also 'shaken' by changes of chance shifts and splashes. There is nature in the process.

Notes on Contributors

Jane Aaron is Professor of English at the University of Glamorgan and co-editor of the series Gender Studies in Wales (University of Wales Press) and Honno Classics. Her latest book, *Nineteenth-Century Women's Writing from Wales: Nation, Gender and Identity*, was published by the University of Wales Press in 2007.

Sam Adams, the author of three monographs in the Writers of Wales series, edited the *Collected Poems* and the *Collected Short Stories* of Roland Mathias and writes a regular Letter from Wales for the Carcanet magazine *PN Review*. His latest book of poems, *Missed Chances*, appeared in 2007.

John Barnie is a poet, fiction writer and essayist. His latest books are: *Sea Lilies: Selected Poems 1984–2003* (2006) and *Trouble in Heaven* (2007). From 1990–2006 he edited the cultural magazine *Planet*.

Tony Brown is Professor of English at Bangor University, where he is also co-director of the R. S. Thomas Study Centre. He was editor of *Welsh Writing in English: A Yearbook of Critical Essays* from 1995–2007. His publications include *R. S. Thomas* in the Writers of Wales series (University of Wales Press, 2006).

Gillian Clarke is a poet, writer, playwright, translator, President of Ty Newydd, and tutor on the M.Phil. course in Creative Writing at the University of Glamorgan. Her poetry is studied for GCSE and A Level throughout Britain. Her latest collection is *Making the Beds for the Dead* (Carcanet).

Tony Conran is a poet, teller of tales for children and ballad scholar. Also (for his sins) an Anglo-welsh critic and translator from the Welsh.

Anne Cluysenaar's poetry includes *Double Helix* (Carcanet 1982) and *Timeslips* (Carcanet 1997). Forthcoming are *Batu-Angas*, a sequence exploring the life and work of the naturalist Alfred Russel Wallace (Seren, spring 2008) and autobiographical poems (Flarestack, October 2008). She founded *Scintilla* and is one of the journal's poetry editors.

Tony Curtis is Professor of Poetry at the University of Glamorgan. He has published anthologies, criticism and nine poetry collections. Recent books include *Wales at War: Critical Essays on Literature and Art* and *After the First Death: an Anthology of Wales and War in the Twentieth Century* (Seren).

Stevie Davies has written extensively on Milton, Vaughan, Shakespeare and Emily Bronte. She is Director of Creative Writing at the University of Swansea. She is a novelist, whose *Element of Water* (2001) was longlisted for the Booker and Orange Prizes. Her latest novel is *The Eyrie* (Orion, 2007).

Roger Ebbatson is visiting professor at Loughborough University. His most recent books are *An Imaginary England* (Ashgate, 2005), and *Heidegger's Bicycle* (Sussex Academic Press, 2006).

Colin Edwards is Senior Lecturer in English and Creative Studies at Bath Spa University. Apart from his interest in Ford and the Modernists, he has strong teaching interests in Creative Writing and Film Studies.

Gavin Edwards is a teacher and researcher in eighteenth and nineteenth century literature at the University of Glamorgan. He previously taught at the University of Sydney and the University of Wales Lampeter. His most recent book is *Narrative Order 1789–1819: Life and Story in an Age of Revolution* (Palgrave).

Matthew Francis is a poet, novelist and critic whose latest collection, *Mandeville*, will be published by Faber in March 2008. He teaches creative writing at Aberystwyth University.

Lee Grandjean (www.leegrandjean.co.uk) is an artist who exhibits widely and is Senior Tutor in sculpture at the Royal College of Art, London. He lives and has his studio in Norfolk.

Philip Gross's poetry collection, *The Egg of Zero* (Bloodaxe) and novel, *The Storm Garden* (OUP) both appeared in 2006, as did *The Abstract Garden*, a collaboration with engraver Peter Reddick, available in a limited edition from The Old Stile Press. He is Professor of Creative Writing at Glamorgan University.

Richard Kerridge is Head of Postgraduate Studies in English Literature and Creative Writing at Bath Spa University. He is co-author of *Nearly Too Much: The Poetry of J. H. Prynne*, co-editor of *Writing the Environment*, and has published articles on writing and environmentalism and contemporary literature. He is currently writing a general introduction to ecocriticism.

Mimi Khalvati has published six poetry collections with Carcanet Press. She is the founder of The Poetry School, where she teaches, and co-editor of the School's anthologies of new writing published by Enitharmon Press. Her most recent book, *The Meanest Flower*, is a PBS Recommendation.

David Lloyd is a poet and fiction writer who teaches at Le Moyne College in Syracuse, USA. His anthology *Other Land: Contemporary Poems on Wales and Welsh-American Experience* is forthcoming from Parthian in 2008.

Peter Lord is an art historian with particular interests in artisan painters, the imaging of industrial society, and theoretical questions arising from the study of visual culture in a nation regarded as marginal to the mainstream. He is the author of the three-volume history, *The Visual Culture of Wales*.

Christopher Meredith is a novelist, poet and translator and teaches at the University of Glamorgan. His novels include *Shifts, Griffri* and *Sidereal Time*. His latest collection of poems is *The Meaning of Flight.*

Wendy Mulford grew up in Wales before moving to Cambridge where she founded the small press Street Editions in 1972. She has worked as a free-lance writer since the mid-eighties; her selected poems, *and suddenly supposing*, were published to critical acclaim in 2002 by Etruscan Books.

Fiona Owen is the author of *Going Gentle, Imagining the Full Hundred* and *O My Swan*. She also co-writes and performs music with Gorwel Owen. She teaches for the Open University and is currently a part-time research student at Bangor University, focusing on ecopoetics.

John Pikoulis recently retired as Senior Lecturer in the Centre for Lifelong Learning in Cardiff University. His publications include *Alun Lewis: A Life*. He is the co-chair of the Welsh Academy.

Sheenagh Pugh (http://sheenagh.googlepages.com) works at the University of Glamorgan. She has published eleven poetry collections, two novels and one critical study of fan fiction (*The Democratic Genre*, Seren, 2005). Her latest collection is *The Movement of Bodies* (Seren, 2005)

Norman Schwenk is a free-lance writer, editor and teacher. His latest book is *The More Deceived*. He is currently at work on a collection of stories, *My Dog can Talk*, and a book of haiku, *Cadillac Temple*.

Sean Street is a writer, poet and broadcaster. He teaches in The Media School at Bournemouth University, where he is Professor of Radio and Director of the Centre for Broadcasting History Research. He has published six collections to date, the most recent being *Radio and Other Poems* (Rockingham Press).

M. Wynn Thomas is Professor of English and Director of CREW (Centre for Research into the English literature and language of Wales), Swansea University. A Fellow of the British Academy, and Chair of the Welsh Books Council, he has published twenty books on American poetry and on Wales's two literatures.

Diana Wallace is Reader in English at the University of Glamorgan. She is the author of *The Woman's Historical Novel: British Women Writers, 1900–2000* (Palgrave, 2005) and *Sisters and Rivals in British Women's Fiction, 1914–39* (Macmillan, 2000).

Jeff Wallace, Professor of Literature and Cultural History at the University of Glamorgan, is the author of *D. H. Lawrence, Science and the Posthuman*, and has published widely in the areas of science and literature, and modernism. He is currently working on the concept of abstraction in modern art and thought.

Foreword

Christopher Meredith

I N the early 1970s, as an undistinguished undergraduate sitting through Eng lit lectures at Aberystwyth, I was struck by the teaching of one youngish lecturer in particular. What was striking had little to do with the lecturer's delivery. His style was without pyrotechnics. In fact (unlike his students) it was sober, thoughtful and rather quiet. But I recall coming out of a lecture on Joyce's *Dubliners* feeling that vertiginous depths of possibility had opened in a text I had thought I was already familiar with, and thinking that there was a bit more to this reading malarkey than I'd supposed. It's barely an exaggeration to say that this was when I started to learn to read.

So I first encountered Jeremy Hooker, as many others have before and since, as a superlative teacher and literary critic who could transform or deepen your view of a text by allowing you to eavesdrop on his intensely attentive and felt reading of it. It was as if the text were a landscape whose meanings and moods you could explore and re-explore. And it was about that same time that he was becoming well known as a poet, with a contribution to the first volume of the Faber *Poetry Introductions* series in 1969 and the collections *The Elements* from Christopher Davies in 1972 and *Soliloquies of a Chalk Giant* from Enitharmon in 1974. These were the first works in a lifetime devoted to literature in general and poetry in particular.

All the biographical notes will tell you that Jeremy Hooker was born in 1941 at Warsash near Southampton and brought up there and at Pennington on the edge of the New Forest, and that he's taught in universities in Wales, England, the Netherlands and the USA. It's clear from his poems that he's travelled elsewhere too, and it's handy, when reading the 'Crossways' poems in *Our Lady of Europe*, to know that he lived and worked for some months on a kibbutz in Israel. An awareness of place, above all else, is central to Hooker's poetry. Just as in his criticism there's a quiet tenacity in his attention to texts, so in his poetry from the

1960s to today, we find, as well as a remarkable consistency of technique, a tenacious focus on place and on the natural and the human and their interplay in specific places. There's often a concern to apprehend the textures of a specific moment on a mountain or a shore, and as often an acute apprehension of the flow of human history and prehistory through a landscape.

Two places in particular, I'd say are important. First there are the liminal and littoral landscapes of the south of England of Hooker's formative years. 'Life could take me anywhere,' he wrote in a journal in 1971, 'but I carry the south inside me.' But second is Wales, and especially west Wales where he lived and worked from about 1965 to the early 1980s. That period, especially from 1969, when he moved with his then wife to the cottage of Brynbeidog, in Llangwyryfon parish, is a crucial phase in his growth as a writer and critic. He's one of a small group of honourable English people to try—and succeed in—grasping something of this complicated country. (Another of them, Peter Lord, is a contributor to this book.) Hooker is the author of some of the most absorbing criticism of Welsh writing in English ever produced. But this period also fed his own poetic engagement with landscape, history, the numinous, and the nature and role of poetry itself. Working among Welsh writers in both languages, he understood the difference of the culture he'd entered, learned from it, and, though he often saw himself as an outsider, he has grown to be partly of it.

A generation has gone by since then, but the importance of this period is borne out when you look at Hooker's poetry and criticism. His two vivid, frank volumes of journals, *Welsh Journal* and *Upstate*, both published in this century, bear witness to its importance too. And in this century Hooker has returned to Wales, though this time to teach at Glamorgan in the south—the south which *I* carry inside me. He'll understand me better than anyone when I say that this volume of poems and essays, apart from celebrating a remarkable career still in progress, also celebrates, a little belatedly, Jeremy Hooker's simultaneous exile and homecoming.

✳

The contributors to this book weren't asked to write specifically about Jeremy Hooker. But it's entirely appropriate that many of the poets have addressed him directly and that the first two critical essays, by Richard Kerridge and Anne Cluysenaar, celebrate him by discussing his poetry. In fact, the broad intention was to gather together work in the two genres in which Hooker excels and which would, how ever glancingly, touch on some of the interests that have preoccupied him. To that end, the poems and essays are very loosely grouped by theme. I'm very aware of some gaps. There's not enough here about David Jones, for instance, and nothing at all about John Cowper Powys, or Edward Thomas, or the American poetry which has been an interest and influence for Hooker. I'm sure, too, that there are other poets and critics who would have wanted to contribute to this book whom we may not even have contacted. I can only apologise to them. In fact, there could have been a whole other volume by different contributors on other topics. As it is, I'm struck by the extraordinary range of material we've elicited. It brings out the realisation that a lifetime in literature can combine singleness of purpose with eclecticism.

I have some important thank yous—first of all to the contributors for their generosity and labours in making this book. That includes the artist and occasional collaborator with Jeremy Hooker, Lee Grandjean, who provided the cover image. Second to Jeremy's wife Mieke, who joined this conspiracy with enthusiasm and helped us to contact many of the contributors and subscribers. Finally, to my co-conspirator Jane Aaron, who put me up to this thing in the first place, and whose understanding of copy-editing is so elastic that she should by right have her name on the title-page as co-editor.

I

Earth and Words

Gillian Clarke

Nettles

For Edward Thomas — and Jeremy Hooker

No old machinery, no tangled chains
of a harrow locked in rust and rising grasses,
nor the fallen stones of ancient habitation
where nettles feed on what we leave behind.
Nothing but an old compost heap
warmed to a simmer of sickly pungency,
lawn clippings we never moved, but meant to,

and can't, now, because nettles have moved in,
and it's a poet's words inhabit this.
And, closer, look! The stems lean with the weight,
the young of peacock butterflies, just hatched,
their glittering black spines and spots of pearl.
And I want to say to the dead, look what a poet sings
to life: the bite of nettles, caterpillars, wings.

Philip Gross

Fantasia on a Theme from IKEA
: seven descants on 'ground',
for Jeremy

WE could see ourselves in one, these half-a-rooms
of dolls'-house lifestyle, life-sized (the books on the shelves
in Swedish). We order by numbers; down in catacombs
a forklift whirrs down the racks of available selves.
We follow the way-marked route at a shuffling shunt
round each turn, like the Ghost Train in a seaside fair—
for miles, then stumble out into…astonishment
to see, after all, it's just a shed. Take a square
box, corrugated over girders; blue and yellow paint;
a brown-field site, a name… And it has become
a world, born of economies of scale, ground rent,
need and desire: the product of the sum
of (as real and recurrent as mist from the stream
the car park buried) *us*—the human dream.

§

Dream on! The girl in the car park snaps
her phone shut. End of story. She folds him away,
the face on a screen like a make-up mirror; slaps
him in her hipster pocket, snug—which may
be as close as he'll get (and yet not know)
to what he's dreamed of. Her, she's had enough.
Behind her, billboards plead: Dream *this*. So
much they need us, dreams. We are such stuff:
flesh, matter. No wonder they can't look away,
all those ideals and angels. Where else to found
their celestial cities but on grit and clay,
hormones and DNA? Where else to ground
their being? The phone in her pocket chirrs, cheep
cheep. Poor lovebird. She puts it to sleep.

3

§

Sleep is something like it: what ground does
beneath our soles. It breathes. Sometimes it seems
to shift or shrug. It's not thinking, and not about us.
We are its slight disturbance - like most dreams
the product of qualms, hungers, physical itches
and aches, sometimes bearing gifts, vignettes
from the flipside of sense; more often, repetitious
buttonholings, boredom. Ground, like sleep, forgets
for a living. It's not that *the worm forgives
the plough*; it gives it *no mind.* (Pain
occurs, in passing.) Faced with a creature that lives
in, digests, shits, *creates* earth…how to explain
your self, this figure that steps from the ground and confronts
you in your own shape, saying: *This, this once?*

§

Once there was a figure who lived in a ground
(the plot was small but it was grand)
with a ditch and a bank and a burial mound.
I'll sing you a lay of the lie of the land,
derry down. He watched the red sun sink.
His shadow grew tall and skewed and thin.
It moved; he stayed; it made him think
and now the past was about to begin
as he looked for himself: where had he gone
while he stood there still as a standing stone
or a figure in chalk, oh, once upon
a down, derry down? But how he'd grown.
Thus time. Space. Relativity.
And so we are lonely, and elsewhere, and free.

§

Freehand, by eye, the master of his art
describes a circle. Without words. And again,
left handed. Bows to the assembled court
in silence. Outside, medieval rain
slows to a tick. Torch-flicker. *Fetch*
the instruments! A glance, cleric to lord,
lord to sergeant at arms. And now they watch
as the charcoal marks are measured, and declared
to be true. Too true. The verdict: theft
from God's perfection—no gift this, but craft,
a dark art. Guilty. Seized and bound.
Outside, a raindrop in the ditch articulates
no end of circles. Tethered to its stake
a cow crops circles from the thistly ground.

§

Groundlings, in the pit. Above, tier on tier,
to the gods, to a circle of sky. It's our sweat
and guffaws, our pulse, that oils the gears
that turn the Globe. The wheel of fire. (Yet
soft, what light?) The music of the spheres
sounds frail without a ground bass. It needs us
like we need a good grand downfall. Cheers.
Our revels now. We sway out, word-drunk, a tinnitus
hiss in our ears, the palpable hush of our blood
or, suddenly, the river. Sounds, crisp, far
apart. Mist does that. Breathes from the mud.
Brings things back. Where the lost streams are.
The ground's half water, like us. Piss at the wall,
slops from a window. It accepts us, one and all.

§

All Souls, tonight… Will that be *us*, those finished
articles, stacked round the shop floor of this life
gazing in: *souls*? Tempting to hope, as we're diminished
bit by (age, chance, illness, surgeon's knife)
bit. We will not be mended. Is that *growing*
up, at last, at least—to know we've begun
to disperse (did, from the start), our moments flowing
out, into and through each other, property of no one
any more than words or water…and into the ground-
swell of the sea like hills, or hills like sea,
in which we'd hoped to stand out like that down-
land figure, though he's just a chalk line round
an absence? We're elsewhere, we're home, if we
could step back far enough, if we could see.

Sam Adams

Poem

for Jeremy

We shook hands in the old way, over books,
I, new to Usk's deep, twice-daily silted trench,
Reaching out to you by Beidog's stream,
A quartz vein slicing down from Mynydd Bach.

Water, for you, sets memory adrift,
Sliding down Itchen, New Forest brooks,
Southampton Water, to yet deeper tides –
Aquamarine flux of time.

I see you, aeons past, beside a shallow sea,
Half-a-mile or more of chalk
Already laid beneath your feet,
With flints and fossils from the great chalk main.

What I meant to say, but haven't said
Till now, is that my boyhood river
Had eels, mud-coloured fish with bristles
For the dark and, once, a silver prodigy –
Solitary trout gasping in a putrid shallow pool.

There was, of course, clean rain, which strung
A cleft in distant hills, advanced and rapped
The sounding boards of roofs and windows:
Harp-like the cleft, strung with the falling rain.

And heaped beyond our garden wall lay tattered
Dog-eared volumes of grey shale, survivors
Of an ancient holocaust. Each split leaf
Revealed the burnished shadow of a fern
As if sun-printed on the stone.

'Leaves that we say are dead'
Jeremy Hooker's ecological imagination

Richard Kerridge

PLACE, land, landscape and nature are big preoccupations in Jeremy Hooker's poetry. In his literary criticism, too, place and what it means to writers has been an abiding concern. It is the topic with which he is most clearly identified and to which he has most often returned. Place, land, landscape, nature: each term brings a different conceptual, aesthetic and political orientation to, essentially, the same subject. Can I add ecology to the list?

Contemporary writing about place and nature can scarcely avoid 'the environment' as a subject, and it is one that poses fundamental challenges to traditional attitudes and genres. Do they help or hinder our understanding of the ecological crisis we face? Must they be revived or revised, or both? Hooker has seldom written of this crisis explicitly, yet the preoccupations of his work lead inevitably, now, to environmentalism, and, given his long poetic and critical meditation on different meanings of place, nature and home, his work should be rewarding territory for ecocritics. What kind of vision of place does he express, and is it at all ecological in character?

How does nature manifest itself in the poetry? This is from 'Present':

> The father walks under the trees
> with his son,
> who is laughing on his back.
>
> And we call this *now*,
> when the man stands still
> in the woods in summer,

on leaves that we say are dead.[1]

We are wrong to say that the leaves are dead, the poem implies, because their falling and decomposition is a stage in the continuing life of trees. Releasing its leaves enables the tree to grow, and their mulching down fills the soil with nutriments, in the energy flow that ecologists identify as the most essential form of inter-relationship between different life-forms in an ecosystem. By implication, a human life too, though it comes to an end, is part of larger cycles and processes that do not. More tenuously, the poem also suggests that if we are wrong to say that the leaves are dead, we may be wrong in a similar way to call the particular, present moment 'now', since it is nourished and constituted by continuities with the past. This is Hooker's other great subject.

Gerard Manley Hopkins's 'Spring and Fall' seems to be a presence behind this and several other poems about trees and falling leaves in *Their Silence a Language* (1993), a collaborative work by Hooker and the sculptor Lee Grandjean. Amongst Hooker's poems and short passages of prose appear drawings by Grandjean and photographs of his sculptures. Hooker's poems and passages are about walking in the New Forest and the forest's place in his life. In crude summary, it is fair to say that Hooker's contributions are very firmly rooted in the realism and specificity of detailed observation and particular moments, while Grandjean's non-realist drawings and sculptures introduce an element of humanist and quasi-Christian symbolism. When the two are put together, Grandjean seems to offer an expansive, abstract and symbolic extension of the realist poems, which in turn, differently expansive, give the abstract sculptures and drawings a connection with the time-bound real. In an afterword,[2] Hooker describes the collaboration, explaining that the works were expressive of the lifelong concerns of each artist. The different works can stand alone, and have done so, but the collaboration enabled the two artists to offer interpretations, implicit extensions, of each other's meaning, leaving an inviting 'space' between the two kinds of work for the reader's interpretative response.

The poem after 'Present' is 'Windless Leaf-Fall, With Emily':

> We find a small, clear pool
> of water on a bed

---

[1] Jeremy Hooker, *The Cut of the Light: Poems 1965–2005* (London: Enitharmon Press, 2006), 206. All further references to Hooker's collected poems are from this edition, hereafter abbreviated as *CL*.

[2] Jeremy Hooker and Lee Grandjean, *Their Silence a Language* (London: Enitharmon Press, 1993), 75–79.

of dead, golden-brown leaves. (*CL*, 207)

Here there is no hesitation in calling the leaves dead, but there is that glint of golden, so inseparable from the brown of earthy decay that the words too cannot be separated. The poem seems to echo Hopkins's ambivalent love of variegated natural colours, dapplings, stipplings and complex patterns of light and leaf-shade in woodland, but, though Hooker, like Hopkins, is fascinated and moved by sudden flares of bright colour, associated with letting go or taking flight, these flares cannot signify transcendence as they do in Hopkins. They do not overcome and burn up the complex mixtures, compromises and ambivalences of the earthy colours. Hooker is not caught, like Hopkins, between love of the variegated world and joy at its fiery dissolution. Dazzle isn't what he wants from light. He doesn't yearn to be overpowered. At the end of this poem, the leaves dance, and the father and child too, but not a whirling, ecstatic dance; this is *windless* leaf-fall.

Flight and dance in several of these poems hint at the possibility of ecstatic release, but the release is not separation from earth and solidity, which are often represented by wood and by complex, textured, subdued colours. In 'Elusive Spirit', there is the 'sudden/ sword dance of one bracken frond', but the bracken stem leads the eye down to the leaf-mould (and, anyway, this dance probably brings to mind Sergeant Troy's flashing sword in the hollow amid the ferns, and look what happened to him). The other whirling flights in this poem are similarly inseparable from earth and its colours:

> dark butterfly that whirls up
> fast and high, out of sight –
> tap tap tap on dead bark,
> the yaffle that flies away
> crying his ancient laugh. (*CL*, 195)

The butterfly is a woodland species, dark in colour; the woodpecker gets his nourishment from invertebrates that live in dead bark and rotted wood. He goes by a traditional name for the common Green Woodpecker, 'yaffle', from village-demotic, a name that roots the bird in locality and belongs to comic alliterative homeliness rather than heroic, elevated diction (as the word's derivation the OED gives the 'echoic' relation to the bird's 'laughing' call). The yaffle laughs. His flight is an alarmed dash that becomes a bouncing glide, short and visibly losing momentum: just enough to carry him to another tree. He doesn't soar like the windhover.

Hooker is fond of this bird, and this name. In an earlier poem, 'Yaffle', from *Solent Shore* (1978), the woodpecker's laugh rings out over the natural detritus, ground litter that is death but also life, to which Hooker's eye frequently drops: 'leafmould/ Brine and dead crab' (*CL*, 101). At bitter moments this detritus is waste and filth, as in 'Black on Gold' in *Their Silence a Language*:

> A dead butterfly flutters in a breeze,
> dances at the window in a filthy web.
> Even when I was a boy (he thinks)
> walking with a rod in April among the trees
> I tasted filth. (*CL*, 186)

What transmutes the fertile detritus to filth seems to be blocked creativity: moments, or, as here, nightmares in which the poet fears a death of his art that will take it outside the energy flow, the cycle of renewal in which the necessary passing and letting go of experience makes new poetry grow. In 'Yaffle', the woodpecker's laugh betokens an exuberant carelessness. He is the 'Don't-give-a-damn/ woodpecker', circling the walker, jerking the man's eyes up from the littered ground; eluding those eyes but leading them to rest in a new place. Butterfly and yaffle, in 'Elusive Spirit', take flight suddenly but in doing so do not transcend the grounding of ordinary life. They fly, but their kinship, and ecological co-evolution, is with the solid, rooted trees that cannot leave the earth.

Angels do appear in Hooker's work, as a recurrent motif, but they too, after a first startling flourish, are revealed as inseparable from the earth. Birds for a moment become angels; angels turn back into birds. There is this one, in *Our Lady of Europe* (1997):

> It is not what we expect
> when a greenshank flying down
> from a fence post lifts its wings
> to reveal white feathers, and is
> for that moment, an angel. (*CL*, 228)

The poem, 'In Drenthe', is about a Dutch landscape whose flatness deceives the walkers into expecting too little, but deceives them kindly, to delight them the more. If the greenshank makes an unlikely angel at first thought, the comparison forces us to search for the vision, thinking harder, if we know, about what a greenshank is like, until we see the two slender wings opening either side of the bird's head in inverted V shapes, like a medieval painted angel's wings. The comparison makes us work to see the bird as well as the angel. In 'Groundwork', the long poem that opens *Adamah* (2002), Norfolk, also (terribly) flat, is 'a land of angels/ carved from wood, and angels/sculpted in stone' (*CL*, 305). The wooden angels in the hammerbeam roof of a church seem to have no congregation to inspire to imagined flight, but if they did, the flight would not be into the heavens but 'swooping/ like gulls in the wake of the plough' (*CL*, 305); like the yaffle's, a flight that even in its exhilarating movement reaffirms the need to return to earth for food and rest.

✷

This impulse to look down, and refusal to banish the earthy and ordinary, might lead us to Hooker's most explicit contribution to ecocriticism, the concept of 'ditch vision'. He introduced the term in 1999, in an article on Richard Jefferies and John Cowper Powys in the rather specialist pages of *The Powys Journal* (Vol IX, 1999, 14–29). It is his name for the characteristic that most distinguishes the British non-fiction nature writing tradition from the North American. In purist definition, and in the US Wilderness Act of 1964, what the Americans call 'wilderness' is land that has not been altered by human activity. This definition is controversial, mainly because of its implication in colonial culture's erasure of the presence of Native Americans in many if not all of these territories. The term raises the same problems in Scotland, where the lands that might now qualify as 'wilderness' are mostly those from which highlanders were expelled in the Clearances. More loosely, though, 'wilderness' means the vast expanses of mountain, desert and roadless forest in North America that enable the intrepid hiker to achieve real distance from human society. Wilderness offers, in addition, a sense of danger, in the remoteness from rescue services and the possibility of exciting, elemental encounters with dangerous animals.

In contrast, the British seeker of Romantic solitude in nature, especially in England and perhaps more especially still in the Southern England that Hooker sees as his poetic home ground, will have great difficulty in finding any place of wild seclusion that is not liable to disturbance by other walkers or nearby traffic; hardly anywhere that is more than a few hours' walk from a town. Nature and seclusion have to be found in the midst of society. This problem, if it is one, was nowhere near so acute in Jefferies' time, yet it is this writer about nature in farmed fields and urban or suburban margins who, for Hooker, represents the domestic wildness of the English tradition. Jefferies' essay 'The Pageant of Summer' (1883), in which a ditch of green rushes is lovingly described, seems to have prompted Hooker to come up with 'ditch vision' as his term for the English imaginative habit of playing with scale in order to discover wildness and infinity in small spaces. The term conjures an image of childhood, too: the absorbed gaze of a child to whom the local world has not yet come to seem small and familiar, and specifically— perhaps now rather archaically, sad to say—the characteristic boyish love of exploring ponds, woods and wastelands. There is a perception now that urban society, with its traffic congestion, over-protective parents and addiction to television and computers, is cutting children off from direct experience of wild nature, even of the 'ditch vision' type. This deprivation now goes, I'm afraid, by the name of Nature-Deficit Disorder. For an ecocritical account of it, see Richard Louv's *Last Child in the Woods.3*

Childhood, in the Romantic imagination, was to be contemplated with joy because children, trailing clouds of glory, retained for a few precious years their sense of living in an infinite world. Adulthood in general, and modern, urban life in particular, would deprive them of this. Wild nature was where that sense of the infinite, in space and time and in the possibilities of selfhood, could be brought to life again. 'Ditch vision', as a concept, continues these Romantic traditions, adding two more elements. The finding of infinity in a small and ordinary place is, in the Wordsworthian tradition, an antidote to the influence of reductive and Cartesian science; the science that treated living organisms as mechanisms. But 'ditch vision' seems cognate as well with Charles Darwin's contemplation of his 'tangled bank' at the end of *The Origin of Species*. A way to a positive view of science is tentatively opened up in the idea that the endless and cosmic process of evolution can be observed, almost made palpable, in such a small, homely, near at hand space. Part of Darwin's reason for writing that passage may well have been a wish for reconciliation with the Romantic imagination. The other element 'ditch vision' brings is a note of ironic self-depreciation or self-mockery; it is *vision*, sure, but *ditch* vision.

One can see how the idea of 'ditch vision' arose from Hooker's poetic and critical interests, but insofar as it suggests immobility—a watcher held, enthralled, in one place, only looking down—it does not describe Hooker's own poetry. The picture is of someone standing safely outside a miniature world and gazing in, and staying put, preoccupied with the local. This only partially illuminates the poetry, and implies a rather different poetic form from Hooker's. 'One tree, a beech, held us for a long time', begins one of the prose passages in *Their Silence a Language,4* and throughout the description that follows this opening I feel the slight tension of a walker who is, precisely, being held, interested in the tree but also wanting to pull free and walk on. The poetic eye in these poems is nearly always an eye on the move, turning to catch, or not quite catch, new events and visitations in a world full of movement. Many of the poems are from the viewpoint of a walker moving through the landscape rather than holding it steadily in view. This is not the

---

3   Richard Louv, *Last Child in the Woods: Saving Our Children from Nature–Deficit Disorder* (Chapel Hill: Algonquin Books, 2005).
4   Hooker and Grandjean, *Their Silence a Language*, 32.

prospect poem, surveying landscape from an elevation, nor is it Wordsworthian recollection in tranquillity. The walk carries the poem on. Hooker's primary tense is the present. Subjectivity is in motion here, and always in the process of dissolving and being remade. Slow growth is at work, in the self's deep intellectual, emotional and cultural gravitation towards what feels like a destined place, but this slow persistence is counterpointed by sudden, sharp, surprise encounters. The contemplation of trees, with their rooted bulk and invisible, slow growth, is disturbed by the startled flight of the yaffle. So the two forces that Hooker's poetry observes, and that in combination give it its dialectical character, are attachment and movement: deep continuity of allegiance and the disruptive contingency of worldly perception.

He is fascinated and deeply touched by the painful alienation felt by late-Romantic nature-lovers such as Richard Jefferies, Edward Thomas and Ivor Gurney. Distressed by the transformations wrought by modernity upon rural England, these writers yearned for a community that would accept them and with which they could identify. Their longing was also for continuity with the historical past, and they tended to imagine and idealise a Shakespearean England of village life that modernity was destroying or had destroyed. All three, in different ways, wrote a late-Romantic pastoral in which nature and historic rural life, as they imagined it, were closely associated in meaning; both were unattainable worlds of organic wholeness, unselfconscious vitality and merriness. The philosopher Kate Soper has called this yearning 'the envy of immanence'.5

Hooker feels it too, but cautions against it as a too dominant mood, one that excludes all others and ends up loving and fortifying the sense of social alienation to which it was a response:

> What one feels very strongly in some of Jefferies' essays is the hysteria which derives inevitably from the love of nature becoming an end in itself. He is free from this in his books on country people [...], but where he is alone with nature the vivid intensity of a love that is more than half pain cries aloud his need for a measure of ordinariness, of human contact and a work-a-day role in communion with people. In my view, the lack of these things contributes to his nervous exhaustion, for he knows, perhaps unconsciously, that there is no place for him, as a writer, in rural society. The worship of nature that transcends nature, or is diffused in it, in Wordsworth, becomes in Jefferies and Edward Thomas, concentrated in it: it is an egress of emotion, a bleeding away of

---

5   Soper used this phrase in a keynote address to the inaugural conference of the UK branch of the Association for the Study of Literature and Environment, at Bath Spa University College in 1998.

energy, that offers in return only a fugitive—and sometimes shattering—
ecstasy. They find in their own work little normality, such as that found in the
fellowship of a common labour, in which to recover bodily, mentally, and
emotionally their expenditure of energy.[6]

This judgement is from 'The Sad Passion' (1970), an early article about Jefferies
and Thomas that seems to have been of continuing and troubling importance in
Hooker's mind, so that more than once in later essays he picks up points from it
for adjustment. How, he asks, is the love of nature, so often identified, since
Romanticism and urbanisation, with solitary alienation, to be re-integrated with
social life, so that it does not isolate the lover still further, as happened to Jefferies
and, to a lesser extent, Thomas? It is an urgent question for environmentalists
today, whose main political problem is their inability to get through to mass
popular consciousness. The question takes us back to 'ditch vision' and Hooker's
distancing of British nature writing from the North American tradition of
Thoreau, Abbey and Dillard: the tradition of searching for spiritual revelation in
wilderness separated liminally from social space. But 'ditch vision' is only part of
the solution, for it still leaves the nature lover immobile and facing away from
social culture. 'Ditch vision' must enter into dialectical and dialogic relations with
other experiences.

The Hooker of 'The Sad Passion' seems to regard the late-Romantic love of
nature as a necessary recourse in an industrialising society, but also a kind of
symptom. He seems to seek a revived Georgic, rather than Romantic, pastoral, or
at least a reconciliation of the two. So he says that what the alienated nature-lover
lacks is 'ordinariness', 'work-a-day' experience and a community formed by shared
labour. Without this, it is as if a whole life could consist of epiphanies. Such a life
would not be tenable in emotional terms, political terms or, interestingly, to take
up Hooker's imagery, in terms of energy flow.

Industrial-capitalist society gives most people in mature industrialised societies
unprecedented material comforts and longer lifespans, but at the expense of forms
of labour that alienate them from each other, from nature and from their own full
provision of natural senses and impulses. This is the problem, according to the
Marxist diagnosis shading into the environmentalist diagnosis. Hooker is quite
close, in implication, to the arts-and-crafts vision of William Morris, or the recent
organic farming and 'slow food' movements, as an alternative, but closer still to
classically Modernist notions of art as the only possibility of salvation from
alienation. So there is a search, throughout his work, for the kind of art that would
begin to make the right connections; art that shades into physical labour for the

---

6   Jeremy Hooker, *The Poetry of Place* (Manchester: Carcanet Press, 1982), 21–22.

provision of material sustenance, and into the human encounter with natural forms and our own naturalness. Hence his fascination with wood sculpture; and hence his comparison of his own poetry to that art. From 'Black on Gold':

> He dreams he is a sculptor hacking
> at the block that is himself.
> It is black, black as rainwater
> from the stump of the tree of knowledge.
> Let me let in the gold (he weeps)
> but the wood rots under his hand. (*CL*, 187)

This is the nightmare version, Hooker's version, perhaps, of the hysteria he says afflicted Jefferies. On the principle that it is wrong to call the leaves dead, it is also wrong to feel horror and panic at the rotting of the wood; that is, horror at mortality. But in nightmare moments we do, and elsewhere, in a different mood, the gold he is trying to force into the crumbling wood becomes itself the sign of mortality and energy flow, when it is the 'dead, golden-brown leaves' of 'Windless Leaf-Fall, With Emily'. At calmer moments, when he can accept this association between epiphanic beauty (gold) and energy flow, the sculpture, and by extension the poetry, find their continuity with other, 'work-a-day' kinds of labour, as here in 'Groundwork':

> Just at this spot,
> standing in a field
> near the barn-studio
> where oak trunks
> are delivered, hitting
> the brick floor with a 'dumb' sound
> that pleases you. (*CL*, 299)

'Barn-studio' is like 'golden-brown': the inseparability of the words means something. In many contexts 'barn-studio' might have the ring of a sneer, mocking the middle-class urban second-homer in a village, who turns the tools of pre-industrial agriculture into objects of nostalgic prettification. But Hooker is attempting to assert a real continuity between the old and new uses of the building (probably Lee Grandjean's studio), which leads us to a continuity, also, between the new sculptures to be made from these oaks and the wooden angels in the church roof whose significance was once so public and communal.

Jonathan Bate, in his work of ecocriticism *The Song of the Earth*, discusses the word 'sawing' as used in Edward Thomas's poem 'Home', and remarks on the fact that this word for a human labour that reshapes the wood and in doing so becomes intimate with it (this is definitely not industrial sawing, as Bate points out) is also a traditional word for the song of the thrush.7 These are the continuities Hooker wishes to find: between art as labour and dwelling as labour, between the artist, therefore, and the communities formed by such labour, and between both kinds of human labour and natural life like that of the bird. He can't quite *unselfconsciously* call the woodpecker 'yaffle', but he can do so as an expression of his wish for continuity with popular community and history, and perhaps, like the bird itself, the word takes him by surprise, coming naturally, suddenly making it easy, but then flying away with a laugh.

In search of these continuities, Hooker writes an English Modernist pastoral deeply influenced by two Anglo-Welsh poets, Edward Thomas and David Jones. His formal antidote to the bleeding-away of energy he diagnosed in Jefferies is the use of Modernist 'open' forms that he learned, especially, from Jones and George Oppen. They enable him to accept the intensities, and visionary quality, of 'ditch vision' without being made immobile by it—to gaze intently and then allow himself to be interrupted and carried away; to be in the world rather than survey it from outside.

*

But how ecological is his vision—or how close to ecology?

In some ways, the combination of concerns and poetic forms described above is consistent with an ecological perspective. Life forms are interdependent, continually making and remaking each other in co-evolution. Ecology came into being as a scientific discipline because of the perception that it was misleading to remove any creature from this dynamic ecological context in order to isolate it for laboratory study. Creatures, plants and natural processes have to be studied in the field, and understood by means of ecological concepts of relation, such as energy flow, food chain and niche. Of course, the poetry is not analytical in this way, nor does it display scientific understanding, except very occasionally. One of those occasions is worth pausing over.

Between the passage about the oak trunks in the barn-studio and the one about hammerbeam roof angels and gulls following the plough, 'Groundwork' has this:

> What I want to argue
> is that poetry and sculpture
> are life sciences.

---

7   Jonathan Bate, *The Song of the Earth* (London: Picador, 2000), 275–276.

It is not that we express
some finished
or constructed self.

The point is to step out
into the space between.

＊

I like the face of this
theoretical physicist
which appeared
                an abstraction
from an unknown and undefinable
totality
and has vanished
leaving us a theory –
a theatre—
in which we sense the whole

Shall we say, though,
a molecule of carbon dioxide
that crosses a cell boundary
                into a leaf
suddenly *comes alive*
and a molecule of oxygen
released to the atmosphere
suddenly *dies.*
Or shall we regard
life itself
as belonging
to a totality. (CL, 303–4)

Hooker's directly stated desire, in what sounds like the opening line of a lecture or academic article, is to align his poetry, and the sculpture to which he often compares it (especially the work of Lee Grandjean), with certain sciences. Next comes an explicit renunciation of the idea of a *completed* self, whether natural or culturally constructed; or, rather, of the idea that artistic achievement might supply this completion where other natural and cultural resources have failed. This sounds like a renunciation, after all, of that early Modernist aspiration that art might heal the wounds to both society and psyche inflicted by modernity, relieving the modern self of its terrible sense of incompleteness and its restless search for wholeness. But, as we have seen, Hooker seems to retain a form of this desire. The crucial difference, aligning him to some extent with an eco-postmodernism, is in the meaning of his open poetic forms. Relief is to be found by giving up the idea of completeness and relishing the step into the spaces opened by incompleteness.

He then, in the passage from 'Groundwork', connects this embracing of incompleteness with certain ideas from theoretical physics. The quotation in italics comes from the physicist David Bohm (1917–94). Presumably the face is Bohm's too. Bohm was a systems theorist and complexity theorist who argued that elementary particles seem so interdependent and inter-related that it is not tenable to think of them as other than a continuous stream, an 'open system' in the sense that it is always in flux and every part is potentially able to lead to every other. He called this system 'the implicate order', and in his book *Wholeness and the Implicate Order* (1980), from which Hooker's quotation comes, he proposed a number of adjustments to our conceptual apparatus to help us perceive that stream, including a radical shift of emphasis from nouns to verbs. If I give a bit more of Bohm's sentence, the sense becomes clearer: '…any describable event, object, entity etc., is an abstraction from an unknown and undefinable totality of flowing movement'.[8] As a theory of the deep physical substance of life, Bohm's 'implicate order' is clearly more consistent with ecology than with the scientific isolation of creatures for study, and Bohm explicitly lent his support to environmentalist arguments for a holistic understanding of the global ecosystem rather than a heedless concentration on economic growth. The poetic form that seems most in tune with Bohm's idea is the Modernist 'open field'.

In the rhetorical question that follows the quotation from Bohm, however—it is another version of the question whether we should call the leaves dead— Hooker's specific scientific reference is not to particle physics but to an ecological process, a familiar one that is essential to the maintenance of our ecosphere. It is photosynthesis: we come back to leaves. Hooker's lines ask us a question about photosynthesis, so it is worth reminding ourselves what the process is: the action by which plants absorb energy from sunlight and use it in their pigments to 'fix' the carbon dioxide they take from the atmosphere, converting the carbon gas to sugars and other carbohydrates. With these they sustain themselves and provide the sustenance of human beings and animals. Molecular oxygen, too, is produced in the reaction; the present atmosphere of the earth is the product of millions of years of photosynthesis. Planting trees is suggested as part of the solution to climate change because photosynthesis extracts from the atmosphere some of the carbon dioxide our burning of fossil fuels pumps out. Destroying huge areas of forest, such as the

---

8   David Bohm, *Wholeness and the Implicate Order* (1980; London: Routledge, 2002), 62.

Amazon and Indonesian rainforests, makes global warming worse in two ways: by releasing the carbon previously fixed in those trees and by depriving the world of the future carbon fixing those trees would have provided.

Thinking about photosynthesis reveals the plant not as a separate organism but as a function of these ceaseless processes of material exchange. I said above that plants 'use' energy from light to fix carbon, but that is to suggest that the plant exists prior to the process and 'uses' it. Independent, active agency is attributed to the plant and passivity to the energy, as if the user could take up the tool and put it down at will. Another, more Bohmian or Gaian way of putting it is that such processes are not a matter of some things being users and others merely used. The plant does not exist except as an effect of the process, an unceasing action that the different elements perform together, a stage in the circulation of energy that makes up a larger system or organism, the ecosphere.

Hooker's question in the poem is a challenge to the exclusiveness of our insistence on divisions, not only between live and dead things (at the back of his mind may be Edward Thomas's preoccupation with death) but also between the things themselves: entities, events and human individuals. He is asking—this consistently self-conscious and autobiographical poet, acutely sensitive to the struggle of the self to find its home—what the emotional, and by implication the cultural and political, consequences might be of allowing physical interdependency and energy flow into our imaginations much more. This is the proto-environmentalism of Hooker's work, almost becoming explicit in the passage I have looked at here.

*

I want to finish with a word about the colour red in his poetry. It always—or that's my impression—appears suddenly. This abrupt red means the sudden and rapid draining of what was blocked. Blood spills, meaning death, and, in the description of Jefferies' 'hysteria', meaning the dissipation of energy for no return, though from the ecological perspective the blood will nourish other life forms and so the energy will flow somewhere. But these sharp appearances of red often bring human death to the foreground, and thus polarize, shockingly, the different perspectives of human mortality and ecological continuity.

Hooker (like his painter father) is a colourist, adept at positioning red as a sudden small flare in drab surroundings. The effect needs the drabness, and needs the red to spring out of quietly descriptive lines, the 'ordinary', the 'work-a-day'. Sometimes there seems to be a direct invocation of Christ's wound, and I have not so far touched upon another preoccupation of Hooker's, the continuing meaning of Christian symbols in a secular world: another thing we should not regard as dead, though his is a resolutely secular perspective. Some of Lee Grandjean's wood figures seem to be crucifixes coming to life, flexing, sprouting, sending out roots or beginning to dance. Red is life too, as here when a sycamore bud gives us bird foetus and human foetus as well:

> curving
> into soft, closed beaks
> that open on their tongues
> and now unfold small hands:
> wrinkled blood red leaves,
> fresh and glistening
> damp (*CL*, 128)

Or here, in a poem in memory of Hooker's friend the poet Les Arnold, a snapshot memory or perhaps a real photograph:

> a man full of life
> pulling a cork
> pouring in our glasses
> red wine. (CL, 372)

Embodied Knowledge
in the Cutting Touch:
A Matrix in Jeremy Hooker's
The Cut of the Light

Anne Cluysenaar

It may be that for each poet there's one imaginative matrix, which everything life brings—new experience, knowledge, the capacity to renew, to reshape, to see again—activates. In a sense, the poet is at work on one poem, or, as I prefer to say, a body of poetry. But the metaphor—it's more than a metaphor: the nature of a matrix is to give birth—must not be allowed to exclude the possibility of real change, in the poet and in the poetry, or of the revelation that transforms.

Jeremy Hooker, Upstate.[1]

JEREMY Hooker concluded his early collection *Solent Shore* with a poem which comes to mind when I consider the distinctive qualities of his poetic achievement.[2] Although 'Gull on a Post' may appear a relatively simple poem when read in isolation,[3] I want to argue that it embodies perceptions central to Hooker's poetic experience, a matrix he has since explored in greater depth. This essay seeks to suggest ways in which this poem may become, as we deepen our understanding of its themes, 'a space dense with meanings'.[4]

---

1 Jeremy Hooker, *Upstate, An American Journal* (Exeter: Shearsman Books, 2007), 85.
2 Jeremy Hooker, *Solent Shore* (Manchester: Carcanet Press, 1978).
3 Jeremy Hooker, 'Gull on a Post', *The Cut of the Light, Poems 1965–2005* (London: Enitharmon, 2006), 105–6; hereafter CUT.
4 Jeremy Hooker, quoted by him in the essay 'Reflections on Ground', *Scintilla*, 10 (2006), 36; hereafter SCINT.

a space dense with meanings

GULL ON A POST

Gull on a post firm
In the tideway—how I desire
The gifts of both!

Desire against the diktat
Of intellect: be single,
You who are neither.

As the useful one
That marks a channel, marks
Degrees of neap and spring;
Apt to bear jetties
Or serve as a mooring;
Common, staked with its like.

Standing ever
Still in one place,
It has a look of permanence.

Riddled with shipworm,
Bored by the gribble,
In a few years it rots.

Desire which tears at the body
Would fly unconstrained
Inland or seaward; settle
At will—but voicing
Always in her cry
Essence of wind and wave,
Bringing to city, moorish
Pool and ploughland,
Reminders of storm and sea.

Those who likened the soul
To a gull, did they ever
Catch the eye of a gull?

Driven to snatch,
Fight for slops in our wake.

Or voice a desolation
Not meant for us,
Not even desolate,
But which we christen.

Folk accustomed to sin,
Violent, significant death,
Who saw even in harbour
Signs terrible and just,
Heard in their cries
Lost souls of the drowned.

Gull stands on a post
In the tideway; I see

No resolution; only
The necessity of flight
Beyond me, firm
Standing only then.

This poem travels between two instances (in verses 1 and 12) of an image which draws into relation gull, post and tideway. The second half of verse one establishes a sense of inner conflict. The watcher is conscious of desiring the gifts of both gull and post, two such different things. The exclamation mark conveys a certain urbane awareness of the reader's presence, even a self-deprecating touch of humour. But the tone becomes more serious when 'the diktat / of intellect' opposes desire by commanding the watcher to adopt a singleness not true to experience. From this point on, the poem seeks to elucidate the genesis of the desire to possess 'the gifts of both'.

The post 'marks a channel' in the tide, a 'way' useful to shipping. It is one of many. Its 'look of permanence' is misleading: 'In a few years it rots.' In so far as the watcher might share its gifts, he may expect to be socially useful and to experience a sense of 'Standing ever / Still in one place' as the tide rises and falls. But he will also be 'staked' with his 'like'. It seems that these considerations lead to a sense that, as the post is 'bored by the gribble', so 'Desire…tears at the body'. If desire 'tears', it is surely because this desire is not only a desire to share the gifts of the post but also to 'fly unconstrained' like the gull. As desire is transformed to something like a gull, flying 'inland or seaward', the watcher recognises that it will always be 'voicing' 'Essence of wind and wave', reminding places inland of 'storm and sea', of the tide that surrounds humanity, in which the post can do no more than mark a 'channel'. The thought emerges of the real gull having, not simply a cry, but a cry capable, like that of a human being, of 'voicing' experience, even 'desolation', and the poem is then brought up short against reality:

> Those who likened the soul
> To a gull, did they ever
> Catch the eye of a gull?
>
> Driven to snatch,
> Fight for slops in our wake.
>
> Or voice a desolation
> Not meant for us,
> Not even desolate,
> But which we christen.

Pauses between these verses create a sense of the mind moving beyond words, towards the bird's real presence, which the phrasing 'Desire…/ Would fly unconstrained/ Inland or seaward' had almost obliterated. Self-correction is part of the process, as the third of these verses makes especially clear. There is perhaps a suggestion that the watcher is tempted to override the real gull in favour of the 'soul' and that this is an effect, both intimate and misleading, of his Christian linguistic heritage.

But 'even in harbour' the 'folk' of the past 'saw' and 'heard' something in gulls which they interpreted as the cry of souls 'drowned' at sea. Is the implication that those who saw and heard in this way did so with an immediacy not now available to most of us? If so, perhaps they had more right than the poet to override reality with metaphor.

At this point the poem returns to its opening image.

> Gull stands on a post
> In the tideway; I see
>
> No resolution; only
> The necessity of flight
> Beyond me, firm
> Standing only then.

The alteration here of the opening line—'Gull stands on a post'—allows for the way metaphors of 'standing' and 'flying' will be combined when 'The necessity of flight / Beyond me' looks to the future: 'firm / Standing only then'.

The 'necessity' discovered by means of this poem is that of combining apparently opposed 'gifts'—initially sensed in gull and post: 'flight' yet also 'firm standing'—but of doing so in a manner uniquely human. It seems the desire from which the poem springs may be satisfied after all, but only through an ability to combine flight 'beyond' the ego with 'firm / Standing' to mark a 'channel' of use to others. In what follows, I intend to explore how this perception may be seen to bear on a matrix central to Hooker's poetry.

a place in words

We have seen that a key phase in this poem's development was the recognition of gull and post as real, not mere fodder for human possession through language, through metaphor. Nevertheless, it is important to notice that it is through words that the watcher has been enabled to explore his experience and by means of the intersubjective validity of words that we, as readers, move through the space offered by the poem. The dual nature of words—their role in enabling human experience, whether through writing or reading, and their inadequacy in face of the non-human, and of certain inner experiences too—is something Hooker repeatedly examines. In 'Arnolds Wood', for example, Hooker explained his intention with regard to Les Arnold, the subject of that memorial poem, but also expressed his sense of the poet's role among readers: 'What I want to make for us / is a place in words / which we might share'(*CUT*, 363).

Poetry's existence as a place in words open to both writer and reader is, I think, a touchstone of authenticity throughout Hooker's work. It reflects (like the exclamation and question marks in 'Gull on a Post', and the honesty of its self-contradictions) a desire to open the poem to others, those 'known and unknown friends…for whom one writes'[5] and ultimately to a community, one which may not now exist in a single place (did it ever?) but does exist as an intersubjective reality shared, potentially, by a language-community. In *Welsh Journal*, Hooker had expressed doubts about the role of the poet: 'What am I giving to anyone, sitting here writing?'(*WJ*, 39). Reaching beyond solipsism, and influenced by the sense Welsh poets have of their role in a community of the living, the dead and those yet to be born, Hooker has often quoted with approval Waldo Williams's words: 'What is love of country? Keeping house / amid a cloud of witnesses' (quoted at

---

5   Jeremy Hooker, *Welsh Journal* (Bridgend: Seren, 2001), 119; hereafter WJ.

the head of 'Variations on a Theme by Waldo Williams', *CUT*, 281). And he himself was able in a recent interview to express his sense of 'personal depths that are shared'.[6]

But Hooker is also sensitive to the inadequacies of language, both as a means of sharing experience with others and as a mode of contact with realities beyond and within the self. So, for instance, he writes 'words at their strongest & most sensitive are a net with great tears'(*WJ*, 211), while 'Both in essence and appearance all life exists outside language; the attempt to capture it thus ends inevitably in despair, for the limits are defined by the reality language itself creates'(*WJ*, 109). Nevertheless, from early in life 'I felt a depth in the world around me, and experienced language as that which could partially illuminate it, and point to what remained essentially mysterious.' A little later, he remarks that 'language is endlessly generative' and again: 'Language changes historically, and retains its history within it. It connects us to the living, but it relates us also to the dead. We repeat words, but because language is metamorphic, we can say new things, too' (*GL*, 9). I am reminded of Shelley's description of poetry as an art which replenishes the imagination with thoughts which 'form new intervals and interstices whose void forever craves fresh food'.[7] Even after death, a writer's images 'flow / in the channel that he made' (*CUT*, 290), and this channel is something future generations may use in their own way: so, for instance, 'A later poet with a different metaphysic may find sustenance in a seventeenth-century predecessor but it may be something quite different from what the earlier poet intended and even alien to his spirit. However, the metaphysical poets of the seventeenth century resist the tendency to disembodiment' and are 'incarnational poets, who base themselves on a sense of full presence; the Word made Flesh. Hence the sustenance their work affords to poets in later ages who seek in different ways to express an animate nature and to ground an image of integral human being upon sacred reality' ('Metaphysical Presence', *SCINT*, 11, 2007, 25). We shall have occasion to consider the conception of ground as it functions in Hooker's own poetry. However, no approach to the poet's role can be of more than decorative value to a community if the writing and reading of poetry really, as Auden supposed, makes nothing happen.

But one can hardly doubt the possibility of at least partial illumination through reading if one has experienced, as did Hooker in his boyhood, the impact reading can make on the imagination. The essays of Richard Jefferies showed him 'thought growing out of natural description & evocation, with poetic echoes & repetitions'

---

6 Fiona Owen, ' "Mystery at the heart of things": an interview with Jeremy Hooker', *Green Letters*, 8 (2007), 6; hereafter GL.

7 P. B. Shelley, *A Defence of Poetry*, quoted in Anne Cluysenaar, *Introduction to Literary Stylistics* (London: Batsford, 1976), 27.

and made him 'recognise how much I owe to his ways of writing and seeing'(*WJ*, 229). So 'It was both in and out of books that I first discovered nature' (*GL*, 4). But Hooker also discovers through his own writing: 'We learn from language as well as with it. I have learned from my own poems, finding, after the event, that they have said something I was unaware of saying, or shown me something I hadn't seen before' (*GL*, 9).

unknowing, yet seeing (GL, 9)

'Gull on a Post' is based on a moment of 'seeing' which initiates processes of exploration and discovery. The poem is concerned with what can be seen and what remains unknown: the relationship between perception, whether through the eye or through language, and 'a depth in the world around me'. Commenting on Mircéa Eliade's observation that 'the more a consciousness is awakened, the more it transcends its own historicity', Hooker writes: 'What is ultimately at issue is not only the conviction that men and women have integral spiritual and material needs, but an enlarged idea of human potential'.[8]

In a poem dedicated to a fellow poet, Roy Fisher, Hooker likens 'seeing' to 'touch', a way of making contact with what is 'beyond the body's reach':

> There is a looking that is
> a kind of touch,
>   a fingering
> beyond the body's reach. (*CUT*, 306.)

'Fingering' evokes intimacy of touch. However, such a way of touching is also sensitive, respectful of the other. 'It is feeling with, feeling into, that respects the other' (*CUT*, 333), and the choice of 'kind' (rather than, let us say, 'sort') is indicative. Hooker comments on Richard Jefferies's essays that 'the intensity with which he sees mere matter, whether it is a flower or the dust, leads him towards a sense of its complete otherness, its existence beyond all perceptions, images, concepts' ('Richard Jeffries: the art of seeing', WL, 26).

In an essay on T. S. Eliot's 'Waste Land', Hooker argues that Eliot, in his early work, seems to have had no faith in the poet's ability to make contact with reality: 'Perception in the early poems cannot make contact with reality because it reflects

---

8   Jeremy Hooker, 'Landscape of Childhood', *Writers in a Landscape* (Cardiff: University of Wales Press, 1996), 7–8; hereafter WL.

only the perceiver's mind.'9 Hooker points out that Imagist views contrast with this extreme philosophical position: 'Pound's idea of the image as the word beyond formulated language implies a faith in the poet's contact with reality, as does (William Carlos) Williams's "no ideas but in things".' Eliot's early solipsism is a psychological tendency Hooker had at times diagnosed in himself and sought to overcome. Experiences such as the following, recorded in *Welsh Journal,* are an important step towards the 'beyond': that sense of 'otherness which may open the mind to the unknown' and even to a 'sacred reality' beyond but also, ultimately, within the self:

> Struggling out of my intense mental coil, by a stream that welled up among the dark-green ferns before again disappearing underground, I had a fleeting sense of the cosmos outside my narrow mind. The sun was a pale yellow disc through cloud, swirling above a jagged range of cloud mountains and boring down upon the rocky mountainous earth—was it the unknowable power of the sun's furnace in the beginning, bringing life out of vast seas? Afterwards, still conscious of the unique particularity of leaves & flowers, I saw them as interdependent parts of the life-stream connected to the sun, which generates it. This is the only sane way to see things: each in its uniqueness yet borne on a river connecting each to each, and all to the forces of sun, wind, rain & earth, while the eye that sees is no less part of the river seen. (*WJ*, 23–24)

We may take a moment to consider the sense here of clouds as a jagged range and of the rocky mountainous earth as being bored down upon by the sun, made porous to its generative force. The vision—profoundly personal, embodied in a particular time and place, on a particular ground—nevertheless conveys a sense of evolutionary change within deep time, the sun bringing life out of vast seas. The unique particularity of small emergent things, 'leaves & flowers', far from being obliterated by such giant forces, makes them 'interdependent parts of the life-stream'. And the eye is 'no less a part'. This last phrase reflects an important perception, one to which Hooker often returns—the right of humanity, no less than of other beings, to exist. And this perception, which is also a literal truth, enables him to avoid the despair Jefferies expressed when he wrote: 'by no course of reasoning however tortuous can I fit my mind to the universe' (WL, 37). In a passage echoing some of the images in 'Gull on a Post' Hooker writes:

> Oystercatchers picking at

---

9   See 'T. S. Eliot: Tradition and the "resident alien" ', *The Presence of the Past: Essays on Modern British and American Poetry* (Bridgend: Poetry Wales Press, 1987), 51; hereafter PP.

the tideline, the gulls
that miss no scrap,
have no more right than mine.
     ('Weston Shore', *CUT*, 174.)

The psychological importance of such an emphasis arises from a recurrent awareness of how one might indeed sense oneself as *not* valuable, or even fully present, in the world. During a walk, for example, sunlight prints the shadow of a fern, then:

A breeze jigs the fern,
And between moments of perfect white
The rock flickers. Then the wind stops
And the fern stiffens, a shadow bedded in rock.
Feeling invisible, I climb on.
     ('Landscape', *CUT*, 27.)

or again, in a different poem,

          standing
On a bank for the view,
I am surprised by a shadow
Comical stick-like elongation
Spanning a small field.
     ('Landscape of the Winter Sun', *CUT*, 42.)

The tone is different in 'As a Thousand Years' when, having seen on a Welsh mountainside 'not a soul', only 'a stubble field, bales / like megaliths',

          then,
     for a breath,
there was no sign of us.
Not a soul, only
light flooding this field,
bright as a marigold.
     ('As a Thousand Years', *CUT*, 121.)

The insetting of the line 'for a breath' embodies in (or rather between) words the moment of realisation, a moment which this time seems neither fearful nor comic but entranced. In the short poem 'Not Newton', a bramley 'bowed down/ under the weight / of big apples', 'a red admiral / feeding on / a windfall' and 'a green woodpecker / flying away / laughing' are all seen as

> nothing
> but
> energy.
> ('Debris', *CUT*, 335.)

Setting of these words in isolation invites us to connect them in different ways—both 'nothing but' and 'but energy'—perfectly conveying the duality of a modern response to material reality. Perceptions such as these seem to partake of the kind of seeing which allows the unknown to be envisioned and at least pointed to by language.

The communal importance of sharing such spaces is well conveyed by these lines from a poem dedicated to the sculptor Lee Grandjean. As the two artists talk by the river, 'creating a body / between us':

> …in my mind I catch
> and loose its images,
> and above our heads
> swifts hawking for mayfly
> unerringly, explosively, glide.
> I would let all go again
> saying—it is perfect without us,
> but we meet here, we share
> words and your hand shaping
> the flow, the brute
> and graceful wings.
> And our feet beat solidly on the bridge.
> ('At Ovington', *CUT*, 160.)

The notion of a bridge appears in other poems too. They are human constructions. Thanks to them we may cross over 'the bodied / escaping appearances, / the bodiless the broken the whole / flowing through' ('A Poem for my Father', *CUT*, 347). So, for example, in 'Crossing the New Bridge', Hooker realises that his father, walking there, looks through the present bridge to 'a gravel track, the floating-bridge, / your father with a pony and trap / on the shore' and comments 'You look through near things, / but not into distance. / The man with the trap, the children, / all the people with you, / were real as the shingle and the sun'. Thanks to his father's ability to see the presence of the past with such immediacy

for me the shore
was firm again as it was
at first, when you said,
'they're part of us, we're part of them'. (*CUT*, 171)

A work of art is a form of conversation which can create something 'between' the artist and reality, and 'between' the artist and other people, enabling us to 'cross over' a shared space onto 'solid' or 'firm' ground. Wallace Stevens has remarked that 'It is not only that the imagination adheres to reality, but, also, that reality adheres to the imagination and that the interdependence is essential.'[10] One of the 'Steps' that form part of 'Groundwork' combines both interpretations of the artistic bridge:

You shape the image:
it is a bridge we cross over
to meet in the world. (*CUT*, 184.)

'You' is here no doubt Lee Grandjean but also, I think, the poet himself, considering the images that may be created by 'a man's embodied knowledge / in the cutting touch' ('Seven Songs', *Land's End*, CUT, 322), of poetic vision. In another section of 'Groundwork' we read:

What I want to argue
is that poetry and sculpture
are life sciences.

It is not that we express
some finished
or constructed self.

The point is to step out
into the space between
('Workpoints', *CUT*, 303.)

upon our pulses

A note in *Welsh Journal* runs as follows: 'the source of my essential insights is

---

10 Wallace Stevens, 'The Noble Rider and the Sound of Words', *The Necessary Angel* (London: Faber, 1960), 33.

particular sensuous experience, whether mine or others'.' (*WJ*, 45) Through such insights Hooker finds himself opened to what, in discussing the poetry of George Oppen, he describes as mystic experience. Having quoted:

> The mystery is
> That there is something for us to stand on

Hooker comments:

> [George Oppen] is certainly a metaphysical poet, and may even be described as mystical, if we take the full force of 'the mystery is / That there is something for us to stand on'. The poem continues, and ends:
>
> > We want to be here.
> >
> > The act of being, the act of being
> > More than oneself.
>
> His poetry is an attempt not to lose himself in the self but to find himself in the world. ('Seeing the World: The Poetry of George Oppen', *PP*, 63.)

The process of thought in Oppen's poems, as Hooker remarks, is 'the seeing of things which is simultaneously a self-enlightenment'.

There can be sensed, in this observation, deep fellow-feeling. And yet, it seems to me, Hooker's own poetry offers a greater intensity of painterly or sculptural vision, a more acute sense of the natural world's existence as distinct from its usefulness or significance to *homo sapiens*. He himself has remarked that 'my instinctive feeling for things and for landscapes is closer to the feeling of sculptors like Moore and Barbara Hepworth, and of certain painters, than to that of most writers' (*WJ*, 64). And that is itself, I believe, a distinctive aspect of his poetic achievement. Consider this account of a walk by the sea:

> Fallen cliffs, breakwaters—rows of stout posts standing out above the sea— gravel, gorse to the very edge of the cliffs: these things move me strongly...
>
> The posts are vaguely human in shape and they stand for a massive effort that is only temporarily effective and has to be renewed over and over again; and at the same time they are completely non-human, insensate, and like a strange thing emerging from the sea. They belong, and they do not belong, they become part of the sea against which they are a defence, the waters they are meant to break. ('So the Old Snake Sheds its Skin', *CUT*, 186).

Here a sense of the posts as 'vaguely human'—they have a role given them by human beings, they 'stand for' a massive but time-threatened attempt to control the uncontrollable—is combined with a touch of horror before their strangeness, their absolute non-humanity. Because of that strangeness, that otherness, they 'become part of the sea', of ultimately unbreakable waters. There is love, here, for the mystery of human life, the 'massive effort' it continues to make (like gorse) 'to the very edge of the cliffs' and beyond. As we saw earlier, there may be either delight or fear before the world out of which humanity has come and the strangeness of the self. And yet, awe is stronger: 'How close the knowledge is / which every thing conceals' ('Ytene', *CUT*, 192).

To have contemplated the evolutionary insights initiated by Wallace and Darwin—to realise that humanity is part of what it sees and knows, and to realise this not just intellectually but 'upon our pulses'[11]—is surely the most secure foundation for an genuine ecopoetics. As my use of Keats's phrase may suggest, this is an aspect of Hooker's world view which results not merely from scientific, philosophical or religious understandings but from the kind of personal experience explored in the passage about those eroded, 'fallen', cliffs.

Hooker's poetry persuades us to honour, in a fully contemporary context, the 'I and Thou' relationship (*GL*, 5), both in order to preserve our own sanity, as individuals and as a species, and to feel in depth and with intensity the wonder of there being, in Oppen's words, 'something for us to stand on'. So, of a painful moment in a walk to Caperneum he writes:

What I feel most is the heat,
and sick at the unreality
of bad art:

a sloppy English poem
which someone has fixed on a wall
at the site of the miracle
of loaves and fishes...

And yet, when

Unreal, in a sweat of heat
and bad blood, I dip
my seamy face in the water...

---

11 '[A]xioms in philosophy are not axioms until they are proved upon our pulses', to John Hamilton Reynolds, 3 May 1818, *Letters of John Keats*, ed. Robert Gittings (Oxford: Oxford University Press, 1970), 93.

there comes that saving sense of the 'beyond':

> A crane—not, thank God,
> a symbol—but a white crane,
> with long wispy hairs at the back
> of its neck, stands
> fishing in the shallows.
> A black lizard looks at me
> over the edge of a black stone.
> ('Walking to Caperneum', *CUT*, 259–60.)

These images are seen with the eye of a painter. The crane is real, it 'stands'; the black lizard looks at the man over a black 'edge', the threshold of its different world in which, black sheltering black, it belongs. Such lines move me to tears, so exactly do they convey a truth of experience, embodied, incarnate, the sense of 'sacred reality'. One must add that the real crane is, by the very fact of its reality, able to fish in shallows where the miracle of the loaves and fishes has given rise to bad art and where the poet himself has felt 'unreal', overcome (in his human world) by 'a sweat of heat / and bad blood'.

In Hooker's work, there is a strong sense of 'the many forms of life each with its own world in the world that human senses perceive' (prose following 'Steps', *CUT*, 185.) These worlds may be that of 'insects under a scale of bark' (prose following 'Steps', *CUT*, 185) , of a hare—'our image / a gleam in dark eyes' ('Debris', *'Hare'*, *CUT* 336) , of deer who 'feel the world as deer' ('Verdun', *CUT*, 239), or of birds who look down at us with yellow eyes ('Reigersbos', *CUT*, 228) (we remember the eye of a gull and that woodpecker 'flying away / laughing'.):

> And what are we who gaze back,
> wanderers over the brink of our own world
> who have stumbled into theirs.
> ('Reigersbos', *CUT*, 228.)

Human beings have a duty to history, and history is explored with appalled honesty in *Our Lady of Europe*. But the Thames 'is also what exists / in the eyes of a cormorant' ('City Walking (1)', *CUT*, 311.)

In Rembrandt's *The Anatomical Lesson* it is the human eye that is in question, and questioning, as we look at the painting and find there 'the man / who looks at us':

> It is not yet only
> a scientific question

that dawns in his dark eyes.

What is man? What am I
who am wonderfully
and fearfully made,
like this dead thing?
('After Rembrandt: *The Anatomical Lesson*', CUT, 232.)

ground in time

Hooker has agreed with David Jones's remark that 'one is trying to make a shape out of the very things of which one is oneself made',[12] emphasising that this process is also one of discovery. The notion of 'things out of which one is oneself made', of 'ground', has been fundamental to all Hooker's work, but for him 'ground' is not a simple concept but one in which the dual effort to 'see' all that is 'present' (including the 'presence of the past'), but also to look 'beyond' what can be seen, is crucial:

> Ground is something I seek to see in its totality, but it also involves seeking connection with energies beyond consciousness, with the life one is part of, and cannot see. (*GL*, 4.)

It is I think for this reason that already, in 1971, Hooker had written:

> At times I feel certain that the 'nature poet', who is close to the life and death mysteries, and whose instinct is to embrace the body of the earth, is more important today than at any other time. (*WJ*, 41.)

The need to 'embrace', to love and touch, 'the body of the earth' is perhaps something few people sensed with as much urgency, thirty-six years ago, as did Hooker. But in this new millennium, ecopoetics and ecocriticism seek to return us to an awareness respectful both of nature and of humanity. There is in Hooker's poetry a deep desire both to place humanity in its context amongst other creatures and to honour human labour and individuality, recognising both the glories and the shames of human history.

Another passage from *Welsh Journal*, written in the same year, emphasises the importance of human continuity and kinship while seeking to look beyond the

---

[12] David Jones, 'Preface', *The Anathemata* (London: Faber, 1952).

'fashion' of any one time. It brings together a number of issues we have been considering and takes a further step towards defining the kind of art, whether visual or verbal, which the poet feels we need most, now and in future. What is in question now is not, after all, personal solipsism but cultural solipsism. Continuity is at least as important as change:

> All the vivid transformations of a changing society, a technology with built-in obsolescence, are essentially superficial as far as the human spirit and emotions are concerned....It should be possible to feel the same kinship with people of the twenty-first century, or the thirtieth century, that we can feel with seventeenth-century or even primitive man...(*WJ*, 43.)

Writing about Vernon Watkins, Hooker noted that Watkins 'had an experience after which he could never again write a poem dominated by time. I don't feel I could ever write a poem that wasn't' (*WJ*, 147). Time however, as it impinges on Hooker's poetic experience, is a complex dimension. It involves awareness both of the historical—involving a recognition of individual and 'massive' human effort, the placing of a 'post...in the tideway'—and of the transhistorical—a sense of what is 'beyond me' and also of evolutionary force 'boring down upon the rocky mountainous earth'. And this is, I think, why Hooker could never have made painting or sculpture his life's work, despite his extreme sensitivity to visual art. As he wrote in an early poem, 'Paint stiffens but the river swims forward' ('Elegy for the Labouring Poor', *CUT*, 35). Even what in Oppen he described as mystic experience is, for him, imbued with movement. So for example, at a time in the late sixties when 'frozen in a state of depression and anxiety', he found himself staying near Hambledon Hill:

> one day, lying down on the grassy summit, I looked down at a wheatfield, which suddenly seemed to 'unfreeze', and appeared to me like a weir of gold. The earth moved! But of course, it always does: mental stasis and self-enclosure is a wretched human condition; we are always connected with our bodily rhythms and our language to the great rhythmic life of nature. I think a lot of my poetry has occurred in the space 'between', when I recognise, as I did in the wheatfield, the greater world beyond me, but which, in some sense, I'm part of. (*GL*, 6.)

This 'greater world beyond me' is the world he envisages finding in 'Gull on a Post'. And yet, in Hooker's own words, 'The modern consciousness is historical even when it is also religious' ('Crossings and Turns: The Poetry of John Matthias', *PP*, 101).

A poem, like music, moves forward in time and is able through words to give a sense of the past in the present, as when Hooker writes: 'There is no bare earth—/ each stone has sucked up blood / and memory inscribes the dust.' ('Tel Gezer', *CUT*, 251.) Temporal awareness must always have linked human beings to both past and future. But as we became aware also of how *homo sapiens* has evolved (and may still be evolving) amongst other animals and changing environments, we also became more keenly aware of humanity's special gifts and unique responsibilities, and also of the importance of *cultural* evolution. And in cultural evolution writers have a distinctive role to play, exploring thought not as part of a philosophical system but as it reaches us with immediacy, 'upon our pulses', in ways that may after all make something happen.

on the brink

Hooker's notion of 'ground' has evolved over the years. The following passage is taken from a note on the 'Groundwork' poems, part of his collaboration with Lee Grandjean:

> 'Ground' is a concept that has obsessed me for many years. At the time of my earlier poems…I identified it with actual ground: chalk and soil and shingle, the material elements of place, which I sought to explore as a total environment, a human and nonhuman world in time and space…
>
> My later work has grown out of my earlier writing, but with a difference. It has become more exploratory, less sure of where I personally 'belong', and of what the human ground (*humus*) actually consists of, and what it rests on, what its foundation is in metaphysical reality…
>
> I am now more aware of groundlessness. This has its positive and negative aspects. It can manifest itself as a sense of emptiness, an underlying void. It can also be felt as what Lee Grandjean calls 'that ground of elemental energy from which all matter emerges and into which all things are eventually enfolded'. ('A Note on the Groundwork Poems', *SCINT*, 2, 1999, 156)

The 'seen' was always on the 'edge' or 'brink' of becoming what one 'cannot see': 'everything as you look, all / that appears solid transforms' ('Elusive Spirit', *CUT*, 195). A bird flying away from the watcher or soaring above land seems to lose its precious but vulnerable 'particularity'. So a pigeon 'flaps away losing shape' ('Seven SONGS', *'Groundless She Walks'*, *CUT*, 324) and, in another poem, a pigeon resolved in heat-haze becomes 'a burr of energy' ('Yellowing Moon, *CUT*, 61) Elsewhere, a lark is 'a black dot / quivering' ('Debris', *'Lark Song'*, *CUT*, 331).

As this awareness grows, there can be felt in Hooker's work an increasingly acute sense of our own selves as 'other'. Otherness was perceived, in his earlier work, as residing primarily, though never exclusively, in observed particulars. But certain poems in *Adamah* engage at great depth with internalised otherness—that is, with the self not as ego but as a form of consciousness upon which ego rides. Even the 'tide' of 'Gull on a Post' has come to be perceived, at times, as 'the place where no one can dwell, / the dark tide that generates' ('City Walking (2)', *CUT*, 317). As this phrasing shows, 'terror at the roots of things' ('Seven Songs', *'Cyane'*, *CUT*, 320) is still sensed, but it is a terror that threatens the ego rather than consciousness, consciousness being part of the tide and having a participatory role to play, voicing its own generative (cultural) presence though language. And yet, even in that role, we may fear that humanity is 'making another earth; / the creatures we drew from the rock / are going back' ('That Trees Are Men Walking', *CUT*, 294). Therefore we must seek understanding of our selves.

In certain poems in *Adamah* what is 'observed' or quite literally 'embodied' is a sense of self which, while still surrounded by other modes of being, explores its own mystery. In *Our Lady of Europe*, there are already passages that wonder at the ability to live (literally) with distances, 'listening, feeling / the pressures of the sea' ('Noordpolderzijl', *CUT*, 221), or explore a dream in which 'there are no words, / no symbol, no metaphor / to bear him over the torrent, / nothing but courage, and his mind / that listens…' ('Variations on a Theme by Waldo Williams', *'Imagining Wales'*, *CUT*, 290.) . But 'Cyane' offers the reader a consciousness that is itself, in the words of an earlier poem, 'the stream within the stream' ('Earth Song Cycle', *'Written in Clay'*, *CUT*, 276):

> …I shake, the being that I was—
>   skin blood bones
> unbinding, flying into drops,
> flowing with a constant tremor,
> plunging down, shattering,
> shaking out long and smooth,
> always broken, always whole.
> ('Seven Songs', *'Cyane'*, *CUT*, 320)

And in *'Groundless She Walks'* a female consciousness, who 'has been at the edge / since first light', walks beside a harvest field. A child moves 'under her heart'. And now her self-awareness takes the form of another world within her, in which she 'sees' her own presence, in a field that is a sea (through not, this time, a 'dark tide'), and hears its voices 'whispering' :

her mind itself the sky
in which a woman lifts up her hands
over heavy-headed wheat,
the whole sea of the field whispering.

But she may not dissolve,
she must absorb the turbulence,
the desire within to be other
is the pressure she must bear.
('Seven Songs', *'Groundless She Walks'*, CUT, 325)

Having a child to bring into the world she 'may not dissolve', yet wonders what world she will be bringing her child into: 'What ground will he stand on? / What humus, or piece of debris / hurtling from the supernova, / the giant star that once was man?' Indeed, wonder at humanity, at 'what we are', receives the final emphasis in *Adamah*:

Think of the birds
flying away. Imagine the sound
of a human kiss
waved into space.
What will it find?
Who will know what we are?
('Thoughts on a Star-Map', *CUT*, 356.)

The significance of Hooker's poetry lies, to my mind, in the courage and consistency with which he has allowed himself to feel upon his pulses a matrix of interconnected issues, whether psychological, intellectual or religious, crucial to our time and to our own and the planet's future. His poems are places in which the reader may discover 'embodied knowledge', realities too simple, too personal, too appalling, too deeply imbued with praise to be easily expressed or shared in twenty-first century Western culture They are therefore a valuable gift. And, in Hooker's own words ('A Winchester Mosaic', *CUT*, 150), 'time does not waste a gift / that opens the heart'.

In the Footsteps of Roland Mathias

Sam Adams

A superficial comparison of the poetry of Jeremy Hooker and Roland Mathias will immediately reveal large differences between the lucid vision of the former and the latter's rugged poetic self-exposure and interrogation. Yet they have two elements in common: important fundamental principles of grace and good living, and rootedness in familiar, well-loved places envisioned in this and other times.

Although he travels poetically, notably to Wales and the Netherlands, the centre of Hooker's world is the south of England. Its topographies are located either side of Southampton Water—the new Forest to the west and, to the east, Netley and the Itchen Valley extending as far north as Winchester; but it has outliers a little further west in places with deeper historical associations, like Avebury and Cerne Abbas.

Mathias's concern with place, often given the extra dimension of history, is measurably large, as the contents list of *Collected Poems* demonstrates. More than a quarter of the titles include a place name, while 'The Flooded Valley', 'A Last Respect', 'New Lease' and many more have, and are to a significant extent referentially dependent upon, readily identifiable locations. They range from Germany and Cyprus to Brittany and the Swiss and Austrian Alps, but cluster thickly in three areas: Oxfordshire, near the family home of his wife, Molly; Pembrokeshire, where roots struck deep in the decade he spent as headmaster of Pembroke Dock Grammar School, 1948–58; and around Brecon, close to his birthplace,[1] where his parents had settled in the 1940s, and where in turn he came to live on leaving the education service in 1969.

There is of course another connection between these two remarkably gifted writers, for Hooker is one of the key critics and interpreters of Mathias, without whose painstaking and timely reconsideration the older poet's work might have remained misunderstood and misjudged.

---

[1]   Mathias was born in Glyn Collwn, above Talybont-on-Usk, near Brecon in September 1915.

I began a pursuit of Mathias in his characteristic landscapes accidentally, as a result of a visit to Cascob. It was not Mathias's strange poem of that name which took me to the isolated Radnorshire hamlet, but my research on T. J. Llewelyn Prichard,[2] who at various times during the second quarter of the nineteenth century had found at the rectory there (the home of his loyal friend, the Revd William Jenkins Rees) rest and succour, and access to a library to assist his own historical studies.

To reach the church at Cascob you leave what passes for a main road in these rural parts and negotiate at a prudent speed a few miles of hazardous narrow lane.[3] When you arrive, you find no provision for parking, so you ease the car onto a gaily floral, weed-covered bank by the red telephone kiosk with the kitchen chair inside. This is the centre of Cascob. Across the road, facing the churchyard gate, you note a small, undistinguished house crouched behind its hedges, and to your left a substantial stone building of vaguely ecclesiastical aspect, which, not unreasonably, you might assume to be the rectory. But you would be mistaken. Formerly the school, it is now (as I discovered later) the home of Peter J. Conradi, friend and biographer of Iris Murdoch. He directed me to the old rectory, about half a mile off, where I found a rather imposing, if sadly altered, whitewashed building in the midst of its fields. The eighteenth century rectory had become a farmhouse.

The church drew me back. As though in preparation for visitors, a few sheep had been turned loose in the graveyard to trim the long grass but, while leaving ample droppings, had hardly begun to get to grips with the task. On a dank day with scudding clouds, I thought it an eerie place, or perhaps recollection of Mathias's poem made it seem so.

> ...the bound
> Of the churchyard circles and the black yews
> Are markers. Each on the circuit ropes and screws
> Giddily, wind having caught it widdershins
> At the clock's three. No true arrest. For two pins
> I'd leave in a hurry, were it not absurd...
>
> Blank wall facing west, belfry of weather-board
> Raised on a druids' mound, none of it
> Reassuring. Within, a brass of familiars, habit

---

2 Thomas Jeffery Llewelyn Prichard, 1790–1862, the subject of a monograph by Sam Adams in the Writers of Wales series (Cardiff: University of Wales Press, 2000).

3 Cascob is about 6 miles west of Presteigne on a lane off the B4375.

Of clergy, *pater pater pater, noster noster noster*
Three times for Saturn, *O save our sister*
Elizabeth Lloyd from spirits, amen. Behind
My back a thin mediaeval tongue, the wind
Carrying it woodward, tang and tone.
Service at three. Who is it coming? Afternoon, afternoon.[4]

Having (at the advice of the rectory farmer) obtained the key from the house across the road, I entered the strangely stunted church. Although there is but one window of any size and the afternoon offered only feeble intermittent sunlight, I quickly found a memorial tablet to the Revd. William Jenkins Rees, 'Priest, Author, Antiquary, Litterateur', whose grave I had sought outside in vain, and displayed on the wall close to it an inscription that I stared at with astonishment—the Abracadadabra Charm, a protective incantation dating from the seventeenth century to preserve 'Elizabeth Lloyd from all witchcraft and all evil…the witches compassed her abought [*sic*] but in the name of the Lord I will destroy them Amen ****** pater pater pater Noster Noster Noster …' Its melding of Christian prayer and astrological conjuring is indeed far from reassuring. We cannot know now what wickedness 'loping beyond the yews' pursued Elizabeth Lloyd, what local wizard pronounced the words, or the reason for their preservation in the church but, in any event, there lay the source of the weird invocation in the midst of 'Cascob'.

Usually, Mathias knew something of the places he planned to visit beforehand. Cascob was an exception. He went there during a family holiday more than fifty years ago.[5] Finding the Abracadabra Charm was as much a surprise for him as it had been for me, and the strange wonder of it is communicated in the eruption of incantation into the poem. Later he learned that the Church of St Michael, one of several so dedicated in the area, is dated possibly from the thirteenth century, and that the mound almost five feet high beside the tower, was reputed to be a druid's mound.[6] The roughly circular graveyard suggests its use as a burial ground extends into a mistily distant pagan past. These features too, and the wind that twirls the trees unluckily 'widdershins', are included in the amalgam of curious lore informing the poem, all tending to heighten the sense of uncertainty about what is to come

---

4   Sam Adams, ed., *The Collected Poems of Roland Mathias* (Cardiff: University of Wales Press 2002), 175. Hereafter *CP*.

5   In the notebook where Mathias copied more or less finished poems, he wrote alongside the text, 'Begun at Builth Easter 1955. Completed 25 March 1957 at 4 Park View Crescent, Pembroke Dock'. It was first published in *The Dragon*, the magazine of UCW Aberystwyth (Summer 1958), 8.

6   Modern scholarly opinion declares it no more than the remains of an earlier collapsed tower.

next, life or death, God or devil.

When I edited the poems, what I should have guessed from his use of italics was quotation, I had found, frankly, inexplicable, but now by chance I had the explanation. The poet himself was unconcerned about the abstruse and unexplained in his work. Does the organisation of the poem impress with its carefully crafted, unobtrusive rhyme? Above all, does it succeed in conjuring up a place and a mood? Of course, it does both. Nevertheless, I was left to ponder how many other allusions I had misinterpreted, or missed, because I had not visited the places that provide the stimulus or point of departure for so much of Mathias's poetry, and decided there and then that, when opportunity offered, I would more deliberately walk where he walked, stand where he stood, re-read the poems and see—quite what I did not know.

Common sense suggested I should try out my project on a few poems and places within comfortable reach of Brecon. The single exception arose again fortuitously. While on a brief visit to Pembrokeshire, I found myself within easy distance of Orielton, a mansion house of ancient origin close to the town of Pembroke, and the subject of one of Mathias's poetic meditations on time and change. I knew that the house and estate (of 260 acres) had been purchased for a song in 1954 by the Cardiff-born naturalist and writer R. M. Lockley, and that it stood empty for a year before the new owner moved in.[7] I knew, too, that the poem was begun in the summer of 1954 and 'completed 6 June 1955' at Mathias's Pembroke home,[8] hence its title 'Orielton Empty'.

Since 1963, when Lockley sold it to the Field Studies Council, Orielton has been a residential study centre for courses on wildlife and the environment. Unable to make contact by telephone, I journeyed there in hope rather than expectation, but I was warmly received. The house, which dates from 1743, is on a slight rise, overlooking woods, ponds and fields. It is very grand, with glorious Georgian symmetry, but not the symmetry presented in the opening lines of the poem:

> There has been burning, identifiable still
> > Behind composure when the shuttered front
> Opens its thirteen eyes.[9]

You look in vain for an arrangement that will disclose 'thirteen eyes' in the rows of

---

7   Ronald Lockley, *Orielton; the human and natural history of a Welsh manor* (London: Deutsch, 1972), 8.

8   The poet habitually recorded such information in the notebooks containing fair copies of poems.

9   *CP*, 174.

eight windows boasted by the two upper storeys and the three great windows either side of the pillared porch, for here, at the outset, Mathias is merging past and present. Eighteenth century engravings of the property reveal that there were then rows of thirteen windows, and the 'burning' refers to a fire that destroyed the north wing in 1809. It was not rebuilt. Rather, the front was remodelled and the main entrance relocated to create 'composure', the well-ordered structure we see today. The evidence of neglect, those lesser depredations of time, the 'corner urn [that] needs/Looking to' and the dropped guttering, which the poet meditates upon, are no longer to be seen.

In his book about the house, Lockley describes his favourite walk 'from the Grecian porch to the Lily Pond, admiring the ancient Japanese maples … [then] … across the causeway damming the lake … [The] dam, long neglected, half overgrown with alder, wild rhododendron, camellia and willowherb, leaked a good deal …' This is much the same view and path that Mathias takes. 'Many of the trees are copper, one/ A beech, a Japanese maple another' he observes, as visitors may today, if they stand, back to the porch, looking over the lily pond and to the wood and lake beyond. On a day of prolonged, almost unnatural mid-February sunshine, there were no flies swarming over the lake, as there were on the poet's late summer survey, but at the foot of a lakeside tree the graves of 'Durgi and Soda, gundogs of the Rosebery age' (with that of another dog we know from Lockley's history to have been named Sancho), each enclosed by a low iron railing, are still to be seen, though Durgi's metal nameplate alone remains; and rhododendrons still 'drink/ Gapingly like mangrove roots from the nearer bank'. It is not proliferating nature that preoccupies Mathias, however, but the desertion of the place, the absence of shaping mind and hand:

> Of the whole circle there is no one left to thank
> For the windbreak, for the island hopes
> Of the heart, for the sickle that blunts and stops.

And as he looks towards encroaching autumn, the darkness of his mood thickens:

> The scar has widened, weeping over fire and century,
> Reds and yellows falling, by and by
> Sodden and historied in leaf and frail.
> Outside the circle the sea winds scut and kill.

There the poem ends but not the mystery. From a large first floor side window I was shown the 'tower fickle with grasses', which once punctuated a boundary wall, a nesting place for kestrels, where, Mathias says 'a beldame and her pack/

Gamed all her guineas away in a round/ Of parties to dawnlight'. No one at
Orielton now could throw any light on this profligate, and Lockley, who
researched the history of the house thoroughly, is silent on the matter. The poet
could no longer remember the source of the tale, but suggested it might have come
from Lockley's wife, who was a 'school governor', and whom he therefore knew
quite well. Identification of the beldame is not necessary to an appreciation of the
poem's purpose and accomplishment, but the lack persists as an itch on the
conscience.

You may have consulted a map beforehand, but in the absence of a road sign
you can pass and re-pass the entrance to the narrow lane running steeply up hill to
Brechfa without seeing it.[10] Once found it conducts you past a couple of farm
buildings and finally over a cattle grid on to a common, a broad, quite flat area of
moor, with scattered half-hearted trees, little semblances of hedge, and rushes and
gorse in clumps. In the midst is a surprisingly extensive pool, surrounded by marsh
and scattered small satellite pools, suggesting the spread of water is sometimes a
good deal larger. Beside an unsurfaced track skirting the pond to the left stands a
chapel, encircled by gravestones behind a low stone wall. From a little distance it
appears very small, and box-like, not much longer than it is wide.

This is the setting of one of the most memorable of Mathias's poems, 'Brechfa
Chapel'. Internal and circumstantial evidence suggest it belongs to the winter of
1977–78. Early drafts were sometimes put aside for a considerable time before a
fresh impulse drove them forward to completion, but the linguistic concentration
and complexity of this poem, the tone, the unflinching focus on the human
condition, in a world where grace and belief are almost overwhelmed by ignorance
and brutal confusion—all convey a concept envisioned and achieved while the
experience of 'this latish day that began with love' was fresh.

> Not a shank of the long lane upwards
> Prepared our wits for the myth, the slimed
> Substantiation of the elements. And the coot
> With his off-white blaze and queasy paddle
> Was an old alarm, the timid in flight
> From the ignorant.[11]

The coot is emblematic, as are the swan, 'dreaming' on a clump of reed, and the
raucous black-back gulls that crowd the margin of the pool, 'a militant brabble'

---

[10] From Brecon, the lane branches off the A470 about half a mile short of Llyswen, and just
after the sign for Llandefalle.

[11] *CP*, 222.

uttering their 'bankrupt/ Hatred of strangers'. The meditative gaze shifts from the water birds to the chapel and its graveyard, where inscriptions on the stones proclaim lives, long or cruelly short, dedicated to the faith.

> A light from this
> Tiny cell brisked in far corners once, the hand held
> Steady. But now the black half-world comes at it,
> Bleaks by its very doors. Is the old witness done?

The question hangs ominously. Mathias noted evidence at least of persistence in the swept gallery of the chapel, the neat stack of books on the pulpit, and Sunday services for farmers who come, not in the close company of family and friends as in the old days, but 'singly', and put 'Their heads to the pews as habit bids them to' What little reassurance that might have given has now gone.

Though still in place, the 'old iron gate' to the graveyard is no longer needed for the wall has been broken down to allow builders' supplies to be dumped on toppled gravestones. Among stones still standing are those remembered by the poet,[12] which, in the certainty of their faith, 'trouble/ The spirit...give look for look!' The chapel has been gutted; soon it will be a house. The commemorative tablets that were once inside are tumbled among the graves outside. One tells of the founding: *'Bethesda was built in the year 1803 by Public Subscription. Wm. Parry of Llyswen, Gent. gave the ground and twenty pounds towards the building and likewise five pounds annually in his last will for the support of the Calvanistic Independents in this place for ever.'* What irony there.

Beyond the wall, in the midst of a sheep- and horse-bitten moor, is the pool, much as Mathias must have observed it. On the day of my visit, it was a disc of rippled silver, the raft of reeds still there, but no swan, and only a dozen or so black-back gulls quietly sitting on the water, heads into the wind. To read 'Brechfa Chapel' there is to realise afresh and intensified its superlative achievement as a profound and moving expression of Nonconformist belief, in the face of dwindling congregations and disappearing chapels. It has a final message: as the old community of faith falls away—

> Each on his own must stand and conjure
> The strong remembered words, the unanswerable

---

12   Mathias was not in the habit of making notes on the spot and the recall of unimportant detail is not perfectly accurate.

Texts against chaos.[13]

It is easy to pass St Mary's Church, Sarnesfield without noticing it, partly because it is located a little way back from the road on a dangerous bend and the driver's attention is occupied.[14] At any event, I missed it and had to retrace my steps. Notices by the gate inform visitors that it is a '12th Century Church' and has benefited from the Heritage Lottery Fund. A narrow, mossy path winds from the simple wooden gate through the graveyard, bending left towards the church porch and the impressive tomb of John Abel, then curving away again to peter out among graves on the south side. The drystone wall surrounding the graveyard needs repair in a few places. A tall, massive yew, festooned with ivy, neighbours the gate, and another, far smaller, shadows the church porch. Other trees, mostly winter-bare grow here and there around the perimeter. Externally the church is a very simple, quite low grey stone building. The windows are small, but several bear coats of arms in stained glass. The tower is remarkable for its crowning glory, a splendid, brightly gilded weathercock.

Mathias recalled clearly that he knew about the mediaeval church at Sarnesfield, just across the border into Herefordshire, before he halted the car there on a sunlit, breezy day in 1962, en route for Belper, Derbyshire, where he had taken up a headship following his departure from Pembroke Dock. He remembered the occasion particularly because one of the children noticed for the first time that they had crossed the border out of Wales, and wanted to go back. It was the end of the Easter holidays.

The poem 'Sarnesfield', which he began drafting soon afterwards,[15] reveals 'five travellers', the poet, his wife and their three young children stepping into the ancient churchyard. The light-hearted mood is reflected in jaunty references to the family—their stature and their startled reaction to the rat-tat-tat of a woodpecker drilling a branch. The tone of the poem appears essentially playful if self-deprecating, not least of the intellectually competitive instinct of the father figure, for whom the woodpecker's drumming is an opportunity to test the children:

---

13   The centrality of Christian belief in Mathias's poetry is discussed in two important articles: Jeremy Hooker's 'Roland Mathias: "The strong remembered words"', *Poetry Wales*, 21/1 (1985), pp. 94–103; and M Wynn Thomas's ' "All lenient muscles tensed": the Poetry of Roland Mathias', *Poetry Wales*, 33/3 (1998), 21–26.

14   Sarnesfield is on the A4112, a stretch of the direct route from Brecon to Leominster, about ten miles from the latter.

15   In the Notebook, the poem is annotated, 'Begun after a visit to Sarnesfield on the return north after the Easter holiday 1962. Pottered at several times since, and finally polished up on 4 & 5 January 1964'.

'You know
He only drills a dead branch, don't you?'
Being alive was incredibly to begin
Warfare again and justification, as though outside the grave
There were no greater wisdom than to win.[16]

Allusions to jungle warfare (the imagined 'gunner astride a fork, hidden, cartridge-loop bellying') are highly unusual if not unique in Mathias's writing, but given the context, at least understandable. What do we understand, however, of the references to John Abel; to the cock on the church tower as 'a gold *achievement*', and to the sun having 'left its *quartering*' (my italics)? Indeed, what are readers to make of 'York Herald in the north-east corner/ With a grass train of Marshalls forming/ In his shade', if they have not been to Sarnesfield? There they would find the huge slab beneath which eight members of the Marshall family are now gathered and, if they ventured into the 'worm eaten church porch' (still much as Mathias beheld it), a notice listing keyholders for the church, among whom is a surviving member of the same clan, who can readily be persuaded to speak about his great-grandfather.

'York Herald' was the title granted to George William Marshall (1839–1905) by the College of Arms. He was an expert in heraldry and one of the foremost family historians of his time. The magazine *The Genealogist*, which he began in 1877 and edited for seven years, was said to have 'found much favour among students of history', whose number might well have included the young Roland Mathias. So, in 'Sarnesfield' in addition to the directional sense, the term 'quartering' carries notions of heraldic quarters, and 'achievement'—conventionally applied to John Abel, seventeenth century architect, so-called 'King's Carpenter',[17] and to the poet himself, whose less substantial works are dismissed as a blow-away dandelion 'Clock of words'—also signifies a complete heraldic device: the weathercock surmounting and completing the colourful escutcheon of the church and its surrounds.

The place, the playful delight in vocabulary, plain and esoteric, and in metaphor, lead to a minor epiphany. The poet seizes for himself a brief interlude of sunlit contentment in the cheerful presence of loved ones, and in knowing about

---

16 *CP*, 181.

17 The lettering of the lengthy inscription on the tombstone of John Abel (c.1578–1675), close to the church porch, has been further worn by the elements and is now barely legible in parts. He is said to have been responsible for a number of elaborately ornamented, timber-framed buildings in the Marches, including the market halls at Hereford, Brecon, Leominster and Kington, all long since demolished. Ledbury's example still stands, but is not among his documented works.

such stuff as York Herald and John Abel:

> Of the five travellers one
> Stood still in the gold pool, fingering
> The mistery in its aery vat, a moment
> Gilder and master. Thus in relief high
> Noon and happy cast can keep a pigmy safe.

Wordplay is a feature of the poem. 'Mistery' is the medieval term for a skilled craft, such as heraldry; 'gilder and master' pointing again to the steeple-top cock, carries also the notion of a craft 'guild', and is the unvarnished admission of a momentary lapse into self-satisfaction. The depreciative 'pigmy' follows hard—a characteristically severe self-judgement to break the spell of the golden moment and echoing the allusions to short stature at the outset. In the self-questioning final lines of the poem, the underlying seriousness breaks through with another reverberating 'bullet-burst' from the woodpecker—

> Shooting the cock full of wry
> Machine gun comment and the tree-bole
> Chock of an almost discernible dust. Which
> Of the splaying limbs could he so easily tell
> Was rotten? In which, sun notwithstanding,
> Had he to drill his condemnatory hole?[18]

'On Llandefalle Hill' is one of the few poems Mathias began writing *in situ*.[19] Until the last half-line, the first three stanzas record observations of the landscape and sky above, on a summer day, which yet has menace in the wind and an approaching 'darker rumpus of clouds,/ Like shifty serpents waiting for their trades'. The 'poor trackland' he describes of bracken, tormentil and 'embittered grass' affords but meagre returns to man and beast living upon it.

And, he seems simply to say, it was ever thus ('All that man was// In history pictures here...'). But woven across the harsh existence of the upland farmer, the imagery introduces concepts of a different order—in the opposition of 'light' and

---

18 Mathias's father suffered a stroke in 1960 and died in July 1962, not long after the Easter holiday visit that, at its end, supplied the circumstances of this poem. The poet's sense of his father's tenuous hold on life colours a work in which his own role as *paterfamilias* is presented.

19 In the Notebook the poem is annotated: 'First draft Jubilee Tuesday, June 7, 1977, on Llandefalle Hill. Worked on at The Wells [a holiday home in Pembrokeshire] June 11 and 12. Completed in Deffrobani [Mathias's Brecon home] June 14, 1977'.

'terror', and in an echo of 'Brechfa Chapel', where farmers pray 'as habit bids them to':

> Reluctant light,
> Parade of a far terror, wind greyhound
> In the mosses. Will he peer
> Cunningly from the *hendre* again, chimney-burned,
> To catch at summer in its hasty round?
>
> Sheep graze, a cart track shows
> Yellower where
> The grass is thin and pressed: habit prescribes
> The way. If God allows
> He spoke once to our fathers, the babes
> Will remember it to the wasted tribes.[20]

We understand that the 'wasted tribes' are the same dwindling congregations of the faithful that were the poet's central concern in the other poem. And having seen that, we look back at a cloudscape imaged as 'a darker rumpus' and 'shifty serpents' and realise that it is as representative of a turbulent and menacing world as were the black-back gulls squabbling over Brechfa pool.

A discreet fingerpost on the road from Brecon to Llyswen points the way to Llandefalle. Should you follow that sign on a November day you will find yourself in a narrow lane deep between banks surmounted with hard-trimmed, bare hedges. It has few passing places and is clearly not intended for motor vehicles. The lane soon forks, offering a route along the foot of the hill, or alternatively, one to 'Llandefalle Hall' and dog kennels—if you are to believe the signs. From the former, fifty yards or so above the lane on the right, you see Llandefalle church, low and grey among its trees. This is clearly not the way to the 'hill'. The other route, yet narrower and rising steeply, does not disclose a 'hall', but eventually, still grinding up hill, you pass a house with kennels and stables. After these few signs of habitation, you cross a cattle grid and find yourself at the top, on a broad common.

In the depths of the wettest winter in a decade or more, it was drenched, marshy even. Brechfa was not far off, if one knew the direction, but the rain, which had been persistent all the way from Brecon, became heavier, while gusts of wind shook the stationary car and the branches of trees a few hundred yards off at what seemed to be a perimeter, and bowed low the flimsier bushes close by. It was not a day for exploring on foot.

---

[20] *CP*, 218.

Confined as I was to the car, there was little enough for me to see: sky unbroken grey across which darker rags of squalls moved swiftly, a grassy moor with rushes sprouting, clumps of dark green gorse, mounds of sodden, rusted bracken and, in the distance, rather faint, in varying shades of darker grey, the Brecon Beacons. I bowed to my books and spread map.

I cannot tell what made me look up, but when I did it was to the astonishing sight of a lone horseman on a tall horse close by the car, pacing into the wind and rain. In a moment man and horse had disappeared, over the grid I supposed, and away. I did not see them again. Somewhat shaken, I gathered my papers, started the car and drove off the hill and carefully back down the lane.

A few days later I described my route and what had occurred to the poet. That was not the place he had visited, he told me, not the inspiration of his poem. He directed my attention to an Ordnance Survey map and a route via Garthbrengy to what was plainly labelled Llandefalle Hill. I had consulted a road map, found Llandefalle and approached the common from the other side. I did not feel entirely vindicated, and soon after, in far better weather, I drove up the way he had directed. After rattling over another cattle grid I found myself on an extensive gently undulating area, much of it bracken covered, with one or two farms, all keeping tight, waiting for the end of winter. I had previously seen only one small, rain-swept corner of this great tract of upland, but I had put that right, and consoled myself that my earlier misdirection had at least led me to perceive a closeness to Brechfa that was borne out by the poem

'Maesyronnen' does not appear in any of Mathias's fair-copy notebooks, and consequently we know nothing definitive about its date and place of composition. It is certainly a poem of his young manhood, in all probability written between 1940, when, his father having retired from the army chaplaincy, his parents moved to Brecon, and 1942 when it was published in *Days Enduring*, his first book of poems.[21] His father had taken him to Maesyronnen the poet told me, a special reason for remembrance,[22] but he had no affection for the poem, which he dismissed as apprentice work. Another view is that it is a piece in which he is beginning to discover that raw and sometimes rugged power of shaping language that is characteristic of his mature writing, trying his strength in a form that differs markedly from the regular, rhyming stanzas that dominate *Days Enduring* (the poem rhymes irregularly and its rhythms are far closer to the rhythms of speech), invoking the historical dimension of a subject and, for the first time, engaging with his Nonconformist belief. It has its quota of flaws, but also youthful confidence

---

[21] Roland Mathias, *Days Enduring and Other Poems* (Ilfracombe: Stockwell, 1942)

[22] The lines 'Hear the free/ Sonority of Welsh come hushing out/ Over the nodding heads' suggests his father was preaching there on this occasion.

and vigour.

Only a short distance from Hay-on-Wye, near Llowes, and clearly signposted,[23] Maesyronnen Chapel is not difficult to find. This year is the three hundred and tenth anniversary of its registration as a place of worship, although a barn on the site had been used by Dissenters for decades before that. The present building, erected around 1696, consists of a plain rectangular chapel fifty feet by twenty-two and a half, with a small house attached to the west end. The huge bent 'A' of a cruck truss between the house and the chapel reveals its antiquity. It is steeped in the history of the faith; little wonder it stirred a response in the poet:

> Across the field, beyond the lordly hedge,
> One side as anciently toward the poor,
> The long white chapel leans, a living pledge
> Left by the men who broke their Babylon,
> The staple of the state.[24]

The chapel stands alone at the end of a steep narrow lane, just below the crest of a ridge overlooking the Wye valley. To left and right near the foot of the hill, are fine farm buildings, and a little further, on the right, the ornamental gates of Maesllwch Castle, its cluster of grey turrets visible through the bare trees. The castle explains why one side of the hedge that almost encircles the chapel is 'lordly', while the other belongs with the generations of rural poor who worshipped in this spot. The chapel has been refurbished in recent years and has a faithful congregation, but when Mathias first visited in 1940 or 1941, its state was far less secure. He saw how 'the roof with four blue feet of sky,/ The half blocked up with boards, lifts ominous', and more evidence of neglect in the blackened stove and dusty hymn books. A family pew brings at once to mind 'braver days', and the chapel furniture, some almost as old as the building, catches his imagination (and stirs something of the manner of his later writing):

> In front set out
> One hoary bench, thick as a quarried flag
> And sagging with the dropsy, bellies back
> Into an older age.
> Upon the pulpit board new bossed with black
> Gleaming with gold leaf, gallant as a page
> On which the day's illumination falls,

---

23 It is off the A438 almost halfway between Glasbury and Clyro.
24 *CP*, 96.

> Start out the names of tens of serving men
> Who launched the lighted Word within these walls
> Three hundred years ago, who flung the gage
> Downhill across the Wye.

It remains simply furnished. There is a piano, a pulpit, the front of which is decorated with simply painted panels declaring the Ministerial Succession from 1640 (the 'board' in the poem) and, facing the pulpit across the narrow floor, family box pews. Below the pulpit are two straight spindle-backed benches, one bearing the date 1728, and a low table. Beneath the cruck beam are several more low, backless benches, gnawed by worm and time and in a generally battered state. A leaflet is available, which tells the history of the chapel and of dissenting religion in the area from the sixteenth century.[25]

At Brechfa Chapel, Mathias meditated upon the decline witnessed in the gravestones from an evangelical past, 'a light from this/Tiny cell brisked in far corners once'; 'Maesyronnen' celebrates an earlier more combative spreading of the Word, against the opposition of the Anglican Church and Roman Catholicism:

> Stand by the door. Be silent, see
> Jogging evangelists come in aflame
> And seeking men stride out of Breconshire.
> [.......................................]
> Up many a lonely cwm for miles around
> The disputatious climb, mouthing the good,
> To rack the Church and curse Her Popish springs.
> Now by each lonely fire the ashes sound,
> The finger in the Book falls on the text
> Weighing the household sin. And lo who sings
> The penitential round...

Lest the reader should think the poet shares, with the same faith, the same harsh disciplines, the final lines remind us that was part of the history of Dissent, a past of struggle and achievement, but also of stern morality and easy condemnation. From the dilapidation of the chapel he takes the sober message of the present:

> This was the anvil. Now the sparks beat out
> In darker hammering and a little dust.

---

25 M. E. Griffiths, *History of Maesyronnen United Reformed Chapel and Surrounding Area* (1987).

The places visited in this small tour of topographies associated with the poetry of Roland Mathias were not pre-selected with the intention of illustrating this or that aspect of his writing. The choice was largely fortuitous. Most, however, are lonely, rather remote and numinous. And the poems that arose out of his experience underline the constant strength and seriousness of his art, and the consistency of his highly individual voice, which was beginning to assert itself as far back in his career as 'Maesyronnen'. These elements, with his sense of history and a response to landscape that is rarely one-dimensional, are dominant characteristics of his writing. Finally, the poems discussed here, as any other selection that might be made, reveal with great clarity that fundamental to all, the man and his work, is his Christian belief.

In Black and White:
Weatherscapes in Joseph Conrad's *The Shadow-Line* and Per Olof Sundman's *Ingenjör Andrées luftfärd*

John Barnie

WEATHER and its larger manifestation as climate shapes our lives. Anyone who doubts this hasn't been listening to the debate about global warming. It also shapes landscape, imperceptibly over decades and centuries, profoundly over the tens of millions of years of geological time. Yet in literature weather tends to be part of the background, even in the poetry of landscape where its effects might be more appreciated. There are nonetheless exceptions and it is two of these, drawn from fiction rather than poetry, that I would like to discuss here.

The first, Joseph Conrad's novella *The Shadow-Line* from 1917, will be familiar; the second, Per Olof Sundman's novel *Ingenjör Andrées luftfärd* (Engineer Andrée's Air Voyage) from 1967 will probably be unknown to readers.

*

More than most fiction writers, Conrad was highly attuned to the weather as a result of his many years as an officer in sailing ships in the merchant navy where a keen understanding of weather was essential and where it became, as it were, part of the sensory texture of an officer's mind. There is an example of this in his memoir, *A Personal Record*. Bound for Australia under sail, Conrad befriends a young passenger with literary interests and asks him if he would be willing to read the unfinished manuscript of his first novel, *Almayer's Folly*. A storm is gathering and as the young man leaves the cabin, he has to watch his chance with the roll of the ship, opening the door and closing it behind him in quick succession. Conrad comments:

> In the moment of his exit I heard the sustained booming of the wind, the swish
> of the water on the decks of the *Torrens*, and the subdued, as if distant, roar of
> the rising sea. I noted the growing disquiet in the great restlessness of the
> ocean, and responded professionally to it with the thought that at eight
> o'clock, in another half-hour or so at the furthest, the top-gallant sails would
> have to come off the ship.[1]

The door is open for seconds, yet the seaman in Conrad has reacted to the
sound of the rising wind and its effect on the ocean and has calculated precisely
when it will be necessary to adjust the sails—not now, but in half an hour. All this
takes place 'in the moment of his exit'; it is a subliminal process as much as a
conscious one, borne out of long years at sea.

Conrad carried this habit of mind over into his second career as a novelist so
that observations on the weather became part of the mesh of his fiction. At the
beginning of 'The Return' from *Tales of Unrest*, for example, the reader is
introduced to Alvan Hervey as he emerges from the London Underground at the
end of a working day:

> He strode firmly. A misty rain settled like silvery dust on clothes, on
> moustaches; wetted the faces, varnished the flagstones, darkened the walls,
> dripped from umbrellas. And he moved on in the rain with careless serenity,
> with the tranquil ease of someone successful and disdainful, very sure of
> himself—a man with lots of money and friends.[2]

Conrad captures precisely here the visual and tactile effects of a needle-fine rain on
a darkening day, but it is more than scene setting. The image of 'silvery dust' finds
an echo in 'a man with lots of money and friends', suggesting the absolute
confidence of Alvan Hervey in his world. But as Hervey and the reader will soon
learn, his confidence is misplaced, for he arrives home to find that his wife has left
him and their loveless marriage. The world he thought so solid turns out to be as
illusory as the expensive-seeming droplets of rain on his clothes.

---

[1] Joseph Conrad, *A Personal Record* (Uniform Edition, London: Dent, 1923), 16.
[2] Joseph Conrad, 'The Return', *Tales of Unrest* (Uniform Edition, London: Dent, 1923), 119.

Examples abound in the detail of Conrad's style. A Dutch trader's eyes are 'pale, like a river mist' in 'Karain: A Memory',3 also from *Tales of Unrest*. In *Lord Jim*, Jim confronts the narrator, Marlow, outside the courthouse where his conduct at sea is under investigation, because he overhears Marlow, as he thinks, talking about him behind his back. Marlow comments:

> To watch his face was like watching a darkening sky before a clap of thunder, shade upon shade imperceptibly coming on, the gloom growing mysteriously intense in the calm of maturing violence.4

Conrad is employing here what the critic Derek Pearsall has called drastic imagery, where a seemingly unbridgeable disproportion exists between the subject and object of comparison. For a moment, as we read, we forget Jim's face as we look into the massing thunder storm, yet the effect is to imprint on our minds in an unforgettable way the pent-up fury mixed with frustration and humiliation which Jim feels and which at any moment might find its release in violence.

*

The Shadow-Line is the story of a young man's first command. The captain of a sailing ship has died at sea and the owners need a replacement to sail her back from (an unnamed) Bangkok where she is laid up, through the Gulf of Thailand to her home port. The first third of the novella is taken up with how the narrator (he too is never identified by name) gets the command while waiting in a colonial port for a passage to England. It takes place in an atmosphere of oppressive heat and the bright sparkling light of the tropical sun on water.

When he arrives in Bangkok, the newly appointed captain finds that there is fever among his crew and he sets sail as soon as he can to avoid the stifling air of the port, in the belief that clean sea air, combined with quinine, is the best way to restore the men's health.

---

3   Joseph Conrad, 'Karain: A Memory', *Tales of Unrest*, 29.
4   Joseph Conrad, *Lord Jim* (Uniform Edition, London: Dent, 1926), 71.

Once in the Gulf, however, the ship is becalmed and the weather, which up to now has provided incidental background, comes to the fore as the captain scans the sea and sky day after day. One moment the ship is under canvas, but the slight breeze drops and it becomes 'impossible to distinguish land from water in the enigmatical tranquility of the immense forces of the world.'⁵ Dawn comes and he looks across at the land to port: 'in the still streak of very bright pale orange light I saw the land profiled flatly as if cut out of black paper and seeming to float on the water light as a cork. But the rising sun turned it into mere dark vapour, a doubtful, massive shadow trembling in the hot glare.' (S-L, 77) The ship is at the mercy of mysterious currents, fitful winds that die away, all noticed in the minutest detail by the anxious captain. A sudden contrary wind takes the ship at speed off course and he reflects: 'if we had been out on pleasure sailing bent it would have been a delightful breeze, with the awakened sparkle of the sea, with the sense of motion and a feeling of unwonted freshness.' But this too dies away as suddenly as it came, and 'the stilled sea took on the polish of a steel plate in the calm'. (S-L, 87)

The crew can survive so long as the quinine holds out, but the narrator discovers that half the ship's supply has been replaced by a worthless powder, the quinine sold off by his predecessor. The crisis deepens, for hardly any of the crew are fit to work the ship, while the first mate, Mr Burns, in a state of delirium, is obsessed with the belief that the late captain's spirit is maliciously preventing the ship from passing beyond the line of latitude where he is buried.

It is at this point that the weather looms over the narrative in the most literal and oppressive way. One afternoon begins like many others:

> It was a terribly lifeless afternoon. For several days in succession low cloud had appeared in the distance, white masses with dark convolutions resting on the water, motionless, almost solid, and yet all the time changing their aspects subtly. Towards evening they vanished as a rule. But this day they awaited the setting sun, which glowed and smouldered sulkily amongst them before it sank down. The punctual and wearisome stars reappeared over our mast-heads, but the air remained stagnant and oppressive. (S-L, 104f)

Instead of dissolving as usual, the clouds begin to fill the sky and Ransome, the ship's cook and the only man apart from the captain to have escaped the fever, remarks that it looks like rain. 'I noticed then,' the narrator recalls, 'the broad shadow on the horizon extinguishing the low stars completely, while those overhead, when I looked up, seemed to shine through a veil of smoke.' (S-L, 105)

---

5   Joseph Conrad, *The Shadow-Line* (Uniform Edition: London: Dent, 1923), 76. All further references to the novella are from this edition, hereafter abbreviated to *S-L*.

The situation is critical because of the lack of able-bodied men—a sudden squall could whip out the ship's sails or even de-mast it. But the cloud, as it envelops the sky above them, takes on a new, more disturbing aspect:

> The impenetrable blackness beset the ship so close that it seemed that by thrusting one's hand over the side one could touch some unearthly substance. There was in it an effect of inconceivable terror and of inexpressible mystery. The few stars overhead shed a dim light upon the ship alone, with no gleams of any kind upon the water, in detached shafts piercing an atmosphere which had turned to soot. It was something I had never seen before, giving no hint of the direction from which any change would come, the closing in of a menace from all sides. (*S-L*, 108)

This oppressive, threatening weather becomes an objective correlative for the young captain's inner fear that he may be out of his depth on this voyage, not up to his commission. 'When the time came,' he fantasizes, 'the blackness would overwhelm silently the bit of starlight falling upon the ship, and the end of all things would come without a sigh, stir, or murmur of any kind, and all our hearts would cease to beat like run-down clocks.' (*S-L*, 108) He describes the effect of this annihilating darkness playing on his mind as 'my moral dissolution'. He has the presence of mind nonetheless to summon the few half-fit men to trim the sails in expectation of the coming squall, even though he knows that 'their weight on a rope could be no more than the weight of a bunch of ghosts.' (*S-L*, 109)

The blackness is now so complete that 'It was impossible to tell when the blow would come. To look round the ship was to look into a bottomless black pit. The eye lost itself in inconceivable depths.' (*S-L*, 110) It is, he recalls, like the 'darkness before creation':

> I knew I was invisible to the man at the helm. Neither could I see anything. He was alone, I was alone, every man was alone where he stood. (*S-L*, 113)

Then the unbearable tension is broken. He hears a random tapping all over the deck. 'While I wondered at this mysterious devilry, I received a slight blow under the left eye and felt an enormous tear run down my cheek. Raindrops. Enormous. Forerunners of something. Tap. Tap. Tap....'

What happens next is so far outside his experience that he struggles for words to describe it:

> Suddenly—how can I convey it? Well, suddenly the darkness turned to water. This is the only suitable figure. A heavy shower, a downpour, comes along,

making a noise. You hear its approach on the sea, in the air too, I verily believe. But this was different. With no preliminary whisper or rustle, without a splash, and even without the ghost of impact, I became instantly soaked to the skin. (S-L, 114)

Just as suddenly the cloudburst stops. A wind flaps the topmost sails, though it is dead calm on deck, and the ship moves forward 'as if of herself'. The cloud clears and the stars become visible again. 'The barrier of awful stillness,' the narrator comments, 'which had encompassed us for many days as though we had been accursed was broken.' (S-L, 121)

The ship sails on course at last, the captain worrying now how he is going to get her into harbour with his debilitated crew. 'Well –,' he reflects, 'it did get done about forty hours afterwards. By the exercising virtue of Mr Burns' awful laugh, the malicious spectre had been laid, the evil spell broken, the curse removed. We were now in the hands of a kind and energetic Providence. It was rushing us on...' (S-L, 125)

It is tempting to make something of the parallels with 'The Rime of the Ancyent Marinere' in this story—the curse of the late captain's spirit (as Mr Burns sees it in his delirium), the ship suddenly moving 'as if of herself', the feeling that an 'evil spell' has been broken and a 'curse removed', as a 'kind and energetic Providence' propels the ship to its destination, all have a parallel of sorts in Coleridge's poem. But it is not what Conrad is about.

In his Author's Note to the Uniform Edition of *The Shadow-Line*, Conrad is at pains to disclaim that he had any intention of making a raid on the 'supernatural' in the novella: 'I believe that if I attempted to put the strain of the Supernatural on it it would fail deplorably and exhibit an unlovely gap,' he remarks. He is too much of a materialist for that:

> I could never have attempted such a thing, because all my moral and intellectual being is penetrated by an invincible conviction that whatever falls under the dominion of our senses must be in nature and, however exceptional, cannot differ in its essence from all the other effects of the visible and tangible world of which we are a self-conscious part. (S-L, ix)

What is happening in *The Shadow-Line* is something much more interesting and in keeping with Conrad's stoic conviction that duty is the measure of a man's worth. In 'An Outpost of Progress' (*Tales of Unrest*) the narrator observes that: 'Few men realise that their life, the very essence of their character, their capabilities and their audacities, are only the expression of their belief in the safety of their surroundings.'[6] This is the testing ground for many of Conrad's protagonists; it is what Jim comes up against in that fateful jump from the stricken, and as he believes, doomed ship crammed with pilgrims.

It is what overtakes the narrator of *The Shadow-Line* when every point of reference, physical, psychological and moral, is stripped away from him in the impenetrable darkness of the squall. As we have seen, the oppressive weather becomes the outward manifestation of a 'moral dissolution' to the captain; the ship itself is a 'bottomless pit' where all normal associations are in abeyance, while the darkness echoes 'the darkness before creation' where the narrator had to reinvent himself as a moral being.

He was luckier than Jim in that he held his ground and did his duty. The shadow-line was not crossed that time around.

*

Per Olof Sundman (1922–92) was born in Vaxholm near Stockholm, but as a young man moved to Jämtland where for many years he ran a small hotel. It was here that he wrote most of his fiction, including his debut collection of short stories, *Jägarna* (The Hunters, 1957), which established him as one of the most promising writers of his generation. Several novels and short story collections followed in the 1960s and '70s, but by Scandinavian standards Sundman was not a prolific writer, and when he turned to politics, becoming a prominent member of the Centre Party in the Riksdag, the fiction dried up.

After his death, it was discovered that he had joined Nordisk Ungdom (Nordic Youth), the Swedish Nazi youth movement, in 1938, when he was sixteen, and had remained a member through the war years. He had kept quiet about this all his life.[7] The parallel with Günter Grass's recent revelation about his past in the Waffen SS is interesting. There was a heated debate in the Swedish press about Sundman's failure to reveal the truth, which led to a further decline in his reputation as a writer—a process which had begun, as it so often does, shortly after his death. A collected short stories appeared in 1998, but currently none of his extraordinary novels is in print. Had Sundman joined the Young Communists, with their allegiance to Stalin's brutal politics, little or nothing would have been said, such is the disparity still between our perception of Communism and Nazism.

---

6   Joseph Conrad, 'An Outpost of Progress', *Tales of Unrest*, 89.
7   This is fully explored by Per Svensson, *Frostviken: ett reportage om Per Olof Sundman, nazismen och tigandet* (Stockholm: Bonniers, 1998).

From the beginning of his literary career, Sundman had a deep fascination with the North and its harsh conditions. The novel *Två dagar, två nätter* (Two Nights, Two Days, 1965) is set in the bleak winter landscape of his adopted Jämtland; *Berättelsen om Såm* (The Story of Såm, 1977) is set in Iceland; he wrote two travel books about Lofoten; and his last significant book, *Ishav* (Arctic Ocean, 1982), is an account of three months spent on *Ymer*, an icebreaker turned research ship which explored the Arctic waters in 1980.

The one exception is *Expeditionen* (The Expedition, 1962), based on H.M. Stanley's disastrous expedition to 'rescue' Emin Pasha and set in the Congo. I don't know if Sundman ever read Conrad, but *Expeditionen* can be compared with *Heart of Darkness* as a depiction of the folly and brutality of Europeans in Central Africa at the end of the nineteenth century.

*

Given Sundman's fascination with the far North, it is not surprising that he should be attracted to the story of the Swedish explorer S.A. Andrée and his attempt to reach the North Pole by balloon in 1897; an attempt which ended in the deaths of André and his fellow balloonists, Knut Frænkel and Nils Strindberg.

The Andrée expedition attracted huge international interest in the 1890s at a time when Arctic exploration and ballooning were both at their height. Andrée's expedition was doomed from the start however. Not only were he and his team comparatively inexperienced balloonists, none of them had any experience of Arctic conditions. Andrée was warned that he could expect to meet hostile weather even in summer, and hardly anyone in the ballooning community believed his claim that his huge balloon, *Örnen* (The Eagle), could stay aloft for at least thirty days. (In the event it was airborne for barely four.) Andrée's innovations of steering lines and a sail to make the balloon partially steerable were also treated with skepticism and in fact the steering lines failed on take-off. *Örnen* flew, or was blown, from its base on Danskøja, one of the islands of Spitzbergen, never to be seen again.

There was much speculation about the fate of Andrée and his companions which became known only when the remains of their last camp were found on the shores of Kvitöja, a small inhospitable island to the east of Spitzbergen. Strindberg, who had evidently died first, was found buried in a cleft in the rocks, his body crudely covered with stones. Andrée and Frænkel's remains were in the expedition's tent. Rolls of film taken by Strindberg were found to be partially retrievable. The year after *Ingenjör Andrées luftfärd*, Sundman published the more starkly titled *Ingen fruktan, intet hopp* (No Fear, No Hope, 1968), a collection of documents relating to the expedition, including Andrée's journal, letters that Strindberg wrote to his fiancée, Anna Charlier, as they marched back over the ice, and Frænkel's meteorological journal, which were also found at the campsite. The book includes some of the expedition's remarkable photographs—the balloon, capsized on the ice; Andrée, rifle in hand, standing beside the first polar bear they shot; the three of them labouring with a sled bearing their canoe over a ridge of pack ice.

The bears were shot for meat since the men's three sleds could not carry enough food to sustain them on their journey South to one of the Arctic islands where they planned to over-winter. The bears were essential for their survival, therefore; but they were also the indirect cause of their deaths.

A few weeks into the march they began to experience disturbing symptoms— streaming catarrh, stomach pains and diarrhea, followed by boils and severe cramp in their arms and legs. Almost certainly they were suffering from trichinosis, caused by the minute hair-like nematode worm, trichina. They had ingested the worm from infected bear meat. (Dried bear meat which survived at the last campsite was found to contain trichinae.) A female trichina can produce up to 15,000 larvae in the host organism and even a mild infection can rapidly produce 50–90 million larvae which spread through the body forming cysts in muscle, including the heart, which weaken it fatally.

*

Ingenjör Andrées luftfärd is narrated in the first person by Knut Frænkel who joined Andrée's team after an aborted launch from Danskōja in the summer of 1896. A vacancy arose because Nils Ekholm refused to take part in a second expedition, expressing doubts (rightly as it turned out) about the airtightness of the balloon and the effectiveness of Andrée's steering mechanism.

In his narrative technique, Sundman was influenced by behaviourist psychology and its tenet that only the external behaviour of an organism can be properly observed. Even when using a third person narrator, therefore, Sundman eschews any assumption of omniscience. The reader is presented with the facts of a character's physical appearance, his or her actions and conversation, as observed by the narrator who, if it is a first person narration, is the only character whose subjective life is known to the reader. We have to deduce that of the other characters (if we want to) for ourselves.

In order to express this, Sundman developed an austere, minimalist style that has been compared to Hemingway's. In fact, it is much closer to the style of the Icelandic family sagas which Sundman had read in some depth. (*Berättelsen om Såm*, for example, is a retelling in a partially modernised context, of *Hrafnkell's Saga*.)[8]

8 Sundman denied the influence of Hemingway though seems to have resigned himself to the comparison. In an early letter, written shortly after the publication of *Jägarna*, he wrote that:

*

Sundman follows the documentary evidence for the 1897 expedition very closely; it is the framework for the narrative. Frænkel is a good choice for narrator as he is in many ways the least known and knowable of the three men. Andrée's diary and Strindberg's series of letters to Anna Charlier, provide a good deal of information about them. Frænkel's meteorological journal, on the other hand, provides only the bare bones of weather conditions, temperature, the course of their march and their position (when it was possible to take a sighting). Consequently, Sundman has a freer hand in creating his inner life as first person narrator and as close observer of his two companions. Frænkel's role as the expedition's meteorologist is also relevant, since a hydrogen-filled balloon is even more dependent on the weather than a sailing ship and awareness of weather conditions is not so much a motif as part of the deep structure of the novel.

Even before joining the expedition, for example, Frænkel shows an instinctive attention to the weather. Walking through a wintry Stockholm two days after his first meeting with Andrée, he notes that the weather is overcast, combined with a 'south-westerly wind, rising temperature, and an enervating drizzle.'

> I took a long walk along Djurgården's many winding paths. The snow was slushy and wet; it seeped through my shoes and was also soaked up by my trouser legs according to the elementary physical law of capillary attraction.[9]

(A translation of *Ingenjör Andrées luftfärd* appeared in 1970 under the title *The Voyage of the Eagle*, though I have never seen a copy. The translations here are my own.)

Exact observation of snow and its effects will become more significant and urgent on the polar ice, where it will not be a question of inconveniently wet feet, but of survival. This passage, like many others in the first part of the novel, prefigures the gruelling journey to come. (Passing a stand of horse cabs, Frænkel notes that the drivers are constructing a shelter of snow and ice, as they do every winter; when he, Andrée and Strindberg are near the end of their strength, they

---

'For me, the choice of a regional subject matter has perhaps involved most of all a semantically deliberate sparseness of language and a rejection of 'psychologising' in favour of a kind of behaviourist physiologising (which I see, without much pleasure, will be taken as Hemingway-inspired.)' (Unpublished letter to Åke Lindström, editor of *Expressen*, 6 Dec. 1957.) See also Birgitta Trotzig, *Per Olof Sundman* (Stockholm: Norstedts, 1993), pp. 17ff, for the influence on his style of the speech patterns of the remote area of Jämtland where he lived in the 1950s.

9   Per Olof Sundman, *Ingenjör Andrées luftfärd* (Stockholm: Norsedt, 1967), 35.

build a hut in the same way on an ice floe, hoping it will save their lives.)

In the early chapters, the weather is constantly glimpsed, as it were, through the interstices of the narrative. Reminiscing about the crowds at the railway station in Stockholm the previous year, Andrée recalls that 'It was a Thursday evening with a clear sky but heavy, close air that threatened thunder.' (*IAL*, 93) As they sail from Göterborg at the start of the 1897 expedition, Frænkel notes that 'the cloud cover had been broken up and dispersed, the wind had slackened to a mild breeze, the sun shone from the West and there lay a heavy, close early summer warmth over Göterborg.' (*IAL*, 98) The first third of the novel is taken up, rather as in *The Shadow-Line*, with events preceding its real subject which is the isolated world of the three men during the brief balloon flight, the decision to land, and the return over the ice on foot ending in their deaths at the winter camp on Kvitöja.

Once the balloon is airborne the narrative closes in on the restricted space of the balloon's gondola as the last vestiges of the civilised world dwindle behind them on Dansköya. Despite the failure of the steering lines, there is an initial euphoria: 'We found ourselves in a total stillness, we were supreme—the Earth was obliged to move beneath us.' (*IAL*, 152) This sense of well-being is short-lived however. Instead of the clear skies Andrée had confidently predicted, they find themselves enveloped in cloud and fog as soon as they reach the polar ice, and they discover the sensitivity of the balloon's hydrogen to temperature change—a fall of half a degree Centigrade causes the balloon to lose 200 metres in altitude. In a sense there is nothing now *except* weather. The favourable southerly wind which they depend on to take them across the Pole veers East, then West, driving them out of their course; the cloud and fog condense on the huge expanse of the balloon's fabric, soak into the ropes. When the temperature falls below zero at night, this freezes to a skin of ice weighing, they estimate, at least a ton and forcing the balloon so low that it bounces in great strides over the ice until they hastily jettison ballast.

After three and a half days they decide that the attempt to reach the Pole is futile and land *Örnen* on the ice. Frænkel begins a new meteorological journal— 'temperature about zero Centigrade, the sky overcast but the cloud cover high, the air remarkably clear despite a fine drizzle, weak gusts of wind from the North-West.' The dry journal notes are rounded out, however, by Frænkel as he looks around at the desolate polar scene with a human eye:

We found ourselves on a large and snow-covered ice floe.
It was impossible to make out the horizon.
The whiteness of the snow dissolved into the whiteness of the fog and the fog became white cloud that slid over us.
It was like sitting under a cupola of whiteness the size of which it was

impossible to estimate. (*IAL*, 193)

As they unload the gondola, Andrée, Strindberg and Frænkel are like arctic Robinson Crusoes. They have with them a huge range of the products of our industrial civilization, from sleds and a collapsible canoe to hunting rifles, a primus stove and tinned and dried food. Unlike Crusoe, however, they are marooned in one of the most inhospitable places on Earth, and their main hope is to march South, either to Franz Josef Land in the South-East, or to Spitzbergen in the South-West. They make a series of sightings and realize that the ice is constantly moving under them with the polar currents, but not constantly in one direction, swinging from South-West to South to South-East. They decide to set a course S-SE for Franz Josef Land.

They now have to negotiate an alien world; the arctic ice cannot be said to be either landscape or seascape; it is a product of the deeply inhospitable polar climate, sculpted by weather; a kind of weatherscape. 'This bloody whiteness,' Frænkel exclaims at one point. 'Fog, snow, snow-covered ice—no shadows, no visibility, impossible to estimate the distance from one ridge of pack ice to the next—fifty metres or two hundred.' (*IAL*, 235) Moving a hundred paces from the camp one day, he can barely see the tent and the sleds: 'I found myself in a little world of whiteness which I knew to be a huge desert of ice and snow and whiteness.' (*IAL*, 239) (When later on the ice is splashed red with the blood of a bear they have killed, it shocks the reader with its vividness, so accustomed have we become to this cold, white, fathomless world.)

On one of the rare occasions when the sun appears and it is possible to take a sighting, they discover that while they have been marching S-SE, the ice has changed direction and has drifted to the West. Despite several days and many kilometres, they are further from their destination than when they set out. They decide therefore to change course once again and head S-W for Sjuöyane, a group of small islands to the North of Spitzbergen.

The journey across the ice is slow and punishing. The ice is riven with channels of open water which they have to cross with the aid of their canoe, loading and unloading each sled in turn; floes that have been lifted over one another by the movement of the ice create long ridges of pack ice several metres high which can take hours to cross with the heavily laden sleds.

Frænkel broods more and more on Andrée's incompetence—their sleds are wrongly constructed; they have out-of-date single shot rifles instead of modern repeaters; the balloon's steering lines and airtightness failed and had been seriously questioned by experts, yet Andrée insisted on going ahead. As they march, travelling in one direction but moving in another with the drift of the ice, Frænkel begins to question Andrée in an increasingly aggressive way. At their first meeting in Stockholm, Frænkel had noticed the rapid oscillation of Andrée's eyes from side to side; on the ice he alone has no need of dark glasses against the glare of the snow. It dawns on Frænkel that Andrée has severe problems with his sight and may even be half-blind; but when he confronts him with this, Andrée avoids answering, just as he refuses to rise to the bait when Frænkel taunts him about his 'scientific' observations as he constantly stops to measure the thickness of the sea ice, collect grit and sand trapped in floes, or a gull's severed head (so its eyes can be dissected to discover what mechanisms it has evolved against snow blindness). Andrée is an engineer not a geologist or biologist. The 'scientific' purpose of the expedition was always a blind to cover the mere adventurism of the enterprise. It descends into farce when, in the last days, as Frænkel and Strindberg work desperately to erect an ice hut where they can over-winter, Andrée takes no part in the exhausting process but wanders around taking measurements and soundings. 'Do you realise,' Frænkel confronts him, 'how insane this whole balloon business was?' And he goes on:

> Badly planned. Badly organised. Badly equipped. Doomed to failure from the beginning. Quite apart from the steering lines and the fact that you panicked when we took off.
>   No, he said.
>   You don't want to see it, I asked.
>   No, he replied. (*IAL*, 321)

Andrée can't be drawn, but it becomes clear to Frænkel that Andrée had determined to take off come what may because he couldn't stand the humiliation of returning to Stockholm a failure for the second time.

During another confrontation, Andrée half admits this and that he knew beforehand that the expedition was bound to fail. Yet he only half admits it. Andrée remains an enigma to the end; a man of immense presence, yet unknowable behind his reserve. Strindberg, too, is remote. He takes little part in Frænkel's one-sided quarrels, pouring his feelings and thoughts into his letters to Anna instead, which he has encrypted so that his companions can't read them. When he stops writing to her it is a sign, we know, that he has given up hope.

As the arctic winter approaches with its sub-zero temperatures and endless night, they build an ice hut on a floe which they consider large enough to be safe. But almost as soon as it is finished the floe is broken up by the violent convulsions of the sea ice and they are forced to relocate their camp to Kvitöya, the desolate island they have been drifting past for several days. The ridges of pack ice are such, though, that it takes them two days to haul the sleds two kilometres to the shore.

From the height of the island's glacier they can glimpse hills to the South which they realize must be Spitzbergen. They discuss how they will reach them over the ice next summer. But there is to be no next summer. A new ice hut is started and abandoned as the trichinosis takes its toll. Strindberg, the youngest and weakest, stops eating and takes to the tent. His last words are a question to Andrée: 'Why the hell were you forced to make this journey?' (*IAL*, 339)

With their last strength, Andrée and Frænkel bury Strindberg in a cleft in the rocks. When shortly afterwards Andrée dies silently, lying next to Frænkel, Frænkel takes stock of his situation. There is bear and seal meat in plenty, but he knows that he will not be able to withstand six months' isolation in the total darkness of an arctic winter. He swallows the expedition's remaining vials of opium and morphine. 'I lay down on my side close to Andrée. His beard was grey, he was an old man.' (Andrée was forty-four.)

'Jag var ännu ung,' he reflects as he lies dying. 'I was still young.' They are the last words of the novel. (*IAL*, 344)

✶

If Conrad's great theme is duty as an expression of stoic integrity, Sundman's is the unknowable nature of our fellow humans. For both novelists, the human condition is grounded in the harsh conditions of the material universe. 'It was one of those dewy, clear, starry nights,' Marlow recalls in *Chance*,

> oppressing our spirit, crushing our pride, by the brilliant evidence of the awful loneliness, of the hopeless obscure insignificance of our globe lost in the splendid revelation of the glittering, soulless universe.[10]

The Shadow-Line and *Ingenjör Andrées luftfärd* are contrasts in nature's black and white. The pitch blackness of the tropical squall projecting outwards the moral and psychological crisis of the young captain. The endless blinding whiteness of the Arctic annihilating everything except the fact of Andrée, Strindberg and Frænkel's fleeting existence as they cross its vastness. Their journey from the start was meaningless, but once begun, it too became a kind of duty, a test of human endurance in an ice-world indifferent to their fate. What made you do it, Strindberg asks as he dies. But in Sundman's world questions rarely receive answers and Andrée doesn't reply.

---

[10]   Joseph Conrad, *Chance* (Uniform Edition, London: Dent, 1923), 50.

Tench's quotations:
the poems you take with you

Gavin Edwards

WHATEVER material possessions people may be able to take with them when they travel from one part of the world to another, they always take cultural ones. They take, in particular, their native language: words, and the attitudes which their words express. Yet these attitudes, and even the meaning of familiar words, are likely to be altered by the encounter with unfamiliar places and situations.

The travel writings of the eighteenth century marine officer Watkin Tench, born in Chester to schoolteacher parents in 1758, interestingly exemplify this interaction between word and world. His three books - *A Narrative of the Expedition to Botany Bay* (1789), its sequel, *A Complete Account of the Settlement at Port Jackson* (1793), and *Letters Written in France to a Friend in London between the month of November 1794 and the month of May 1795* (1796) - show us that, in addition to his native language, Tench took with him a good knowledge of Latin and French, Anglican religious beliefs and whig political ones, and a conventional enlightenment vocabulary of social classification. However, it is one particular cultural possession that concerns me here: the poems that he knew, passages from which appear in his books as quotations or allusions. The poets' words helped to shape his response to his experiences as a traveller and soldier – to landfall, the encounter with other peoples, exile and slaughter – but their words acquired new meanings in the process.

Although *A Narrative of the Expedition to Botany Bay* was published in London, it was wholly written in New South Wales. Tench sent the manuscript back on the first boat to leave for England, while he himself stayed on in the new colony. Any poems which he quotes in the *Narrative* must therefore be quoted from memory or from books he took with him. By contrast, parts of the *Complete Account* may draw on material available to him back in England where it was completed. As for the *Letters Written in France*, Tench lost most of his material possessions—including, presumably, his books—in the fighting which led to his capture by the French. But while these 'letters written in France' may be exactly what they say they are—letters written as a prisoner of war in republican France—they may also have been written up, from a journal, after he returned to England in May 1795.

The poem to which he most frequently alludes—usually in the form of unattributed quotations—is *Paradise Lost*. Lines and, quite evidently, whole passages from Milton's poem came to his mind as he attempted to give meaning and shape to his experience. The *Narrative* records the departure of HMS *Supply* from Portsmouth on May 13, 1787:

> By ten o'clock, we had got clear of the Isle of Wight, at which time, having very little pleasure in conversing with my own thoughts, I strolled down among the convicts to observe their sentiments at this juncture. A very few excepted, their countenances indicated a high degree of satisfaction, though in some the pang of being severed, perhaps forever, from their native land could not be wholly suppressed. In general, marks of distress were more perceptible among the men than the women, for I recollect to have seen but one of those affected on the occasion. 'Some natural tears she dropp'd but wip'd them soon.' After this the accent of sorrow was no longer heard; more genial skies and change of scene banished repining and discontent, and introduced in their stead cheerfulness and acquiescence in a lot now not to be altered.[1]

Tench does not tell us where the words in quotation marks come from, but they certainly depend for their full effect on our knowing their source and context, the final lines of Milton's poem:

> Some natural tears they dropp'd, but wip'd them soon;
> The World was all before them, where to choose
> Their place of rest, and Providence their guide:
> They hand in hand with wand'ring steps and slow,
> Through Eden took their solitary way.[2]

Tench's allusion places the events in which he is participating into a grand redemptive narrative encompassing the whole of time and space. The exile of the convicts—and to some extent his own departure—becomes a repetition of the

[1] *Sydney's First Four Years, being a Reprint of 'A Narrative of the Expedition to Botany Bay' and 'A Complete Account of the Settlement at Port Jackson', by Captain Watkin Tench*, ed. L. F. Fitzhardinge (Sydney: Library of Australian History, 1979), 13-14. All references to the *Narrative* and the *Account* are to this edition.
[2] Book XII, lines 645-9. Text taken from John Milton, *Paradise Lost*, ed. Christopher Ricks (Harmondsworth: Penguin, 1989).

original exile of Adam and Eve from Eden. *Paradise Lost* makes it possible to think of the banishment of the convicts as both an experience of irreparable loss and the prelude to a new life. Moreover, as an English version of the Genesis story, the poem allows Tench to associate Eden rather specifically with his own native land.3

But if Milton's lines shape Tench's perception of the present, the realities of the present also lead Tench to modify Milton's lines. Milton's 'they dropp'd' becomes 'she dropp'd' because, perhaps contrary to his expectations, Tench sees more 'marks of distress' among the men on board the *Supply* than among the women: only one woman is in tears and she 'wipes them soon'.

An allusion of this sort, which draws on but also differentiates itself from an earlier text, assumes, or pretends to assume, that author and reader share a literary inheritance. But if this is so, what effect does the allusion have on the relationship between us (author and reader) and the convict woman herself, the immediate subject of the allusion?

On the one hand, the allusion to the exiled Eve elevates the convict woman, and links author and reader to her through our common descent from 'the Mother of Mankind' (I. 36). Furthermore this is, indirectly, an allusion to a biblical story that most people on the ship—officers, marines, sailors and convicts—would know. To that extent the allusion sustains a common culture. On the other hand, drawing most of its words specifically from Milton's retelling of the biblical story, it belongs to the culture of a minority, a minority which would almost certainly exclude the convict woman. Tench's allusion tells us that we are all in the same boat, but not all on the same deck.

Tench frequently quotes lines of verse to mark moments of crisis and heightened emotion, of joy or grief or both. Allusion to Milton marks the moment of departure; allusion to Homer and Addison herald the moment of arrival:

> When day appeared we had lost sight of the land and did not regain it until the 19th at only the distance of seventeen leagues from our desired port. The wind was now fair, the sky serene though a little hazy, and the temperature of the air

---

3   He made the association again, more explicitly, in the *Letters Written in France*: ' "Oh! For a bridge to pass over two hundred thousand *sans-culottes!*" I hear often exclaimed. Not that bridge which, according to Milton, Death consolidated over Chaos, could be more fatal to the remaining innocence of our first parents, than such a structure, in the shape of a superior fleet, would prove to their English descendants' (28). All quotations from the *Letters Written in France* are taken from Watkin Tench, *Letters from Revolutionary France*, ed. Gavin Edwards (Cardiff: University of Wales Press, 2001). Tench is alluding here to *Paradise Lost*, X, lines 301-5 which describe the devils building 'a bridge/ Of length prodigious joining to the wall/ Immovable of this now fenceless world/ Forfeit to Death; from hence a passage broad/ Smooth, easy, inoffensive down to hell.'

delightfully pleasant. Joy sparkled in every countenance and congratulations issued from every mouth. Ithaca itself was scarcely more longed for by Ulysses than Botany Bay by the adventurers who had traversed so many thousand miles to take possession of it.

'Heavily in clouds came on the day' which ushered in our arrival. To us it was 'a great, an important day', though I hope the foundation, not the fall, of an empire will be dated from it. (31-2)

In the second paragraph Tench is quoting, or misquoting, from the opening lines of Addison's play, *Cato* (1713):

> Heavily in clouds brings on the day,
> The great, the important day, big with the fate
> Of Cato and of Rome.[4]

An allusion to this play about the fall of the Roman empire obviously needs Tench's gloss on it ('I hope the foundation, not the fall, of an empire will be dated from it'). As for the reference to the *Odyssey*, it is understandable that Tench, after a voyage of eight months, should associate his longing for landfall at Botany Bay with Ulysses' longing for landfall at Ithaca after his long voyage from Troy. On the other hand, there is an irony in the allusion too: Ulysses was returning to his native Ithaca whereas Tench and his fellows have left their native land and are about to 'take possession' of somebody else's. It is a difference Tench became sharply aware of in subsequent months.

What Tench certainly does appreciate is that, from the moment the fleet enters the Pacific, and throughout his stay in New South Wales, the poems to which he alludes are, like himself, a long way from home. He invokes an ancient Greek poem about a Mediterranean voyager to describe his own Pacific landfall many centuries later. Allusion always transfers words from one text to another, one time to another; when Tench alludes to European texts in the antipodes, we are often aware that the words have also been transferred from one part of the globe to another.

This is made very clear in a passage from the *Complete Account* describing an expedition inland in May 1791. Tench and three colleagues encounter a group of 'natives' (he calls the indigenous people 'natives or 'Indians') who help them to cross a river. After commenting on the 'patience' and 'courtesy' of these men, he concludes:

---

4   Joseph Addison, *Cato*, in *Five Restoration Tragedies*, ed. Bonamy Dobree (Oxford: Oxford University Press, 1928), ll. 1-3.

Let the banks of those rivers 'known to song'; let him whose travels have lain among polished nations, produce me a brighter example of disinterested urbanity, than was shown by these denizens of a barbarous clime, to a set of destitute wanderers, on the side of the Hawksbury. (236)

This passage includes at least three kinds of linguistic transfer: of proper names, of verse, and of a specific descriptive vocabulary. The river had been named after Lord Hawksbury, President of the Board of Trade when the fleet left England for Botany Bay in 1787. 'Known to song' is presented as a quotation: I have not been able to find an exact source for it, though there are approximations to it in early eighteenth century verse.[5] In any case, the river is unknown to the kind of European song in which the phrase 'known to song' might appear. The particular force of the allusion, however, derives from what follows it, the description of the 'disinterested urbanity' of 'these denizens of a barbarous clime'.

These words—'urbane' and 'barbarous', along with 'polished' and 'Indian'—belong to the European vocabulary of social description which Tench took with him (he also took 'European'). This vocabulary does not derive from any one source and Tench's use of it therefore does not count as allusion; nevertheless, it shares characteristics with the kind of allusion I have been discussing. In particular, the application of the phrase 'disinterested urbanity' to the men who help the Europeans cross the river can be compared with the application of Milton's line 'Some natural tears they dropp'd but wip'd them soon' to the tears of the convict woman on the *Supply*. This is not only because the words 'disinterested urbanity' honour the indigenous men as Milton's words honour the convict woman, but because the actions of these men, like the actions of the convicts, alter the meaning of the words invoked to describe them.

By describing the men's actions as urbane, Tench foregrounds and questions the equation between cultivated courtesy and urban civilization which the word 'urbane' took for granted.[6] This happens because he is applying the word to natives of a land without towns, without *urbs*. The actions of these men discover a faultline in the vocabulary of social description which Tench has brought to bear upon them.[7]

5   John Armstrong in his poem 'The Art of Preserving Health' (1744) refers to the river Liddal as 'till now, except in Doric lays/ Tuned to her murmurs by her love-sick swains/ Unknown in song.' I am grateful to David Skilton for this reference.

6   William Empson argued that all complex words make 'equations' of this sort between different semantic elements. See William Empson, *The Structure of Complex Words* (London: Chatto and Windus, 1951).

7   For an interesting discussion of the ways in which the agency of Pacific peoples makes itself felt in European representations of them, see Bronwen Douglas, 'Slippery Word,

Tench's third book, *Letters Written in France*, begins with an account of the sea battle off the coast of Brittany in which he was 'taken by "the insolent foe"' (5). Being 'taken by the insolent foe' was an episode in 'the story of my life' which Othello told to Desdemona and then to the Venetian Senate in Act 1 of *Othello*. At the time, this was a speech much quoted, for instance by Wordsworth who frequently referred to Othello's tale of 'moving accidents by flood and field' as he attempted to distance his own poetry from Othello's world of heroic adventure.[8] Tench, by contrast, is identifying himself with Othello, as a soldier-storyteller, converting Othello's insolent Ottoman foe into his own insolent French one.

Tench then goes on to describe the sea-battle itself in a literary context that is both epic and tragic:

> I left the deck and descended into the bread room. There I had in the morning deposited one of my trunks, out of which I filled a clothes-bag with such necessaries as I thought would be most useful to me, and left it in the charge of my servant, while I endeavoured to save a part of what a very large trunk, lodged in the marine store-room, contained. But this resolution I was incapable of effecting. The cock-pit, which I was obliged to pass through, presented such a scene of misery, as banished every feeling, but sorrow and pity. I found myself encompassed at once by the dead and the dying. The groans of the latter, joined to the cries of the wounded, on whom operations were performing by the surgeon, and to the blood which overflowed my feet, filled me with horror and disgust.
>
> > "Sight so deform what heart of rock could long
> > Dry-ey'd behold?"— MILTON
>
> It "quelled my best of man;" and, after two ineffectual attempts to penetrate across this stage of woe, I returned to my servant, and made a few farther arrangements of what was left to me. (6-7)

The two quotations here—the first, unusually, attributed to its original author— are taken from the same passage in *Paradise Lost*. The surgeon at work in the cock-pit of the *Alexander* has brought to Tench's mind the passage in which the

---

Ambiguous Praxis: "Race" and Late 18th-Century Voyagers in Oceania', *Journal of Pacific History*, 41 (2006), 1-29. For a fuller discussion of Tench's vocabulary and his interest in language, see Gavin Edwards, 'From Chester to Quimper via Sydney: Watkin Tench in Revolutionary France, *Literature and History*, 11, 2 (2002), 1-18.

8   See Gavin Edwards, *Narrative Order 1789-1819: Life and Story in an Age of Revolution* (London: Palgrave, 2001), 100-122.

Archangel Michael shows to Adam in a vision the consequences of the Fall, representing humankind's fallen state as a hospital where

> ...despair
> Tended the sick busiest from Couch to Couch;
> And over them triumphant Death his Dart
> Shook, but delay'd to strike, though oft invok'd
> With vows, as their chief good, and final hope.
> Sight so deform what heart of Rock could long
> Dry-ey'd behold? Adam could not, but wept,
> Though not of Woman born; compassion quelled
> His best of Man, and gave him up to tears
> A space, till firmer thoughts restrained excess.
>   (XI. 489-98)

This passage raises with particular force an unanswerable question which is raised by all of Tench's quotations: when did the lines of verse come into his mind? It is perfectly possible that lines from Homer and Addison came into his mind as the *Supply* approached Botany Bay, and not only when, on shore later, he wrote his account of the episode. On the other hand, even if we could be certain that these really are 'letters written in France', it seems unlikely that lines of Milton came into his head as he attempted to cross the *Alexander*'s grim operating theatre. And yet *Paradise Lost* was so much a part of his being—he may have known it by heart— that we cannot be sure its words and episodes would not have come to his aid in a situation like this.

In any case, what those lines from *Paradise Lost* suggest to him, as he tries to cross—or describes himself trying to cross—'this stage of woe' is that he is not in fact alone in his feelings of sorrow and fear: such feelings, such events, have precedents and are part of a wider action. In this respect it is important that Tench always alludes to epic or dramatic verse, never to lyric. The kind of poetry he quotes lends itself to the expression, but also the control, of strong feeling. You are led from grief back into a continuing action. You shed tears but wipe them soon. This is poetry which allows you to weep a space, but which restrains excess. The road of excess does not, for Tench, lead to the palace of wisdom. Tench's Milton is not of the devil's party.

Tench quotes Milton in his description of the cock-pit as a way of telling us that he broke down in tears, but of telling us indirectly. The sight 'quell'd my best of Man'; but we may only know from the original context that this means that Tench 'wept', 'gave him up to tears/A space'. 'Some natural tears she shed, but wip'd them soon' was more literal and open; nevertheless, the elevated literary form in which the convict woman's tears appear does in itself do something to shield the rawness of her grief.

If we put these two episodes together—the episode on the *Supply* and the episode on the *Alexander*—we can see that Tench is torn between two understandings of masculinity and weeping. On the *Supply*, 'the marks of distress were more perceptible among the Men than the women', while on the *Alexander*, Tench's tears need the precedent of Adam who cried 'though not of Woman born'. On the one hand, Tench knows from observation and introspection that men are quite as prone to tears as women. On the other hand, he believes that it is against their nature to be so: it is unmanly, unsoldierly. The allusions to *Paradise Lost* allow Tench to articulate this tension. Milton's poetry helps to shape Tench's experience, but Milton's meanings, and even his words, are altered in the process.

II

Landscapes, Warscapes

Matthew Francis

Letter from West Wales

for Jeremy Hooker

HOUSE next to the main road:
the trucks grunt, on and off
dogs bark in a farm van,
a man up in the glass
cab of some great wheeled beast
sails to Spar to buy fags.

The hills crouch in the gorse.
Phone wires slice up the sky.
There is smoke in the air:
the dark malt of coal fires,
the cough of blown ash where
March burns in the damp yards.

The sea shows in the gaps,
its blue blurred with the mud
of the land it has gulped.
The low cliffs are pressed sand,
the beach is jags of black.
Dead fish and cans lodge there.

The fields are strips cut to
a plan from the Black Book.
Spiked tools rust in the weeds.
Strange sheep with furred brows mooch
by the bare pole whose flag
was ripped off by the wind.

Lime kilns are squat huts where
no one dwelt but scorched stones.
A gate stands on a slope
with no fence to frame it.
Once I found a sheep's shin,
in the grass, still with skin.

This is their land. When night
comes and the trucks' grunt stops
sheep song fills up the dark.
Each one has its own bleat;
their highs and lows map out
the lived shapes of the hills.

Norman Schwenk

After Kikusha-ni

(1753–1826)

1. Is the wind Spirit?
   It is like: invisible,
   pulling down great trees.

2. Are clouds Illusion?
   They are like: hiding the road;
   cars appear like wraiths.

3. Is the moon Knowing?
   It is like: through wind and clouds
   hinting a bright face.

David Lloyd

Various Restrictions

for Jeremy Hooker

IF you stand long enough in one place
and speak few or no words and no names

and restrict movement to necessary breaths,
even the hairs on your arms still;

and if you try not to remember
that cup of coffee this morning or last week

or the path you walked to arrive at this place;
and if you face the wind, your back to the afternoon sun,

your skin sweating off its scent,
your clothes green or brown or better yet

no clothes at all, not even folded nearby; then
creatures you have never heard or seen

or imagined will arrive out of air and the long grass
to reveal to you their secret markings.

They'll do this in silence.
They'll do this as if you are one of them.

'Inwards where all the battle is':[1] Alun Lewis's 'The Jungle'

John Pikoulis

DESPITE its significance, Alun Lewis's 'The Jungle' has attracted surprisingly little critical attention. The poem was written after Lewis went on a reconnoitring mission in south west India in his role as Intelligence Officer of the 6th Battalion, the South Wales Borderers from mid-December 1943 to January 1944. It touches on a variety of themes; it is at once a narrative of the jungle, both as a place and a state of mind, a contrast of the East and West, a personal confession and a description of the existential emptiness of life. At the same time, it constitutes a Bloomian argument with the literary predecessors who weighed most heavily on him at this critical juncture of his life. Within six weeks, on March 5th in Burma, he killed himself.

I

The jungle fascinated Lewis as well as awed him. In a letter to his wife, Gweno, on August 12, 1943, he wrote: 'I feel now that the only place worth going to is the Jungle'.[2] Frustrated by the 'bare necessities of soldiering' (*ITGT*, 55) and by 'the conventional life of the Mess', he longed for a world of pure contemplation, the source of his poems and stories. 'I'm not busy, you know. I'm just at something or

---

[1] Alun Lewis, *Letters to My Wife*, ed. Gweno Lewis, (Bridgend: Seren Books, 1989), 415 (hereafter *LW*). This offers a fuller version of Lewis's correspondence with his wife than *In the Green Tree* (London: George Allen and Unwin, 1949), which has been reissued in a revised version in the Library of Wales series as *In the Green Tree: The Letters and Short Stories of Alun Lewis* (Cardigan: Parthian, 2006). Since the text of the latter is likely to be more available to readers, I have quoted from that wherever possible.

[2] *In the Green Tree* (Parthian edn.), 46 (hereafter *ITGT*).

other all the time' (*LW*, 405). He had written little of late and what he had struck him as being 'poor second-rate stuff' (*ITGT*, 63):

> although war is so monstrously arbitrary and violent that personal values seems so futile and ineffectual as 'art for art's sake' I still hold them, like the thousands of others, because there is nothing else to save one or make one worth saving. (*ITGT*, 60-1)

The jungle helped him recover 'personal values', being a 'separate world, remote, unperturbed, indifferent, serene' where 'your own troubles and fears fall away and remain outside in the world of roads and spaces' (*ITGT*, 61), where there still existed a 'humanity that imperialism and snobbery haven't spoiled' (*ITGT*, 66).

The jungle, however, also served as a metaphor to describe his own depression. He told his wife, Gweno, in April 1943: 'I love you very much indeed and never lose you, thank God, in the jungle of my mind' (*LW*, 322). When he enlisted in the war four years before, it was because it seemed to him the necessary means of defending democracy—a sufficient motive to override his pacifist scruples. Now, though, it struck him as no more than 'the sprawling gamble of big empires grappling for blood and oil and palm nuts' (*ITGT*, 47), the defence of a society that was rooted in class and race: 'oh, the temptation of the wilderness, darling; for it is the wilderness into which we have gone' (*LW*, 382). The war he was fighting no longer seemed to him justifiable.

The jungle thus accurately reflects his state of mind at the time. It was a means of escape but it also reflected on what he was escaping from, being an 'absurdly unreal little elysium'. 'You can imagine the boyish pleasure of it all—and the unreality of it also, for I find myself suddenly thinking, 'What *is* happening—behind this?' The jungle liberated him but it also disconcerted him for he could never shake himself free from the 'dark foreboding [that] comes with me to the river when I slip away to swim by myself and lie in the sun' (*ITGT*, 64). Its peace was deceptive, for it seemed only to delay the inevitable. Such ironical ambivalence permeates the poem. The point was made in a different way when Lewis returned to the battalion only to find himself immersed in everything the jungle had freed him from.

The jungle's happiness is thus confounded even as it arrives. The opening description in lines 4-10 is eloquently sustained in long cadences, the breath held:

> The crocodile slides from the ochre sand
> And drives the great translucent fish
> Under the boughs across the running gravel.
> Windfalls of brittle mast crunch as we come

> To quench more than our thirst—our selves –
> Beneath this bamboo bridge, this mantled pool
> Where sleep exudes a sinister content…

The elevated diction and sinuous syntax combine to produce a grave rhetoric. The soldiers come to the jungle to find themselves renewed physically and spiritually; they 'quench' their thirst but also their inner selves, their uncertain or fraying identities. 'Quench', however, also suggests termination as well as satisfaction. The pool refreshes but also induces in the soldiers a sense of an ending.

The usual effect of irony is simple: one statement is made but carries its own immediate contradiction or qualification. In 'The Jungle', the effect is more complicated: statement and counter-statement exist but fail to achieve resolution. Either, or both, could be true: neither successfully contradicts or counters the other. In any event, the soldiers' salvation is queried by the allusion to Narcissus in the picture of them resting gazing into the jungle pool. Beauty mixes with menace, as is evident again when the crocodile dives after the 'translucent' fish, its insidious intention granted a surprising sheen by 'slides', 'ochre' and 'translucent'. In the ensuing stalemate, nature's law appears harsh but remains picturesque, as is demonstrated by 'Windfalls of brittle mast', a rich crunch of syllables emphasising the fragility of things.

The soldiers then fall asleep. Their sleep persists for the rest of the poem, which then emerges as the displaced expression of their thoughts (if, that is, they could be said to have any). 'The Jungle' is an oneironic reverie, though unusually articulate. 'Dream' also implies visionariness, particularly in a man like Lewis, possessed of an 'aesthetic passionate impulse'[3] and more than usually responsive to the pool's 'sinister content'. It remains unclear whether the accent in 'content' falls on the first or second syllable. If it is on the first, it implies 'burden' or 'significance' to men grown wary of the dangers of relaxation after so many months of intense training; if it falls on the second, it suggests 'satisfaction' at being able to cast care aside even as battle approaches.

But the question immediately arises: is the pool's kindness subversive, undermining the soldiers' will to fight, or does it only reactivate the men's awareness of the reality of death after years in which it has become blunted by army routine? The jungles of Burma loom in the jungles of India. For the first but not the last time in the poem, kindness is confused with enmity, pleasure intermixed with danger. Of such is the men's ironic haven.

> Windfalls of brittle mast crunch as we come

---

3   Alun Lewis, *Collected Poems*, ed. Cary Archer (Bridgend: Seren, 1994), 194 (hereafter *CP*).

> To quench more than our thirst—our selves –
> Beneath this bamboo bridge, this mantled pool
> Where sleep exudes a sinister content
> As though all strength of mind and limb must pass
> And all fidelities and doubts dissolve…

The men lose their identity as mind and limb, all previous loyalties, 'dissolve' in the 'green indifference of this sleep', which they greet with 'the nonchalance of a laugh'. ('*Ha! Ha! Among the Trumpets*', the volume in which 'The Jungle' appeared, refers to the episode in Job when the horses, sensing battle, charge exhilaratedly towards it.) In their exhausted state, they shed their strength in order to regain it:

> The weighted world a bubble in each head,
> The warm pacts of the flesh betrayed.…

The world has become no more than a bubble or round 'O' to them.

'Betrayed' is a warm word to express this dissolution of the ties. The men reject 'the warm pacts of the flesh' in favour of their 'green' sleep. Once the foundations are disturbed, however, it is not easy to cure the resulting instability. Sprawled about their pool, the men unravel the knitted sleeve of care and savour for the first time the universal indifference.

> To die, to sleep –
> No more; and by a sleep to say we end
> The heart-ache and the thousand natural shocks
> That flesh is heir to. 'Tis a consummation
> Devoutly to be wish'd. To die, to sleep;
> For in that sleep of death what dreams may come,
> When we have shuffled off this mortal coil,
> Must give us pause.

Hamlet's soliloquy seems never very far away.

The third section of the poem reprises men's arrival at the pool only to establish a connection between it and the migrations of teal and quail over the Himalayas. The same law governs the chase of crocodile and fish, of predator and prey, of friend and enemy; it is the law inherent in the cycle of life and death within the wider suspension of time the jungle provides. As the soldiers relax by the pool, they come across an enemy who is also a friend, one who is closer to them than their loved ones. Distinctions that are normally regarded as discrete or opposed entities are revealed by the jungle to be part of the eternal doubleness of things.

This insight is given fresh support by the allusion to T. E Lawrence in the phrase 'warm pacts of the flesh'. It is Lawrence's engagement with Arab fatalism and nomadism that the men presently imitate, an 'Arabism' that Lawrence defined in a letter to a friend thus:

> It is the old, old civilisation, which has refined itself clear of household gods [compare 'The warm pacts of the flesh'], and half the trappings which ours hastens to assume. The gospel of bareness in materials is a good one, and it involves apparently a sort of moral bareness too...In part it is a mental and moral fatigue.4

'The Jungle' explores just this 'fatigue'. In doing so, it raises two questions: what is the value of life, and how does one find one's 'quietus' from it? Two years earlier, Lewis employed Lawrence's phrase 'the warm ones about us' in his story 'Dusty Hermitage', which is an account of his visit to Lawrence's home in Dorset, Clouds Hill, during the summer of 1942, when his battalion was based in Bovington. The visit occurred 18 months before 'The Jungle' was written; in terms of experience, however, it is an aeon away. Lawrence again:

> I find myself wishing all the time that my own curtain would fall...There is something broken...my will, I think...As for fame after death, it's a thing to spit at; the only minds worth winning are the warm ones about us. If we miss those we are failures.5

A man about to depart this life looks back at 'the warm ones about us'—just as the men in 'The Jungle' do.6

In the poem, Lewis eroticises 'warm ones about us' to 'warm pacts of the flesh', no doubt as a result of his experience in July 1943, when he met and fell in love with Freda Aykroyd on leave in Coonoor, southern India. For him, his love for Freda ran parallel with his love for Gweno—hence the plural 'pacts', though the word adds a public dimension to the argument, as does 'world'. That is because, for

---

4   *Letters of T. E. Lawrence*, ed. David Garnett (London: Jonathan Cape, 1938), 244.
5   Alun Lewis, *The Last Inspection and other stories* (London: Allen & Unwin, 1943).
6   This theme of separation from loved ones was first sounded tentatively by Lewis in 'All day it has rained...': 'Yet thought softly, morosely of them, and as indifferently/ As of ourselves or those whom we/ For years have loved, and will again/ To-morrow maybe love'. This was then hardened in 'To Edward Thomas' to: 'and growing clearer,/ More urgent as all else dissolved away,/—Projected books, half-thoughts, the children's birthdays,/ And wedding anniversaries as cold/ As dates in history.' (*CP*, 23 and 30)

Lewis, there was no 'private' realm that existed separately from the 'public' one, a perception that marks him out as a keen reader of W.H. Auden who, four years previously, had stated in '1st September 1939': 'There is no such thing as the State/And no one exists alone'. Like the 'dream beside this jungle pool', love may help one overlook disaster but cannot prevent what is happening—another key Audenesque perception. Like T.E. Lawrence, Lewis tries to hold out against the times but the mantled pool insists on the in/fidelity of love.

'The Jungle''s opening lines are relevant here:

> In mole-blue indolence the sun
> Plays idly on the stagnant pool
> In whose grey bed black swollen leaf
> Holds Autumn rotting like an unfrocked priest.

This description plays off beauty against rankness, the fallen and disgraced; the death of the year brings with it the death of hope. 'Mole-blue indolence' alludes to the woods that surrounded the Aykroyds's house in Coonoor which Freda and Lewis liked to walk in. They would stand there looking at a stream that wound its way through the eucalyptus trees (the 'tall blue saplings swaying' of 'Wood Song'). Because of their purple iridescence, Lewis said that was where the moles lay, 'dappled moles of warm blue sunlight' (*LW*, 387). Coonoor's trees exist within the trees of 'The Jungle'. This suggests that after love comes betrayal, just as, after life, comes dreaming about life.

En route to India in late 1942, Lewis told Gweno that, in the midst of everything that was happening to him, 'at the centre my thoughts and emotions form their altering patterns and make their music' (*ITGT*, 17). Now that love has faded to the periphery, he surrenders to 'this mammoth jungular world of the East' (*ITGT*, 40). Yet, far from weakening him, it gave him the strength to write his greatest poetry.

The alienation induced by India may be said to have begun twelve months before in January 1943, when Lewis broke a jaw following a football accident. The pain he suffered while he lay in Poona Hospital having the jaw reset, together with the effects of the dysentery he caught there and his medication, precipitated a depression, as the poems he wrote there show. These, together with the story 'Ward 'O' 3 (b)', illustrate the increasingly important part water played in his work and the way the image of the beloved changed from the sweet golden wife to a siren-like 'beautiful singing sexless angel'.

When the battalion reached Lake Karakvasla just before Easter 1943, Lewis wrote a sequence of six poems including this, called 'Water Music'. It ends:

> Hurry not and fear not
> This oldest mystery,
>
> This strange voice singing,
> This slow deep drag of the lake,
> This yearning, yearning, this ending
> Of the heart and its ache.

The 'strange voice' that sings to him here is another version of the 'sexless angel' of 'Burma Casualty' (one of the Poona Hospital poems):

> Her hands so soft you scarcely feel her touch
> Gentle, eternally gentle, round your heart.
> She flatters and unsexes every man.

In July 1943, Lewis wrote 'The Orange Grove', a story which comes to a climax when the truck that Staff-Captain Beale drives carrying the body of his dead driver in it stalls in a stream that is being forded by a tribe of gipsies. He surrenders the body of the driver to them before he joins them himself in their endless migrations about the earth. (We recall the teal and quail of 'The Jungle'). The story ends: 'He wished, though, that he knew where they were going…. Maybe they weren't going anywhere much, except perhaps to some pasture, some well.' (*ITGT*, 125) 'The Jungle''s ironic method is perfectly exemplified by the qualifiers 'perhaps', 'maybe', 'some'. These words imply hope while effectively denying it. C.B. Cox likens Beale's passage at the end to that of 'a soul to Hades'.[7]

Water, water everywhere and all of it poisonous. The 'well' that lures Beale, like the river his truck stalls in, implies rebirth but is actually tainted, as are the siren's lake and the hospital pool of 'Ward 'O' 3 (b)'. Like 'The Jungle''s pool, this is 'mantled', i.e., has branches that hang over it. A toad sleeps beneath its mosses whose back is 'rusty with jewels' (c.f. 'The Jungle''s 'mole-blue' water). As Lt Weston sits on the pool's ledge, he drops his hand into the water and sends out ripples to the edge as well as 'against the most withdrawn and inmost ledges of his being'. These ripples are evidently meant to be restorative but are described as 'a series of temptations in the wilderness' (*ITGT*, 139–40). Weston believes he has been fortified against the 'darkness' that has claimed his fellow wounded soldiers, but we are not so sure.

This sequence of watery imagery reaches its apogee in 'The Way Back', the

---

7   *The Spectator*, 18 November 1966, 654.

poem that most memorably records his love for Freda Aykroyd. In that poem, he describes himself revelling in her 'naked' lake, in anticipation of the moment when he will be 'squandered' and 'hurled' back to her in some unspecified act of violence. The poem presents the lovers as they are about to part, he to return to the war, but anticipates the moment when they will be reunited. A few weeks later, Lewis was in Karachi and there experienced the same feeling of a violent end while he was singing in the showers. He sensed an 'enormous and dreadful joy' come over him, one that 'said something quite final and terrible to me & I laughed and sang it back.' The next morning, he is 'delighted that I can sing it & not shudder over it.'[8] (All that singing!)

The nature of this disturbance is suggested by 'final' and 'terrible'. As in 'The Jungle' and 'The Way Back', an approaching release excites but also terrifies, mixing dread with elation. Lewis shouts 'Ha! Ha! Among the Trumpets' again. He expounded this idea again in this journal entry he wrote straight afterwards: 'The jungles of Burma came towards me & flowed round me familiarly & I could count the days that remained neatly...'[9] 'The Jungle' fills just one such day.

Lewis tried to versify the thought, specifying the precise number of days that he believed were left to him:

> Now after all the groping and revulsion
> Come clear at last entertain my death
> ....
> And this sweet joy of writing is the right spending
> Of one day that remains me out of ninety.[10]

'Ninety' takes us to the late autumn of 1943, when the battalion was expected to launch an amphibious attack on Burma. This was subsequently delayed and then became an overland assault scheduled for early 1944. It was in preparation for this that Lewis was sent to the jungle. His agon neared resolution.

II

In section two of the poem, Lewis describes the world he leaves behind.

> Wandering and fortuitous the paths

8 John Pikoulis, *Alun Lewis, A Life* (2nd edn., Bridgend: Seren, 1991), 189.
9 Ibid., 190.
10 Ibid.

We followed to this rendezvous today...

('Rendezvous' implies a predestined encounter, despite 'Wandering' and 'fortuitous'—another ironical moment.)

> ...to this rendezvous today
> Out of the mines and offices and dives...

'Dives' suggests an American ambience, as in Auden's '1st September, 1939', the most celebrated retrospect of the 1930s.[11].

> I sit in one of the dives
> On Fifty-second Street
> Uncertain and afraid
> As the clever hopes expire
> Of a low dishonest decade:

These words resonate as much now in India as they did then in New York.

> Waves of anger and fear
> Circulate over the bright
> And darkened lands of the earth,
> Obsessing our private lives;
> The unmentionable odour of death
> Offends the September night.

And it does again Lewis's January night.

Lewis's version of Auden's 'low, dishonest decade' is one of the best things he did; it emulates Auden without imitating him, though there is still plenty of Auden in it, as is right, for Auden is part of the story he has to tell:

> Out of the mines and offices and dives,
> The sidestreets of anxiety and want,
> Huge cities known and distant as the stars,
> Wheeling beyond our destiny and hope.
> We did not notice how the accent changed
> As shadows ride from precipice to plain

---

11   The word is not unknown in British literature of the period, e.g. Graham Greene's *A Gun for Sale* (1936): 'He didn't know what dives to raid, what clubs and dance halls', but always, as here, with the influence of Hollywood apparent (Harmondsworth: Penguin, 2001) 69.

> Closing the parks and cordoning the roads,
> Clouding the humming cultures of the West—

Compare this with Auden's 'Consider this and in our time': 'You cannot be away, then, no/ Not though you pack within an hour,/Escaping humming down arterial roads' or 'As shadows ride from precipice to plain/Closing the parks and cordoning the roads'. Auden, too, is the source of Lewis's panoramic stance ('As the hawk sees it or the helmeted airman'), his cautionary eloquence, the aphoristic style, the sense (implicit in '1st September 1939' with its reference to 'Imperialism's face/And the international wrong') of an end to an era, which Lewis captures brilliantly with the Audenesque-sounding yet still quintessentially Lewisian phrase 'the humming cultures of the West'.

'Humming' suggests activity of a bee-like kind, repetitive and numbing, like mining or welding: 'The day shift sinking in the sun,/The blinding arc of rivets blown through steel'. As it happens, Lewis's childhood was overshadowed by the General Strike of 1926, which coincided with his departure from the valleys for Cowbridge Grammar School. In the obvious as well as more personal sense, mining and welding then ceased for him. In 'Ward 'O' 3 (b), Lt Weston recalls how he 'used to watch the wheel of the pit spin round year after year, after school and Saturdays and Sundays; and then from 1926 on I watched it not turning round at all, and I can't ever get that wheel out of my mind.' (*ITGT*, 131) Nor could Lewis. When mining and welding started again with the approach of war, the circumstances had grown even direr.

'Humming' also reflects Lewis's puritanical aversion to popular music, associated in his mind with casual fraternising and camp concerts, 'chichi' girls dancing to Hawaiian guitars or Eurasians mimicking jazz songs: 'I can't see any value at all in yankee music and it becomes a disease when transplanted to Eastern peoples,' he wrote (*LW*, 405).[12] Both tap dancers and jazz musicians struck him as representatives of a 'phoney civilisation' (LW, 407), unlike the performers in the rituals he observed in the jungle and which he found so moving. When he read a *The New Statesman* review of his volume of short stories, *The Last Inspection*, he declared:

> They're obsessed with the 'isolation of the Intellectual' and his 'guilt complex' and the 'conscious left wing' writer. Well—maybe I used to be. I'm not so now and never will be. I seem to have stepped outside all that. That's just a bit of froth on England's whirlpool. There's all the patient suffering world beside, and I'm in that now for better or for worse. (*LW*, 315)

---

[12] See, too, the 'swing music' of 'urbane permissive ballrooms' in *The Orange Grove, IGT*, 149.

'The humming cultures of the West' just about sums up the 'froth on the whirlpool'.

It is surprising Auden does not appear more prominently in the work of Welsh writers in English of this period. There is plenty of D.H. Lawrence but not his most significant disciple, the poet who charted the collapse of industrialism and Empire and recorded the rise of fascism, who pricked the conscience of a generation with descriptions of refugees marching in 'bankrupt countries where they mend the roads/Along the endless plains' ('Easily, my dear...'), who said that 'men are changed by what they do' ('The Malverns') and urged the 'Death of the old gang' ('1929') in favour of 'New styles of architecture, a change of heart' ('Petition'), who coined the phrase about 'Glamorgan's glove-shaped valleys' ('O Love, the interest itself...'). Yet the valley writers themselves signally failed to return the compliment, with the exception of T. Harri Jones and Alun Lewis. There is no Auden in Glyn Jones (who, in some ways, was the most politically conscious of these writers) or Gwyn Thomas or Idris Davies or Lewis Jones. The reason for this may be suggested by a review Lewis wrote for *Tribune* in 1942 when he referred to 'the dead hand of the living Auden, who has educated *and* destroyed so many...young writers'.[13]   Auden was the poet other poets wanted to avoid, though even Dylan Thomas cannot help sounding like him from time to time.

Lewis's farewell to the humming cultures of the West is to a world well and truly lost and is done with a weary frustration that mounts to a barely-controlled anger:

> Wandering and fortuitous the paths
> We followed to this rendezvous today
> Out of the mines and offices and dives,
> The sidestreets of anxiety and want,
> Huge cities known and distant as the stars,
> Wheeling beyond our destiny and hope...—
> The weekly bribe we paid the man in black,
> The day shift sinking from the sun,
> The blinding arc of rivets blown through steel,
> The patient queues, headlines and slogans flung
> Across a frightened continent, the town
> Sullen and out of work, the little home
> Semi-detached, suburban, transient
> As fever or the anger of the old,

---

13   19th June, 1942, 14.

The best ones on some specious pretext gone.

This passage is the most impressive literary description of the Depression that we have in Wales. No more compelling definition of a people's suffering has ever been attempted. The cataloguing style is once again out of Auden, just as Auden's 'Get there if you can...' was out of Tennyson's 'Locksley Hall', but now fully absorbed. There is in Lewis none of Auden's flamboyance, his sense of fixing a scene before departing from it, something more earnest and more lived in as it is acrid—and 'humming' is the last word one would want to use about it.

The last line in my quotation above recalls what was so often said about the young who left the Welsh valleys for Slough and Dagenham and America. Oddly, Lewis ascribes a 'specious pretext' to them. Was this because he believed their attempt to secure an economic future for themselves was doomed? All roads, after all, led to war. Looking back, he is profoundly disillusioned with a world 'known and distant as the stars', though, in his earlier poetry, Lewis often drew comfort from the stars as a symbol of his relation to his loved ones, with whom he shared a sense of beauty and moral values. Now, they are subsumed in 'this tinpot civilization that is so easy to export by radio and gramophone and film... it devalues everything'. (*ITGT*, 72–3)[14]

> But we who dream beside the jungle pool
> Prefer the instinctive rightness of the poised
> Pied kingfisher deep darting for a fish
> To all the banal rectitude of states...

As Lewis's social commitment faded, he was drawn to an abstract, reified sense of beauty. Of course, he had always been attracted to nature but it now becomes something separate from the human, an absolute outside of time. To one who enlisted in the war for humanitarian reasons, the rejection is final.

Adrift from his community as from his loved ones, Lewis discovered that the only authentication of self he could find was that provided by the jungle. He knew he could never really 'enter' India—it was too vast and strange, too resistant to any hope for social improvement. The jungle encouraged instead an identification with such items as the 'dew-bright diamonds on a viper's back' and in them he sensed compensation enough for 'the slow poison of a meaning lost/ And the vituperations of the just'. In India, political progressivism was finally revealed to be a chimera; everything that a childhood in the south Wales valleys had induced in him vanished before this perception: nothing alters, nothing matters—*kuchh fikr*

---

14 Something of this feeling was also voiced by George Orwell in *Burmese Days* (1934).

nahin. So Lewis turned from the 'banal rectitude of states' in favour of the 'instinctive rightness' of 'the most vivid kingfisher you've ever dreamed of, a wonderful, brilliant little flying rainbow' (*ITGT*, 24). Here was something he could believe in.

A month before entering the jungle, Lewis told his parents that, when he returned to Wales, he would learn more about 'the law, the police, the insurance, the hospitals, the employment exchanges, the slums' and apologised for having 'always enclosed myself in an impalpable circle of seclusion' (*ITGT*, 68). That seclusion is now complete. Life appeared to him to lack all 'shape or plot or purpose', a strange belief for a man fighting a war to entertain: 'When I consider how my days are spent! They go and go and go. Nothing to show for them either.' (*ITGT*, 57) The cause he was fighting for vanished; the army 'organizes only to destroy', he said (*ITGT*, 70), for it works 'among things that crumble as they are made and meaningless in history and in the heart' (*ITGT*, 66). The point was made in a different way when he read Graham Greene's *Brighton Rock* and recoiled from his account of the 'detailed disintegration and instability and bewilderment of modern humanity' (*ITGT*, 67).

Before he came to the jungle, Lewis wrote: 'The world is much larger than England, isn't it? I'll never be just English or just Welsh again!' (*ITGT*, 28) In this perspective, neither nationalism nor latitude matters, neither capitalism nor Marxism. Lewis enters the heart of darkness.

> There *is* such a thing as freedom, and in Europe *we are* liberators at the moment. In the East it is less so, alas. Liberty isn't the point at issue, and neither side offers it. That's what makes it so hard to accept. (*LW*, 393)

III

The third section of 'The Jungle' opens with a passage of private reflection that corresponds to the public retrospective which opened the preceding section (a good example of the careful patterning of the poem, sustained over 99 long lines). Lewis's literary mentor here is W. B Yeats, whose poems he carried with him to war alongside Edward Thomas's, specifically Yeats's 'A Dialogue of Self and Soul':

> What matter if I live it all once more?
> Endure that toil of growing up;
> The ignominy of boyhood; the distress
> Of boyhood changing into man;
> The unfinished man and his pain

Brought face to face with his own clumsiness...

Lewis's version reads:

> The vagueness of the child, the lover's deep
> And inarticulate bewilderment,
> The willingness to please that made a wound,
> The kneeling darkness and the hungry prayer;
> Cargoes of anguish in the holds of joy.

The passage is characterised by an astonishing intensity. Even now, readers cannot appreciate why this should be so and critics cannot offer a truthful account of it. Suffice to say that Lewis is agonised by a sense of failure so abject as to render the absence of specifying detail less distracting than it might be. All his life, he was dogged by this sense of failure and it lay at the root of his depression. The confession of culpability in this third section is thus free of Yeats's sense that he is describing something that is passed. Lewis's boyhood, however, continues to rankle; it has accompanied him into adulthood and now causes as much pain as it did then. His description, therefore, does not so much recall pain as re-enact it, sensing in it an all-encompassing 'oceanic tide of Wrong', a striking quasi-Freudian phrase which is in its way as memorable as the 'humming cultures of the West'. Lewis drowns in a sense of error so vast as to lie beyond alteration.

An even greater discovery awaits him in the poem, however, and is revealed in the lines: 'though the state has enemies we know/The greater enmity within ourselves'. A Japanese soldier assuredly lurks in Burma but an even greater menace exists in the jungle: the 'smooth deceitful stranger in the heart'. This stranger is Lewis's alter ego, Hamlet struggling against the cursed times that are out of joint, T. E. Lawrence undermined as a soldier by his intellect and imagination, Auden rejecting his youthful beliefs which he escapes from by sailing across an ocean, or Yeats, losing himself in a provisional series of masks or personae.

When Lewis confronts the 'stranger in the heart', all distinctions between inner and outer, friend and foe or anguish and joy vanish. The stranger is what is left once the conflict between 'rectitude', 'rightness' and 'just' (on the one hand) and 'Wrong', 'wrack', 'poison' and 'unfrocked' (on the other) is over. He is what is disclosed in the 'black spot in the focus' of the jungle pool, one that 'grows and grows'.

For a last time, Lewis begs forgiveness in propria persona from all he deserts:

> Oh you who want us for ourselves,...
> Forgive this strange inconstancy of soul,

> The face distorted in a jungle pool
> That drowns its image in a mort of leaves.

'Mort' is an interesting word, signifying death but also a mass or number. As the soldiers look at themselves in the pool's distorting reflection beneath a mound of leaves, they realise they are as good as dead. They have become 'ghosts'. Like the gibbering monkeys in the trees, they are 'ignorant and wise'—ignorant to be wise and well out of it. Another ironic moment.

IV

The poem nears its end with the noise of these monkeys in section four. Soldiers and monkeys are alike 'anonymous, unknown' (note the reference to the 'unknown soldier'). In the 'trackless wilderness', the soldiers find new direction in their moral confusion.

> The killing arm uncurls, strokes the soft moss;
> The distant world is an obituary,...

As they sleep beside the pool, they lose their occupation. Separated from the 'humming cultures' and 'the warm ones about us', they exist in an insistent present tense that is without past or future and prepare for their departure from it, too:

> The act sustains; there is no consequence.
> Only aloneness, swinging slowly
> Down the cold orbit of an older world
> Than any they predicted in the schools....

The poem has traced this passage from warmth to cold, from human solidarity to nature's 'coldness and pride' (*ITGT*, 63). Here is the existentialist dilemma in a nutshell. Adrift in a meaningless universe, the soldiers go beyond the theology lectured on in the schools of the mediaeval divines to experience the wisdom of an 'older world' instinct with the wheeling of the elements, the traffic of stars and the migrations of people and birds within the cycle of life and death that exists within space-time. There is, apparently, that which is—and then that which is not. *Kuchh fikr nahin*—nothing matters. As he contemplates the universal nothingness, Lewis holds steady. His fortitude and lucidity are exemplary. A lesser man would have been undone by the revelation, no matter what the circumstances. At the full stretch of his imagination, he achieves a final definition of self.

The last lines of the poem lead insistently to an 'overwhelming question':

> ... if the mute pads on the sand should lift
> Annihilating paws and strike us down
> Then would some unimportant death resound
> With the imprisoned music of the soul?[15]

The question had long haunted Lewis: 'What survives?':

> there doesn't seem to be any question more directly relevant than this one of
> what survives of all the beloved, I find myself quite unable to express at once
> the passion of Love, the coldness of Death (Death is cold)...(*ITGT*, 30–1)

The same thought reappears in 'Peasant Song': 'If I should go/...Would you hear my plough still singing?'. In other words, would the potential he possesses survive his death, offering compensation for all he had failed to achieve in his life, or does death simply signify the end of all things?

As if by way of answer, the poet imagines an encounter with a tiger or panther, investing it with the same incongruous voluptuous beauty of the crocodile and fish. He thereby lends the notion of death an odd allure. (Lewis may be echoing Blake's tiger here or his own early poem, 'The Tiger of Camden Town'). The tiger brings death by 'annihilating paws', a phrase that suggests less a tragic accident than the consummation of a devout wish. The paws re-appear in the closing couplet:

> ...does the will's long struggle end
> With the last kindness of a foe or friend?

'End', appearing at the end of a line connoting closure, again implies merciful release, though mercy of an ambiguous quality. Is the death promised an act of kindness or hostility? Or is hostility simply another mask for kindness? Only kindness, after all, could confer such a benefit.

The enemy within and enemy without confront each other, separate but conjoined. The long struggle of life ends in this embrace of life and death or life-and-death. There is, apparently, the death that is in life and the life that is promised by death, the poem's ultimate irony. Something, it seems, *will* survive. This conclusion holds on the plane that Lewis found himself in, one where time does not matter:

---

15 R.S. Thomas echoes the last line in his 'Sure' (1992): 'Where a soul perishes/what music?'.

Even if it were to end like that, would time end for me? Wouldn't that search, oh deep as child-hood or adolescence or soldiering, the *intermittent* search—wouldn't it be taken up again in the clearer less bounded incorporeal space of endlessness? I don't know whether it will be or not—I seek no consolation—nor am I compelled to imagine some compensating dream world…I can afford to lose all I am losing…for an indeterminate time. Because I know that there is something indestructible in me…(*LW*, 379)

It is in the 'clearer less bounded incorporeal space of endlessness' that readers, now as then, may find him.

Dancing in the Mud:
Bunting's Documentary Tradition and
the Anecdotage of Ford Madox Ford

Colin Edwards

'I have a large presence and can overawe trouble-makers as a rule. And I like to see people enjoy themselves.' (*It Was the Nightingale*)[1]

W RITING about the weekly parties he used to throw in the Boulevard Arago, Paris, in his role as Editor of the *Transatlantic Review* in the 1920s, Ford Madox Ford explained that they had a function that perhaps was invisible to his guests: 'I can think my private thoughts while they go on nearly as well as in the Underground during rush hours—and if any one is present that I like and there is a shortage of men, I dance.' (*IWTN*, 306)

By this stage in his career, Ford was happy to allow his American guests to let off steam: he was also relatively at home with the scandals that resulted. We can imagine that prohibition was a factor in the explosiveness of these literary fiestas: 'I was dancing with a girl of seventeen, who appeared to be enthusiastic and modest. And suddenly—amazingly—she dropped right through my arms and lay on the floor like a corpse.' (*IWTN*, 306)

Ford had not always been able to dance his way out of embarrassing situations. During the ugly aftermath of Ford's split from his wife in the London of the before-the-war years, he and his consort, Violet Hunt, had both learned to count the cost of flouting the proprieties (losing, respectively, their close friendships with one-time collaborator, Conrad, and—a temporary freezing out for Violet—with the Master, Henry James). But even when Ford's 'personal affairs might be in an

---

1   Ford Madox Ford, *It Was the Nightingale* (London: Heinemann, 1934), p. 307. Hereafter *IWTN*.

agonizing muddle...' still, 'A distinction must be drawn between Ford's relations with the people with whom he associated, and his "life of the mind".'[2] That was how his observant friend and sub-editor, Douglas Goldring, was to write in his memoirs of Violet's home in Kensington, South Lodge, which became the resort of sundry tennis-playing Vorticists like Ezra Pound (who, according to Ford, was a 'galvanized agile gibbon', while Lawrence made a fast and agile ball-boy).[3]

In this essay, I wish to consider the strange and often misleading potency of some of these kinds of image: to reflect upon the ways in which Ford liked to employ *vignettes* of the fleshly self in the literary reminiscences which formed such a significant part of his *oeuvre*, and to reflect, too, upon the ways in which the life of the body (particularly when relaxed) can infiltrate one significant portion of the poetry-writing traditions in England, now as well as in the heyday of Modernism. A tradition of 'documentary' will be shown to be instrumental to this writing: a tradition, or an idiom indeed, which has been written about in assorted writings of Hugh Kenner on Ford and his legacy. These are ideas that spanned a considerable period and included Kenner's writings in his final thoughts on the Modernists in *A Sinking Island*; they are a key source to which this essay is indebted.[4] And beyond Kenner, the direct link to Ford, for a way of writing which can be both light on its feet and also have the grainy physicality and stress of verbal life which recalls Ben Jonson, is Basil Bunting.

It is indeed possible that the style of life allowed for in the Parisian quarters, where Ford lived with Stella Bowen and their baby daughter, was conducive to just the sort of equilibrium that this particular writer needed. This is a view that Bunting would have been able to deny or affirm: he was in a position to know! In fact, he shared the apartment, and (as he recorded, for a radio interview in 1974) supported the editor's household with a broad range of domestic skills:

Besides the obvious duties of assistant editor I did all sorts of other things ... I corrected not only the proofs of the magazine but those of the current novel, which was *Some Do Not* [first part of the War tetralogy, *Parade's End*], and some of Conrad's work. Finally, when there was nothing else that needed doing, I would sometimes bath the baby.[5]

---

2 Douglas Goldring, *The Last Pre-Raphaelite*, 163; quoted in Max Saunders, *Ford Madox Ford, A Dual Life*, i (Oxford: Oxford University Press, 1996), 367.
3 Ford Madox Ford, *Return To Yesterday*, (New York: Liveright, 1972), 409; quoted in Saunders, 367.
4 Hugh Kenner, *A Sinking Island, The Modern English Writers* (London: Barrie & Jenkins, 1988), 86–97. Hereafter *ASI*.
5 Alan Judd, *Ford Madox Ford* (London: Collins, 1990), 350.

Bunting makes his first entry into Ford's reminiscences as a 'studious and bespectacled young man...really near starvation' (*IWTN*, 301–302). He had been thrown (literally thrown, if we are to believe Ford) out of his lodgings, by an irate concierge. Here is the prelude to Ford's colourful account of the 'studious' youngster's arrival at the Boulevard Arago:

> The young man walked round a block and tried again. Things were worse. The strange concierge blocked the way. The young man knocked him down... Outraged by their offences against the laws of hospitality the young man smashed some windows, defiled the staircase, yelled at the top of his voice, and got into bed with the concierge's wife...
>
> Ezra's proposition now was that I should pay [Bunting's] fine and approach the authorities with assurance of the excellence of the young man's poetry... (*IWTN*, 302)

It is possible that Ford was more attracted towards situations involving domestic stress, than he was fully aware! Certainly his best fiction powerfully attests (in relation to the situation of Captain Tietjens, in *Parade's End*), that involvement with the private muddles of the lower ranks almost becomes a counterfeit way of dealing with his own intractable family problems ('in the end, these were his own affairs...Money, women, testamentary bothers. Each of these complications...were his own troubles').[6] In fact, the reader comes to see that this kind of distraction, by others, from his own pressing anxieties about home is a subliminal way of dealing with these very issues. I shall return to *Parade's End* (one hopes that this novel sequence benefited from Bunting's proof-reading!) in order to consider further how the management of life's daily stresses seems to be linked, in Ford's case, with the achievement of moments of luminous tranquillity. His ability to represent the mind when it is apparently most besieged does seem to relate to the *writerly* habits of the man: not only was his judgement (as editor) clearly felt by his peers to be instinctive—he worked (or his subterranean mind worked) unusually well when life was at its most flurried.

This was not always without personal troubles, however. It is reasonably clear that the twin ignominies of business failure (of his two celebrated literary *Reviews*) and a complex pattern of personal infidelity were central ingredients in the story of both *The English Review* and the *Transatlantic*. But Ford's ability to cope with (or otherwise evade) stress levels seems to have been quite significantly better when in France, than in England. For a record of one of the gloomiest of Ford's London

---

6 Ford Madox Ford, *Parade's End* (*No More Parades*), (Manchester: Carcanet, 1997), 322. Hereafter *PE*.

days, we have to thank the testimony of Violet Hunt. She may not represent Ford in his finest hour (and we may feel that Ford's elaborate plans for a disguised act of suicide might have proved to be less than efficient), but we are given a record of the vivid imagination when it was truly overheated:

> How to manage? He had it all ready. The great 'buses rolling down the hill from Notting Hill Gate went straight past his door—I could hear them as he spoke—and he would throw himself under one of them after having taken poison, and no one would think of having an autopsy of the mangled corpse.[7]

Alarmingly, this is from Violet's account of what happened *before* Ford's most terrible years! For it was from 1910 to 1914 (the kernel of the events turned by Violet into *The Story of My Flurried Years*) that Ford garnered his worst life-experiences, as well as the most fruitful ones for his subsequent writing life. Those just-before-the-war years were spent on the run from his English trials: notably, being dragged through the law courts by his Catholic wife, Elsie Hueffer. There was a prolonged period spent in Germany, where he failed to obtain a German divorce.[8]

But the most interesting escapes—flights of the mind from domestic and public calamity—were those recorded in his fiction and poetry of the period: *The Good Soldier*, and in 'On Heaven', one of Ford's best poems, written for Violet. She had said: 'I want no beauty, I want no damned optimism; I want just a plain, workaday heaven that I can go to some day and enjoy it when I'm there' (*MFY*, 218). And Ford was listening.

We know that Ford always had kept one ear open to the possibilities of street-level and demotic speech. He had imbibed the language of his pre-Raphaelite forbears and pointedly turned his back on that poetic legacy: the kind of euphonious utterance which Hopkins had, similarly, rejected when he named it 'Parnassian'.[9] No, it was a much rawer combination of physical gesture and street balladry that appealed to Ford. Goldring was to write—fascinatingly—about Ford's attendance at the London Music Hall, the Shepherds Bush Empire: this had been yet one more of the gregarious, sociable contexts in which the mind of the Editor could both relax *and* apparently make his editorial decisions! During the performances, wrote Goldring, 'I duly recorded them. But when someone really

---

7   Violet Hunt, *The Story of My Flurried Years* (New York: Boni & Liveright, 1926), 65. Hereafter *MFY*.

8   Saunders, *Ford Madox Ford*, i, 338–345.

9   John Pick ed. *A Hopkins Reader*, (London: Oxford University Press, 1953), p. 74: 'Letter to Baillie' (1864): 'The second kind I call *Parnassian*. It can only be spoken by poets, but is not in the highest sense poetry.'

worth listening to—the late Victoria Monks for example, or 'Little Tich' or Vesta Victoria—appeared on stage, the cares of editorship were for the moment laid aside.'[10]

So, when Ford in his poem for Violet, took her to a 'workaday' heaven, it was a place in which they still had plenty of crowds around them (street entertainers indeed) and it was one that was situated in Ford's beloved Provence:

> And all the world is afoot after the heat of the day,
> In the cool of the even in Heaven…
> And it is here that I have brought my dear to pay her all that I owed her,
> Amidst this crowd, with the soft voices, the soft footfalls, the rejoicing laughter.
> And after the twilight there falls such a warm, soft darkness,
> And there will come stealing under the planes a drowsy odour,
> Compounded of all cyclamen, or oranges, or rosemary and bay,
> To take the remembrance of the toil of the day away.
>
> So we sat at a little table, under an immense plane,
> And we remembered again
> The blisters and torments
> And terrible harassments of the tired brain,
> The cold and the frost and the pain,
> As if we were looking at a picture and saying: 'This is true!
> Why this is a truly painted
> Rendering of that street where—you remember?—I fainted.'[11]

Kenner drew attention to the 'trouble it cost Ford to *devise an idiom*' (my emphasis) as well as to the poem's 'diffuse, leisurely sentences, the intimacy with the reader, the colloquial ease, the many—too many—words: this was trouble taken that he might "render his own times in terms of his own times" ' (*ASI*, 92). Kenner's choice of words here ('diffuse', 'ease', 'too many words') will distress one kind of critical reader: *Was the great editor not able to edit out the superfluous words?* might well be their first question.

We need to consider the mindset of the poem's speaker, with reference to his addressee. He is, in these lines, engaged as much (or more, in my view) with an act of seduction as he is with an implied mental alertness. So, it is the touch and stress (alternately light and plangent) of words, we may need to respond to: words that

---

10   Douglas Goldring, *South Lodge, Reminiscences of Violet Hunt, Ford Madox Ford and the English Review Circle*, (London: Constable, 1943), 32.

11   Ford Madox Hueffer, 'On Heaven', *On Heaven & Poems Written On Active Service* (London: John Lane, 1918), 79–110. Hereafter *OH*.

imply a voice of urgency and coaxing and pleading, in a kind of continuous spell. Then, there is the wonderfully drowsy physicality of 'such a warm, soft darkness,/ And there will come stealing under the planes a drowsy odour,/ Compounded of all cyclamen'. In its call to self-abandonment (is it an invitation to dance, without the dance itself?), and in its plaintive note of distress (the 'terrible harassments of the tired brain') we are taken to emotional territory, involving consolations and remorse, where we are apt to feel a little queasy!

Perhaps, for some readers, the poem's problematic intimacy (where, for some, that becomes cloying) is to be related to the shifting ground on which it was squarely built. In its collision of English prudentialism (the poem refers to 'Worries, tongue-clackings, nonsenses and shame/ For not making good', *OH*, 89) with a warmer climate of mediterraneanism in the south of France, Ford arguably transports the particular crises of his intimate life into a transnational arena.

Adventurously uneasy as it is in its exploration of emotion, and difficult to excerpt as it is too, 'On Heaven' has the combination of drama and nonchalance in it that Kenner, back in 1972, had found in Ford's earlier poem, 'The Starling'. And it was in writing about the latter that he had discovered the specifically 'documentary' quality he wished to draw attention to more largely: a tradition which violates the dominant post-Romantic aesthetic to which most poetry readers are already—more-or-less unconsciously—the paid-up subscribers. The events of poetry which is contaminated with 'documentary', he argues, will be events which poets have been conditioned to distrust:

> These events are imagined like incidents in a novel. Juxtaposed, they do not state the poem's revelation; rather, they are occasions on which to meditate; meditating on them, the poet arrives at a revelation which he then explicitly states. It isn't a profound revelation, but the revelations at which one arrives by thinking seldom are. They need their specific occasions to lend them poignancy.[12]

In Kenner's view, the dominant—and, after T.S. Eliot's example in both criticism and verse, the *presiding*—tradition in English poetry has become the 'aesthetic-Symbolist' one (*ASI*, 93). The tradition of Eliot is, he argued, always likely to take issue with those who are inclined to use the 'exact unspectacular' idiom of documentary. Yet Kenner is prepared to uphold in Ford a habit of mind which values the speech-patterns of prose. He notes that Ford's best effects in verse 'require time in which to take hold' (*ASI*, 92). Slowness, he implies, is a virtue too:

---

12   Hugh Kenner in 'The Poetics of Speech', from Richard Cassell ed. *Ford Madox Ford: Modern Judgements*, (London: Macmillan, 1972), 177.

one that, in the context of verse writing, does not have to imply, in any sense, either sonorousness or aesthetic ineptitude.

So, 'documentary' verse—by contrast with the 'aesthetic-Symbolist fusion'— goes against the grain in showing a 'distrust of imaginative leaps' (*ASI*, 92), and it has not easily attracted the support of the sophisticated. However, if we choose to ignore it, we do so at our peril—partly because in doing so we are averting our gaze from too many poets who value the existence of the prosaic inside the world of verse:

> Along with Kipling of the brassy finish and Hardy of the studied awkwardness, [Ford] derives from Browning, who derived from Wordsworth...Crabbe, and, standing behind Crabbe, the Augustans; and behind them all stands Ben Jonson (*ASI*, 92–93).

While noting the special and generally overlooked qualities of the aforementioned poets, we should also make it clear (as Kenner does in the same passage) that it was a poet of his own generation—Ford's secretary and baby-minder Basil Bunting—whose conversations had been the original source for Kenner's understanding of the 'unrecognized' documentary tradition.

✼

It was towards the end of the Great War, and before he changed his name to Ford, from the Germanic 'Hueffer', that 'On Heaven' was first published in book form, in *On Heaven and Poems Written On Active Service*, 1918; after so many deaths, Ford realised that the poem had come to answer to a different set of public needs. He felt that the ground had shifted under his feet, and might have echoed a common emotion when he assumed the posture, as ex-combatant, of now being 'unliterary'. He wrote in his short introduction to the volume, that 'I am no longer a writer and have no longer any place in the world of letters' (*OH*, 8–9). He wishes to add a note of doubt, perhaps, to the view of Pound, who, when the poem had first been published in *Poetry* magazine in 1914, had praised it as 'the best poem yet written in the twentieth-century fashion'.[13]

If the version of heaven that had been offered to Violet did not prove to be to her taste—it was a love, she wrote later, 'without breadth, depth, or thickness, without dimension. Subjective, purely' (*MFY*, 220)—still, by 1918, it could be offered to a wider public, and could thus be revisited (as it were) in a different context. 'For we *must* have some such Heaven to make up for the deep mud and the

---

13   See Saunders, *Ford Madox Ford*, i, 398.

bitter weather and the long lasting fears' (*OH*, 8), as Ford's introduction insisted.

The post-war years were those in which Ford, as artist, had 'taken shelter' in a cottage that 'leaks through its thatch' (as Pound recorded of him, in 'Hugh Selwyn Mauberley'[14]), but his slow subsequent emergence from the Sussex backwater where he lived with Stella Bowen, the young Australian artist he first met in 1917, was unquestionably spent—apart from raising some prize goats—in writing. That was the story of his life: he never stopped writing.

By the time that Ford, Stella and their new baby daughter arrived in Paris in 1922, Ford had, indeed, already resumed the habit of writing personal reminiscences—with *Thus To Revisit*. With its many relaxed, companionable anecdotes about those who in London he had called 'Les Jeunes'—'the Vorticists, Cubists, Imagistes, Symbolists, Vers Libristes, Tapagistes…the fine, young Cocks of the Walk!'[15]—Ford started to pick up the threads of connection with the world that had ended in 1914.

'The truth' behind writers' personal reminiscences from the 1920s, notably concerning the *'Génération Perdue'* (notoriously—and, when dealing with Ford, grotesquely—recorded by Hemingway in *A Moveable Feast*[16]) will not easily be arrived at. However, the recent account of *Ford Madox Ford and the Regiment of Women*, by Joseph Wiesenfarth, has been most helpful in giving attention primarily to the *work* (painting as well as writing) achieved by (amongst others) Violet Hunt, Stella Bowen and Jean Rhys. Wiesenfarth weighs the evidence—notably about Bowen—judiciously. For example, he claims that 'in spite of his complete dependence on Bowen to manage every domestic difficulty, Ford never ceased to encourage her, at the same time, in her work as an artist.' [17]

Although we do not have conclusive evidence, we can hope to sift the substance out from the half-truths. Bunting's testimony on Ford's behalf is quietly persuasive: he wrote that Hemingway's portrait of Ford 'is another sort of lie, one deliberately assembled' and that 'I , for instance, who knew them both, would never have guessed the unlaughable caricature was meant for Ford if Hemingway had not named it.'[18]

Anecdotes (as I hope to have indicated) can however, and indeed should, make the lives even of the Literary Great seem to smack of the ordinary. When Ford

---

14   Ezra Pound, *Collected Shorter Poems*, (London: Faber, 1952), 212.

15   Ford Madox Hueffer, *Thus To Revisit, Some Reminiscences*, (London: Chapman & Hall, 1921), 139.

16   Ernest Hemingway, *A Moveable Feast*, (Harmondsworth: Penguin, 1966), 61–68 ('Ford Madox Ford and the Devil's Disciple').

17   Joseph Wiesenfarth, *Ford Madox Ford and the Regiment of Women, Violet Hunt, Jean Rhys, Stella Bowen, Janice Biala*, (Wisconsin: University of Wisconsin Press, 2005), 98.

18   Alan Judd, *Ford Madox* Ford, 349.

went on, in later life, to recall the meetings he had with Joyce in Paris during his period as editor of *The Transatlantic Review*, he must have been highly conscious of Joyce's status: he knew he had been in the presence of the writer of *Ulysses!* But when he settles into a discussion of Joyce's ailments, and gossips about his theories concerning the link between poor eyesight and drinking too much white wine, he seems to be talking about a fellow writer, and of a man we too might come to know—of one, indeed, who had just championed the life (in Leopold Bloom) of *l'homme moyen sensuel* (*IWTN*, 267–271).

There is something about this sort of engagement with the lives of those he knew that was—in its simplifying of circumstances, in its use of broad brushstrokes—always going to be apt preparation for representing people in all their ironic helplessness, yet also for seeing them without malice. To represent a man as object of a public and a shared gaze (flawed, eccentric, desperate) and to recognise simultaneously the possibilities of an enlarged spectrum of his interior desires—the possibilities of grandeur *within* his ordinariness—was a part of the boldest project of Ford's writing life, *Parade's End*. It was to be written in a new kind of prose—*not* by any means Joycean—which would also, at its best, exhibit the virtues that Kenner has found within Ford's verse.

The finest sequences of *Parade's End* are not only those (by any means) which are about the experience of being under fire. No, it is rather that the 'bombardments' which *do* make this war fiction so memorable are impossible to disentangle from experience of a 'normal' time-continuum. They don't so much loom over, or burst upon, his character's head: rather, they work quietly from within the mind, to nag and gnaw upon the ground of an uncannily shared disequilibrium: that of men who struggle, in common, in the mud. They come from inside the head of Ford's protagonist, in the form of domestic worries and ordinary anxieties. We might say that the shared fears of a sudden death experienced by Captain Tietjens and his 'rag-time army' are only there like an anecdote ironically foretold: such things are really of less account than the truly durable, specific and intractable desires and griefs that make us the time-bound and human creatures we are, wherever we find ourselves.

In the culminating phase of the bombardments fictionalised in *A Man Could Stand Up* (the third novel in the sequence), Tietjens' day begins, unexpectedly, with music:

The key-bugle remarked with singular distinctness to the dawn:

>   *dy*
> *I know a la   fair   kind*
>   *and*
>   *Was never face*

so   mind
      pleased my
                  y

    A sudden waft of pleasure at the seventeenth-century air that the tones gave
to the landscape went all over Tietjens.... Herrick and Purcell!... Or it was
perhaps a modern imitation. Good enough. He asked:
   'What the devil's that row, Sergeant?' (*PE*, 564)

The experience (pleasure; barked involuntary response) is then worked by Ford—
seamlessly, yet with the acknowledgment of awkwardness granted via its use of a
documentary poetics—into the diurnal pattern of the character's shifting attention:
alternately to the Sergeant, and back to his own apparently unhurried lucubrations.
The musical motif doesn't impart a special atmosphere to the episode: the writing
fails to acquire a kind of sealed-against-time *claritas*, or the aesthetic self-sufficiency
to grant it (to make use of the more familiar Joycean term) an *epiphanic* status.
Thus, the 'singular distinctness' of the key-bugle, sounding across the trenches, is
apprehended sensuously, intellectually, and—simultaneously—in a way that
transports its musical cadences *deeply into* a quite personal, as well as literal,
landscape.
    Tietjens then makes the connection from his emotion upon hearing the song in
his head ('the remembrance of those exact, quiet words') to another, darker
emotion associated with subterranean digging of the Germans ('they were exact and
quiet. As efficient working beneath the soul as the picks of the miners in the
dark.'). He is making precisely the sort of link that keeps his insight *documentary* in
quality. The connection is heavily ironic in nature (the threat of counter-mining is
real, but hardly one to inspire connection with Purcell) and belongs to a mind not
without quirks and idiosyncrasies! The thought then loops back to the time and
place where he is standing: his mental formulations allow him to reconnect,
seamlessly, with the quite ordinary knowledge 'that it was O Nine Griffiths [for
Tietjens is in charge of a Welsh regiment] practising on the cornet' (*PE*, 565). At
this point, the thought-sequence is allowed to expand outwards towards the 'good
taste' of the oblivious bugler (perhaps he might 'save the fellow's life, for his good
taste!') before struggling upwards, towards a flight of the mind, away from
terrestrial matters. A flight that is soon brought back to earth:

    What had become of the seventeenth century? And Herbert and Donne and
    Crashaw and Vaughan, the Silurist?...Sweet day so cool, so calm, so bright, the
    bridal of the earth and sky!...By Jove, it was that! Old Campion, flashing like a
    popinjay in the scarlet and gilt of the major-general, had quoted that in the
    base camp, years ago. Or was it months? Or wasn't it: 'But at my back I always

hear Time's winged chariots hurrying near,' that he had quoted? (*PE*, 565)

The unexpected provenance of the Marvell quotation in his memory (the name Campion is by no means a happy accident, or any kind of brush with the poetic: General Campion is in fact Tiejens' rival—as he hasn't fully realised—for the affections of Mrs Sylvia Tietjens!) brings his dalliance with well-weighed syllables back down to the well-churned ground. A sufficiently familiar ground of family scandal and marital infidelity—that has beset him even in France. And yet…

> The land remains…It remains!…At that same moment the dawn was wetly revealing; over there in George Herbert's parish…What was it called? What the devil was its name? Oh, Hell!…Between Salisbury and Wilton…The tiny church…But he refused to consider the plough-lands, the heavy groves, the slow high-road above the church that the dawn was at that moment wetly revealing—until he could remember that name. (*PE*, 566)

Tietjens' mind—the very ground of this fiction—is pitted with gaps and interruptions to the flow of these jerkily not-quite-poetic flights and tumbles of the besieged mind. Thoughts, here, are allowed to be as lumbering as the body. Collection of 'meal-sacks' as he is, his inspection of the regiment's trenches, today, will by no means be a military cakewalk!

Tietjens—shell-shocked—grasps hold of different worlds of ideas only by stages. He will allow his mind to articulate ideas as fast, or as slowly, as his tongue can navigate its way, falteringly, over a world of half-lost names:

> The name *Bemerton* suddenly came on to his tongue. Yes, Bemerton, Bemerton, Bemerton was George Herbert's parsonage. Bemerton, outside Salisbury…The cradle of the race as far as our race was worth thinking about. He imagined himself standing up on a little hill, a lean contemplative parson, looking at the land sloping down to Salisbury spire. (*PE*, 567)

Ford is able, in this sequence, to turn the intimate thoughts and emotions of his protagonist into the stuff of true pathos: a pathos that dares to be absurd at the moments where it is also struggling for illumination. And it is prose that, within its time-bound, physical constraints, still yearns for the clarity of musical notes: to find the 'singular distinctness' of the key-bugle which was its source, or well-spring.

But, prose it is ('exact and quiet'): responsive to the incomparable words of the 16th and 17th century poets and knowingly tinged with desperate nostalgia.

*

Our response to Ford's anecdotes—*unquiet* as his reminiscences can be—should share, with the narrative techniques described above, a strong sense of their ironic and provisional status: documentary poetics will present us with a highly particular angle of vision upon a set of events. Like the emotional 'truths' which we discover as the tetralogy moves to its end (as witnesses to the relationship, outside marriage, of Tietjens and Valentine within and beyond the Wartime world), personal events are disclosed in partial stages. Frequently, in the act of revisiting a particular, poignant day or place, its significance comes to be re-configured. We learn to keep an open mind and eye upon the horizons of a shared past. It is the kind of mindset that, in his *Writers in a Landscape*, Jeremy Hooker has asked us to imagine as a kind of shared gift: the gift that writers like Ford's near-contemporaries, Thomas Hardy and Richard Jefferies, still can and do bestow upon the world, in 'their simultaneous expression of impassioned subjectivity, manifested in imagery of particular places and things.'[19] This is a subjectivity that will have instinctive recall and humane sense of the indwelling traditions of place, as well as of documentary poetics. Documentary methods of the Fordian kind are about deepening our sense of what is knowable, whether about a landscape or a crowded room: not about discovering 'its truth'. Sara Haslam, in her recent study of *Fragmenting Modernism*, puts it thus:

> The external vision is ordinary; what is extraordinary is the technique of regressively pursuing the incident to a much more profound level. Ford's adoptive style is that of deepening the reader's understanding, making it more complex, rather than progressing it; he constructs parallel lines of narrative.[20]

✣

Let us now return to Ford and Stella Bowen's party at the Boulevard Arago. In the Fordian way of 'revisiting', this account will be from a different witness, Harold Loeb. (The atmosphere is so chaotic that it's even possible that we're not at the same occasion![21]) It certainly represents Ford as being 'quite calm' (able to think his own thoughts) in a setting that has most of the ingredients of a celebration amongst friends:

---

[19] Jeremy Hooker, *Writers in a Landscape*, (Cardiff: University of Wales Press, 1996), ix.

[20] Sara Haslam, *Fragmenting Modernism, Ford Madox Ford, the Novel and the Great War*, (Manchester: Manchester University Press, 2002), 53.

[21] Saunders, *Ford Madox Ford*, ii, 146: 'One particularly eventful [party]—it may even be the same one at which Ford's dancing partner collapsed—was described by Harold Loeb and Stella Bowen—their quite different accounts showing how reminiscing inevitably reinvents the past.'

The main room was full of dancers, expounders, strollers, music and smoke...As I started down to her, Silvia Goff kicked Mary Butts' behind...

Stella roared up from below, 'Miserable man, he's spoiling my party by committing suicide!'...

I...was dancing with a tall, elegant Swedish girl when Berenice Abbott fell on her back in the middle of the floor...

Some of the guests seemed confused but Ford was calm.[22]

How very close the scene we find here is to the sort of mêlée of soldiers in which Ford, at the end of *A Man Could Stand Up*, situates Tietjens: ' "Good old Tietjens! Good old fat man! Pre-war hooch! He'd be the one to get it!" No one like Fat Man Tietjens. He lounged at the door.'

Ford ends this part of his Great War sequence on Armistice Day, with Tietjens surrounded by smashed glasses, and chaos. It is Valentine who is given some of the novel's last words: 'His right hand was behind her back, his left in her right hand. She was frightened. She was amazed. Did you ever! He was swaying slowly. The elephant! They were dancing!' (*PE*, 674)

I think we can know that this dance would be a slow one. But it is a dance (amongst the muddle and the turmoil of a complex modern world) which will help the dancer to find exact words and the contemplativeness to render his world properly. It would be a dance—whether in prose or verse—to require, and take, its time.

---

[22] Alan Judd, *Ford Madox Ford*, 343.

Prophetic Landscapes:
Thomas Hardy and Richard Jefferies[1]

Roger Ebbatson

Poor flourishing earth, meek-smiling slave,
If sometime the swamps return and the heavy forest, black beech and oak-roots
Break up the paving of London streets;
And only, as long before, on the lifted ridge-ways
Few people shivering by little fires
Watch the night of the forest cover the land
And shiver to hear the wild dogs howling where the cities were,
Would you be glad to be free?

Robinson Jeffers, 'Subjected Earth'

THE messianic or prophetic voice is characteristically muffled, undeclared or ambivalent in the period of modernity. According to Walter Benjamin, before 'prophecy or warning has been mediated by word or image it has lost its vitality'. Benjamin goes on, in terms peculiarly applicable to the thought of the Victorian nature writer, Richard Jefferies, 'To turn the threatening future into a fulfilled now…is a work of bodily presence of mind'.[2] The allegorical gaze, in Benjaminian terminology, reveals both nature and history as a devastated terrain subject to inexorable decay, and this imaginative formation marks the powerful trope of landscape representation in Hardy and Jefferies. In this structure of feeling we may diagnose capitalism itself, in Benjamin's phraseology, as 'a phenomenon of nature whereby Europe once again fell asleep and began dreaming' in a process

---

[1] This paper develops and reinflects the argument first put forward in chapter four of my study, *Heidegger's Bicycle* (Brighton: Sussex Academic Press, 2006).
[2] Walter Benjamin, *One-Way Street and Other Writings*, tr. E. Jephcott and K. Shorter (London: Verso, 1985), 98, 99.

which, he claims, brings about 'a reactivation of mythic forces'.3   The prophetic
revelation of sacred texts is replaced, in the secularity of late-Victorian England, by
the more limited non-doctrinal revelation of the literary text, and specifically by
the idiomatic intensity of landscape evocation and description. In a context
characterised by the 'disappearance of God', Hardy and Jefferies seek, in places, to
frame a concept of spiritual renovation. Such textual effects possess not truth value
but aesthetic richness in a spiritually impoverished world. It is the intensity and
constitutive metaphoricity of these descriptions which, therefore, replace the
literalness of the sacred text. The polarities of landscape depiction in Hardy and
Jefferies represent a new inflection of what George Steiner designates 'the inspired
duplicity of the prophet's task'.4   Whilst a mystically projected text like Jefferies'
The Story of My Heart (1883) is cast in that dominant prophetic syntax identified by
Steiner as 'one of "future present", of anticipation that is also, at every historical
moment, remembrance and tautology', celebrating 'that which is now as being that
which is not yet',5 in countervailing texts such as *After London* (1885) or *Tess of the
d'Urbervilles* (1891) Jefferies and Hardy explore those qualities, 'illusory or
menacing', which are evinced, as Steiner observes, 'through human failure, through
departure from the law'.6 It is this catastrophic failure which is mirrored in the
dichotomies and distinctions embedded in the polarity between the epiphanic and
blasted landscapes represented in this writing, a disjunction which stages a modern
version of prophetic voicing. In his study of prophecy, Martin Buber stresses that
the deity is always 'the God of the earth, the God of its history, of the biblical
history of men', and he argues further, in terms resonant with implications for the
reading of Hardy and Jefferies:

> The important thing here is that the earth comprises the soil (*adaman*), and that
> this is dependent on man (*adam*), formed out of it, and looking to him to
> cultivate it, to 'serve' it. The earth is dependent on man not in a figurative sense
> but most actually. Man's rebellion brings the curse upon the earth. When man
> 'corrupts his way' the land is 'corrupted'.7

The prophet's role, Buber argues, involves 'the full grasping of the present,

---

3   Cited in John McCole, *Walter Benjamin and the Antinomies of Tradition* (Ithaca: Cornell
University Press, 1993), 282.
4   George Steiner, *After Babel* (London: Oxford University Press, 1975), 147.
5   Ibid., 148, 217.
6   Ibid., 148.
7   Martin Buber, *The Prophetic Faith*, tr. C. Witton-Davies (New York: Harper & Row, 1949),
90.

actual and potential'.[8] Buber's distinction between 'a prophecy of salvation and a prophecy of disaster' is germane to the function of landscape evocation in both Hardy and Jefferies:

> In days of false rewriting a shaking and stirring word of disaster is befitting, the outstretched finger pointing to the historically approaching catastrophe, the hand beating on hardened hearts.[9]

In the duality between the effulgence of the utopian landscape of the South Country and the desolation of the landscape of modernity staged in this body of writing, we may identify what Steiner designates 'the optative, future indefinite character of the Messianic prophecy'[10] in its 'weakened' Benjaminian form.

Mikhail Bakhtin adumbrated the hypothesis that, during the classical period, 'the forms of drawing-room rhetoric acquired increasing importance', instantiating 'a new private sense of self, suited to the drawing-room'. As the process got underway, Bakhtin contends,

> Even nature itself, drawn into this new private and drawing-room world, begins to change in an essential way. 'Landscape' is born, that is, nature conceived as horizon (what a man sees) and as the environment (the background, the setting) for a completely private, singular individual who does not interact with it.

Thus it is, under this Bakhtinian diagnosis, that 'Nature enters the drawing-room of private individuals'.[11] In the modern period, that is since the Middle Ages, Bakhtin's literary 'chronotope' designating time-space comes to dominate the reading experience: 'Time, as it were, thickens, takes on flesh, becomes artistically visible; likewise, space becomes charged and responsive to the movements of time, plot and history'.[12] The literary representation of space in the nineteenth century reinforces the *Biedermeier* effect in response to the industrial revolution and the human domestication of nature. The *Biedermeier* assimilation of nature, as embodied in the overdetermined interiors of Balzac, Dickens or Ibsen, dialectically calls into existence a reversal of the nature/culture dichotomy which rejects enclosure both agricultural and horticultural in favour of a Ruskinian evocation of landscape space

---

8   Ibid., 175.
9   Ibid., 178.
10 Steiner, *After Babel*, 147.
11 M. M. Bakhtin, *The Dialogic Imagination*, tr. C. Emerson and M. Holquist (Austin: University of Texas Press, 1981), 143, 144.
12 Ibid., 84.

as freedom. The antitheses of nature and culture, rural and urban, simplicity and sophistication coalesce in a renegotiation of the spaces of earth under the impress of technology—witness the trains which Thoreau can hear in the distance at Walden Pond, or the counterblast from the Welsh quarry which disturbs the close of Tennyson's 'The Golden Year':

> He spoke: and high above, I heard them blast
> The steep slate-quarry, and the great echo flap
> And buffet round the hills, from bluff to bluff.[13]

A reading of the literary landscapes of a semi-mythicised 'South Country' may be framed by Gaston Bachelard's proposal that 'We dream before contemplating', and that any landscape is 'an oneiric experience before becoming a conscious spectacle'. According to Bachelard, 'We look with aesthetic passion only at those landscapes which we have first seen in dreams'. The unity of a landscape thus 'appears as a fulfilment of an oft-dreamed dream'.[14] The literary quest identified here was for a specifically redemptive space identified with and located in the English South Country, that mythical/real location or Foucauldian 'heterotopian' space spectrally inhabited by such figures as George Borrow, Richard Jefferies and Thomas Hardy, and then belatedly by W. H. Hudson and Edward Thomas. We may wish to define landscape here, in W. J. T. Mitchell's terms, as 'a process by which social and subjective identities are formed' in a potent instantiation of 'cultural practice'.[15] Thus conceived, the landscape spaces prophetically framed in this instance become what David Matless, in his study *Landscape and Englishness*, designates 'a vehicle of social and self identity', functioning as 'a site for the claiming of a cultural authority'. As Matless observes, the 'ideal southern landscape is significantly highlighted as a mythic ideal contrasted with "disfigured" contemporary landscapes'.[16]

In his well-known essay, 'The Story Teller', Walter Benjamin annotated a process of mutism which, he claimed, had begun with the Great War. 'Was it not noticeable', he asks, 'at the end of the war that men returned from the battlefield grown silent—not richer, but poorer in communicable experience?' And Benjamin went on to analyse the generational change which had taken place from the end of

---

[13] 'The Golden Year', in *Tennyson: A Selected Edition*, ed. C. Ricks (Harlow: Longman, 1989), 210, ll. 74-6. For a reading of the proleptic qualities of this poem see Roger Ebbatson, *An Imaginary England* (Aldershot: Ashgate, 2005).

[14] Gaston Bachelard, *On Poetic Imagination and Reverie*, tr. C. Gaudin (Dallas: Spring Publications, 1987), 36.

[15] W. J .T. Mitchell, *Landscape and Power* (Chicago: Chicago University Press, 1994), 1.

[16] David Matless, *Landscape and Englishness* (London: Reaktion, 1998), 12, 18.

the nineteenth century:

> A generation that had gone to school on a horse-drawn streetcar now stood
> under the open sky in a countryside in which nothing remained unchanged but
> the clouds, and beneath these clouds, in a field of force of destructive torrents
> and explosions, was the tiny, fragile human body.[17]

We may trace here something of the transition from a sense, in the late-Victorian
period, of the earth as a nurturing physical and metaphysical space towards the
cataclysmic 'field of force' and blighted terrain of No Man's Land, taking as
exemplary or symptomatic texts some key passages from Richard Jefferies and
Thomas Hardy. The issue, then, is to propose a dialectical relation between the
luminosity of the South Country and the degradation of modernity epitomised in
the Western Front.

In Jefferies' 1883 spiritual autobiography, *The Story of My Heart*, the open or
'empty' space of the Wiltshire Downs enables him to project himself towards the
earth in a potently redemptive or prophetic gesture:

> Lying down on the grass, I spoke in my soul to the earth, the sun, the air, and
> the distant sea far beyond sight. I thought of the earth's firmness—I felt it bear
> me up; through the grassy couch there came an influence as if I could feel the
> great earth speaking to me.[18]

Jeremy Hooker has appositely identified Jefferies' 'capacity to both ennoble and
defamiliarise the lowly object, and also with near vision, to enlarge the world',[19]
and there is a curious juxtaposition in this writing of the transcendental—the
response to earth, sun and space—and the quotidian—that 'dry chalky earth'
Jefferies lets fall through his fingers, a heady combination which leads to the
spiritual afflatus, the mystical union, attained as he hides his face in the grass.
Later, in Sussex, he discovers 'a deep hollow on the side of a great hill, a green
concave opening to the sea': 'Silence and sunshine, sea and hill gradually brought
my mind into the condition of intense prayer' (SH, 31). These experiences lead to
the annihilation of time in which he can affirm, 'Now is eternity; now is the
immortal life' (SH, 39). Such writing, unlike the registration of social change in his
fine radical novel *The Dewy Morn* or the sociological essays, is defamiliarising and

[17]   Walter Benjamin, *Illuminations*, tr. H. Zohn (London: Fontana, 1973), 84.
[18]   Richard Jefferies, *The Story of My Heart* (Dartington: Green Books, 2002), 18-19;
subsequently cited in the text as SH.
[19]   Jeremy Hooker, *Writers in a Landscape* (Cardiff: University of Wales Press, 1996), 17.

transcendental, a kind of revelation of being. Jefferies' posture is clearly Transcendental in the technical sense, drawing upon the New England doctrine of the 'universal mind' or 'Oversoul', and the desire, as Emerson puts it, to do away with the 'preposterous There and Then and introduce in its place the Here and Now'.[20] In his seminal essay, 'Nature', Emerson adumbrates many of the concerns of Jefferies' autobiography:

> Standing on the bare ground,—my head bathed by the blithe air, and uplifted into infinite space,—all mean egotism vanishes. I become a transparent eyeball; I am nothing; I see all; the currents of the Universal Being circulate through me; I am part or parcel of God.[21]

Following the publication of *Being and Time* in 1927, Martin Heidegger expounded his later philosophical project as a wish 'to open up to the vastness and at the same time be rooted in the dark of the earth',[22] and it is his thought, especially the 1936 essay 'On the Origin of the Work of Art', which may offer a productive philosophical framework through which to interrogate Jefferies' sense of earthly space. This is a form of writing, in Heideggerian terms, created out of nothing:

> Truth is never gathered from things at hand, never from the ordinary. Rather, the opening up of the open region, and the clearing of beings, happens only when the openness that makes its advent in thrownness is projected.[23]

If the 'Being of beings comes into the steadiness of its shining', then it is 'Upon the earth and in it' that 'historical man grounds his dwelling in the world' (BW, 162, 172). Jefferies seeks the clarification of Heidegger's 'earth', his ascent up to the downs bestowing access to Heidegger's famous 'clearing', an 'open centre not surrounded by beings': 'rather, the clearing centre itself encircles all that is', and beings, Heidegger postulates, 'stand within and stand out within what is cleared in this clearing'. 'In the midst of beings as a whole an open place occurs. There is a clearing' (BW, 178). Indeed, Heidegger affirms what Jefferies and other writers of the late-Victorian period such as Edward Carpenter gesture towards: 'At bottom, the ordinary is not ordinary; it is extraordinary' and the truth is arrived at through a 'clearing of the paths of the essential guiding directions with which all decision

---

20 *The Portable Emerson*, ed. M. van Doren (Harmondsworth: Penguin, 1977), 144.
21 Ralph Waldo Emerson, *Nature, Addresses and Lectures* (London: Routledge, n.d.), 15-16.
22 Cited in Rüdiger Safranski, *Martin Heidegger: Between Good and Evil*, tr. E. Osers (Cambridge, Mass.: Harvard University Press, 1998), 3.
23 Martin Heidegger, *Basic Writings*, ed. D. F. Krell (London: Routledge, 1993), 196; subsequently cited in the text as BW.

complies', to the extent that, as Heidegger expresses it, 'Earth juts through the world and world grounds itself on the earth' (BW, 179, 180). Just as Jefferies sinks to the earth, so Heidegger ponders the weight of the stone in its heaviness, and the way earth 'shatters every attempt to penetrate it'. All art, Heidegger claims, is '*in essence, poetry*', taking place in 'the open region which poetry lets happen', so that beings 'shine and ring out' (BW, 172,197). The ground in which man 'bases his dwelling' Heidegger designates 'the *earth*', an open region in which, he proposes, 'The Being of beings comes into the steadiness of its shining' (BW, 168, 162).

Jefferies' vantage points on the Wiltshire or Sussex heights are similarly saturated with a sense of space, light and sun. In such writing, as Heidegger puts it in 'The End of Philosophy' (1969), 'Light can stream into the clearing, into its openness', but he goes on to insist that 'light never first creates the clearing': 'Rather, light presupposes it'(BW, 442). And Heidegger's citation from Goethe here is apposite to Jefferies' project: ' "Look for nothing behind phenomena"', writes Goethe, ' "they themselves are what is to be learned"' (BW, 442). In *The Story of My Heart*, Jefferies strives towards Heidegger's postulate that the clearing, in its 'free openness', will ultimately bestow 'pure space and ecstatic time'. There is 'No outward appearance without light', and 'no brightness without the clearing'. It is in that clearing that 'possible radiance' is to be found, that is, 'the possible presencing of that presence itself' (BW, 442, 444, 445). Jefferies' strange spiritual autobiography, we may argue, 'lets the earth be an earth' in the sense that this writing compels us by the obscure and resistant weight of its language. Heidegger thus shares with Jefferies a sense of the earth not as a resource for agricultural or industrial exploitation but as a dwelling place which is 'sheltering and concealing' (BW, 172). Both writers seek out the clearing, the attainment of a 'lighting centre' which 'encircles all that is and which enables beings to be unconcealed'. Jefferies' late essays are deeply inflected with this concern for being, which produces, as in his essay 'On the Downs', an ecstatic, celebratory mode of responding to landscape space in tracing the effects of light on the sea and the hills. The mind, Jefferies insists, must allow itself to 'rest on every blade of grass and leaf', and he goes on:

> *Stoop and touch the earth*, and receive its influence; touch the flower, and feel its life; face the wind, and have its meaning; let the sunlight fall on the open hand as if you could hold it. Something may be grasped from them all, invisible yet strong. It is the sense of a wider existence—wider and higher.

This sense of 'absorbing something from the earth' is 'like hovering on the verge of a great truth'.[24] Four years later, in his last illness, Jefferies was still seeking what

---

[24] 'On the Downs', in *Jefferies' England*, ed. S. J. Looker (London: Constable, 1945), 94, 96.

he termed 'the Beyond', 'Soul-Life' or 'Sun-Life', again adumbrating a phenomenological world-view:

> No theory, philosophy, religion, meets the labourer rough and red, the woman to the draw-well, the invalid on his bed, the omnibus driver: all speculation, they do not touch the real.[25]

Yet the quotidian is ineluctably linked, in these moving final ruminations, with transcendence, 'The sun in silence rising over the sea' connecting Jefferies with 'a sense and a sympathy with some larger life'. This gives what he terms a 'great view of the greater earth—*putting soul—thought into the greater sphere*'. Although in his last reflections he feels 'utterly abandoned', it is the 'intense beauty and love of nature—every grain of sand',[26] which dominates these meditations:

> I fetish Nature. Sea, sunshine, clear water, leaves. If I can see why not—if they cannot see I cannot help that—I see the sands and the stars, and subtle cosmical material far up, and feel through, and the more I touch these the greater grows my soul life and soul touch.[27]

In his last note Jefferies offers a summation of his philosophical journey: there is, he avers, 'Nothing for Man. Unless he has the Beyond', and he concludes, '*I dream of Ideality*'.[28]

It is this sense of aspiration for 'the Beyond' which Walter Benjamin examines in a gnomic section of 'One-Way Street' entitled 'To the Planetarium'. Here Benjamin suggests that what distinguishes ancient from modern man is 'the former's absorption in a cosmic experience scarcely known to later periods', and he goes on, in terms cognate with Jefferies' project:

> The ancients' intercourse with the cosmos had been different: the ecstatic trance. For it is in this experience alone that we gain certain knowledge of what is nearest to us and what is remotest to us, and never of one without the other. This means, however, that man can be in ecstatic contact with the cosmos only communally. It is the dangerous error of modern men to regard this experience as unimportant and avoidable, and to consign it to the individual as the poetic rapture of starry nights.

---

25 *The Notebooks of Richard Jefferies*, ed. S.J. Looker (London: Grey Walls Press, 1948), 230.
26 Ibid., 233, 264, 280.
27 Ibid., 283.
28 Ibid., 290.

Such rapturous communion is not simply individualistic, 'unimportant and avoidable'; to the contrary, Benjamin avers, 'its hour strikes again and again', as was made manifest 'by the last war, which was an attempt at new and unprecedented commingling with the cosmic powers' in a form of degraded sublimity:

> Human multitudes, gases, electrical forces were hurled into the open country, high-frequency currents coursed through the landscape, new constellations rose in the sky, aerial space and ocean depths thundered with propellers, and everywhere sacrificial shafts were dug in Mother Earth.

In this historical conjuncture, as the logical consequence of the industrial revolution, the 'lust for profit of the ruling class sought satisfaction' through this ecstatic union, and thus 'technology betrayed man and turned the bridal bed into a bloodbath'. In this catastrophic process, the ancients' rapport with nature is replaced by a different response, so that 'In the nights of annihilation of the last war the frame of mankind was shaken by a feeling that resembled the bliss of the epileptic'.[29]

Edward Comentale has suggested that 'the attempt to establish a certain authenticity, a new perspective, a transcendent consciousness, depends upon the presence of some fallen other, some decadent or marked double'.[30] The 'ideality' which imbues Jefferies' late thoughts, and the potential of a pantheist sensibility in relation to landscape, space and earth was to be re-examined to powerful effect in Hardy's *Tess of the d'Urbervilles* (1891), a text in which the paradisal or metaphysical properties expounded in Jefferies' autobiography are as it were fictionalised in the experiences of Angel Clare and Tess at Talbothays Dairy only to be cancelled and reversed in the wasteland of modernity at Flintcomb-Ash. As she enters the valley of the Froom, Tess's 'hopes mingled with the sunshine in an ideal photosphere' (TD, 109),[31] and she appears even to possess some of the afflatus or visionary intensity of Richard Jefferies, telling Dairyman Crick how, by fixing her thoughts upon a star, she can find herself 'hundreds o' miles away from [her] body' (TD, 124). It is in this setting that the well-known harp-scene brings an ecstatic courtship to a head:

> Tess was conscious of neither time nor space. The exaltation which she had

---

29 Benjamin, *One-Way Street*, 103-4.

30 Edward Comentale, *Modernism, Cultural Production, and the British Avant-Garde* (Cambridge: Cambridge University Press, 2004), 4.

31 Thomas Hardy, *Tess of the d'Urbervilles*, ed. J. Grindle and S. Gatrell (Oxford: Oxford University Press, 1988); subsequently cited in the text as TD.

described as being producible at will by gazing at a star, came now without any determination of hers; she undulated upon the thin notes of the second-hand harp, and their harmonies passed like breezes through her, bringing tears into her eyes. The floating pollen seemed to be his notes made visible, and the dampness of the garden the weeping of the garden's sensibility. (TD, 127)

Hardy had already, however, adumbrated the inauguration of a quite different type of landscape, writing in *The Return of the Native* (1878) of the evolution of a taste for 'a gaunt waste in Thule':

The time seems near, if it has not actually arrived, when the mournful sublimity of a moor, a sea, or a mountain, will be all of nature that is absolutely in keeping with the moods of the more thinking among mankind.[32]

Thus it comes about, in *Tess*, that the 'oozing fatness and warm ferments of the Var Vale' (TD, 151) give way, following Angel's rejection of Tess on the wedding night, to a landscape of exposure and suffering at the 'starve-acre place' of Flintcomb-Ash (TD, 277), where the rich potency of the Froom water-meadows is reinflected as a landscape of naked aggression, 'almost sublime in its dreariness' (TD, 275), personified in the sexually predatory farmer, Mr Groby:

The swede-field, in which she and her companion were set hacking, was a stretch of a hundred odd acres, in one patch, on the highest ground of the farm, rising above stony lanchets or lynchets—the outcrop of siliceous veins in the chalk formation, composed of myriads of loose white flints in bulbous, cusped, and phallic shapes…the whole field was in colour a desolate drab; it was a complexion without features, as if a face from chin to brow should be only an expanse of skin. (TD, 277)

Here Marian and Tess are transmuted, 'two girls crawling over the surface' of the field 'like flies' (TD, 277). As Roger Webster has noted, the colouring and sense of 'indistinct and nebulous' light effects associated with the dairy are here 'reversed' so that 'hard forms or outlines replace the softness of the light and colour effects'.[33] The emphasis is upon space as an emptiness in which the labourers are exposed to the elements; as the narrator laconically remarks, 'to stand working slowly in a field, and feel the creep of rainwater, first in legs and shoulders, then on

32 Thomas Hardy, *The Return of the Native*, ed. S. Gatrell (Oxford: Oxford University Press, 1990), 4.
33 Roger Webster, 'From Painting to Cinema: Visual Elements in Hardy's Fiction', in T. R. Wright, ed., *Thomas Hardy on Screen* (Cambridge: Cambridge University Press, 2005), 30.

hips and head...and yet to work on till the leaden light diminishes', 'demands a distinct modicum of stoicism' (TD, 278). This vacant space is invaded by a type of premonitory natural sign—the arrival of Arctic birds classed as 'gaunt spectral creatures with tragical eyes' which had witnessed 'scenes of cataclysmal horror', scenes 'of a magnitude such as no human being had ever conceived' (TD, 279-80). Here and elsewhere in the Flintcomb-Ash sequence Hardy appears to reinflect Ruskin's 1884 lecture on the premonitory 'Storm Cloud of the Nineteenth Century' which elicits a 'Blanched Sun,—blighted grass,—blinded man', phenomena there interpreted as 'the physical result of your own wars and prophecies', an omen that 'the Empire of England, on which formerly the sun never set, has become one on which he never rises'.[34] On her first arrival at Flintcomb-Ash, Tess had enveloped her beauty in a 'grey serge cape' and 'whitey-brown rough wrapper' (TD, 272), and now, across the denuded and endless space the female field-labourers, in Hardy's bleak vision, 'trudged onwards with slanted bodies' (TD, 280), proleptically anticipating in posture and anguish Wilfred Owen's Great War soldiers, 'Bent double, like old beggars under sacks,/Knock-kneed, coughing like hags',[35] or Ivor Gurney's regiment, 'Bent, slouching downwards to billets comfortless and dim'.[36] Each of these literary figurations stages the way in which, in Adorno's resonant diagnosis of the administered society, 'mankind still keeps dragging itself along' in 'an endless procession of bent figures chained to each other, no longer able to raise their heads under the burden of what is'.[37] In a potent reinscription of natural space, the two young women 'often looked across the country to where the Var or Froom was known to stretch' (TD, 279). Walter Benjamin's notion of the 'aura' as 'the unique apparition of a distance', and his notation of its modern 'decay',[38] is movingly embodied in Marian's plaintive remark to Tess: ' "You can see a gleam of a hill within a few miles o' Froom Valley from here when 'tis fine"' (TD, 278)—a moment reinflected in the youthful Jude's vision of Christminster as 'points of light' which 'gleamed' 'like the topaz'.[39]

Ensuing on this bleak scene of exposure, the 'calvary of labour' of the steam

---

34 'The Storm Cloud of the Nineteenth Century', in *John Ruskin: Selected Writings*, ed. D. Birch (Oxford: Oxford University Press, 2004), 277.

35 'Dulce Et Decorum Est', *The Collected Poems of Wilfred Owen*, ed. C. Day Lewis (London: Chatto & Windus, 1967), 55.

36 Ivor Gurney, 'Canadians', *Collected Poems*, ed. P. J. Kavanagh (Manchester: Carcanet, 2004), 143.

37 T.W. Adorno, *Negative Dialectics*, tr. E. B. Ashton (London: Routledge & Kegan Paul, 1973), 345.

38 Walter Benjamin, *Selected Writings*, vol. 4, ed. M. Bullock, H. Eiland and M. Jennings (Cambridge, Mass.: Belknap Press, 2003), 255.

39 Thomas Hardy, *Jude the Obscure*, ed. P. Ingham (Oxford: Oxford University Press, 1985), 17.

threshing-machine enacts and stages the principle of mechanisation and the new relations of production which will transform the space of the landscape in conformity with the laws of capital and exchange. Whilst the field-labourers serve 'vegetation, weather, frost, and sun' (TD, 315), the steam-thresher is serviced by the blackened engine-man with his 'strange northern accent' and his 'iron charge' (TD, 315, 316). It is a relatively short step from here to the climactic scene at Stonehenge set in a landscape of 'open loneliness and black solitude' (TD, 378). Here on the Great Plain 'the whole enormous landscape bore that impress of reserve, taciturnity, and hesitation' (TD, 381) which, paradoxically at this prehistoric site, announces the onset of modernity with the arrival of the agents of the law. As the black flag is raised above Wintoncester Gaol to signal Tess's execution, the 'two speechless gazers', Angel and Liza-Lu, 'bent themselves down to the earth' (TD, 384) in a gesture which parodically or tragically reduplicates Jefferies' life-affirming posture in *The Story of My Heart*. Jefferies himself had also, in *After London*, already envisaged or prophesied the wasted landscape of modernity in imagining the disappearance of London under the great lake which, at its eastern end, becomes 'a vast stagnant swamp' exhaling a 'fatal' odour. In this dystopian vision the blackened water 'bears a greenish-brown floating scum, which for ever bubbles up from the putrid mud', and the scene is dominated by a low cloud which hangs ominously over the 'oily liquid', in a premonitory figuration of what has been designated the 'slimescape' of the Western Front:

> For all the rottenness of a thousand years and of many hundred millions of human beings is there festering under the stagnant water, which has sunk down into and penetrated the earth, and floated up to the surface the contents of the buried cloacae.[40]

In *Tess of the d'Urbervilles*, Hardy focuses upon those issues—forces of production, class consciousness, base and superstructure—which inform the Marxist analysis of capital, and the entire Flintcomb-Ash sequence may be fruitfully placed in conjunction with some of Marx's reflections in the *Economic and Philosophical Manuscripts* of 1844. Thus the 'despotic demand' which the threshing-machine makes on the labourers (TD, 315) is a precise staging of the way, in Marx's writing, the worker's labour 'becomes an object, an *external* existence', 'something which is

---

40 Richard Jefferies, *After London* (Oxford: Oxford University Press, 1980), 37-8. On the 'slimescape' created by the Great War see Santanu Das, *Touch and Intimacy in First World War Literature* (Cambridge: Cambridge University Press, 2005), ch. 1.

'hostile and alien'.[41] It is just such alienation that leads to the recurrent harking back to a pre-industrial time, the older men talking 'of the past days when they had been accustomed to thresh with flails on the oaken barnfloor'—a time 'when everything ...was effected by hand-labour' (TD, 316). Here and in the earlier swede-cutting scenes Hardy meditates upon the issues surrounding human labour in the open landscape of Wessex, the experience of Tess and her fellow-labourers enacting Marx's contention that 'the more the worker by his labour *appropriates* the external world, sensuous nature, the more he deprives himself of *means of life*'.[42] This appropriation leads towards the naked exposure of the swede-field, or of that 'wide and lonely depression' in the natural space of the Berkshire Downs where Jude acts ineffectually as bird-scarer, a space where the human culture and memory of the folk is obliterated:

> 'How ugly it is here!' he murmured.
> The fresh harrow-lines seemed to stretch like the channellings in a piece of new corduroy, lending a meanly utilitarian air to the expanse, taking away its gradations, and depriving it of all history beyond that of the few recent months. [43]

Such exploitation and representation of earthly space prophetically embodies the establishment and representation, within a generation, of No Man's Land. Men work, Marx argues, to convert nature into a world of objects. In looking at nature men see only 'the bitterest competition among plants and animals'. Men and women here form the link between the instrument of labour and its object. The natural space of the South Country, that is to say, is here the subject/object of labour, human forces stamping their impress upon the face of nature even in the arid uplands of Flintcomb-Ash. The swede-cutting scenes introduce a direct transaction between the human and nature in which exchange-value dominates, as it does not at Talbothays Dairy. At the dairy, the rustic group come to regard themselves, in Marxian terminology, as *'communal proprietors'* of the enclosed valley, 'members of the community which produces and reproduces itself by living labour'.[44] The sense of communal ownership in Talbothays, already undermined by the arrival of the railway in the valley, is shattered under the impress of the modernity which produces the 'utilitarian' empty space of Flintcomb-Ash, the 'vast

---

41 Karl Marx, *Economic and Philosophical Manuscripts of 1844*, in Marx and Engels, *Collected Works*, vol. 13 (London: Lawrence & Wishart, 1975), 272.

42 Ibid., 273.

43 *Jude the Obscure*, 8.

44 Cited in Alfred Schmidt, *The Concept of Nature in Marx* (London: NLB, 1971), 130.

concave' of Jude's bird-scaring, or the miasmic swamp of Jefferies' prophetic fantasy.

Hillis Miller has suggested that as a form the novel comprises 'a figurative mapping', tracing a space 'based on the real landscape, charged now with the subjective meaning of the story that has been enacted within it'.[45] In *Topographies*, he argues that Heidegger (and, we might suggest, Jefferies on the downs or Tess at Talbothays) 'is beguiled by the dream of a harmonious and unified culture, a culture rooted in one particular place', whilst in contrast Hardy's work demonstrates 'that such an apparent unity, even in rural cultures, is riven by divisions and disharmonies'. He adds that, for Hardy, 'the human predicament, even in relatively stable and unified local society is to be alone'.[46] The juxtaposition of *The Story of My Heart* and *Tess of the d'Urbervilles*, therefore, might be further interrogated in terms of the countervailing representations of landscape space, and the reading of these texts framed and problematised here by fuller consideration of the Heideggerian thesis. Miller is right to claim that Heidegger's topographical thinking 'cannot be detached from the complex of ideas about language, thinking, building and dwelling', ideas symptomatically expounded in the 1951 essay, 'Building Dwelling Thinking'. The crucial starting point for Heidegger here is his contention that 'Man acts as though *he* were the shaper and master of language, while in fact *language* remains the master of man' (BW, 348). The German '*bauen*', 'to build', originally signifies 'to dwell', so that, Heidegger contends, 'To be a human being means to be on the earth as a mortal'—'It means to dwell' (BW, 349). But the modernising activities of 'cultivation and construction' predicate that 'dwelling' 'falls into oblivion' (BW, 350), and Heidegger seeks to relocate this sense of dwelling in relation to his fourfold terms, earth, sky, divinities and mortals. It is the latter who have the power to 'save' the earth by refraining from its exploitation: 'Saving the earth does not master the earth and does not subjugate it, which is merely one step from boundless spoliation' (BW, 352)—a process already underway in Hardy's threshing-machine scene or Jefferies' polluted inland sea. To preserve, to the contrary, 'means to take under our care' (BW, 353). In the second part of the essay Heidegger focuses upon the image or symbol of a bridge over a river, conceived as the essence of true building which 'enspaces' and '*gathers* to itself in *its own* way earth and sky, divinities and mortals' (BW, 355). The construction of a bridge, in this argument, creates what Heidegger designates a 'locale', and locales are said to 'allow for spaces' (BW, 356). The German term for space, *Raum*, means 'a place freed for settlement and lodging', or for 'something that has been made room for': 'Space is in essence that for which room has been made' (BW, 356).

---

45 J. Hillis Miller, *Topographies* (Stanford: Stanford University Press, 1995), 19.

46 Ibid., 55.

Heidegger concludes by positing that the 'essence of building is letting dwell'. He contends that '*Only if we are capable of dwelling, only then can we build*', and illustrates his point by the example of an ancient Black Forest farmhouse:

> Let us think for a while of a farmhouse in the Black Forest, which was built some two hundred years ago by the dwelling of peasants. Here the self-sufficiency of the power to let earth and sky, divinities and mortals enter *in simple oneness* into things ordered the house. It placed the farm on the wind-sheltered mountain slope, looking south, among the meadows close to the spring. It gave it the wide overhanging shingle roof whose proper slope bears up under the burden of snow…It did not forget the altar corner behind the community table; it made room in its chamber for the hallowed places of childbed and the 'tree of the dead'—for that is what they call a coffin there…A craft that, itself sprung from dwelling, still uses its tools and its gear as things, built the farm-house. (BW, 361-2)

We might contextualise this hymn to dwelling, to the human enclosure of domestic space, by recalling some of Hardy's interiors—for instance, the tranter's cottage in *Under the Greenwood Tree*, the Great Barn in *Far From the Madding Crowd*, or indeed the dairy in *Tess*. Traces of such 'dwelling' mark even the bleak field of Jude's bird-scaring, in which 'to every clod and stone there really attached associations', and 'echoes of songs from ancient harvest-days', 'of spoken words, and of sturdy deeds'.[47] Such a 'constellation' is no longer available to mankind, in Heidegger's diagnosis, because of the onslaught of modernity: building, he argues, 'never shapes "pure space"' (BW, 360), but the '*proper plight of dwelling*' goes back, he argues, to a period 'before the world wars with their destruction'. Man's existential 'homelessness' is the refusal, ultimately, of the summons to 'dwell' (BW, 363). Heidegger is proposing that the poetic encounter with nature is crucial to an authentic inhabitation of the earth. The sense of poetry insisted upon here is not an aesthetic luxury but a primary condition of that 'dwelling' which is threatened and undermined by contemporary technology. It is, in this argument, mankind who create 'a place for space by making sites and locations that surround themselves with a landscape', as Hillis Miller puts it.[48] The thinking is complex here and refers back to *Being and Time*, where Heidegger reads space as dependent upon time. Being, or *Dasein*, 'as temporality is ecstatico-horizontal in its Being' and thus 'it can take along with it a space for which it has made room'. Heidegger adds in portentous italics, '*Only on the basis of its ecstatico-horizontal temporality is it possible*

---

47 *Jude the Obscure*, 9.
48 Miller, *Topographies*, 241.

for Dasein to break into space[49]—a knotted Germanic version of the spiritual afflatus of Jefferies' communing on the downs.

The organisation of space creates the landscape, in this argument—an act of creation dependent upon the notion of '*Raum*', founded in the notion of clearance. Hillis Miller glosses this by suggesting that the 'site organises space around it from a horizon', so that it 'goes out to make the border from which a space is cleared'.[50] But it may be that Heidegger's anti-metaphysical reading of space, with its resonant pre-echoes in Hardy and Jefferies, contains, as Hillis Miller notes, disturbing connotations in terms of the importation of 'the monolithic, one-fold, culture of a people (*ein Volk*) sharing the same language, laws, and cultures, and dwelling in one particular place'. As Miller asserts, 'Such topographical assumptions would underwrite a uni-cultural nationalism'.[51] Does the cultivation of a transcendental landscape space in late-Victorian England, therefore, dialectically call into being or prophesy the abyssal landscapes of modern technology and warfare? Certainly, it is impossible to overlook the reactionary undertones in *The Story of My Heart*, when for instance Jefferies longs for 'an iron mace' with which he 'might crush the savage beast and hammer him down' (SH, 80). Perhaps more ominous is the cult of Julius Caesar, conceived as the one man 'truly great of all history' who attained 'the ideal of a design-power arranging the affairs of the world for good' (SH, 65-6). We are, it may be, here not too distant from Heidegger's notorious invocation, in his rectoral Freiburg University lectures of the early 1930s, of 'the forces that are rooted in the blood and soil of a *Volk*', and his concept of a '*fierce battle*' to be waged by teachers 'in the National Socialist spirit', in a project 'to build a *living bridge* between the worker of the "hand" and the worker of the "head"'.[52] The Führer, Heidegger suggested there, 'asks nothing of the people', only what he terms 'the will to the self-responsibility of the people', or 'the *Dasein* of our people'—in this way were the German *Volk* to 'find the greatness and truth of its determination'.[53] This entire structure of feeling, with its existential concomitants, forms part and parcel of an ideological position that Adorno would caustically define as the 'tragic Hitlerian pose of lonely valour' which, 'posturing as metaphysical homelessness', serves to 'justify the very order that drives men to despair and threatens them with

---

49 Martin Heidegger, *Being and Time*, tr. J. Macquarrie and E. Robinson (Oxford: Blackwell, 1962), 420-21.

50 Miller, *Topographies*, 244, 245.

51 Ibid., 253.

52 These phrases are drawn from three lectures of 1933-4, reprinted in *The Heidegger Controversy*, ed. R. Wolin (New York: Columbia University Press, 1991), 33 ff.

53 Cited in Jürgen Habermas, *The Philosophical Discourse of Modernity*, tr. F. Lawrence (Cambridge: Polity Press, 1987), 157.

physical extinction'.54

The longing for a return to natural landscape spaces took the form of a response to the bourgeois experience of alienation in a mass society, but the premonitory possibilities of such a 'return' were persuasively laid bare in a 1937 essay on the Norwegian nature-novelist, Knut Hamsun, by a member of the Frankfurt School, Leo Löwenthal. Drawing upon Ibsen, Löwenthal argues that the 'path to nature' took the form, not of a flight from reality, but rather a trajectory towards liberation. However, in the late-nineteenth-century manifestation of this impulse of which Hamsun, a writer much admired by Heidegger, is an exemplar, Löwenthal argues that 'this new type of submission to nature is closely related to political submission', with the result that 'communion with nature is transformed from sentiment to sentimentality, and then into brutality'.55 In bourgeois liberal cultural readings, nature is transformed 'by organised societal enterprise', Löwenthal suggests, becoming 'an object for scientific and practical control', whereas in the nature-mysticism embodied by Heidegger (or, we may postulate, Jefferies or Emerson), the individual 'consecrates his life in rapt surrender and even in mystical identification' to generate what Löwenthal designates 'a jumble of mawkish sympathies for both natural objects and spiritual difficulties', to the extent that Hamsun's world, in Löwenthal's critique, 'foreshadows the affinity of brutality and sentimentality' which would characterise the twentieth-century German war-machine.56 In such a structure of feeling, as Comentale remarks, 'divine pattern concedes to the inhuman face of technological domination'.57 Walter Benjamin would concur with this evaluation, noting how 'In the face of the landscape of total mobilisation, the German feeling for nature had an undreamt-of upsurge'.58 The evocative and spellbinding conjuration of a transcendental 'rootedness' in the spaces of earth thus paradoxically prophesies its opposite, so that, with the onset of the Great War, in Benjamin's haunting diagnosis, the 'pioneers of peace' are 'evacuated' from these landscapes with the result that, 'as far as anyone could see over the edge of the trench, the terrain had become the terrain of German Idealism'. The allegorical gaze, in Benjaminian terms, reveals both nature and history as a devastated landscape subject to irresistible decay. As Benjamin puts it,

---

54 T. W. Adorno, *Negative Dialectics*, tr. E. B. Ashton (London: Routledge & Kegan Paul, 1973), 89.

55 Leo Löwenthal, 'Knut Hamsun', in *The Essential Frankfurt School Reader*, ed. A. Arato and E. Gebhardt (Oxford: Blackwell, 1978), 320, 321, 322.

56 Ibid., 326, 328.

57 Comentale, *Modernism, Cultural Production*, 96.

58 Cited in John McCole, *Walter Benjamin and the Antinomies of Tradition* (Ithaca: Cornell University Press, 1993), 179.

every shell-crater had become a problem, every wire entanglement an antinomy, every barb a definition, every explosion a thesis; by day the sky was the cosmic interior of the steel helmet, and at night the moral law above. Etching the landscape with flaming banners and trenches, technology wanted to rescue the heroic features of German Idealism...Deeply imbued with its own depravity, technology gave shape to the apocalyptic face of nature and reduced nature to silence—even though this technology had the power to give nature its voice.

War is, in this interpretation which resonates with our texts, 'nothing other than the attempt to redeem, mystically and without mediation, the secret of nature, understood idealistically, through technology'.[59] Both Hardy's imaginative juxtaposition of Talbothays Dairy and Flintcomb-Ash, and Jefferies' projection of the South Country and its inundation under the great lake, stage and enact Benjamin's ruminative remark that 'nature is messianic by reason of its eternal and total passing away'.[60] As Esther Leslie argues in her study of the German chemical industry, the natural experience of the Benjaminian aura 'becomes inceasingly a social experience that either excludes aura, or reweaves it according to false pattern'. Paradoxically, as Leslie argues, technology itself 'generated a sort of aura', 'on the battlefields of the Great War where chemical gases fuzzed up the European landscape':

> It destroys the vista of nature as a place of contemplation. In altering the rules of war and hazing up the battlefield something akin to aura, a haze, is reproduced, but its qualities are quite different: this is aura after aura. It takes its place alongside those other entities that generate not aura but fake aura, the rotten shimmer of the commodity fetish or untimely artwork. At the end of auratic experience, in modernity's new denaturing, is aura's reinvention as synthetic.[61]

In contemplating the transmutation of the visionary landscape of Jefferies or of Hardy's Vale of the Great Dairies into the abyssal spaces of modernity, it is worth recalling Benjamin's contention that there is 'no more insipid and shabby antithesis than that which reactionary thinkers' posit 'between the symbol-space of nature and that of technology'. Rather, Benjamin suggests, 'to each truly new configura-

---

59 Walter Benjamin, 'Theories of German Fascism', in *Selected Writings*, vol. 2, ed. M. W. Jennings, H. Eiland and G. Smith (Cambridge, Mass.: Belknap Press, 1999), 318-19.

60 Walter Benjamin, 'Theological-Political Fragment', in *Selected Writings*, vol. 3, ed. H. Eiland and M. W. Jennings (Cambridge, Mass.: Belknap Press, 2002), 306.

61 Esther Leslie, *Synthetic Worlds: Nature, Art and the Chemical Industry* (London: Reaktion Books, 2005), 226.

tion of nature—and at bottom, technology is just such a configuration—there exist new "images"'.[62] This transmutation effect, from transcendence to obliteration, traces the contrast between being, permanence and the identical, and history, which is a movement of becoming. Historical knowledge—in this instance, the knowledge of war—is marked by a discontinuity and fragmentation born out of the opposing trope of being and identity, as Paul de Man has explained:

> A consciously created *being*, whether it be a work of art or a historical fact in general, is unstable in its being, and it negates itself to be reborn in another *being*. The two are separated by the abyss of a negation (in organic language: a death), and the passage from one to the other is essentially discontinuous.[63]

The 'new images' which Benjamin envisages being created by technology are thus ineluctably related to the immanence of natural space in the transcendental tradition. In the Great War the sacramental spaces of the late-Victorian and Edwardian South Country undergo a final catastrophic transformation into that No Man's Land where, for instance, Benjamin's fellow Freiburg student, Martin Heidegger, would serve as a meteorological observer:

> Hideous landscapes, vile noises, foul language and nothing but foul, even from one's own mouth (for all are devil ridden), everything unnatural, broken, blasted; the distortion of the dead, whose unburiable bodies sit outside the dug-outs all day, all night, the most execrable sights on earth. In poetry we call them the most glorious.[64]

Wilfred Owen's account points towards, not only some of his own work, but also the more expressionist landscapes of Georg Trakl's final poems; indeed, it has justly been said that 'Abendland' ('The West'), composed in May 1914, 'ends with lines which seem in retrospect to be a prophetic anticipation of the coming war'[65]:

> You great cities
> Reared of stone

---

[62] Walter Benjamin, *The Arcades Project*, tr. H. Eiland and K. McLoughlin (Cambridge, Mass.: Belknap Press, 1999), 390.

[63] Paul de Man, 'The Temptation of Permanence', in *Critical Writings, 1953-78*, ed. L. Waters (Minneapolis: University of Minnesota Press, 1989), 32.

[64] Wilfred Owen, letter of 1917, cited in Jon Stallworthy, *Wilfred Owen* (Oxford: Oxford University Press, 1977), 159.

[65] Richard Detsch, *Georg Trakl's Poetry: Toward a Union of Opposites* (University Park, PA: Pennsylvania State University Press, 1983), 60.

In the plains!
Speechless with dark brow
The homeless man
Follows the wind,
Bare trees by the hillside.
You far-flung fading rivers!
Fearful sunsets
In tempest clouds
Inspire mighty dread.
You dying nations!
Pallid wave
Breaking upon night's shore,
Falling stars.[66]

It has been observed that in Trakl's later verse, composed before his suicide on the Eastern Front, nature 'far from being a secure refuge for men, is itself involved in the universal process of decay and destruction', so that many of the images function 'as prophecies of the actual destruction which was soon to be visited upon civilisation'.[67]

As Andrew Webber has noted, in relation to 'Abendland', 'through the historical lens of the First World War and the textual lens of Spengler's *Der Untergang des Abendlands* (*Decline of the West*, 1922), Trakl's poem seems to assume a prophetic, apocalyptic character'.[68] The elegiac tone adopted by Trakl, that is to say, is modified by 'the radically forward-looking character' of his poetic diction.[69] Whilst 'Abendland' appears to reject the city of modernity in favour of the natural landscapes explored by Jefferies and Hardy, as Webber remarks, 'its anti-urban topography is profoundly conditioned by the experience of simultaneous dislocation…that characterises urban modernity'.[70] The five war poems composed by Trakl are prophetic in tone and replete with the imagery of ruin and desolation, but we may close with one instance, 'Im Osten' ('In the East'), a text in which the prophetic and ecstatic voice adopted in the nature rhapsodies of Richard Jefferies reaches its brutal and cataclysmic reversal in the ultimate desacralisation of the natural world:

---

[66] Georg Trakl, *Poems and Prose*, tr. Alexander Stillman (Evanston, Ill.: Northwestern University Press, 2005), 99.

[67] Detsch, *Georg Trakl's Poetry*, 122.

[68] Andrew J. Webber, *The European Avant-Garde* (Cambridge: Polity, 2004), 73.

[69] Ibid., 74.

[70] Ibid., 82.

A people's gloomy wrath is like
Wild organs of a winter storm
The scarlet wave of battle,
Of leaf-stripped stars.

With shattered brows, silver arms,
Night beckons dying soldiers.
In the shade of the autumn ash
The spirits of the vanquished sigh.

Thorny wilderness girds the city.
The moon hounds frightened women
From bleeding steps.
Wild wolves burst through the gate.[71]

---

71 Trakl, *Poems and Prose*, 125.

III

Welsh Women Writers

Anne Cluysenaar

Change

So heavy with time,
these long leaves
have turned slowly to stone.
It seems they must have fallen
while still green
through shadowed light,
a camera-click
of wet silt
washing away air, warmth, sound,
sunk into darkness, becoming ground.

Hard it is,
with such a slab
resting cold on my knee,
so hard to believe
(what I know) that
nothing exists
of the past —
no far
real place, like a walkable landscape
distantly framing the human face.

Letter by letter,
word by word,
the poem fails to catch up
even with this, the one
moment of earth
between past and future.
Stone leaves,
live leaves.
There's a pulse that lasts, through change
after change, out of which everything came.

And will come.
The night sky
shines with fossils of light.
As day succeeds night,
light blinds,
and the distant suns
vanish.
I will,
all the same, seek to imagine those clouds
of matter, sparking, seeding worlds out.

Wendy Mulford

Question

About the shadow and the lip
                    there may be
Scar tissue
                    never mind that
Somewhere
                    the river runs down
Where's home
                    the trees answer
                        *
Such a poise can put the
                    whole life in
question
                    hesitancy holds
the clue
                        *
Engage such a
                            question
how do you know
                            the size of the ocean?
ask again
                    then plunge

                        *
If the moon rises
                    above this cliff
does it rise too
                    in your parlour?

                        *
So.   There is a clearing.
                    one tall pine   bending
in the wind's commotion.

Soon the heart
will make its obligatory entry
                    sighing pining creating
more commotion

                    *

There are more words here than are needed
                    . . .
And still their prison hulks disgrace us

                    *

Take me down
                    the winds
don't stop their howl

                    *

It is not the place of time to tick
                    what's worth five minutes
bliss?   a song, a tale
a joke of
                    eternity

                    *

So one leg's this side
        the estuary runs deep and cold
we may never reach the other

Fiona Owen

Squirrels and other things

You must not ever stop being whimsical—Mary Oliver

RED berries on the cotoneaster and a bank of ferns.
That's my window view today. When it comes to poems,
one man says tight discipline is right. Another advocates sprawl.
Boxed in by perspectives, I could fall mute—but a squirrel leaps
through the branches of an oak tree and something in me
leaps too. So who is clichéd—the squirrel or me? Anonymous
grey creature, vermin and disposable? Boring trope
of nature's overused language? The world out there
makes me love it by being itself. When a robin
lands on a twig, why not write it in? It hasn't landed there
for my sake and can't help being a romantic symbol of winter.
It flits in with its showy breast. Then: its goneness.

Whatever life is, it's like that.

The poem, the squirrel, the robin and me
fuse at this point. There is also a bramble hedge
and beyond, electric wires, a transformer
and a word in red: *danger.*

'A personal isolated odd universe': Dorothy Edwards and her short fiction

Tony Brown

I

IN a short essay entitled 'On Writing', which she contributed in 1925 to *Cap and Gown*, the student magazine at University College, Cardiff, Dorothy Edwards recalls reading in her childhood, a book entitled *The Lure of the Pen: A Book for Would-be Authors*. The advice of the book's author, Flora Klickman, to her 'would-be authors' is to write about what you know'.[1] In her essay, however, Edwards describes how she herself had felt that she did not have much first-hand knowledge that would provide her with suitable material for fiction and had decided that 'the obvious solution was to write about far-off distant things, and be very symbolic'. In a later letter Edwards again addresses the issue of subject matter in fiction: 'You must be a realist or you must invent a personal isolated odd universe composed exclusively of your own experience'.[2] As is immediately evident

---

[1]   The essay appeared in *Cap and Gown* 23.1 (1925), 11–12. It is referred to in Luned Meredith, 'Dorothy Edwards', *Planet* 55 (1986), 55, and also in Lucy Stevenson, 'Loneliness and Isolation in the Life and Fiction of Dorothy Edwards (1903–1934)', unpub. MA dissertation, University of Wales [Bangor], 2004. I am grateful to Lucy Stevenson for many discussions of aspects of Edwards' work, which have helped me to focus my own ideas about this enigmatic writer. Edwards' copy of Klickman's book, which was published in 1919, is inscribed 'To dear cousin Dorothy, with best wishes for her success!'

[2]   Quoted in S. Beryl Jones, 'Dorothy Edwards as a Writer of Short Stories', *Welsh Review* 7.3 (1948), 187. Jones does not give the date of the letter; it is likely that the recipient was herself since Edwards, Jones and their mutual friend Winifred Kelly, remained in touch from their days at university until Edwards' death in 1934. A significant number of letters from Edwards to Jones and Kelly are in the Dorothy Edwards Papers, held in the Archives

from her fiction, set as it is in her version of a rural, essentially timeless England populated by cultured members of the English middle classes who seem to have nothing to do with their time but read, walk and converse together, Dorothy Edwards did not in fact write whereof she knew when she published her collection of short stories *Rhapsody* (1927, just two years after her *Cap and Gown* essay) or her novel *Winter Sonata* (1928). Ultimately, the present paper will argue, the cultured 'far-off' world which she portrays in her fiction is both 'very symbolic' and yet deeply rooted in her own experience.

The reality of Dorothy Edwards' early years was the industrial South Wales which was to be drawn so vividly in the work of the (male) writers of her generation in the years after her death. As Claire Flay has recently pointed out in providing the context for Edwards' upbringing, when Edwards was born in Ogmore Vale in 1903, there were five working coal mines and the community was culturally dynamic, with the round of chapel-based and leisure pursuits with which such coalmining communities alleviated the pressures of their lives.[3] Edwards' father, Edward Edwards, was a school master and also a prominent activist in the Labour movement locally, and was acquainted with several of the leaders of the British socialist movement; visitors to the Edwards' home included Keir Hardie, Bruce Glasier, George Lansbury and the prominent American socialist, J. Stitt Wilson.[4] But as was the case with so many writers bred by industrial South Wales in these years—Glyn Jones, Alun Lewis, Rhys Davies—the father's job essentially meant that while Edwards was brought up in a working-class community she was in many ways set apart from it. The headmaster's family, for instance, as Claire Flay has pointed out, could take lengthy holidays in England and France, a far cry from the miners' day trips to Porthcawl or Barry Island.[5] In 1916, the cultural distance between Edwards and the day-to-day life of industrial Ogmore Vale widened to the point of total disconnection when she became, at the age of thirteen, a pupil at Howell's School, the prestigious private school for girls in Llandaff, Cardiff, having won a scholarship. (While it would seem counter to Edward Edwards' socialist principles to have his daughter attend a private school, we can only assume that he was unwilling in any way to handicap her prospects of

---

Department, University of Reading. (These papers are referred to in subsequent notes as 'Reading'.)

3 Claire Flay, 'Strange Music: A Study of the Life and Writings of Dorothy Edwards', unpub. MA dissertation, U. of Glamorgan, 2004

4 See Stevenson, 4, and Harold M. Watkins, 'Dorothy Edwards', *Wales* 6 (1946), 43. Watkins recalls Edwards as a schoolgirl reciting a poem by William Morris at a socialist rally in Cardiff. On Edward Edwards' Socialism, see also Flay, 12–13.

5 Flay, 13.

a career on her own terms, without having to settle for a life of domesticity.)[6]
From Howell's, Edwards went to what was then the University College of South
Wales and Monmouthshire, Cardiff, graduating in 1924 with a degree in Greek and
Philosophy.

In fact the move from Ogmore Vale had become complete before she entered
university, when Edward Edwards died. It was in many ways a crucial event for his
daughter; the loss of a parent can be disorientating for any teenager but Dorothy
Edwards lost a parent who was clearly a powerful and active presence in her life.
Moreover, her father's death ultimately created economic and emotional pressures
which were to become increasingly overwhelming in the remaining years of her
short life. After his death, Dorothy and her mother moved to Rhiwbina, Cardiff's
new garden suburb, which became home to a number of teachers and academics
associated with the University, including the Professor of Welsh, W. J. Gruffydd,
Professor Gilbert Norwood and several members of the English Department,
including Kathleen Freeman and Catherine Macdonald Maclean, the latter a
distinguished Wordsworth scholar. Kate Roberts was another resident.

Edwards had involved herself fully in the undergraduate life of the university in
her years there; she played the role of Raina in a production of Shaw's *Arms and the
Man*, she wrote poems, essays, stories and reviews for *Cap and Gown*, took an
interest in musical activities (she had a fine singing voice) and made a number of
close friends.[7] She also fell in love with a young lecturer, John Thorburn, to whom
she seems to have become briefly engaged; the distress caused by the break-up of
this relationship is indicated by Harold Watkins, a friend and neighbour, who
recalls this as 'a difficult time for her': 'She walked the hills alone for hours at a
stretch, day after day, week after week, working off her "nerves", trying to find
calm'.[8] The nervous stress and the loneliness were symptomatic; indeed the break
with Thorburn exacerbated the isolation which Edwards was already experiencing
after graduating. Close friends, including Sona Burstein, Beryl Jones and Winifred
Kelly, had left for jobs in other parts of the country: Jones and Kelly took up
teaching posts in Yorkshire and continued to live together. There was virtually no
literary scene in Cardiff outside the university. In 1925, in another part of the city,
another budding writer was experiencing a similar sense of isolation. Glyn Jones
had returned to his parents' home after teacher training college in Cheltenham to

---

6   That Dorothy Edwards in fact attended Howell's on a scholarship has recently been
    discovered by Claire Flay; I am grateful to her for this information.

7   The production of Shaw is reviewed by Prof. Gilbert Norwood in *Cap and Gown* 18.2 (1921),
    3.

8   Watkins, 47. The relationship with Thorburn, which seems to have been an uneasy one, is
    documented in Edwards' letters to her friends Beryl Jones and Winifred Kelly, now in the
    Reading archive. Some of these are quoted in Stevenson, 10–12.

take up a teaching post in Cardiff; his parents had moved from Merthyr while he was away and Jones found himself with no like-minded friends or acquaintances: 'Cardiff was for me then an extremely lonely place. [. . .] No literary or artistic life existed in the Welsh city'.9 Literary journals like *Wales* and *The Welsh Review* would not be established for another decade; Edwards was sending her stories to London, where some of them were published in *The Calendar of Modern Letters*. Rhiwbina neighbours, academics from the Welsh and English Departments, were significantly older, though they did provide a continued, and clearly vital, link with the University. In 1926, *Cap and Gown* reports that 'Miss Dorothy Edwards, B.A.' had given a paper on Anton Tchekov to the English Society10 and it must have been shortly later that the undergraduate Gwyn Jones (himself the son of a collier, we recall) glimpsed her

> swanning along a College corridor [. . .] in a broad-brimmed black hat, grass-green costume, the longest ear-rings this side of Tiger Bay, and a cigarette-holder whose fifteen inches of elephant ivory ensured that you got more of the smoke than the smoker.11

But the sophistication of this figure is itself a marker of her isolation; actuality was altogether more humdrum and more stressful. Behind the constructed stylishness money was short: Edwards and her mother were living on Edward Edwards' pension. Her mother, not unreasonably, wanted her daughter to become a teacher, like several of her friends; Harold Watkins was well aware of these domestic pressures:

> Dorothy was afraid that teaching would absorb all her energy and stultify her art. Her plan was to devote all her time to writing. [. . .] 'An author Dorothy wants to be, you know,' [her mother] once said to me in a tone implying there was no alternative.12

---

9 Glyn Jones, *The Dragon Has Two Tongues: Essays on Anglo-Welsh Writers and Writing*, ed. Tony Brown (1968; Cardiff: University of Wales Press, 2001), 28–29. Even as late as 1939 Jones could write in his journal: '[. . .] being an artist in Cardiff is like playing an away match—there's no-one to raise a shout for you'. Quoted in The *Collected Stories of Glyn Jones*, ed. Tony Brown (Cardiff; University of Wales Press, 1999), xxx.

10 Elizabeth M. Henney and A. Prosser, 'English Society', *Cap and Gown*, 23.2 (1926), 40, quoted in Stevenson, 43.

11 Gwyn Jones, Introduction, *Classic Welsh Short Stories*, selected by Gwyn Jones and Islwyn Ffowc Elis (Oxford: Oxford University Press, 1992), ix.

12 Watkins, 43-4.

Presumably it was to escape the pressures of her Rhiwbina home, as well as to broaden her artistic horizons, that Edwards twice went abroad in the period 1925–27. Six months were spent in Vienna, where according to Harold Watkins, she lived with a socialist bookseller and his wife, teaching them English in exchange for bed and board; shortly afterwards she visited Italy for nine months, staying mainly in Florence, probably financing her stay with translation work.[13] On both occasions she returned to Rhiwbina full of accounts of the beauty of the places she had visited and of the cultural life she had experienced. But inevitably she returned to the same domestic situation: life with her mother and her anxieties about their financial situation:

> [. . .] my Mother wilts before the gaze of the bank clerk every time she cashes a cheque. [. . .] [She] is not a rational human being—so that if I started to write one article a week to pay the rent etc. we should be in exactly the same state that we are now—i.e. she would be asking—not without justice—for more and I would be slinking about weighted down by furtive guilt, so it seems to me that the only thing to do is to write a lot of articles at once and a get a lot of money at the same time.[14]

In fact during this period, 1927–29, while attempting to write a novel, Edwards was reviewing regularly for the *Western Mail*. As a reviewer Edwards was usually shrewd, discriminating, and remarkably informative, given the limited space available to her. She could also be acerbic: 'I am faced at this moment with a book which arouses in me no emotion whatever' (on the memoirs of Walpurga, Lady Paget); 'The author states in the introduction that she is not a writer. This is perfectly true' (on a book of sketches of the Far East). For Edwards, this regular reviewing was, as her letter suggests, for the most part sheer hackwork. She was called upon to review everything from collections of ghost stories and illustrated children's books to biographies of French kings, accounts of travels in the Balkans and histories of the Indian Mutiny. She frequently had to review more than one book, including portmanteaux reviews of four or five novels at a time. On at least one occasion her frustration shows: 'I know that it is fashionable for reviewers to find or invent an underlying common theme in the books they review together, but I defy even the most ingenuous and least scrupulous to find one in this miscellany'.[15] But at the same time the reviews rarely seem merely dutiful; one

13 Watkins, 44.
14 Letter to S. Beryl Jones and Winifred Kelly, 4 Sept. [c. 1929], packet 2, letter 2, Reading.
15 The five books in this review were books whose subject matter ranged from an account of early Portuguese travels in Abyssinia to the memoirs of a lady in waiting to the Russian royal family when in exile in Siberia, *Western Mail*, 17 April 1930, 9. The reviews quoted

encounters a mind which is thoughtful, witty, well-informed (capable, for instance, of comparing the quality of translation in a new edition of Montaigne's diaries with that of previous translations) and able to reflect with seemingly genuine interest on subjects as unfamiliar as the effectiveness of tribal bush schools as part of the cultural rituals of West Africa ('This is an extraordinarily good book').[16]

Thus, in the years after graduation, Dorothy Edwards, still determined to be a writer, lives a life, relieved only by her travels in Austria and Italy, in which domestic life is frequently tense, given her mother's anxieties about their finances and her increasing ill-health. Edwards has no close friends, her one romantic relationship has ended painfully, and cultural outlets, save for her occasional contact with the university, are almost non-existent. Indeed, having been cut off from any sense of cultural roots in Ogmore Vale, Dorothy Edwards, once she has left University, has no real sense of a social or cultural context by which to define herself; attempts to find a national identity, to establish a Welsh selfhood came later. She is essentially isolated, unhomed. And yet it is in these years that Dorothy Edwards produced the two volumes which established her reputation as a writer, the collection of short stories *Rhapsody* and the novel *Winter Sonata*; indeed, it is the contention of the present paper that the fictional world of those books is essentially the *product* of these years, her 'personal isolated universe'.[17]

Both of Edwards' books received what must have been enormously satisfying reviews in the London press.[18] One response above all must have seemed to have offered Edwards not only the possibility of new, broader horizons but an entree into the world of English letters of which a young writer could only dream. In November 1928 she received a letter from David Garnett, well known as a novelist, especially of *Lady into Fox* (1922), and a prominent member of the Bloomsbury

---

appear, respectively, in the *Western Mail* on 3 January 1929 and 18 October 1928. From April 1927 to July 1930 Edwards published some thirty reviews; from April 1928 to Nov. 1929 she was reviewing at least once a month. One notes, given that her mother was a Christian Scientist, that Edwards sees 'the undoubted religious genius' of the movement's founder, Mary Baker Eddy, as 'too typically American not to appear irresistibly comic from this side of the Atlantic', *Western Mail*, 14 November 1929, 9. Edwards' attempts to write a novel are referred to in the letter to Jones and Kelly cited in note 15.

16 *Western Mail*, 6 February 1930, 11.

17 *Rhapsody* (1927; London: Virago, 1986) and *Winter Sonata* (1928; London: Virago, 1986). Both volumes contain an introduction by Elaine Morgan. Further references are included in the text. Three of the short stories in *Rhapsody* had previously been published in *The Calendar of Modern Letters*: 'A Country House' in August 1925, 'The Conquered' in April 1926, and 'Summertime' in July 1926.

18 Very positive reviews came from Arnold Bennett and Gerald Gould (whose *Observer* review referred to her as a genius); see S. Beryl Jones, 184. The *Western Mail* (1 Nov. 1928) referred to *Winter Sonata* as 'mesmeric'; while reminiscent of Tchekov, 'her genius is her own'.

Group; his praise was unreserved:

> I admired *Rhapsody* very much indeed. [. . .] In *Winter Sonata* you have shown
> that you are a great writer, and an absolutely original one [. . .][A]fter reading
> you all living novelists have sunk in my estimation, much as though with the
> book you had created a new scale of values. [. . .] I cannot tell you in a letter
> like this how deeply I admire your work, how much pleasure it has given me, or
> how important it is that you should go on writing.[19]

Garnett's letter expresses his wish that they meet and in January 1929 she visited
him in London; Edwards' consciousness of what Garnett and his friends might
make of her is evident in the letter she wrote before this meeting: 'I shall have a
grey cloak and a slightly provincial air'.[20] The meeting seems to have gone well, for
some three months later Edwards stayed with Garnett and his wife, Ray, at their
home in Huntingdonshire. However, Garnett's account of his relationship with
Edwards, albeit written over thirty years later, makes for uncomfortable reading.
He shows himself to have been acutely aware of her background—'Her father had
been a poor schoolmaster in a Welsh village [. . .] She had always been extremely
poor. She lived with her mother in a suburb of Cardiff upon a pittance' (Garnett
87–8)— and there is an unpleasant air of condescension: 'Though Ray and I did
not seem rich to ourselves [. . .] to Dorothy we represented the bourgeoisie, able to
enjoy luxuries. [. . .] In our company she could enjoy a glass of wine, a drive in a
private car, or a seat in the pit at the theatre' (Garnett 88. One assumes that wine
and cars were not unknown among Edwards' academic acquaintances in Rhiwbina.)
However, Garnett's admiration for Edwards' work was genuine; he seems to have
been keen to show her off to his Bloomsbury friends as his protégée, his discovery
from the provincial wilderness:

> One of the pleasures of adopting a Welsh Cinderella [. . .] is in introducing her
> to the world. Naturally if Cinderella is a talented writer, the pleasure is all the
> greater. [. . .] I introduced her to Virginia Woolf who seemed vague but full of
> friendly astonishment. (Garnett 92)

At various parties and gatherings, Edwards also met other members of the
Bloomsbury Group; in rather typical Bloomsbury fashion, Garnett wanted
Edwards' opinions of his friends, but found her response disappointing.

---

[19] David Garnett, letter to Dorothy Edwards, 22 Nov. [1928], packet 3, letter 6, Reading. A
xerox of the letter appears in Flay, 85.

[20] David Garnett, *The Familiar Faces* (London: Chatto & Windus, 1962) 87. Further references
are included in the text.

What I wanted were her impressions of Lytton Strachey and Virginia Woolf, but I got none. Later on Ray drew Dorothy out more subtly and discovered that her impressions of Lytton and Virginia and indeed of Duncan Grant, Clive Bell, Roger Fry and Vanessa Bell were precisely nil. She had noticed nobody, had observed nothing, but had come away having enjoyed herself enormously. (Garnett 92–3)

In fact Garnett underestimated the shrewdness of his 'Welsh Cinderella'; while confessing to Beryl Jones and Winifred Kelly that 'I have fallen slightly in love with David himself', it was with them that she shared her thoughts on the Bloomsbury circle. Her perceptions are clear-sighted and vivid: 'Virginia Woolf is like a steel greyhound, swift enough to be gentle. I loved her'; Lytton Strachey 'is absolutely charming. [. . .] He is short-sighted long and thin, with a beautiful beard and rather fair long straight hair so that he looks like a very young man dressed up in spectacles and false beard to play a grandfather in amateur theatricals. He has a high pitched voice and thin high laugh, almost a giggle'.[21]

The return to Cardiff, and life with her mother, after her excursions to Bloomsbury, was inevitably disconcerting: 'It is awfully queer to be home again. It is like cutting a hole in a beautiful coloured not very meaningful canvas and slipping behind it to a dull dingy sordid existence full, comparatively, of struggle and hatred'.[22] It is a revealing passage. Clearly Edwards' reaction to Bloomsbury is not one of unqualified admiration. At the same time one notes the strength of feeling about the domestic situation to which she has returned. Moreover, contact with Bloomsbury seems to have awoken new self-consciousness about her identity as a Welshwoman: the letter continues 'I am trying to see Wales and Welshies with new eyes and I see lots of queer things that I hadn't noticed before'. She felt she had been snubbed sometimes at Bloomsbury gatherings: 'It is partly because I know I am badly dressed [. . .] And it is partly nationalism'.[23] After returning to Cardiff, she reflects in another letter:

The English are very Mandarinish—ask them their opinion of something and they can nod with taciturn certainty or wag their solemn heads from side to

---

21 Letters to S. Beryl Jones and Winifred Kelly, Sunday, n.d. [c. 1929], packet 3, letter 19; n.d. [c. 1929], packet 2, letter 17; 29 April [c. 1929], packet 3, letter 17, Reading. The descriptions of Woolf and Strachey are quoted in Lucy Stevenson, 'Two Drafts of an Unpublished Story by Dorothy Edwards', *Welsh Writing in English: A Yearbook of Critical Essays* 10 (2005), 173.

22 Letter to S. Beryl Jones and Winifred Kelly, n.d. [c. 1929], packet 2, letter 2, Reading. Quoted in Stevenson, 2004, 28–29.

23 Letter to S. Beryl Jones and Winifred Kelly, n.d. [1929], packet 2, letter 2, Reading. Quoted in Stevenson, 27.

side in confident negation. Welsh people can give you their opinion passionately, ardently, embroidered with fancy and phantasy—and behind it a grimace of desperate entreaty to God or the Gods or the empty heavens hoping it is true.[24]

It is presumably in recalling such letters that Beryl Jones comments that Edwards was not only 'very consciously Welsh' in her outlook but could be could be 'at times very consciously anti-English'; Jones quotes a striking passage from a letter Edwards wrote to their mutual friend Sona Burstein:

> I think because I am Welsh that I am a kind of natural saint and genius mixed, as a compensation for being cut off from action in the English sense of it— which I suppose means cutting a few niggers to pieces and stealing their rubber.[25]

Jones does not give the date of this letter, but it not only shows Edwards' own firm identification as Welsh but also a graphic association between Englishness and imperialism, with perhaps a sense of herself as a member of a subaltern culture.[26] It is likely that the letter dates from the early 1930s, since in 1931 she attended an election rally addressed by Saunders Lewis and afterwards sent him an enthusiastic letter of support: 'I was completely carried away by the sincerity, the genuine depth and the courageous and firm grasp of the exact, present state of life in Wales in its very fullest sense, which you showed last night'.[27] In her letter she refers to her socialist up-bringing, but she evidently thinks that Plaid Cymru was equally capable of responding to the 'present state of Wales'. Watkins suggests that she got to know Lewis well—'She told me she thought he was a "great" man'—and notes that Edwards had Welsh lessons from a neighbour, Mrs Gwenda

---

[24] Letter to S. Beryl Jones and Winifred Kelly, 4 Sept. [c. 1929], packet 2, letter 17, Reading. Quoted in Stevenson, 27.

[25] S. Beryl Jones, 'Dorothy Edwards as a Writer of Short Stories', 184.

[26] As Stevenson has pointed out, Edwards' story 'The Conquered' shows an awareness of imperialism and a unpublished story refers to the impact of English culture on India. In her 1933 Journal, written the year before her death, Edwards writes 'I hate Winston Churchill and the British Empire, and I like any one who is really suffering from an injustice, political or social'. See Stevenson, 'Two Drafts', 168.

[27] Letter to Saunders Lewis, 22 Oct. [1931], Saunders Lewis papers, NLW. On Edwards and Lewis, see Katie Gramich, 'Gorchfygwyr a Chwiorydd: storïau byrion Dorothy Edwards a Kate Roberts yn y dauddegau', DiFfinio Dwy Lenyddiaeth Cymru, gol. M. Wynn Thomas (Caerdydd: Gwasg Prifysgol Cymru, 1995) 80–95.

Gruffydd.[28] To what extent this new awareness of her Welshness reflects a reaction to Bloomsbury is unclear. One might, relatedly, suggest that it manifests a search for identity in the emptiness of her life in Cardiff, a search for roots and meaning; the tone of her letter to Lewis is highly emotional and one wonders if some part of that search for meaning involved an unconscious search for an authority figure, missing in her life since the death of her socialist father.

For by 1931 Edwards was experiencing periods of acute stress. She wrote to Garnett in January 1931:

> I do hope there was nothing queer in the letter I wrote you because apparently I was on the verge of a breakdown and a day or two afterwards I went completely dippy and for two days I thought you were the March Hare and the White Rabbit and I was Alice, and then [. . .] I was God and you and two of my friends archangels. I scarcely ever have anyone to talk to so I didn't say any of it aloud fortunately. (Garnett 98)[29]

Her mother was becoming increasingly immobile from rheumatism, and as a Christian Scientist would not seek medical assistance. Illness added to her anxieties about their financial future; in one letter Edwards describes living with her mother as 'like living with an electrified wet blanket'.[30] Edwards had to take over the running of the house, further hampering her capacity to write, which in turn added to her own distress; she wrote to Sona Burstein in the summer of 1932, 'From morning to night I am likely at any moment to be rowed [. . .] (Can't get anything done.) [. . .] I get depressed and nervy and restless'.[31] In response to another 'rather desperate letter' in 1933, Garnett and his wife invited Edwards to come and stay with them (Garnett 96) and she did so for some months, living in their attic. But as is evident from Garnett's account, the visit was a disaster: his 'Welsh Cinderella' was struggling to write anything at all and her level of anxiety caused repeated friction until Garnett found her presence 'almost intolerable'; he was convinced that she was 'either insane or mentally abnormal' (Garnett 96–7).

Her journal of 1933 is dedicated, and partly addressed, to Jackson Stitt Wilson, the prominent American socialist who had been a friend of her father and with whom, to judge from letters to her friends, Edwards felt herself in love, though he

---

28 Watkins, 45. Watkins recalls that Edwards tried to recruit him to Plaid Cymru—he was an economist— and that she insisted 'that one could be a good Welsh Nationalist without being able to speak Welsh fluently, or even at all'.
29 Edwards wrote a very similar letter to Beryl Jones and Winifred Kelly; see Flay, 54.
30 Letter to S. Beryl Jones and Winifred Kelly, n.d. [c.1932], packet 4, letter 22, Reading. Quoted Stevenson, 33.
31 Letter to Sona Burstein, 30. Aug. 1932, packet 3, letter 30, Reading. Quoted Stevenson, 34.

seems to have been unaware of the fact; born in 1868, he was of her father's generation and, it would seem, another potential source of security and assurance. (She referred to him as her 'prophet'.) At the same time Edwards fell in love with Ronald Harding, a professional cellist in a Cardiff orchestra—'He is adorably Welsh and [. . .] I have fallen in love with him'—but Harding was married and the relationship quickly ended.[32] There are references in her letters to depression and another bout of 'dippyness': '[. . .] it seems more likely than not that I shall go completely and permanently dippy some day. I know there aren't any jobs, but I don't feel I can write anything anymore'.[33] In retrospect the route from here to her suicide on the railway line near her home in January 1934 seems almost inevitable; the note she left read 'I am killing myself because I have never sincerely loved any human being all my life. I have accepted kindness and friendship, and even love, without gratitude and given nothing in return'.[34] The statement would seem to be untrue, but the loneliness was finally unavoidable.

II

What is striking about the short stories of Dorothy Edwards is not merely their not being 'realist' in the sense that they do not engage with the reality of south Wales in the 1920s, but that, while supposedly set in England, the actual locations themselves seem oddly unreal. Consistently there is a lack of geographical specificity or place names: 'A Garland of Earth', for example, opens in 'one of the northern towns' (R 149) before the acquaintance of the narrator, Mr Leonard, invites him to come to stay in 'a little village on the coast'. Moreover, the houses in which these stories are set are themselves consistently remote and usually in the countryside. The large house where Leonard goes to stay stands on a hill above the village and is reached 'after a short climb' (R 151). The house to which the narrator is invited to stay in 'Rhapsody' is 'far from the village', its roof 'just visible above

---

32 On Edwards' relationships with Wilson and Harding, see Stevenson, 12–15. In her introduction to the Virago editions (xi), Elaine Morgan comments on how the men that Edwards 'admired' were 'all safely married, or father figures, or half a world away, or otherwise unobtainable. Dorothy had not been reared to dwindle into a wife'. But this is rather to miss the point; by 1931–3 Edwards' loneliness was profound and she was desperately in need of the stability and company she felt a romantic relationship would provide.

33 Letter to S. Beryl Jones and Winifred Kelly, n.d., packet 3, letter 20, Reading. Quoted Stevenson, 66.

34 The note was quoted in press reports of the inquest: *Western Mail* and *South Wales News*, 10 January 1934; *Cardiff Times* 13 January 1934.

the trees' (*R* 16, 28); in 'The Country House' the eponymous, and substantial, house is 'a long way from a town'; in 'Sweet Grapes' Ferris seeks a period of solitude and rents a house 'somewhere in the Peak district, and situated [. . .] right on top of a hill' (*R* 132).[35] Usually these houses are rented for the summer, or are being visited by the narrator/protagonist. There is no real sense of domesticity, of these houses as homes; they are temporary sets on which the events of the story are performed. With the exception of one or two characters who are writing books, the cultured tenants of these houses are on holiday; they read French and Russian novels, play music or go for walks in the sun-filled countryside. As Christopher Meredith has pointed out in the most perceptive reading of Edwards to date, these houses are 'like houses in dreams'.[36]

There is, to pick up Meredith's point, an element of uncanniness about these stories, a 'not-quite-realness', in which what ought to be real has become defamiliarized. The effect is added to by the slight oddness and/or unEnglishness of characters' names: Trenier, Laurel, Gallon, Chalen, Wolf, Froud, Chenery, Rahel Coleman and (in 'The Problem of Life') Primrose Montgomery and Anthony Delcage. The unreality of the stories is further enhanced by the almost cartoon-like method by which Edwards sketches some of her characters: 'Mr Gallon was a small man, with a head which was flat at the back like a Dutch doll's' (*R* 99); Mr Wendover has 'a grey moustache that drooped down on either side of his mouth like the horns of a cow' (*R* 72); Mr Froud has 'a small, wide face, with round eyes almost like a frightened owl' (*R* 154). Such a consciously exterior viewpoint, added to in a number of stories by the detached first-person narrator, can make for an uneasy mixture in tone, of the comic and the sardonic.

The stories are also, in a sense, unsettling in that so little actually happens in terms of what we would normally consider plot events. For the real concerns of these stories are the emotions beneath the surface of the social rituals the characters undertake—shared meals, visits for tea, walks, concert-going—and even then the significance of what has happened is usually unspoken and curiously decentred. David Garnett refers to the stories' being the result of 'the closest observation, and of sympathy with many different kinds of people, but perhaps chiefly with silent, repressed and gentle people of the kind who are apt to be put upon by the egoism of others' (Garnett 89); Christopher Meredith makes a similar point in commenting on the 'strained, claustrophobic relationships' and the 'atmosphere of

---

35   The settings of the stories Edwards wrote after *Rhapsody* are equally remote and rural: 'Mutiny' (*Life and Letters To-day*, 9 (1934), 325–46) is set in the summerhouse of an old Abbey on a hillside and both versions of the late unpublished story about Mrs Fornwood are set in a remote house on a cliff; see Stevenson, 'Two Drafts'.

36   Christopher Meredith, 'The window facing the sea: the short stories of Dorothy Edwards', *Planet*, 107 (Oct.-Nov. 1994), 65.

extraordinary emotional tension' in the stories.[37] To get closer to the core of these stories, though, we must return to Edwards' comments about the writer inventing 'a personal isolated odd universe composed exclusively of [her] own experience' and about the writer being 'very symbolic'. In the majority of the stories there is a female character, frequently isolated, usually emotionally unfulfilled. She is invariably, it is worth noting, part of a family structure which lacks one or both parents, adding to her emotional insecurity or vulnerability: the mother of Rahel in 'A Garland of Earth' has died and she lives with her father, as does the teenaged Elizabeth in 'A Throne in Heaven'; Elizabeth's namesake in 'Sweet Grapes' lives with her cousin and the cousin's frequently-absent husband in their remote house; in 'Mutiny' Primrose lives with her elderly grandfather, a missionary, her mother being dead and her father away mining in South Africa. Not all of the females are young girls: there are isolated wives in 'Rhapsody' and 'A Country House'. However, in almost none of the stories are we allowed inside the consciousness of these women. They are consistently seen from the outside, frequently through the eyes of male, first-person narrators whose limited emotional sensitivity becomes apparent to the reader; in many respects these males represent the social proprieties and gender conventions of the patriarchal society in which these women live.[38] (At the same time we should note that there are lonely males in these stories: seventeen-year-old Sidney Mihail in 'A Throne of Heaven' has no parents or 'guardian, properly speaking, only the lawyers' (R 167), while it is Mr Wendover's lack of friends which causes him to attach himself, while on holiday, to the supposedly married couple in 'Treachery in the Forest'.)

'A Country House' was the first of Edwards' stories to be published and, though in many respects typical of the stories' concerns, is perhaps less subtle in its effects than those that followed. Again, we never have access to the thoughts and feelings of the woman at the core of the story for it is told by her husband, who by both his words and his actions reveals his emotional inhibition and (consequently) his insensitive and possessive attitude to his wife. (He never tells us her name, referring always to 'she' or 'my wife'.) The large isolated house lacks electricity and is lit by candles and lanterns: 'I have lived here since I was born. I can find my way about in the dark. But it is natural that a woman would not like it' (R 32). Richardson, the electrical engineer whom he calls in to organise the construction of a water turbine system to provide electricity, has an 'almost military appearance, only he was shy, reserved, and rather prim' (R 33). At the same time the narrator

---

37 Ibid.

38 For a reading of gender issues in some of Edwards' stories—albeit it is asserted that the 'stories show little explicit awareness of gender issues'—see Teleri Williams, ' "Women like sibyls" and "whisps of things" ', *New Welsh Review*, 43 (1998–9), 63–66.

seems curiously intimidated by Richardson's unusually deep voice and comments on it at several points in the story. Richardson, invited to stay in the house through the summer to oversee the work, shares the wife's love of music, though she is, as the husband is aware, no longer able to go to concerts as she did before they were married: 'We [are] so far from everywhere here' (R 43). But when, on Richardson's first evening with them, she plays the piano in the drawing room, her husband is shocked by her choice of Chopin's nocturnes, though his views go unspoken:

> [T]o play Chopin to a stranger that you meet for the first time! What must he think of you? [. . .] Night is a distorter. These nocturnes come of never having spent his nights alone, of spending them either in an inn or in someone else's bedroom. (R 38)

While telling us nothing of Chopin, the husband's emotional insecurity, and the first hints of sexual jealousy, are all too evident. At the end of the nocturne, as Richardson asks her to play another, the narrator bursts out: 'Night isn't like that. Night is a distorter'. We notice that the wife's only reaction is to look out 'into the darkness outside the window' (R 38); we can only speculate on her thoughts, which presumably are not about the nature of the darkness but about the nature of her life with such a husband. Despite the husband's outburst, every night through Richardson's stay, the wife plays and he sings. Music features in many of the stories and here, as Christopher Meredith has pointed out, 'music acts as a metaphor for liberation and a sexuality which is hardly ever otherwise expressed'.39 The husband, unsurprisingly, has no sensitivity to music: 'He sang some Brahms. It was quite nice' (R 43).

His emotional insecurity and resultant drive for control are demonstrated when he has the wild water meadow, which his wife loves, cut. She is deeply upset; he merely tells the reader 'A place must be tidy' but then goes on:

> What more must she have? [. . .] And I suppose I am insensible to beauty because I keep the place cut and trimmed. Nonsense! Suppose my wife took off her clothes and ran about the garden like a bacchante! Perhaps I should like it very much, but I should shut her up in her room all the same. (R 41)

Lack of restraint, in nature or in human emotion, especially in the female, is a threat to be controlled. As Richardson's stay comes to an end the husband overhears a conversation between his wife and Richardson—she, not insignificantly, recalls the concerts she attended in London before she was married.

---

39 Christopher Meredith, 65.

It is evident that Richardson has indeed developed affection for the wife, but has chosen not to act on his feelings: 'People do not change their lives suddenly [. . .] except in literature' (R 48). As Richardson leaves, the narrator is triumphantly raising a flag up the flagstaff; he sardonically reflects that his wife thinks Richardson will accept her invitation to 'come again, call, and listen to her playing Chopin'. Her actual future is clearly bleaker, though the narrator seems unaware of the emptiness of his own life: 'Up above the flag waved senselessly in the wind' (R 52).

Music is even more central to 'Rhapsody', where again it becomes a medium for the expression of previously inhibited sexual feelings. Elliott, the narrator, himself depressed and lonely in London while on leave from his job abroad, is invited by the music-loving Mr Everett to share a holiday in a remote house in Scotland. This time it is Everett who is unable to get to concerts, because of the poor health of his invalid wife, once herself a pianist; Elliott wonders in fact 'if she had awakened one day to find that he had married her because she was a beautiful pianist, and perhaps she took a dislike to music from that day?' (R 7). In fact Everett is portrayed by Elliott in terms which are both comic and, as the story develops, increasingly unsympathetic. The young woman tutor who is hired by Everett to coach his son during the stay in Scotland is evidently hired less for her ability in arithmetic than for her capacity to play the piano; she is small, timid and badly dressed, but when Everett discovers that she also has a beautiful singing voice, he becomes increasingly besotted with her to the exclusion of all else, including his wife and son. The passion of the physically unprepossessing Everett and Antonia is seen by Elliott as faintly absurd and his impatience grows: 'And all this roused him to such a pitch of excitement that he even insisted on singing himself, in a ridiculous thin whisper of a tenor voice' (R 21). The incongruous comedy becomes even more darkly ambiguous when Elliott reminds us of Mrs Everett, whose health steadily deteriorates during their stay; her husband is merely dutiful and only Elliott goes to spend time with her in her room, while elsewhere in the house they can hear Antonia singing to Everett. By the end he and Antonia are blatantly waiting for Mrs Everett to die. Again, Mrs Everett's inner thoughts are not revealed directly to us, but her pain is evident in her urging Elliott to stay with her, and in her request to him that she not be buried 'anywhere near here' but that she be taken home (R 30), albeit it has clearly been no true home in the sense of a place where she could be truly herself, feel fulfilled.

'Cultivated People' is somewhat atypical of these stories in being set not in rural holiday isolation but in an unnamed but seemingly dull provincial town. The 'cultivated people' are the small circle who run the local Music Club: '[. . .] the ladies and gentlemen on the committee exchange musical confidences in public which they would in any case have exchanged in their calls upon each other' (R 94).

Into this self-important group the club president, Mr Challis, introduces a recent acquaintance, Miss Wolf, a German lady, a spinster who teaches German and music. Proving herself to be a skilled violinist, she is befriended both by Challis and his fellow committee members, Mr and Mrs Gallon. Even less happens in terms of plot events in this story than in those already discussed: they visit each other for teas and dinners, there is inconsequential conversation, they play music. But, beneath the polite surface, Challis and Gallon are jostling for Miss Wolf's attention. The (unnamed and ungendered) first-person narrator notes an expression on Mrs Gallon's face; s/he does not explain but it is the reader's first clue as to Mrs Gallon's inner life:

> Sometimes when she was alone or sitting unnoticed at the club her face would set into the most extreme ugliness [. . .] and the misery expressed on it at those moments would never, even if it had been noticed, have caused any comment, because it is already something of a metaphor to describe it as misery. (*R* 100)

Her rage at her unfulfilled life, and her husband's attentions to Miss Wolf (though this is only delicately hinted at by the narrator), finds its outlet just once when, at the end of the story, staring at the wall, she plays the piano with such force and passion that the other members are taken aback: '[. . .] how is it she can makes such sounds? She has never played as well as this before at the club. She must have practised this piece very hard, perhaps for months.' (*R* 113).

But it is another unfulfilled woman, the lonely Miss Wolf, who is more central to the tensions of the story. She tells Mr Challis of her feeling 'homesick', albeit she has lived in England for ten years and where 'home' is in Germany is by now unclear. Late in the story, and again untypical of Edwards' usual narrative method, the narrator allows us insight into Miss Wolf's thoughts, her alienation not just from the club but from the emptiness of her life:

> She was thinking, 'Why am I here? But wherever I were I should feel like this. The world is the same everywhere. [. . .] If I do go home the stones and the trees are not likely to know me. It is all the same that I stay here. Oh, my God!' (*R* 112)

For just a moment we glimpse the emotional anguish which underlies so many of these stories of lonely, unhomed people. When the tedious Mr Challis, minutes later—as Mr Gallon hovers nearby—makes a characteristically stilted and convoluted attempt to suggest the possibility of a more intimate friendship, Miss Wolf's response is one of utter, desperate exasperation: 'Oh, for Heaven's sake!' But her lonely life goes on: Challis escapes on holiday, she calls on Mrs Gallon only when her husband is out, and she continues to play at the club, though by now—the last sentence of the story—'people are beginning to say that she plays too often there' (*R* 114).

The tone of 'Summer-time' is altogether lighter and returns us to the more characteristic Edwards setting of a sun-filled summer holiday in the country; ostensibly the story is that of a middle-aged man making something of a fool of himself in flirting with a young girl, but again there are stronger, more complex feelings beneath the surface of the story. Beatrice, 'well over thirty' (*R* 115), invites the protagonist, Joseph Laurel, who is nearly forty (*R* 126) to join her at her sister's family home, to continue the games of tennis which the pair have been playing regularly through the summer months. Since Beatrice is a very good player and Laurel rather 'prides himself on his bad tennis' (*R* 116), we can assume that Beatrice has in mind a partnership which extends beyond the tennis court. But Laurel becomes increasingly attracted to Beatrice's niece, who has just left school, and he fantasizes that his feelings might be reciprocated until he sees her kissing her handsome young cousin. Reality comes crashing in on Laurel. Not only does he realise how foolish he has been, but the meaning of the 'little smile of malice and veiled amusement' (*R* 124) which he has previously glimpsed on Beatrice's face becomes shockingly clear. For Beatrice has disappeared to the margins of his attention, as she has to the margins of the narrative. Laurel is horrified when he, like the reader, begins to consider what Beatrice has been thinking and feeling, how her hopes and expectations have been not only disappointed but utterly ignored. This time we are given no direct insight into her feelings but when she and Laurel play one last game of tennis he is disconcerted by the vigour with which she plays: 'Balls seemed to be hurled at him from every direction, and everyone of them seemed to be expressing contempt' (*R* 130). At the end, unable to face further meetings with Beatrice, he goes abroad. Once again the woman is left to get on with her life as best she can.

A number of the isolated women who haunt these stories are far younger. The housekeeper's nineteen-year-old cousin, Elizabeth, in 'Sweet Grapes' lives in a situation akin to a fairy story: alone with her sister in an 'an ugly little castle' on the top of a hill (*R* 132). Here again it is a first-person narrator who tells the story of his acquaintance, Hugo Ferris, a young writer who rents the castle in his pursuit of undisturbed solitude, and indeed the narrator comments on Ferris's response to the attentions of the young girl. The narrator is all too aware of the way in which this girl who 'has lived so much alone without friends and has dreamed about the future and about love and all that sort of thing' will react when a young man 'who is not only a dream but also a fact' enters her world (*R* 135). However, the uptight Ferris, albeit not unaware of Elizabeth's attractiveness, resists her attentions, even her kisses on the top of one of the towers. But the narrator is bemused by Ferris's 'boredom' and his lack of regret at leaving the castle. It is the narrator who in the closing sentences of the story shows his awareness of the pain Ferris has caused:

> I do not think that it has occurred to him that she probably cried in the night. Of course it was all very awkward for him [. . .] and yet it seems a pity that something so like a flower, like a young rose, you know, should have to cry all night. (*R* 148).

An isolated tower, this time in ruins, clings to the top of a cliff in 'A Garland of Earth', while on the pier in the bay beneath is 'a black tower [. . .] very much like a chess castle but without a castellated top' (*R* 151). The young girl in this story is Rahel, the seventeen-year-old daughter of Mr Coleman, and it is to the Colemans' remote house that the elderly narrator comes to visit. For Coleman his daughter, a botanist, is 'another Curie [. . .] a genius' (*R* 152, 158) and she, wrapped in her stained overall, assists her father and the enigmatic Mr Froud in the laboratory attached to the house. But for the narrator there is 'something strange and sad in this pale girl'; he sees her as 'pale and strained' (*R* 158, 160). When they visit the black tower on the pier, they find that it has two windows, one looking out to sea and one to land; Froud asks each to choose, if they were imprisoned there, which window they would have:

> 'The sea one,' said Rahel, without hesitating [. . .]
> 'The land window,' I said [. . .] 'One would at least see one's fellow creatures.'
> 'But that would make it worse,' said Rahel. (*R* 156)[40]

One feels that Rahel can imagine this bleak situation all too easily. The scene in many ways sums up her plight, and that of the imprisoned, lonely lives of so many of the characters in these stories, most of them women.

In *Winter Sonata*, Olivia Neran experiences, late in the book, something like a negative epiphany:

> A sudden feeling of loneliness had come upon her, so intense, that the place and the people around her, the hard, stony garden and the trees, stood out empty and bare. [...] She felt in that moment an almost intolerable distaste for life, a kind of nausea. (*WS* 207)

The grey monotony of the English winter which the leisured, middle-class

---

40 Christopher Meredith, 66, suggests that this scene 'might stand for the human predicament as Edwards sees it all through the book'.

characters pass in a rural English village has by this point become emblematic of their dull empty lives. In this lethargic world, the revelation of the depth of Olivia's anguish comes as something of a release to the reader, a momentary revelation of the pent-up feelings which we sense all through the book; the world for Olivia is Other, defamiliarized, empty. The bleak landscape of the novel in this sense acts as the grey counterpoint to the summer world of the stories. But both clearly express the painful 'personal isolated odd universe' with which Dorothy Edwards was all too familiar, a world whose pain is distanced, controlled, and ultimately disguised in the stories by her use of first-person narrators who are male and/or rather languidly detached, and whose lonely figures are frequently decentred, their anguish only hinted at. But the pain was real, and it persisted. The posthumously-published 'The Problem of Life' is more lyrical in its evocation of the natural world than the earlier stories, but at its heart is the romantic young Adrian:

> [He] was very conscious of this feeling of being shut out, but it was something he sometimes experienced. It came inexplicably and went again; it brought with it a kind of melancholy somewhere deep down in his soul, too far down for him to find it and cast it away.[41]

---

41 'The Problem of Life', *Life and Letters To-day*, 10 (1934), 671.

Rhapsody's lost story

Christopher Meredith

DOROTHY Edwards's fiction—just one collection of stories and one novel, both published by the time she was twenty-five, and a few other short pieces—has an extraordinary degree of coherence of imagery and theme. It's as distinctively its own strange world as any writer's work could be. Some of its energy and interest come, I believe, from a couple of paradoxes which I'll examine in this essay. First, it shows scant concern for verisimilitude or autobiography, yet, I would argue, it frequently if obscurely reflects—even foreshadows—some aspects of Edwards's life. Second, despite its oddity, we can see now how it may be positioned in the mainstream of European modernism, following Chekhov, whom she read and admired, and pointing towards Beckett and others with its tautly reduced scenarios and the combination of absurdist ironic humour with a pessimistic vision. This vision is of essential human loneliness in the face of the strangeness both of the world and of other people. For all her quirkiness, she explores, by 1928, territory that was to become quintessential to much art and literature in the twentieth century.

I'll start by looking in more detail at a passage touched on by Tony Brown at the close of his essay in this volume. Consider this from the fourth and final section—or movement—of her novel *Winter Sonata* (1928). The two Neran sisters are in their garden with their cousin George Curle shortly after snow has thawed:

> Olivia was silent and her dark eyes gazed abstractedly at the trunks of the fir trees and at the light, hard earth of the garden. George came across the grass in a black suit with his hands in his pockets.
>
> "What's the matter?" he asked.
>
> Eleanor lifted her blue eyes to him and smiled. "Only snowdrops," she said. "Come and see."
>
> George walked up to them in a dignified manner, and after passing a glance at the little snowdrops, he began to talk about something else. With his hands in his pockets he looked across the garden down to the road.

Olivia did not listen to what he was saying, nor to Eleanor answering him. A sudden feeling of loneliness had come upon her, so intense, that the place and the people around her, the hard, stony garden and the trees, stood out empty and bare as though without any deeper implications, as though she had withdrawn into herself all the imagination and affection which could have given them life and depth. She felt in that moment an almost intolerable distaste for life, a kind of nausea.[1]

Out of its context, this loses much of its resonance and tone-colour—the musical terms are peculiarly appropriate. But what I want to notice here is the shock the modern reader may get from that last paragraph and its last word. The word 'nausea' in such a context brings Sartre immediately to mind. In a precise vignette Edwards realises something of his apprehension of a world whose materiality somehow precludes meaning or significance, 'deeper implications' as she puts it. This is built on the fact that in the opening pages of the novel, at the beginning of the winter that's just about to finish in the passage above, we see the Nerans' house and its three fir trees from afar in a way that establishes the expectation of symbolic possibility:

...on the hill, three little fir trees stood up in front of a white house. Against the whiteness of the walls they looked a deep green. Olivia, the elder of the two sisters who lived there, came down the hill in a white woollen dress. ...it was difficult to tell whether the white figure was more like summer going sadly away from the earth or like winter stealing quietly upon it. (*WS* 8)

The business of language is to convey meaning. *Winter Sonata*, in its sombre musical patterning, constantly deals with the possibility of meaning, as in this early passage, of 'deeper implications', with the possibility of characters arriving at some point of significance, usually involving them connecting with some other character, and then with that possibility vanishing. What's left is music, shapes in the air that don't have meaning as language does, but rather structure and perhaps mood. Olivia's mood in the first passage above is of the Sartrean kind, and it was written ten years before the publication of *La Nausée*.

But Edwards is careful to say that Olivia's feelings were 'in that moment'. Eleanor is delighted with the coming flowers and George barely sees them. Unlike *La Nausée*, *Winter Sonata* doesn't privilege one point of view. It's impossible to name one character as central. It's an ensemble piece and only occasionally focalises

---

[1]   Dorothy Edwards, *Winter Sonata* (London: Wishart & Co., 1928, reprinted London: Virago, 1986), 206–7. Hereafter *WS*. Page numbers refer to the Virago edition.

through one character with anything approaching the intensity of the passage quoted. When such focus happens, isolation is invariably the keynote.

The novel closes with an absurd little scene in which a character picks his way across the lawn in starlight, trying, at Eleanor's injunction, to see and avoid treading on the new-sprung crocuses. It's a scene of comic indignity in which characters yet again don't quite get together, yet it has people trying, dimly, to apprehend what's out there, and to respect it. (Its imagery also connects brilliantly with one of the best stories in her earlier collection, *Rhapsody*, 'A Garland of Earth', in which the narrator, old Mr Leonard, wishes to see clearly the flowers at his feet.[2] And note the similarity of his name and Eleanor's in *Winter Sonata*. Edwards's work is haunted by such echoes.)

Olivia's nausea and withdrawal are counterbalanced by her sister's will to pleasure and engagement. Notice how the light/dark contrast is underlined by reference to the contrasting colour of their eyes. Edwards's pessimism lies in her intuition that opportunities for that engagement between people are either missed, refused, or botched. But the very ensemble nature of the novel works against that sense. The characters move in concert. It's as optimistic as Edwards gets. In the absence of any 'deeper implication' than that, in *Winter Sonata* we're left with pattern made from the interweaving of different characters' isolations, harmony—music.

*

I've been trying to show how Edwards's work, for all its uniqueness, touches on some of the main threads in art and literature in the modern era. It deals with loneliness, and puzzles over the meaning of experience and vacillates between withdrawing from and engaging with it. She pulls off the double of making it new and making it true. And this is perhaps more strikingly true of *Rhapsody*.

This time, music itself is one of the motifs, and isn't, as it is in the novel, the actual stuff of the work. In *Winter Sonata*, the novel *is* the sonata, whereas 'Rhapsody' is the title story of the collection, and neither it nor the collection as a whole can be called rhapsodic. The title is the book's greatest irony. In *Rhapsody* music often represents the unstated emotional lives of characters, and often an otherwise unexpressed sexual passion. It becomes a kind of code for the possibility of connection, for instance in 'Rhapsody' and 'A Country House'. The collection also inhabits that distinctive, non-realist world of emotional isolation and unspoken tensions and longings that we could call Edwardsland.

---

[2]   Dorothy Edwards, *Rhapsody* (London: Wishart & Co., 1927, reprinted London: Virago 1986), 149–165. Hereafter *R*. Page numbers refer to the Virago edition.

I've argued elsewhere that the gap between Edwards's real experience of industrial south Wales and her fictional world is more apparent than actual.[3] Edwardsland partly arises out of her reading and education and is coloured by the power of the English cultural ascendancy of her day. I suspect it partly arises also from the fact that she wasn't interested in writing about herself. At its best her work is as disconcertingly impersonal as great art is capable of being. But Edwardsland, as Brown's discussion shows, is something of *her* inner landscape and inescapably those connections, more or less coded, intended or not, are there. For the rest of this essay I'll discuss the light that may be shed on the connections between Edwardsland and Dorothy Edwards's actual situation by looking at a story which she decided not to include in *Rhapsody*. It may be possible too to see how these link with the big themes I've started to touch on above and with a rather more political and sociological reading of her work.

The uncollected story, first published only in 2007, is 'La Penseuse'.[4] Research by Claire Flay has shown that this was originally intended for *Rhapsody* but dropped. Flay dates the story to about 1925–7.[5] This makes it different from the other three known uncollected and more or less complete stories, all of which seem to have been written after *Winter Sonata* and are more sophisticated. We can tentatively say that 'La Penseuse' sits somewhere early on in the period of intense creativity that produced her two books, and it turns out to be a piece of peculiar interest.

In 'La Penseuse' two young men living in a small village both form an attachment with a girl called Mary, who it quickly becomes clear is the female thinker of the title. She 'was possessed by a perfect fever for acquiring knowledge' ('LP' 1.) Sidney Mertris, a medical student, and Richard Warnham, a student of languages, become the means by which she can live an intellectual life. The

---

3 See Christopher Meredith, 'The window facing the sea: the short stories of Dorothy Edwards', *Planet*, 107 (1994), 64–67; and Christopher Meredith, 'Foreword' in Dorothy Edwards, *Rhapsody* (Library of Wales edition, Cardigan: Parthian, 2007).

4 I've included 'La Penseuse' along with two other previously uncollected stories, 'Mutiny' and 'The Problem of Life', both of which were published in *Life and Letters Today* shortly after Edwards's suicide in 1934, when editing additional material for the latest Library of Wales reprint of *Rhapsody*. (See previous note.) The only other known Edwards story in near-complete drafts has been published in scholarly form in two versions with a useful introductory essay by Lucy Stevenson in *Welsh Writing in English*, 10 (2005), 160–189.

5 I'm grateful to Claire Flay for this information from her ongoing research and for drawing my attention to 'La Penseuse'—hereafter 'LP'. I'm also grateful to the University of Reading Library, which houses the Dorothy Edwards papers and holds her typescript of the story. Page references are to the typescript, as the Library of Wales edition of *Rhapsody* including 'LP' is not available at the time of writing.

neighbours assume, wrongly, that Mary is biding her time in nailing one of these men: she lives with an invalid aunt surviving on a poor income whereas the young men are of higher status and have their minds on careers. In fact Mary 'considered wasted every moment she spent with them in which they did not impart to her something interesting and instructive.' ('LP' 2) This goes on for three years, until Mary is nineteen, when Richard goes to Italy and Sidney goes off to medical school. Before he leaves, she rejects Richard's physical advances. He makes a strange speech, talking about love and Shelley, and accusing her of being unjust. Confused and feeling guilty she immediately encounters Sidney, who, showing her some of his new text books, traps her hand in the covers of one of them and asks her to marry him ' "if I become a famous surgeon" ' ('LP' 6). She accepts and her guilt leaves her. But this all happens in an atmosphere of perplexity rather than ardour. Richard vanishes from then on and eventually Sidney's letters and gifts of books peter out. Seventeen years pass and on the death of her aunt she briefly travels abroad as a lady's companion and then seeks a job as a housekeeper in London. She's sent to keep house for Sidney, now a successful surgeon. The arrangement suits them both and as well as keeping house she satisfies her need for thinking and knowledge by helping Sidney to write his books on surgery. Sidney has kept in touch with Richard, who's travelled to Rome and Tibet and written books on aesthetic matters. A visitor from their home village calls, and, assuming she's stumbled across a minor scandal, carries the rumour back home. Shortly afterwards Sidney's brother, also a doctor who still lives in the village, visits, evidently checking up on them, and they learn of the unjustified rumours. Sidney is angered by the news, but Mary, who couldn't care less about the gossip, is deeply upset by his response. Later Sidney tells her not to leave on account of gossip—he doesn't say as much, but he really wants her to continue helping him with his book. She hadn't thought of leaving, but as soon as he says it she decides to go. But a message arrives announcing that Richard is to visit and this gives Sidney a day's reprieve as Mary stays on to prepare dinner for them. After the visit, during which the now monk-like Richard makes some strange, gnomic assertions about the nature of love, Mary stays on and helps Sidney with his book. After it's finished, Sidney finds a woman he deems suitable to marry, Sybil, 'the daughter of one of the richest surgeons in England.' ('LP' 18) After this, Sidney buys back Mary's old cottage in the village and packs her off there with a pension.

That's it. My crassly reductive summary makes the story sound clunkier than it actually is, though it helps to suggest some of the thinking behind cutting the piece from the book. There's a fairly laborious chunk of exposition at the beginning of the story for instance, the musical motif is absent, and the whole piece hinges implausibly on the big coincidence of Mary's being sent to keep house for Mertris. It's the sort of coincidence you'd expect in a Victorian novel. Of incidental interest is Edwards's attempt to construct a big complete, and plotted story-arc in something like conventional storytelling terms in a piece of five thousand words while pursuing her familiar themes. To do this she has to employ an apparatus of messengers and incidental characters markedly absent in the rest of her work. It's very different from the achievement of, say, 'A Garland of Earth' or 'Days', the final story in the collection, in which *nothing* is there merely for plot purposes, and every image and figure plays in the shape and meaning of the piece. It's an indicator of how Edwards worked to pare away the conventional and naturalistic in creating her world.

But there are familiar Edwardsland elements in 'La Penseuse'. An opposition is set up between Sidney and Richard: the former is involved in the mechanics of the body, and, it seems, is incapable of thinking beyond career and reputation; the latter is grown priestlike. At dinner they argue over the nature of materialism, Richard asserting that what Sidney calls his (Richard's) mysticism is actually the greater materialism, the greater engagement with the actual. It's a meeting which disconcerts Sidney and calms Mary into staying with him. Such oppositions recur in Edwards's fiction, as for instance in Eleanor and Olivia, discussed above. There's also, when Richard calls, the promise of a very particular triangle that recurs in her stories—the bully-victim-rescuer triangle familiar to psychologists. Such triangles occur with shades of difference and ambiguity in 'A Country House' and 'Treachery in a Forest', for instance. In 'La Penseuse', we could be forgiven for expecting the returned Richard to be the rescuer of Mary, so obviously being exploited by Sidney, who's determined to hang on to her. But the expectation is disconcertingly subverted and some of the story's strangeness resides in that. Not only does Richard fail to 'rescue' her, but he doesn't even try.

But more interesting than any of that is the fact that had Edwards included 'La Penseuse', it would have been the only story in *Rhapsody* which absolutely unequivocally had a woman at its centre.

Tony Brown has drawn attention to the persistent figure of the isolated woman in the *Rhapsody* stories. In fact, this isolation is pretty much Edwards's view of the human condition generally, but its treatment in 'La Penseuse' underlines the value of Brown's specific observation about female characters. He notes how we're seldom—almost never—given access to these isolated women's minds. The fact that Edwards almost invariably adopts or implies a male point of view when using the first person plays a part in this, of course. This could lead us to think of Edwards the writer as somehow detached from female experience. Elaine Morgan, in her astute introduction to the Virago *Rhapsody* says:

> Dorothy never completely internalised the "feminine" role. Whenever she
> writes a story in the first person it is a man who is the narrator. She once

wrote: "Women like sybils [sic], with strength like iron, do not exist any more. Goddesses now are wisps of things."

She herself was not a wisp of a thing. (R x.)

Morgan links this state of mind to Edwards's tomboy years as a child in Ogmore Vale before she was sent off to a girls' school at the age of thirteen. There's strength in the idea that that's a little old to start learning conventional femininity and that this might have contributed something to Edwards's affinity with outsider figures. I think it would be a mistake, though, to conclude that she seldom enters feminine viewpoints because she doesn't feel at home there. And in fact as I've said, in some stories the gender of the narrator isn't absolutely clear, though these are stories in which the narrator plays no part, and when there is evidence it tends to suggest a male.

Morgan's quotation comes from *Rhapsody*'s wonderful final story, 'Days' and it's worth discussing it a little more fully. 'Days', written in the third person, tells of the novelist George Morn, who starts, at forty, to write about the area where he was born and brought up. He returns there to live with his wife Leonora (note another variation on a familiar name) who's a musician, and various people visit them in their new home. Significantly, we're told 'George Morn came *here* in January' (R 185, my italics). The otherwise impersonal narrative gives us this one little clue of being located in the backwater Morn returns to, rather than belonging to the cosmopolitan life he's left behind. The landscape is a stony and typically bare tract of Edwardsland, and unlike 'La Penseuse' has no apparatus of plot demanding messengers or incidental characters. It's hilly country with farms, but there's no mention of fields or hedgerows. A river in which nowadays 'there are probably no fish' (R 210) suggests pollution, and we could speculate a landscape transformed in the imagination from unenclosed upland south Wales. (Edwards was to retreat from this distinctive bareness in the more richly drawn and perhaps more English landscapes of *Winter Sonata* and her late stories, *Mutiny* and *The Problem of Life*.) Leonora is a variation on the recurrent isolated and perhaps trapped female figure, though whether or not she *is* trapped is hugely ambiguous and handled with greater nuance than in any of the other stories. A visiting friend, Alexander Sorel, a composer, is the outsider/potential 'rescuer'.

In the passage Morgan quotes, Leonora plays one of Sorel's compositions-in-progress on the cello:

Sorel sat at the piano and looked round at her. The 'cello rested against her white dress. Her head was bent in an attitude of strength and the position of her arms gave her shoulders breadth. There is something strange about a woman playing the 'cello. Women like sibyls, with strength like iron, do not exist any more. Goddesses now are whisps [*sic*] of things. But there are still women who play the 'cello. She began to play the Greek dance.

All the time while Sorel played, while the melody fell wailing away from his fingers, and then at the end when only the dark rhythm of the dance was left, he could see Leonora quite clearly in the air in front of him. And when it was over he looked round in time to see her with her head still bent carrying the bow slowly away. (*R* 216)

Here's the familiar figuring of characters' longing for connection, for one another, emerging in music.

But what's most interesting is that Morgan's comment about point of view works against her own quotation. 'Days' adopts the third person, and then, like *Winter Sonata*, hints at shifts into various points of view with some subtlety. Edwards was learning the craft of narrative technique in this piece. In the passage above, it's not at all clear that it's Edwards who holds that 'Women like sibyls...do not exist'. It's not the intervention of an omniscient author. The verb of operation in 'Sorel sat at the piano and *looked* round at her' establishes him as the temporary point of view, just as Olivia's 'dark eyes' gazing at the wintry garden establish her point of view in the first passage quoted from *Winter Sonata*. When we look at the white dress and the 'attitude of strength' we look with Sorel's eyes. It's at best ambiguous whether the following four sentences, shifting into the generalising present tense, are his thoughts or assertions made by no one in particular. The final sentence of the paragraph is neutral as far as point of view is concerned. Then the next paragraph moves unequivocally into Sorel's head. We have his mind's eye conjuring the woman. In the first sentence there's a rare flourish in Edwards's usually bare and often deliberately awkward prose, with the repetition of 'while' and its musical echo in 'wailing away', and those three clauses building towards what it is that he imagines while he plays. The sentence *enacts* both the music and his unwilled conjuring of Leonora. We can go back to those sentences about 'women like sibyls' now, and see them as the thoughts of a man who, we surmise, longs for this strong female archetype. Edwards herself tells us nothing.

Both Sorel and Leonora are isolated here, and the focus in this passage is the man, though elsewhere, generally more tentatively, the focus resides in other characters, including Leonora.

Subtle narrative manipulation of this kind is much less evident in 'La Penseuse', but its heavy plotting and that unusual centrality of a female character could help us re-examine the way women are portrayed, mostly not centre stage, in the other stories.

'La Penseuse' starts in the first person, but the narrator is invisible and not a player in the story. It's an approach Edwards uses in a couple of other stories:

'Cultivated People' and 'Sweet Grapes'. In 'Rhapsody' her narrator, Mr Elliott, plays a part in the story, but is largely an observer on our behalf of the pathetic but ruthless manipulations of the unlikely bully-figure, Mr Everett. In 'Sweet Grapes' the narrator is a friend of the central male character, Ferris, and tells the story presumably at second-hand from him. So we get the narrator's rather sceptical account of Ferris's version. It seems likely that the narrator is male, but it's not made explicit. He struggles unconvincingly to be sympathetic to his friend, but his tale is of Ferris's casual emotional cruelty to a young woman whose point of view our more thoughtful narrator occasionally tentatively guesses at. 'Cultivated People' is the closest to 'La Penseuse' in its handling of the first person. In both the narrator is used for a sort of establishing shot. 'Cultivated People' starts: 'In our town we have a music club...' (*R* 94) and 'La Penseuse': 'In the village in which I was born...' ('LP' 1) Shortly afterwards in both cases the 'I' disappears and we go on to be privy to scenes and to characters' thoughts no narrator could have access to. (In this respect the structure resembles *Madame Bovary*.)

It's as though, in these and other first person pieces, Edwards is experimenting with the possibilities of persona and narrative technique. In 'Sweet Grapes', for instance, the technique allows her to veil nineteen year-old Elizabeth's emotional suffering in the narrator's slight attempts to imagine them while trying not to be critical of his (or perhaps her) friend, Ferris. It's a technique that enables in specific and complicated ways Edwards's favourite modes of understatement and irony.

In 'La Penseuse' there's a hint that the narrator may be male: 'I do not mean to speak slightingly of her [i.e. Mary] though, because she was a pretty little thing and very intelligent.' ('LP' 1) The casual dismissiveness of 'she was a pretty little thing' is compounded by the way 'and very intelligent' is tacked on as an afterthought. There's also the implication of the alarming corollary that it's okay to speak slightingly of women who aren't brainy or pretty. It seems to me that in that opening page there's an attempt to set up an opposition between the male domain of the two young men (who 'both fell in love with a girl in the village, because, after all, young men must do something in the vacations') with its engagement with the world outside the village and entitlement to an intellectual life, and the literally and intellectually impoverished female domain of Mary and her aunt. The stark, schematic directness of this opposition is vitiated, ironised by the male-seeming voice.

But the voice doesn't seem controlled and the first person quickly vanishes. In this story the persona, the mask, slips in this and other ways. Uniquely among Edwards's stories, this one, in its very title, proclaims itself to be about femaleness. It's the only story whose title draws attention to a specific character, and the character is a woman.

'La Penseuse' may be an ironic feminising of 'Le Penseur', the emphatically male sculpture by the macho Rodin. The iconic sculpture might still have passed as modern, though not contemporary, art in the 1920s. And it's worth remembering that Rodin's alternative title for the piece was 'The Poet'—it had originally been intended as a representation of Dante. A figure representing intellect and poetry would seem to combine some of the mysterious opposition of the mechanical and the metaphysical embodied in Sidney and Richard. Mary is potentially a figure who can make this synthesis but who's disabled by class, gender, and the almost universal emotional stasis that's characteristic of Edwards's work. So the piece can *almost* be read straightforwardly as a fable about the casual and continuing subjugation of women. It's the most overtly political piece of fiction she wrote.

I don't want to suggest that cutting this piece was some kind of political self-censorship. I've mentioned several plausible reasons for the cut, and another is that the narrative voice is unresolved as the piece shifts away from the ironic opening to focus more and more on Mary in a kind of short anti-bildungsroman. The strains of attempting to comprehend a conventional Victorian-style novel structure in a short compass with such a modern sensibility and mix of themes were perhaps too great. It remains a story with a powerful thrust and some resoundingly strong moments. At the end there's deadly power in the quiet sentence: 'Mary sat before the fire and began to think about her life.' ('LP' 20) Out of context it would seem empty and flat, but of course the key word is 'think', echoing the title and the whole theme of intellectual engagement. The terrifying word 'began' understatedly implies a life not lived until it was too late.

There's no room to explore this in detail here, but I believe that the insight afforded by a close reading of 'La Penseuse' may help us to go back to the other stories and look at Edwards's portrayal of women, gender-relations in general, and the manipulation of point of view more discerningly. 'A Garland of Earth' in particular will make an interesting comparison, dealing as it does, though more typically of Edwards in a rather indirect way, with a brilliant young woman surrounded by men. It's possible that we may find more irony at work in the deployment of male voices and rather more suggested about female viewpoints than we suspected.

We have no way of knowing if this was part of the reason for dropping it, but there's no doubt that 'La Penseuse' can also be read as more personally self-revealing than any of Edwards's other fiction. Without knowledge of 'La Penseuse', Elaine Morgan wrote of *Rhapsody*: 'The likelihood is that her own emotional experiences at that time were far too raw and unassimilated to be allowed to surface.' (*R*, Introduction, xiv) It may be that they were a little more assimilated than any of us could have supposed. At the beginning of 'La Penseuse' we see Mary living in a village with an ailing aunt on a small income. This is close, perhaps uncomfortably so, to Edwards's own position, living in a Cardiff suburb with her

ailing, widowed mother on a tiny pension. Something of the dreariness of this
relationship, which played its part in Edwards's eventual breakdown, is hinted at in
the story. The cold realities of money and class, as well as gender politics, chill this
piece for almost the only time in her work. Edwards was possibly as young as
twenty-two when she wrote it. Was she, perhaps, taking an appalled look at how
her life might be to the age of about forty?

Reading the story this way, we can see Sidney and Richard as projections of her
opportunities for the intellectual life which she loved. In reality, we could see these
as being represented in part by her late father's socialism, that male world of the
Independent Labour Party and meetings of which she seems to have seen quite a
lot until her father's death when she was fourteen. (The absent parent motif,
hinting at the trauma of that loss and the motif of adolescent girl and older man
recur in coded variations many times in the other stories.) The other part of her
intellectual life was in her time at Cardiff University, where she studied Greek and
philosophy. Although more open than they'd ever been before, the universities were
still of course largely male preserves. These are male worlds which admit women
but fail to take them seriously and retain their own power. Perhaps Sidney and
Richard are strange, distorted Edwardsland versions of these, encoding, roughly
speaking, science and art respectively, the analytical and the contemplative.

Strangely, we can perhaps also see in Mary, the woman who discovers late that
she's not allowed to be equal to men and who becomes an ambiguous, spurned
lover/servant figure, a kind of foreshadowing of what became of Edwards in her
relationships with various men, including David Garnett. And there's another
darker and startling foreshadowing in 'La Penseuse'.

When Richard makes his pass at Mary early in the story and is pushed away, he
makes that strange speech I mentioned:

> 'You take my love and live on it, and love is something tangible which you
> would understand if you read Shelley properly, so that it is possible to steal it,
> and you do that and give nothing in return.' ('LP' 6)

There are a couple of points of interest here.

First, this is an odd reversal of what seems to be happening—it seems as though
it's the men who've been taking from Mary and giving nothing in return, and that's
certainly what emerges about Sidney later on. Of course we can read this as an
ironic portrayal of male selfishness, even manipulation, but it could also be that
Richard is suffering here as much as Mary is to later, though off-stage, so to speak.
How ever ironic the speech may be in the power-structure of the story, the man's
anguish seems real.

Second, the word 'tangible' is very telling. It connects with the older Richard's equally strange speech later on when he defends what Sidney calls his 'mysticism' as a kind of materialism. ' "[W]hen I touch a stone in Rome" he says, "am I not in some way touching your hand or Mary's?" '('LP' 17). He seems to have reached a kind of peace with himself in which he doesn't expect the world to reciprocate love, an expectation which he thinks leads to '"conflict"' (ibid.). This, I believe, gives some insight into the constant offerings of and withdrawals from physical contact which recur so often in Edwards's fiction.

But most extraordinarily of all, the younger Richard's speech foreshadows some sentences, already quoted by Tony Brown in this volume, which Edwards was to write seven or eight years later:

> I am killing myself because I have never sincerely loved any human being in my life. I have accepted kindness and friendship and even love without gratitude, and given nothing in return.[1]

It's astonishing to discover aesthetic echoings at work not only inside her fiction, but between her fiction and her life—and death. This heartstopping shift of point of view between fiction and fact seems to vindicate a reading of Edwards's work as growing somehow from her own turmoil, in which characters' sufferings—and particularly female characters' sufferings—are presented indirectly through veils of comic irony and displaced viewpoints.

Whether this was all in fact 'too raw' or not for 'La Penseuse' to be included in *Rhapsody* I don't know. I'm inclined to think that in refining her art, Edwards saw that she needed to be ruthless with her material, and so the cut. Perhaps too ruthless for her own good. She was moving towards compositions which, in stories such as 'Days' and *Winter Sonata*, achieve in a unique way a completeness of effect in apprehending the comic melancholy of the human condition that's comparable with the plays of Chekhov or the films of Bergman.

---

1   Quoted in the *Glamorgan Gazette*, Friday 12 January 1934, 8

'Mixed marriages': three Welsh historical novels in English by women writers

Diana Wallace

OF the first nine novels published in Parthian's 'Library of Wales' series of classic Welsh novels in the autumn of 2006 only one—Margiad Evans's *Country Dance* (1932)—is by a woman. Given the claims that this series makes to bring back into print representative but neglected texts ('the best of Welsh writing in English'), it is interesting that *Country Dance* is also the only historical novel (in that it is set, in Sir Walter Scott's famous phrase, 'sixty years since' or more[1]). It is perhaps not a coincidence. In the twentieth century women have frequently turned to the historical novel as a form in which they have had more freedom to write than in other genres.[2] Yet such novels have tended to be dismissed as 'popular' or 'middlebrow'. Since Anglophone Welsh fiction, as Jane Aaron has pointed out,[3] has tended to be associated with male writers writing about workers in the coal mines and iron and steel industries of South Wales, it is not surprising that little attention has been given specifically to Welsh women writing historical fiction. Until recently the three novels I want to discuss— Margiad Evans's *Country Dance* (1932), Eiluned Lewis's *The Captain's Wife* (1943) and Hilda Vaughan's *Iron and Gold* (1948)[4]—were out of print. While *Country*

---

1   Walter Scott, *Waverley; or, Tis Sixty Years Since* (1814; London and Glasgow: Collins, n.d.)

2   For some of the ways in which British women have used the historical novel form in the twentieth century see Diana Wallace, *The Woman's Historical Novel: British Women Writers, 1900–2000* (Basingstoke: Palgrave, 2005).

3   Jane Aaron, Introduction, *A View Across the Valley: short stories by women from Wales c. 1850– 1950* (Dinas Powys: Honno, 1999).

4   Margiad Evans, *Country Dance* (1932; London: John Calder, 1978), Eiluned Lewis, *The*

Dance has just been republished by Parthian, and *Iron and Gold* was republished by Honno in 2002, *The Captain's Wife* is, sadly, still not available.

Since any historical fiction entails some kind of engagement with history and geography in its decision to choose a specific time and place for its setting, even the most popular of historical novels often has interesting things to say about national identity. A sense of national identity is framed and defined in important ways in terms of history and geography, or to put it slightly differently, in terms of time and place: where and for how long the borders of a 'country' or a 'nation' have been established or disputed, for instance. These are issues which have been at the heart of the historical novel since its inception, most famously in Scott's *Waverley* (1814) set against the conflict between English and Scotland around the 1745 Jacobite rebellion. Discussion of Scott as the putative founder of the historical novel has been strongly influenced by Georg Lukács's Marxist study *The Historical Novel* (1962) which takes Scott's novels as a model of the 'classical historical novel'.[5] More recently there has been considerable interest in what Linda Hutcheon termed 'historiographic metafiction': that is, postmodern historical fiction which self-consciously draws attention to the difficulties of representing the very history it depicts.[6] The focus on these two areas, both of which might be expected to have attractions for critics of Welsh writing in English has, however, obscured a body of historical fiction by women, particularly from the years between 1920 and 1950, which appears to fit neither category.

Of the three novels I am discussing, it is perhaps most contentious to call *Iron and Gold* a historical novel. It would not qualify under, for instance, the criteria used by Avrom Fleishman in *The English Historical Novel* (1971), who suggests that what defines a historical novel is 'the active presence of a concept of history as a shaping force'; a setting in the past (40–60 years ago); the inclusion of '"historical" events', particularly in the public sphere; and the inclusion of at least one '"real" personage'.[7] These criteria, however, tend to exclude novels by women since women, historically confined to the private sphere, have been less likely to be involved in 'public' historical events or to be or interact with 'real' historical personages. Women's historical novels are often *about* the ways in which women are

---

Captain's Wife (London: Macmillan, 1943), Hilda Vaughan, *Iron and Gold* (1948; Dinas Powys: Honno, 2002). All pages references are to these editions and are given in parentheses in the text.

5   Georg Lukács, *The Historical Novel*, trans Hannah and Stanley Mitchell (1962; London: Methuen, 1983)

6   Linda Hutcheon, *A Poetics of Postmodernism: History, Theory, Fiction* (New York and London: Routledge, 1988).

7   Avrom Fleishman, *The English Historical Novel: Walter Scott to Virginia Woolf* (Baltimore and London: Johns Hopkins Press, 1971), 15, 3.

excluded from (public) history.

Country Dance, The Captain's Wife and Iron and Gold are all novels which are concerned with the issue of Welsh identity but which also explore in detail the gendering of national identity. They ask what it means to be a Welsh *woman*. All three novels are what Raymond Williams called 'history written from below'[8]— that is, history seen not from the point of view of kings, lords, or politicians, the dominant classes of society, but from that of workers, women, even children, who take little part in the public events which make up recorded history. There is now a considerable body of work which looks at the ways in which women have been, in Sheila Rowbotham's phrase, 'hidden from history.'[9] Welsh history, Raymond Williams suggested, has been similarly erased: 'Actual stories are told by both winners and losers. Yet what becomes history is a selection by the winners.'[10] Historical fiction often plays an important part in re-imagining these lost histories.

The central motif of each of these three novels is what Eiluned Lewis calls a 'mixed marriage' (106). In *Country Dance*, which uses the classic rival-suitor plot of nineteenth-century novels such as *Wuthering Heights* (1847) or *Far from the Madding Crowd* (1874), Ann Goodman, herself the child of a Welsh mother and an English father, must choose between two men—the Welsh farmer Evan ap Evans and the English shepherd Gabriel Ford. *Iron and Gold* retells the Welsh folk legend of the fairy bride of Llyn y Fan Fach, in the western Brecon Beacons, and her marriage to a mortal farmer. Finally, the 'Captain's Wife' of Lewis's novel is the Welsh Lettice Peters who has married the sea captain John Peters, a monoglot English-speaker. All three novels explore the ways in which for women the choice of a husband is a far-reaching decision about identity—English or Welsh, fairy or human. Lettice becomes the 'Captain's wife'; the fairy bride becomes a downtrodden housewife; and Ann is murdered.

These novels are asking about the meaning of national identity for women if that identity is subject to change on marriage. In the 1930s and 1940s the issue of mixed nationality marriage was of particular importance to women since a British woman who married a foreigner could not legally retain her British nationality. Although feminist groups agitated for reform of this legal inequality during the inter-war period, it was not changed until the 1948 British Nationality Act. While these novels are exploring an issue which was of contemporaneous importance

---

8   'People of the Black Mountains: John Barnie interviews Raymond Williams', *Planet* 65 (1987), 7.

9   Sheila Rowbotham, *Hidden From History: Rediscovering Women in History from the Seventeenth Century to the Present* (1973; New York: Random, 1976).

10 Raymond Williams, *People of the Black Mountains: vol. 1: The Beginning* (1989; London: Paladin, 1999), 325.

(particularly during the Second World War), their historical settings possibly helped to disguise a contentious topic by placing it safely in the past.

On the other hand, the motif of the 'mixed marriage' in these novels can also be read as a metaphor for the complex relationship between England and Wales. An increasing political focus on Welsh nationalism during this period is indicated by the formation of Plaid Cymru in 1925. A flexible metaphor, 'mixed marriage' has the potential to suggest a range of possibilities from a harmonious mutually-beneficial partnership, to a vexed, oppressive, even deathly conflict between two unequal bodies. The ways in which it is deployed in these three novels vary, partly according to their moment of publication (particularly in relation to the war), but partly according to the circumstances and personalities of the writers themselves.

'Margiad Evans' was the *non de plume* of Peggy Whistler, an Englishwoman (although her paternal grandmother, Ann Evans, was believed to be Welsh) who developed a strong affinity with the Welsh border area as a child. Her credentials as a 'Welsh' or, more accurately, a Border writer ('I'm not Welsh and never posed as Welsh […] I am the *Border*—a very different thing,' she wrote to Gwyn Jones[11]) have been the subject of debate. Claire Morgan has argued that Evans is not a Welsh writer at all but a Neo-Romantic one, who displays the outsider's nostalgic 'desire to appropriate the rural, and particularly the Celtic, past in terms of the anxieties of the present and the uncertainties of the future.'[12] Evans, she argues, is 'fantasizing Welshness' (115).

In a more sympathetic essay, Tony Brown has argued that Wales and the Border 'seemed to have answered some deep personal need in Evans herself', becoming emblematic of 'stability and rootedness in a life which provided her with no permanent sense of home.'[13] Evans's formative years were shadowed by insecurity, partly because her father lost his job (possibly as a result of alcoholism). The family life endured by Arabella in Evans's semi-autobiographical second novel, *The Wooden Doctor* (1933), suggests a childhood shaped by conflict between alcoholic father and embittered mother.[14] It is the *imaginative* use Evans made of Wales and Welshness, particularly in relation to conflicts over identity (both national and gender), which is important.

Evans's emotional and intellectual identification with Wales is also a political

11 Quoted in Ceridwyn Lloyd–Morgan, *Margiad Evans* (Bridgend: Seren, 1998), 32.

12 Clare Morgan, 'Exile in the Kingdom: Margiad Evans and the Mythic landscape of Wales' in *Welsh Writing in English: A Yearbook of Critical Essays*, 6 (2000), 113.

13 Tony Brown, 'Stories from foreign countries: The short stories of Kate Roberts and Margiad Evans' in Alyce von Rothkirch and Daniel Williams, eds, *Beyond the Difference: Welsh Literature in Comparative Contexts* (Cardiff: University of Wales Press, 2004), 23.

14 Margiad Evans, *The Wooden Doctor* (1933; Dinas Powys: Honno, 2005)

identification with the underdog, with a defeated and conquered people. As Raymond Williams has put it, 'To the extent to which we are a people, we have been defeated, colonised, penetrated, incorporated.'¹⁵ The sexualised nature of his metaphor—'penetrated'—suggests the way a defeated people is feminised. Incorporation, too, recalls the concept of the *feme covert*—where the married woman's identity was legally incorporated into her husband's, as Lettice Peters is identified as 'The Captain's Wife'. *Country Dance* is an example of what I have elsewhere called 'histories of the defeated'¹⁶, which are typical of British women's historical novels in the 1930s when writers such as Naomi Mitchison, Sylvia Townsend Warner and Rose Macaulay wrote novels which took the sides of defeated and conquered peoples, in part as a way of exploring the gendering of power inequalities. Above all, they show how in any conflict between two opposing forces it is always women who are most vulnerable. These 'histories of the defeated' disappear in the 1940s when an emphasis on defeat might have been seen as counter-productive to the war effort.

Much of the power of *Country Dance* lies in the rendering of Ann's voice in the main body of the text, presented as her diary and written in the present tense which gives great immediacy to her account of everyday rural life. Yet there are tensions and inconsistencies between this and the framing narrative where Evans presents the manuscript she claims to have 'discovered'. A framing narrative introducing a 'found' manuscript is a common technique in the historical novel, usually used to assert authenticity. Evans suggests that Ann's diary offers us 'the facts', the 'true knowledge of a tragedy' which has been 'distorted by tradition' (vii) so that the figures of the rival suitors have been accentuated while Ann herself has become 'curiously nebulous and unreal, a mere motive of tragedy' (vii). Evans's book is thus in the long tradition of women writers who have given a voice to those women 'hidden from history'.

Yet Ann Goodman is represented from the first sentence of the framing narrative as representative rather than individual: 'The struggle for supremacy in her mixed blood is the unconscious theme of Ann Goodman's book' (vii) Evans writes. This struggle is acted out by the two suitors who battle for her. Ann's status as emblematic figure is reiterated in the epilogue where the 'underlying narrative' of Ann's book is interpreted as the record of a mind in which 'two nations' were 'at war' and which 'represent[s] the entire history of the Border, just as the living Ann must have represented it herself—that history which belongs to

---

15 Quoted in Kirsti Bohata, *Postcolonialism Revisited* (Cardiff: University of Wales Press, 2004), 14.

16 Wallace, *The Woman's Historical Novel*, Chapter Three: 'Histories of the Defeated: Writers Taking Sides in the 1930s', 53– 77.

all border lands and tells of incessant warfare' (95).

Evans goes on to assert:

> Wales against England—and the victory goes to Wales; like Evan ap Evans, the awakened Celt cries: 'Cymru am byth!' with every word she writes. (95)

There is an interesting slippage here from character to author. It is difficult to see in what way Ann Goodman's fate represents any kind of 'victory'. Although her final choice of Evans as her lover symbolises her allegiance to Wales (tellingly, her mother's country), her ending is tragic. She is murdered, her body found in a deep pool with a great wound on her temple. It is important that *both* men are suspected by the community although Evans says that 'Gabriel was undoubtedly the murderer' (94). The 'awakened Celt' writing here would seem to be Evans herself who has through her identification with Wales found a voice as a writer.

The stark assertion that 'the victory goes to Wales' also seems at odds with the intricate patterning of the novel, which like the eponymous 'country dance', shows people crossing and re-crossing the border, and works to break down any sense of nationality as straight-forward and easily defined. Ann is brought up in Wales but by English relatives living on a farm with an English name, while the Welsh Evan ap Evans lives on the English side of the border. Ann's book suggests that national conflicts are both male-driven and deathly for women, and the only hope lies in the toleration of difference represented by the border. When a fight nearly breaks out over national loyalties at a supper it is Gwen Powys who defuses the situation by toasting 'the border' (61). The border is thus simultaneously presented as both a place of 'incessant warfare' (95) *and* a symbol of the possibility of harmonious co-existence. Women are potentially both victims and peace-makers.

Ann's diary is precisely dated to 1850, yet as Catrin Collier notes in her introduction,[17] there is no sense of the national or international events which we normally think of as 'history'. It is less than a decade after the Rebecca Riots, for instance, while John Davies pinpoints the middle of the nineteenth century as a turning point for Wales as the growth of industry and the coal trade led to a decline in the rural population.[18] To put it slightly differently, this is not a historical novel which depends on archival research, although Evans did 'research' Welsh rural life, customs and language by staying with the Lloyd-Jones family at

---

17 Catrin Collier, 'Introduction', Margiad Evans, *Country Dance*, Library of Wales series (Cardigan: Parthian, 2006).

18 John Davies, *A History of Wales*, first published as *Hanes Cymru* (1990), (1993; London: Penguin, 1993), 397.

Coch-y-Big near Pontlyfni.[19] (Moira Dearnley suggests that the sheepdog trials depicted in *Country Dance*, based on trials Evans attended there, are probably an anachronism.[20])

Instead, *Country Dance* offers a history based on 'memory', 'tradition', 'hearsay', a past strongly tied to a sense of place. The rural way of life which Ann documents is presented as both timeless and yet lost, symbolised by the ruin of the cottage where she was born. This actually seems to reflect the strong sense in the 1930s that, as A. J. P Taylor notes, 'rural communities were supposed to enshrine historic England.'[21] This led to subsidies for British agriculture which aimed to preserve such communities but, ironically, helped to erode them as improvements and mechanisation led to a fall in rural employment.[22] Evans represents the Welsh rural community in a similarly emblematic way, documenting a 'traditional' way of life which she sees as vanishing. The final paragraphs of the epilogue suggest the fading of all old stories—'painted in greys and lavenders' (96)—but asserts that they retain more of their colour in their original places, which are haunted by 'the dead who hold tenure of lands that were once theirs' (96)—the 'defeated' in other words. The 'echoes' of their lives may only be audible to 'native ears attuned' (96). Aware of her status as an outsider—one who by 'liv[ing] awhile' (96) in the area may just catch those 'echoes'—Evans nevertheless found in the Welsh border an imaginative space which fired her creativity as a writer, partly because it connected with her concern with insecure identities and with the defeated.

If Evans was an outsider, Hilda Vaughan and Eiluned Lewis were insiders, members of an Anglicised Welsh upper-middle-class. Born in Builth Wells to a successful solicitor and his wife, Hilda Vaughan married Charles Morgan, the novelist and drama critic of *The Times*. They lived in Chelsea and were part of the literary set known by Lewis, who edited Morgan's letters. *Iron and Gold* was written and first published (as *The Fair Woman*) in America where Vaughan and her children were staying for safety during the war. It is a kind of a disguised war novel and its concern with violence between dialectically opposed elements can be read in that context.

As I suggested earlier, it is perhaps contentious to call *Iron and Gold*, a retelling of the legend of the fairy bride of Llyn y Fan Fach, a 'historical novel'. While Evans and Lewis date their novels precisely, Vaughan appears purposely to frustrate any attempt to pin down the historical period in which *Iron and Gold* is

---

19 Moira Dearnley, *Margiad Evans*, Writers of Wales series (Cardiff: University of Wales Press, 1982), 9.

20 Ibid., 11.

21 A. J. P Taylor, *English History 1914–1945* (1965, Harmondsworth: Pelican, 1975), 424.

22 Ibid, 425.

set. This is, of course, appropriate for a legend which is, by implication, timeless. However, John Williams in his version of the legend in *The Physicians of Myddfai* (1861) dates it to 'when the eventful struggle made by the Princes of South Wales to preserve the independence of their country was drawing to its close in the twelfth century,'[23] thus also linking it to Welsh nationalism. Vaughan does not follow this—references to one character carrying a pistol, for instance, suggest a later date, possibly the nineteenth century. In the frame narrative the bard who tells the fable to an audience of children, and claims to have seen the fairy bride, can remember when 'the land was green and whole' before 'the young men [...] were gone to the Pits to hew coal' (1); that is, before the Industrial Revolution. When a child repeats the suggestion that the fairy bride appeared when 'the Welsh was fighting some wicked old Norman kings' (1), his mother dismisses the whole legend: 'There's a deal o'such hearsay spoken.' (2). This again is history as 'hearsay', memory, tradition but even the boy's pragmatic mother won't dismiss it as 'lies' commenting, 'Can I judge what be truth to a poet?' (2). The fable, then, contains a truth which is of continuing historical relevance.

Vaughan uses the techniques of the historical novel—detailed realistic descriptions of a specific place, psychological realism, an evocation of a rural way of life and customs—to flesh out the legend to a full-length novel. As Jane Aaron suggests in her introduction, Vaughan does not so much re-write the legend as bring to the surface its latent psychological themes.[24] These realist techniques are countered by the non-specific historical setting and the supernatural elements (the fairy bride and her magical cattle) but all three work to distance radical material— it was not until the 1970s that feminists highlighted the issue of domestic violence, for instance—and to open up the possible interpretations of the central metaphor.

As critics have noted, ill-matched marriages are a recurring theme in Vaughan's work.[25] *Iron and Gold* uses the theme of the 'mixed marriage' to weave a parable about otherness and the difficulties of 'marrying' two widely differing, even opposite, elements whether iron and gold, human and fairy, man and women, English and Welsh. It is also about the potential for violence which haunts such 'marriages', whether domestic or national, and about the loss to all when otherness is suppressed and erased. As Aaron notes, it is the fairy bride's 'otherness' which provokes her husband, Owain, into striking her with iron on three occasions, on the third of which she 'dies' as a mortal and returns to her lake home (xv). While the novel might superficially be seen as a retreat into history, myth or the domestic as a way of ignoring the events of the Second World War, Vaughan's fable actually

---

23 Vaughan, *Iron and Gold*, Appendix, 206.
24 Jane Aaron, 'Introduction', Vaughan, *Iron and Gold*, x.
25 Ibid., viii.

has significant resonances at a time when racial, religious or national otherness in Hitler's Germany meant a journey to the death camps.

Moreover, Fascist ideology in the 1930s and 1940s emphasized the difference between the sexes as complementary but unequal opposites. As early as 1934 Winifred Holtby was pointing to the way in which Germany was preaching the doctrine of 'Kinder, Küche, Kirche' and demanding that women conform to an ideal of domestic interests and psychological docility.[26] To call Owain a Fascist would be to go too far but it is a matter of degree. Vaughan makes it clear that it is Owain's desire that his fairy bride become a 'dutiful housewife' (59) confined to domestic servitude rather than roaming free on the mountain, which erodes what is 'rare in her' (her difference), and makes her 'commonplace' (62). 'As you desire me so shall I become,' she warns him (30). In a key metaphor, Owain sees his wedded life as a map of possession: 'the whole acreage of enclosure in which wealth was made sure and beauty held a constant captive' (50). Like Owain's mother, the fairy refers to her husband as 'Master' and allows him to name her: 'Glythin Martha' (46). That this is a fable about what happens to many women in marriage is made clear when Owain's mother tells her:

'I've made you grow like to myself. [...] When I'm gone, you'll be taking my place quite natural. [...] That's how it has been. How 'twill ever be. A chain o' women. All alike. Every link. That life may hold unbroken.' (105–6).

In this double metaphor women are the 'chain' which holds 'life' together (as they give birth to and sustain new life), but they are also en-chained, held captive, by that role. At the end of the novel when Glythin, struck a third time by iron, ages visibly she appears to become Owain's mother, suggesting the inter-changeability of women in the maternal role: 'Mother, Mother! What's on you!' Owain cries before correcting himself, 'No, no, 'tis *wife* I do mean! Sweetheart as you were once. You that did use to set me singing, wherefore is your magic dwindled' (193, 194). As he indicates here, Owain's creativity as a bard is linked to his ability to acknowledge and appreciate her otherness. It is not her magic that has dwindled but his capacity to see it.

Vaughan emphasizes the narrowness of small rural communities where the outsider in a mixed marriage is regarded with suspicion. The neighbours jeer at Owain for being 'wedded to a stranger' (61), while his brother Dan accuses him of being 'bewitched' by his 'strange' wife (118). Unable to ignore their comments Owain increasingly forces Glythin to conform. Their relationship is a contrasted with another mixed marriage: Owain's brother Madoc has married an

26 Winifred Holtby, *Women* (London: John Lane, 1934), 154.

Englishwomen, a rich but ugly 'Saxon' (8), and lives over the border, for years refusing to allow his mother to see her grandchildren. The use of the word 'Saxon' here locates this story within a wider history, one shaped by conflicts—Celt /Roman, Celt/Saxon, Saxon/Norman, English/Welsh and so on—which have frequently entailed the violent suppression of the defeated 'other'. It is the strength of Vaughan's novel that what on the surface seems to be a simple folk tale allows such varied and suggestive readings.

In contrast to Evans and Vaughan, Lewis emphasizes the positive aspects of the hybrid identities which come from mixed marriages in a novel which has its roots in her own family background. Lewis's childhood was spent in Glan Hafren, a large Georgian house near Newtown in Montgomeryshire, where J.M. Barrie was a visitor and George Meredith was godfather to her brother. Her Cambridge-educated father was a landowner and owner of a Newtown tannery, while her Welsh-speaking mother, who had an MA from London University and had been headmistress of Newtown Girls' School, was from Pembrokeshire. As depicted in Lewis's autobiographical novel, *Dew on the Grass* (1934)[27] it was an idyllic childhood. Lewis went on to work on newspapers in London where her memoirs convey her pleasure in being at the centre of a literary world.

Published in 1943 but set in 1880–1 in 'St Idris' (a lightly disguised St David's), *The Captain's Wife*, as the dedication acknowledges, is a 'mixture of fact and fancy' based on material provided by Lewis's mother, Eveline Martha Lewis, the model for Lettice Peters's daughter, Matty. Lettice herself is based on Lewis's maternal grandmother, who travelled the world with her sea captain husband and gave birth to her first child in Calcutta.[28]   This is, then, a *matrilineal* and familial history. Lewis's book is a tribute to the value of (his)stories passed from mother to daughter. As she puts it elsewhere: 'that is the way all legends are born: from the stories told us by our mothers.'[29]

Lewis stresses the hybridity and fluidity of national identity. Incomers and 'mixed marriages' are generally presented as positive, although one character regards a 'mixed marriage' to an Englishman as 'a doubtful blessing' (106). Although Lettice's own family have lived at the family farm, Nantgwyn, for generations and the graves of her forerunners lie in the shadow of the cathedral (3), they are descended from a West Country man who fled to Pembrokeshire to escape the Bloody Assizes (27). As Lewis put it in her radio play 'September Day'[30], also

---

27 Eiluned Lewis, *Dew on the Grass* (1934; Dinas Powys: Honno, 2006).

28 Eiluned Lewis, *A Companionable Talent: Stories, Essays and Recollections* (Goudhurst: Finchcocks Press, 1996), 69.

29 Ibid., 65.

30 Lewis, 'September Day' (broadcast 1995), in *Talent*, 121–33

based on her Pembrokeshire ancestors, 'we're visitors here, like everybody else.'[31] While John Peters has an English name and is a monoglot English speaker, he has Norse blood and a Scottish grandfather who married a Welshwoman (191). Their marriage is presented as a source of strength for Lettice, whose love for her husband is the 'central core of her life' (152).

Lettice's bilingualism is presented as another aspect of this hybridity:

> [Lettice] spoke English to her husband and children, Welsh to her servants, and both in turn to her farmer cousins [...] but she could never repeat a word of the Bible in anything but Welsh. (3)

This glosses over and normalises a class-based language divide which reflects an Anglicisation of the Welsh upper and middle classes, but Lewis's use of Welsh in the novel is complex and more partisan than this initial analysis suggests. A comparison with Margiad Evans's use of Welsh words and phrases in *A Country Dance* is interesting. Used by Evan ap Evans to Ann, Welsh signifies intimacy and a shared national identity (hence Gabriel's jealousy when he hears Evans calling Ann 'dear names in Welsh' (46)) while the 'Cymru am byth!' cried by the 'awakened Celt' (95) in the Epilogue suggests political nationalism, although safely distanced in the past. Kirsti Bohata has suggested that Evans mainly uses 'extrinsic code-switching' (the use of 'foreign' words or phrases, usually italicised, to provide local colour).[32] Evans's use of direct translation implies and privileges a monoglot English audience.[33] In contrast, 'political code-switching'—the use of untranslated Welsh—would assert the validity of the language and stress cultural boundaries. A third variation would be 'organic code-switching'—the use of foreign words (usually italicised, and often with an explanation/glossary) for which there is no equivalent translation. [34]

In *The Captain's Wife*, Lewis uses variations of all of these. On the surface the text seems to privilege a monoglot English audience: the first spoken words in the text, given in English are spoken 'in Welsh' (5). Some words—'"set fawr" (big seat)' (88)—are marked off by quotation marks and translations given, but others, particularly endearments—'Matty fach', 'cariad'—and exclamations - 'oh duwch, duwch' (21)—are given untranslated. Perhaps more important are the symbolic loads carried by the language. For Lettice, Welsh is the language of emotion and

---

31 Ibid, 125.

32 Bohata, 121

33 These translations have been omitted from the Parthian edition. I am indebted to Jane Aaron for pointing this out to me.

34 Bohata, 118.

intimacy, and of her deepest religious beliefs. It is telling that the only Welsh chapter heading, taken from a hymn, is given to the chapter which tells of the death of her youngest son Philip: 'Bydd myrdd o ryfeddodau ar doriad bore'r wawr' (180).35 It is also significant that Lewis dedicates the novel to her mother with the words: 'Ti wyddost beth ddywed fy nghalon' ['Thou knowest what says my heart'36]. These are given without translation, marking the intimate bond between Welsh-speaking mother and daughter, kept secret from the English reader. Overall, and within the context of the novel's emphasis on hybridity, Lewis's use of both Welsh and English reads more as a generous inclusivity than a capitulation to the needs of the English audience.

Lewis's interest in a national identity which is both Welsh *and* hybrid seems to come from her pleasure and pride in her own ancestry. (Interestingly, she married Graeme Hendrey, a Lowland Scot.) However, such a positive view of the hybridity which goes to make up the varied peoples in the British Isles might also have contributed to a sense of national unity during wartime. As another disguised war novel, *The Captain's Wife* offered its audience both nostalgic escape to a former period and, as the jacket blurb of the 1943 edition suggests, contemporaneous relevance: 'This is the story of a woman's heart, of true love and anxious waiting— a theme which belongs to all time and especially to the present day.' The long absences of Captain Peters on his voyages leave the house in 'the quiet mood of a woman's rule' (4)—a female and matrilineal space. The title may suggest the subordination of Lettice's identity into that of her husband but this is countered by the narrative. Lettice has a clear and strong sense of both her national and local identity, based on her position as 'the centre and mainspring' of her own household (12) and on her responsibilities in the wider community.

The Captain's Wife is a novel with a strong sense of history but it is a woman's eye view of history and also a child's eye view, as much of the novel is focalised through Matty. The children, for instance, prefer to walk along the tops of the 'hedges' (grassy banks) rather than in the road with the grown-ups and from there they have 'the best of the view' (6). The ruined Bishop's Palace provides a favourite playground, but one which is (like Evans's border landscape) haunted by the 'echoing past' (94). Matty feels that if she turns her head quickly she will see 'knights in armour, ladies wearing wimples and long pointed sleeves, and pages in slashed velvet' (95).

This is not, however, a narrow point of view. Lewis stresses both the

---

35 An English version of this hymn is given in the text but a literal translation would be 'There will come a host of wonders at the breaking of the day'. I am indebted to Chris Meredith for this translation.

36 I am indebted to my father, Nigel Wallace, for this translation.

importance of the local and the now, and a strong sense of its location within a wider world and the span of history. Here and in 'September Day' Lewis shows how Pembrokeshire, 'sea-girt' on three sides, has historically looked out to the wider world. As a sea-captain's wife Lettice has 'travelled round the world' (3). Moreover, although she

> lived in days that seem to us now incredibly peaceful and serene yet her grandparents had helped to cut off the lead pipes from the Cathedral to cast bullets when the invading French landed a few miles away. (3)

Thus Lewis emphasises women's role in national and even international history: Nansi Richards's mother, 'it was said, had worn a red cloak and marched along the shore to frighten the French when Napoleon tried a landing in Wales' (11). For readers in the early 1940s, the memory of such a successful repulsion of invasion must have been comforting, as well as encouraging women's sense of their potential contribution to the war effort.

Perhaps also comforting was the stress Lewis laid on the continuity represented by natural landscape and children:

> St Idris has outlived many convulsions in men's history and still each year the wild flowers return to the sheltered banks of the lanes and the children of the new generation still smell the heady wine of the flowering gorse along the cliffs as they run joyfully to the sea. (3)

Children, like the past, strong religious belief or a happy marriage—all key themes in this novel—are extremely difficult to write about without falling into either banality or sentimentality. Here Lewis counters the risk of sentimentalising the past with realism about its harshness. As she puts it in 'September Day', 'Don't sigh too much for the past. Our forebears had their trials as well as their fun.'[37] In the penultimate chapter of the novel, the funeral of Lettice's father is followed by the death of her youngest son Philip from a fever, an almost unbearable loss, only barely mitigated by the discovery that she is pregnant again.

Of these novels, *The Captain's Wife* offers the most positive treatment of the 'mixed marriage' motif through its emphasis on the hybridity of the Welsh and the British (we are all 'visitors here'), but it also comes closest to sentimentalising the past. Both *Iron and Gold* and *Country Dance* offer darker analyses of the risks run by the weaker partner in any unequal 'marriage'. *Country Dance*, however, comes close to eulogising the defeated. Kirsti Bohata has rightly argued that we should be wary

---

37 Lewis, 'September Day' (broadcast 1995), in *Talent*, 129.

of nostalgia for lost origins and of a glorification of the past which is 'always a picture of defeat' and has suggested that we need instead to create a 'useable past'.[38] One way of creating such a 'useable past' is through the comparative re-reading of novels such as these which seek in varied ways to engage with the construction of national and gender identity within history.

---

38 Bohata, 16, 14.

IV

Literature and Art

Seán Street

For Jeremy Hooker

ALWAYS this dancing:—
  light through glass, chalk's ancient life,
Itchen growing towards tide
like the being in the wood emerging—
always, always this dancing.

The still, fragile act
of a poem begins here,
the spirit of place passed on
from a father's painter's eye intact,
and the past living as fact

to teach, informing
each day—a benediction
on all these things, like carving
that brings forth intact through a breaking
in the end this true making,

                    this dancing.

Sheenagh Pugh

Men of Iron

Anthony Gormley's 'Another Place': Crosby Beach, July 2005

L AND at his back, he scans
the beach, the breaking surf

where, ankle-deep, his likeness
mirrors his stance, staring

at his own double, immersed
up to the waist, eyes fixed

far out, on a dark head
showing above the waves.

All along the bay's curve,
between high-water mark

and low, a hundred cast-iron clones
stand, paddle, wade;

you would not know them
from us, at a distance,

until sun sets and the beach
empties, and they wait

still, as the slap and suck
of tide on gleaming sand

ebbs from their feet. They bear
the day's decorations,

handkerchiefs knotted on their heads,
genitals spray-painted,

and the rust's graffiti
spreading like a bruise,

while they, enduring,
keep watch for the ones

further out, the spaces
where no heads show.

Come November
they will be gone,

and folk who know
they are in New York

will still be narrowing
their gaze, as if a keen eye

might catch the last of them
walking out to sea.

Tony Curtis

DJ visits Waterloo

FROM the top of the stiff lion's hill
  the easterly cuts you to the bone
        on such a man-made moel,
coming from where the maps show Blucher
        and his Huns rushing in to save the day.

Wellesley held there
        a fine CO who'd cut his teeth in India
and the Peninsula against the Imperium,
mercenaries, no doubt, on all sides
together with the press'd and conscripted,
        all become Wealcyn.

Seems that Tommy, the good Huns and Orangemen
saw Boney turn heels on that long and bloody'd day
and slouch back to an island confine
                where, it is said,
the arse-nick'd wallpaper did for him.
A rum story.

Cluster'd bleak stone monuments *sans grace* –
Victor Hugo, General Gordon, Hanovarians, Belges.
It's in the nature of such stuff to make heroes of the brass
while infantry chaps, thousand on 'em,
go into the ground unsung,
                strip't of tunica and boots
and patted down with the flat of a spade.
Memento etiam Domine.
They prized out their teeth for false 'uns.

One feels that neck-tingle
and the pricking of a tear at Hougoumont Farm
where the stout grenadiers – Coldstreams and Jocks,
cursed themselves for hacking down doors
to fire their billy-brew the night before
    that would've been musket rests and firing cover-
but we held the gate against a hard, long day's assault
by Boney's Garde Imperial. They who fell in ranks
within the termini of the farm walls.

Now glimpsed through the grill of the tiny chapel
the feet of our Lord singed that day
are singed for ever.
      Arglwydd - crucified black and grey.

A hundred years peace – until our own Show –
I suppose, was won at that Farm.

    Out on the fields the red line squared up,
bayonets knelt before muskets
    saw their cavalry repulsed
so the poor beasts piled up into bloody parapets.

No need for trenches,
    'cept to bury the fallen –
poor, stripped buggers forever etc.
    some corner of a Belgian field.
Uniforms and personals filched by the infernal followers.

Hand to mouth, hand to hand, the bad breath of the kill.
(Things hardened into the mechanical in our Show
with death dealt out distant, through gun sights)

One moment: old Wellie snapping shut his telescope,
then waving his hat to send our chaps after their rout,
standing high in his stirrups
    on the bay Copenhagen
to survey the confusion.

Men ploughing the mud
                    with their sweet faces.
In paradisium deducant te Angeli
For there had been no help on that open plain
save the embrace of the enemy.

Fig. 1: Archie Griffiths, *On the Coal Tips, c.* 1930–32
Private collection

Fig. 2: Archie Griffiths, *Drawing for 'Tro yn yr Yrfa'*, 1928

Fig. 3 Evan Walters, *Bydd Myrdd o Ryfeddodau*, 1926

Fig. 4: Evan Walters,
*Drawing for 'The
Communist'*, c. 1932

Fig. 5: Vincent Evans, *Trimming after Charge*, c. 1936

Fig. 6: Vincent Evans, *Drawing for 'A Welsh Family Idyll'*, c. 1935

Fig. 7: Ceri Richards,
*La Cathedrale engloutie
profondement calme*, 1962

Fig. 8: Ceri Richards, *The Pianist No. 1*, 1948

Fig. 9: Ceri Richards,
Souvenir de la cathedrale engloutie,
1960–62

Fig. 10: Josef Herman, *Autumn*, 1946

Fig. 11: David Jones, *Capel Landscape*, 1925

Fig. 12: Merlyn Evans, *The Refugees*, 1946

Biblical and Marxist rhetoric in the painting and literature of the Depression

Peter Lord

As its subtitle states, Idris Davies' 'The Angry Summer' is 'A poem of 1926'. Similarly, Evan Walters' *The Welsh Collier* is a picture of 1926. Indeed, it is a picture of the summer of 1926, and as such its subject matter is close to that of Davies' poem:

> What will you do with your shovel, Dai,
> And your pick and your sledge and your spike,
> And what will you do with your leisure, man,
> Now that you're out on strike…
>
> And how will the heart within you, Dai,
> Respond to the distant sea,
> And the dream that is born in the blaze of the sun,
> And the vision of victory?[1]

It would have been difficult for anyone to paint a Welsh miner in the summer of 1926 without also painting the coal strike, and for Evan Walters it would have been impossible. Though never a miner himself, Walters was born into a working class family in a mining community a few miles to the west of Swansea in 1893. He was thirty-three years old when the strike began and full of confidence as a painter. His title for the picture, under which it was exhibited at the National Eisteddfod at Swansea and won the painting prize, leaves us in no doubt as to his intentions. The sitter's name, William Hopkins, appears only in brackets after the generic title of

---

[1]   Idris Davies, *The Angry Summer: A Poem of 1926* (London: Faber, 1943), 11.

The Welsh Collier. William Hopkins represents more than himself.

Given the intensity of the surrounding circumstances it is not surprising that there are correspondences to be found between 'The Angry Summer' and *The Welsh Collier*, as there are between many other literary and visual works of the period. Evan Walters' younger contemporary, Archie Griffiths, from Gorseinon, who had indeed worked underground, graduated from the Royal College of Art in 1926 and over the summer of that year he made many drawings in the Swansea Valley. None survive in the original, but two were published in the *Cambria Daily Leader*, a local newspaper. *Looking for Coal in an Old Tip* presents a scene which became a familiar motif in the literature of industrial society during the Depression. It is the setting both for a central incident in Gwyn Thomas' *Sorrow for Thy Sons*, and for a moment of revelation in Gwyn Jones' *Times Like These*.

Nevertheless, although the expression 'works of the period' may be used in a general way to encompass both visual imagery and literature, there is a fundamental difference of circumstance between the two which must mediate the interpretation of such correspondences. Notwithstanding its overall hardness, Davies' writing in 'The Angry Summer' occasionally reveals a degree of sentimentality which is surely a product of the softening effect of an eighteen year perspective on the world which he evokes. When the poem was published in 1943 there were miners beginning work for whom the strike was the experience not only of their fathers but also of their grandfathers. On the other hand, Walters' picture, in which 'Miners' leaders threatening/And royalty owners cursing' is implicit, was painted as the conflict evolved. For Evan Walters and for Archie Griffiths the number '1926' had no more resonance than '2007' has for us, since it simply denoted their present. However, by the time Idris Davies wrote 'The Angry Summer', to say 'nineteen twenty-six' was to name a crucial moment in British and Welsh history and to evoke a world. For Davies personally it evoked both a dark and a golden age.

In August 1926 a reporter for the *South Wales Daily News* noted that Walters' *The Welsh Collier* depicted 'a striking (or locked-out) collier, for whose temperament the artist had considerable regard, and into whose eyes the circumstances of the time brought occasionally a certain fierceness'. The cautious phraseology captured an important aspect of the present of the period which is absent from the accounts of Idris Davies and of Gwyn Thomas, and indeed from all the accounts given in what has become the canon of Welsh literature in English in the inter-war period. In a study of art and revolution in France in 1848, T. J. Clark suggested that 'We shall not understand Delacroix or Daumier or Baudelaire until we put back doubt into the revolution; put back confusion and uncertainty, a sense that everything was at risk'.[2] The same is true of Evan Walters and of Archie

---

2   T. J. Clark, *The Absolute Bourgeois* (London: Thames &Hudson, 1973), 16.

Griffiths. It is not true of Idris Davies and Gwyn Thomas, who must be understood differently, as engaged in the construction of history. To point out that Davies did not write about the strike as it happened in 1926 is not to criticise him, of course. It was as a result of his experience of the strike that he went to college and turned to literature. Nevertheless, he did not fully emerge as a writer until 1938, when *Gwalia Deserta* appeared, which was towards the end of that extraordinary five years of publishing which created the canon. Jack Jones' *Rhondda Roundabout* was published in 1934, and Bert Coombes' *These Poor Hands* and Lewis Jones' *We Live* appeared in 1939.

For Archie Griffiths, as for Idris Davies, the consequence of the enforced idleness of a strike had been a fundamental change of direction in life. However, it was the strike of 1921 which turned Griffiths' mind towards painting. Furthermore, public exposure to images of the mining communities of south Wales, painted from the inside, had begun at least a decade before that. It was in 1911 that the first substantial group of industrial images painted by an artist from the working class had been exhibited. These were the early works of Evan Walters, and their significance was powerfully noted at the time by the equally youthful journalist John Davies Williams of the *Cambria Daily Leader*. Notwithstanding the dogged repetition of the myth of the primacy of the word, in fact it was the visual image that broke the ground of working class political and social art in our culture, some twenty-three years before the first of the canonical literary works of the Depression was published.

The relatively early emergence of the visual imagery owed much to the philosophy and practical drive of William Grant Murray, who was appointed in 1909 as Principal of Swansea School of Art. From his own training in Scotland, Murray had inherited the principles of the Arts and Crafts Movement, mediated by Patrick Geddes. The social dimension of the philosophy of the movement disposed Murray to develop the abilities of students from a working class background and, in practical terms, to provide them with a modern art and craft education which would enable them to earn a living. He encouraged his students to draw on their personal experience of life as subject matter. Evan Walters was his first success, and he was soon followed by Vincent Evans from Ystalyfera, who started his training in 1911. In 1920 the *Western Mail* reported that Evans had been one of seven children, living with his mother and father, who was a monumental mason. 'In the case of Vincent, he used to change immediately he came home from the colliery and proceed to the art school at Swansea, where promising students are given lessons for a moderate fee...His studio is his mother's front room, and upon entering one is struck with the reality of a large unfinished canvas facing the door. It is called 'The Double Parting' and depicts a haulier encouraging his horse with a tram of coal while a collier is silhouetted holding his light for guidance.'³

Not only did William Grant Murray offer the opportunity for working class students to acquire a sophisticated art training locally, but he enabled them to pursue their training further in England. In particular he opened access to the Royal College of Art, where Sir William Rothenstein, Principal from 1920–1935, held similar social views to his own. Murray created a professional pathway which took young painters in two steps from working class communities (and in the cases of Evans and Griffiths, literally from the coalface) to the most sophisticated artistic centre in London. No remotely comparable professional pathway existed for aspiring writers. Furthermore, even as the painters were emerging they received further encouragement from a literature of reportage about them. Vincent Evans was a very early recipient of the newspaper appellation 'Miner Artist'. Unfortunately, by emigrating to New Zealand in 1924, he was not in a position to take advantage of the brief period of fashion among metropolitan intellectuals for working-class painters, which reached its height in the aftermath of the General Strike. Archie Griffiths was better placed. By the time of his graduation in 1926 he had been the subject of several newspaper articles, and his work had been extensively reproduced. The *Cambria Daily Leader*, now edited by John Davies Williams, may not have been the *Charivari* (which carried Daumier's visual commentary on the revolution of 1848 in Paris) but in 1924 and early 1925 it commissioned from Griffiths a long series of drawings of the industrial scene in the Swansea Valley. It regularly noticed his professional progress, and used his work to illustrate articles of general local interest. Furthermore, in 1928 Griffiths was eulogised in print by Rothenstein in an exhibition catalogue, and in 1932 by Geraint Goodwin in *The Welsh Outlook*. The motivation for all this literary attention is suggested by the fact that Ceri Richards, who won a scholarship to the Royal College of Art in the same year as Griffiths and who graduated with him, received almost none. Richards had not been a miner, and neither did he paint miners.

Archie Griffiths was the beneficiary, if not the product, of a romantic agenda which drove in subtly various ways William Grant Murray, John Davies Williams, William Rothenstein and Geraint Goodwin. They all turned him into a symbol of the battle of genius against adversity, in the context of social deprivation. For the writers, industrial society represented paradise lost, and Griffiths' struggle exemplified the human condition after the Fall. Although they presented their ideas as reportage, biography and criticism, in fact Griffiths was used much as the novelists of the next decade would use their fictional characters. Many years ago, Dai Smith memorably described *How Green was My Valley* as 'a parable about the Fall from Grace'. Unlike the patrons and promoters of Griffiths, Smith did so

3 'The Collier Artist', *Western Mail*, 28 April 1920.

particularly to condemn a book which he scorned, presenting it as an outsider's projection onto reality. This interpretation became, for many years, the received wisdom and a piece of Welsh political correctness which kept *How Green was My Valley* firmly locked outside the canon. However, with a longer perspective it has become clear that the same parable informs much of its contemporary literature. The opposition of pure and defiled Valleys landscapes as a vehicle in which to convey the idea of Paradise Lost is hardly confined to Richard Llewellyn. Climbing up onto the unspoiled mountain from the polluted industrial town, generally for the purpose of homily, in the best Judeo-Christian tradition, is a common motif. A particularly clear example from the heart of the canon is the opening passage of *Cwmardy*. In filmic terms, it is the all-important establishing shot. The hero, Len, and his father, Big Jim, are walking on the mountain. As he recalls his personal paradise lost, the beautiful land of north Wales, it becomes apparent that Jim is a refugee from the great strike of 1900-3 in the slate industry. In a fragmentary way he also recalls a larger mythic national history. As they descend, Len observes 'the sheep-track winding its way down the mountain breast like a tortuous vein. He saw where it buried itself in the murk and hid as if ashamed of its eventual destination. It was just there, Len knew, that the grass ceased to be green'.4 The resonance with the title of the excluded work, *How Green was My Valley*, is curious.

Within this general construct the particular case of Archie Griffiths seemed to characterise a contrast between the sensitivity of the artistic soul and the brutality of the pit in which it was confined. Rothenstein saw Griffiths, 'whom the urge of creation drove from the Welsh mines on to the narrow and difficult road of the artist' as possessed of 'rare gifts' of 'dramatic and lyrical promise'.5 Goodwin saw him as a mystic—as a pilgrim going to the Vanity Fair of London where 'on every booth, was art':

> But this Art was not the Art he felt; the Art he knew was very much closer to him, was indeed so much a part of his life that he preferred to speak of Life than Art, and to let his mind dwell on the sombre and desolate mountains of his home; the grim out-works of Industry; the fine shouting life that he loved transfixed on this awful gibbet.6

William Grant Murray's aspiration to create a professional pathway for his artists

---

4 Lewis Jones, *Cwmardy and We Live* (Cardigan: Parthian, 2006), 7.
5 William Rothenstein, Introduction to the *Catalogue of Paintings, Drawings and Etchings by Archie Griffiths A.R.C.A* (Swansea, 1928).
6 Geraint Goodwin, 'An Artist of Vision: The Work of Rhys Griffiths', *The Welsh Outlook*, XIX (1932), 79. Archie Griffiths was baptised Archie Rees Griffiths. In about 1931 he took to using his middle name, with Welsh spelling, for professional purposes.

also extended to aftercare. In 1920 Evan Walters became the first former student to be offered by him an exhibition at the Glynn Vivian Gallery, and the benefits were lasting. The show was seen by Winifred Coombe Tennant, who immediately became his patron. At the exhibition she bought *Mother and Babe*, and it is clear from her description of the picture as 'the typical Madonna and Child of industrial Wales' that she had immediately recognised and responded to one of the essential elements of Walters' work. From his Welsh-speaking Nonconformist upbringing the painter had absorbed deeply the imagery of the bible and the sermon. It had become integrated into his imaginative processes. Walters was no devotee of organised religion and, indeed, some of his pictures suggest that he was cynical about its practices. Among his close friends he counted Caradoc Evans.7 Nevertheless, he remained a believer, whose use of Christian reference was purposeful and direct, reflecting the primitivism of eighteenth-century Nonconformism rather than its late nineteenth-century sophistication. In his picture of *The Introduction to Christ* he portrayed himself in the company of St Mark and Jesus: 'I was reading St Mark one night', he observed, 'and I thought that this was the best introduction to Christ, so I painted St Mark introducing myself to the Almighty.' Walters' straightforward Christian reference resonated strongly with his admirers. In Kate Bosse Griffiths' novel *Mae'r Galon wrth y Llyw* the character Arthur takes his prospective lover Doris to an art gallery to look at an exhibition of the painter's work. Duly inspired, Arthur embarks on an impassioned flight of fancy about pictures he himself would like to paint. Among them would be '*Madonna'r Cwm Glo*; a young mother nursing her first-born son in a shawl...and *Mater Dolorosa'r Cwm Glo*, a mother holding a dead collier in her arms'. The second of Arthur's proposed works, like the first, had in fact already been painted by Walters—*The Dead Miner*.8

If Evan Walters' Christian faith was challenged, it was not by the pretensions of organised religion, but by the stress of the Depression. At the National Eisteddfod at Swansea in 1926 he exhibited one of the most startling Welsh paintings of the twentieth century, *Bydd Myrdd o Ryfeddodau* (fig. 3) Few critics ventured to comment upon it in print. The following year he showed the work, retitled in English as *A Welsh Funeral Hymn*, in London, where he had been given an exhibition at the Dorothy Warren Gallery. Although not a 'miner-painter', as some newspapers reported, much to his irritation, the coal strike certainly stimulated the great

---

7   'It was always a pleasure to be in the company of Evan Walters, the famous Welsh painter, and to hear him expound his iconoclastic theories. Walters was playfully cynical while his prototype in literature, Caradoc Evans, was bitterly cynical...' Unidentified press cutting c.1951, NLW 18428E, f. 127.

8   I am grateful to Dr. Jasmine Donahaye for this reference.

interest which the English art world showed in his pictures. Press comment on the exhibition was extensive, but *Bydd Myrdd o Ryfeddodau* again bemused the critics. One ventured to describe it as 'a mystical composition', which he thought 'extraordinarily impressive', but most commentators were unwilling or unable to engage with it. The reason is to be found both in the universality of its social criticism and in the particularity of its cultural reference. As a general critique of the Depression it proceeded beyond the depiction of individual hardship presented in other pictures in the exhibition, such as *The Convalescent Collier Tom Rees*, with whom the critics could un-controversially empathise. On the other hand, it was set in the context of a very particular Christian tradition. Walters intended the cultural specificity of the picture as a part of its meaning. He described it as 'among his most Welsh pictures'. It was painted at a time when the expression of Welshness had become a matter of importance to him, probably encouraged by Winifred Coombe Tennant and William Grant Murray, both of whom were formed intellectually in the cultural nationalism of the turn of the century. However, Walters correctly anticipated that, for all its Welshness—or rather, as in the celebrated case of his friend Caradoc Evans, precisely because of its Welshness— the picture would not prove popular with his own people:

> I do not think many Welsh people will approve of this. I consider it to be about my best work, but my friends in Wales will hardly think so, I'm afraid. And yet it is quite true. Here you see the dark group in the hills; below, the grave, with its young white bodies. There is no sign of happiness or resurrection in the singing. All is hopeless, dreary, dark, and it rends the hearts of the spirits as they hear it, so melancholy and mournful are the sounds.
>
> 'Bydd Myrdd o Ryfeddodau' is an expression of my mind when looking at a group of people standing around a grave singing 'Bydd Myrdd', etc. That group of mourners is in the back ground in front of the little chapel. While the boys in the fore ground represent the expression of (and not an illustration) Pan ddelo plant y tonnau/Yn iach o'r cystudd mawr/Oll yn eu gynau gwynion/Ac ar eu newydd wedd/Yn debyg idd ein Harglwydd/Yn dod i'r lan o'r bedd.
>
> The colour of the picture you will notice is rather in the minor key like the music in the hymn. The picture is an expression of the whole thing—the chapel—the graveyard—the people and their voices—the tune and the words—all combined...9

Bydd Myrdd o Ryfeddodau is not a picture illuminated by the hope of the hymn from which it takes its title, and which, certainly in the period, was one of the most

---

9 Evan Walters to Winifred Coombe Tennant, undated, c.1927, private archive.

resonant in a culture in which the hymn remained a potent art form, as the literature frequently reminds us. The hymn has a biblical source, in Revelations:

> And I said unto him, Sir, thou knowest. And he said unto me, These are they which came out of great tribulation, and have washed their robes, and made them white in the blood of the Lamb …
>
> They shall hunger no more, neither thirst any more; neither shall the sun light on them, nor any heat.[10]

The boys in Walters' painting bear the stigmata, though whether Walters says that they die at the hands of capitalism or that their suffering is a manifestation of the fallen condition of humanity in general is unclear. In other words, is their fate the consequence of a particular sin—the sin of covetousness, manifested in exploitation by capitalists—or does it arise from the human sinfulness in which all share, in the Christian view of the world. The picture questions the concept of eternal life in another world as a response to the waste of human life in the terrible social conditions which were developing in parts of Wales, but it is probably unresolved as to the answer. In 1926 Walters presented the uncertainty of revolution. In common with many other people, he pondered the dominant theological question of the period, 'The Question of the Kingdom'. Was it the destiny of humanity patiently to await, in adversity, the Kingdom of God, to expedite its coming through Christian Socialism, or, indeed, to pursue a godless earthly paradise through Communism?

In the literature, the question addressed by Walters, the divisiveness of which was often bound up with class and generational allegiances inside communities and families, was presented by Lewis Jones in a passage which does not loose its power to shock after many re-readings. In *We Live*, the shopkeeper, Evans Cardi attacks his son, Ron, who is now an 'infidel, an unbelieving Communist', with the biblical rhetoric of tribulation. Ron leaves the house. With a razor Evans slashes the throat of his wife, Maggie, and commits suicide.[11]

Among the young people who in real life turned to Communism was Gwenallt. At the 1926 Eisteddfod he won his first chair with his poem 'Y Mynach'. More significantly in the present context, in 1928 (two years after Walters painted *Bydd Myrdd o Ryfeddodau*) he failed to win with 'Y Sant', a work whose unconventionality caused a major row in literary circles. It was 'a heap of filth', according to John Morris-Jones. In a famous passage from *Credaf*, written in 1943 (and therefore from precisely the same temporal perspective as Idris Davies' *Angry Summer*) Gwenallt

10 Revelations 7: 14–16
11 Jones, *Cwmardy and We Live*, 617–9.

looked back on the death of his father and his rejection of Christianity:

> Years later my father's body came home after he had been burnt to death by
> molten metal, and that unnecessarily. When, in the funeral sermon, the
> minister said that it was God's will, I cursed his sermon and his God with all
> the haulier's swear-words that I knew, and when they sang the hymn Bydd
> Myrdd o Ryfeddodau at the graveside, I sang in my heart the Red Flag.[12]

For Gwenallt as for Walters, the hymn was a potent focus for the crisis of faith
which they experienced—the Question of the Kingdom. Walters was probably not
singing 'The Red Flag', but he was certainly asking the same question that was
asked by Gwenallt and by Lewis Jones. Immediately after the completion of *We
Live* Lewis Jones died, committed to the achievement of the Kingdom in human
terms alone, through Communism. In 1939, outwardly at least, he was not troubled
by the uncertainty of revolution. Gwenallt returned to Christianity, of course, but
retained from his early experience a 'hatred for the dehumanising tendencies of
industrial capitalism'. His Nonconformist upbringing provided him with a
language and a reservoir of images with which to express his beliefs. Dorian
Llywelyn Smith has remarked that:

> He does not shrink from a propagandist's application of biblical images to
> present political realities. The modern crisis of Wales is seen in biblical terms,
> familiar biblical terminology used emotively, morality being the common
> ground between religious and political concerns.[13]

The same was true of Walters, six years his senior, and of Archie Griffiths, three
years his junior. All three grew up in the same Christian tradition and in mining
communities only a few miles apart, and quite clearly manifest the same artistic
vocabulary and moral framework.

In 1927, a year after his graduation from the Royal College of Art, Griffiths
remained in London and almost certainly saw Walters' exhibition at the Warren
Gallery, and *Bydd Myrdd o Ryfeddodau*. In the same year his competition piece for
the Prix de Rome was *The Expulsion*, in which the equation between industrial
society and the Fall was explicitly made. Geraint Goodwin described the
background against which the naked Adam and Eve were set as 'a Welsh mining
village, a little cross with its poor jar of daffodils, a shrunken tree, the outworks of
a pit and behind a strange, glowering sky! That the sky was instinct with drama—a

---

12 Gwenallt, 'What I Believe', *Planet* 32 (1976), 3.
13 Dorian Llywelyn, *Sacred Place: Chosen People* (Cardiff: University of Wales Press, 1999), 121.

strange brooding, other-worldliness such as he conveys again and again—was not the point. The judges, we should imagine, were appalled, and Griffiths did not get the prize ...', though he did make the shortlist of four.[14]

On leaving the Royal College, Griffiths' work was shown by William Grant Murray at the Glynn Vivian Gallery. Repeating the pattern of her patronage of Evan Walters, Winifred Coombe Tennant bought *Miners Returning from Work*. To express his thanks, Griffiths gave her the drawing for what was generally regarded as the most impressive picture which he had painted at that time, *Tro yn yr Yrfa* (fig. 2). The painting itself is lost and no photograph survives, but the drawing shows that it depicted a miner's funeral, crossing the mountain between one valley and another. The image would reappear powerfully in the literature, both in the funeral of Si Spraggs in *We Live*,[15] and in 'The Angry Summer':

> All his long and luckless days are over,
> And the broken old body in the plain deal coffin
> Will be deaf to all the birds above the hill,
> The larks that sing and sing in the cloudless sky
> As the men move away in slow black clusters
> Down on the road to the colliery town.[16]

Although transposed from its original context among the common people of rural Wales, the funeral image had a long pedigree in Welsh visual culture. Whether Griffiths made a conscious reference to David Cox's *The Welsh Funeral* is unclear, but there can be little doubt about his intention to make an art historical reference in *Testing a Collier's Lamp*, painted in 1932. He refers to Christ as the Light of the World through the medium of Holman Hunt's picture of the same name, which was among the most familiar art images of the period, reproduced in large numbers to dignify the pious parlour. The familiarity of the image was exploited again, some seven years later, by Caradoc Evans, though to a different end. In *Morgan Bible*, the eponymous hero arrives at night at the chapel house of Salem, the home of Miss Lewis, his intended sexual victim. When she answers his knock on the door, she sees 'a stranger stood thereat with a pack on his back and the light of a bicycle lamp shining on his face. "Light of the World I am not", he announced, "but the spreader of Light"'

Again, Griffiths' *On the Coal Tips* (fig. 1) has strong visual precedents, though they are to be found mainly in the documentary tradition of the wood engraving,

---

[14] Goodwin, 'An Artist of Vision', 79
[15] Jones, *Cwmardy and We Live*, 429–32.
[16] Davies, *Angry Summer*, 31.

rather than in high art. The image of collecting small coal on the tips had been used to make both political points about the exploitation of working people, and moral points about the role of women in society. However, in lino-cut and in oil-painted versions of the subject, Griffiths made different use of the image through a simultaneous biblical reference. The three women collecting small coal on the tips resonate with the three women who, according to the gospel of Saint Mark, visited Christ's tomb the day after the crucifixion and found it empty. Like Walters' *Bydd Myrdd o Ryfeddodau*, the meaning of resurrection in the context of the Depression—the Question of the Kingdom—is the subject matter, and also in a similar way to Walters, the response in the picture is unresolved. The women, who at the end of the day approach their own place of rest, are preoccupied with the tribulations of their existence. The promise of resurrection is remote. Similarly, in a second version of *Miners Returning from Work*, painted in 1931, Griffiths combined the simple realism which characterised his earlier picture with the image of the meeting of Jesus and the disciples on the road to Emmaus. Jesus, the hope of new life, is unrecognised by men driven to introspection by their concern with the day to day difficulties of their existence—their 'tribulation' in the language of Revelations in the King James bible.

The loss of faith, and consequently of hope—a public mood which was reflected personally in Griffiths' own morose introspection—was carried into the most important commission of his career. Through the good offices of William Rothenstein, in 1931 he was given the opportunity to paint a mural at the Working Men's College in Camden Town, London. The crucified Jesus is present at the centre of the everyday life of the mining community—at childbirth and at death underground. However, Griffiths suggests that the participants both in these dramas and in the more mundane affairs of the allotment and recreation, which he also depicts, appear to have lost their awareness of a larger context for their lives.

In *The Communist* (fig. 4), Evan Walters used the simplest possible formal device also to suggest the unseen presence of the Passion. His orator stands with arms outstretched, a crucifixion without a cross. As with Griffiths, his Christian reference was reinforced by an art reference, in this case to Daumier's *Ecce Homo*. Walters entwined Christianity and Marxism, equally cynical, perhaps, about the hope offered by both. He presented an image of pathos as a comment on the impossibility of the situation—if it was not, indeed, a comment on what Dai Smith called 'the absurdity of it all'. Among the most notable Communist orators of the period was Lewis Jones, and it may be that Walters had Jones in mind in this work. However, there is no documentary evidence for this idea, and it must be said that Walters' context is usually the western coalfield, and not the Rhondda of Lewis Jones.

Both in its narrative and in its pictorial structure, Archie Griffiths' work utilised the conventions of medieval painting, and in that it differed from the work of Walters. In *The Communist*, Walters' time frame was unambiguously the present. In the Camden Town mural, and in other works, Griffiths presented simultaneously events separated in real time. His work may also have drawn on that of Diego Rivera. Although his reputation was still largely dependent on work done in his native Mexico after the Marxist revolution, by 1932 Rivera had painted his first murals in San Francisco. Given the sophistication of the art circles in which Griffiths had moved as a student, it seems unlikely that he did not have some sense of what was afoot, though how much of the work he had seen in reproduction is unclear. The left-wing politics of Rivera's work would have provided a sympathetic context for Griffiths' painting, but there is also a less obvious parallel, which is Rivera's use of Christian reference, transmitted through an interaction of Roman Catholicism, native religions and pantheism. Christian iconography is very widespread, but is always mediated by the particular cultures in which it is manifested. The distinct characteristics of the Nonconformist Christian tradition of Griffiths and Walters, as of Gwenallt, are among those things which make their work important, if we remain concerned at all with the idea of cultural particularity. It was the bible which provided the grammar of their thought—but it was the Welsh bible, Nonconformist understandings of it, and the difficulties which arose from those understandings in the Depression in Wales. Given the depth of the penetration of Nonconformist thought into the psyche of the Welsh painters of the period, the presentation of a straightforward Marxist agenda was easier for others. Jack Hastings' mural at the Marx Memorial Library in London has as its central figure a Welsh miner. On his right stand not only Marx but William Morris (who was of Welsh parentage) and Robert Owen of Newtown. Yet Hastings was both English and upper-class. Here the work of Diego Rivera and the polemical art of the political left presents a contrast to, rather than a parallel with what was happening in Wales. Hastings had been an assistant to Rivera in San Francisco in 1930–1. His Welsh miner is an icon of class struggle, constructed pictorially exactly as Rivera constructed the central iconic figures in his own murals. Though based on a real person, he has become superman rather than flesh and blood, and represented a very different vision to that of Walters or Griffiths who, whether in portraits of individuals or in generic portraits, present miners as flawed human beings in the Nonconformist Christian tradition. In Griffiths' work they clearly represent the sombre depression of fallen humanity, probably close to the painter's own depressed self-image. In the work of Walters, the Fall presents itself more often as confusion or absurdity.

However, although these attitudes certainly reflect cultural characteristics which can be identified as particularly Welsh, they cannot be presented as definitively representing the Welsh position. For instance, whether written by Lewis Jones or, from a different perspective, by Lily Tobias, the polemical novel in which a political agenda drives the narrative and shapes the characterisation, also presents itself sufficiently often as not to be marginalized as exceptional. In the visual culture the later work of Vincent Evans seems to be closer to this literature. The relevant work was all made after Evans' return from living in New Zealand in 1932, and most of it comes from the second half of the 1930s and therefore from the period of the publication of the novels of the literary canon.

Evans did not use Christian symbols. Indeed, his lost picture, *The Miners' Federation Meeting Underground*, might be taken as a repost to the mythologising of underground prayer meetings. On the face of it, Evans seems to be working in the Socialist Realist manner though, while Soviet art (alongside that of Rivera) cannot be discounted as an exemplar, his idealisation of the physicality of the miner in works such as *Repairing Main Roadway* of 1936 is more closely related to his sense of Classical art. The colliers who place the heavy roof timber over their heads clearly derive from Atlas. Surviving drawings suggest that the medium for the transmission of the classical tradition to him was Puvis de Chavannes, who worked in France at the end of the nineteenth century. Nevertheless, of the three Swansea-trained painters, Evans was undoubtedly closest to the formal labour movement. Before the Great War, his home town of Ystalyfera was a place of remarkable intellectual activity. *Llais Lafur* was published there and, indeed, Evans drew a few cartoons for the paper. He was a close friend of Jim Griffiths, President of the South Wales Miners' Federation and, as a consequence, the union bought his work. However, his friendship with Griffiths is important in moderating the temptation to see Evans as the Welsh Socialist Realist, in the Soviet sense. Jim Griffiths was a Christian Socialist who retained his allegiance to the Nonconformist tradition, and whose description in *Pages from Memory* of the Nine-Mile Point stay-down strike resonates very strongly with what we know from Geraint Goodwin of Archie Griffiths' lost picture *Preaching in the Mines*:

> The scene at the pit bottom that day remains vivid in my memory. The nine days below had left their mark; the elderly looked weary—the young had grown beards. I was greeted by the 'patriarch' who had opened and closed each day with prayer, and in between had transformed the stay-down strikers into a choir.[17]

Jim Griffiths' description also resonates with the stay-down strike described in *We Live*, where Lewis Jones talks of the 'cathedral', notwithstanding his Communism. Furthermore, he particularly emphasises the Welshness of the events underground

---

[17]   James Griffiths, *Pages from Memory* (London: Dent, 1969), 38.

by describing an Eisteddfod, adjudicated by Big Jim who, we should remember, was also associated with a sense of pre-industrial Welsh identity through history in the opening scene of *Cwmardy*. A late-nineteenth century sense of Welsh national identity is strongly present in the canon of Socialist literature. The fact has been somewhat obscured as a result of the recovery of that literature by historians who were working from a perspective of Labour history informed by the politics of the 1970s. They sought to present the internationalism of the Welsh Socialist tradition as a justification for contemporary anti-Nationalist party politics within Wales. This was a construct of tradition flawed by selective use of the internal evidence of the canonical texts, and by ignoring some material entirely. For instance, until the Great War, *Llais Llafur* persistently conjoined national rhetoric and the rhetoric of the labour movement. Coming from that same intellectual context in Ystalyfera, but working in the 1930s, the novelist Lily Tobias was explicitly and sympathetically engaged in her writing with the question of Welsh Nationalism, from her unusual Jewish perspective. Vincent Evans, the contemporary of Tobias in the town, unquestionably saw his mining imagery in a Welsh national context, as well as in a Socialist context. When offering *Repairing Main Roadway* and *Trimming after Charge* (fig. 5) for sale to the National Museum, he remarked in a letter of 1936 to Cyril Fox, the Director, that 'The subjects are essentially from Welsh inspiration and of Welsh life'.[18]

The title of Evans' most ambitious picture, *A Welsh Family Idyll* (fig. 6), reinforces the point. He probably began work on it in about 1936, and it celebrates the values of the kind of community, at the western edge of the south Wales coalfield, in which he grew up. In *A Welsh Family Idyll* Evans eschewed the clichés of national life, such as the chapel and the choir, and also pre-industrial national symbols. He painted a picture which was thoroughly modern in its period, for all its promotion of timeless values. The main themes were continuity within the extended family and community, and harmony between people and the earth. *A Welsh Family Idyll* is a landmark in twentieth-century Welsh painting, because it marks the high-point, and the terminal point, of the history of attempts to make large, inclusive and definitive artistic statements of national identity. Earlier attempts, such as Christopher Williams' *Wales Awakening*, were limited by their failure to address the industrial society in which most of the Welsh people lived. In expressing the unity of industrial and rural contexts, Evans' picture came close to the only kind of art that could reasonably claim to be inclusively national.

Here we may return to Gwenallt for confirmation of the particularity and coherence of the social, political and national context, which is the source both of the literature and the painting of the period. Although 'Morgannwg' was first

---

18   Vincent Evans to Cyril Fox, 26 June 1936, NMW Artists' Files, Vincent Evans.

published in 1951, it was rooted in the pre-war experience of tensions between what were perceived as contradictory forces:

> Nid oedd y gweithiwr ond llythyren a rhif
>   Yn rhyw fantolen anghyfrifol draw;
> Ni osodai ei ddelw ar lif y metel;
>   Marw oedd cynnyrch ei law:
> Iechyd fin-nos oedd twlc mochyn a gardd
>   A thrin morthwyl a chaib a rhaw.[19]

> Only a letter and a number named the worker
>   On some careless balance sheet there;
> The flow of the metal did not record his image;
>   The product of his hand was dead:
> Pigsty and garden, the hammer and working the pick and shovel
>   Were his end of day salvation.

Gwenallt was in two senses a national poet. Firstly by virtue of his place in national tradition, as presently constructed, and secondly as a poet who wrote about the idea of Wales—that is, for whom the nation was a subject. He repeatedly wrote about Wales as a divided unity. Therefore, on the basis of his Christian iconography, the parallel between him and Walters and Griffiths, may be extended to include Vincent Evans, notwithstanding the absence of Christian reference in that painter's work. Both Gwenallt and Evans, at any rate in his *Welsh Family Idyll*, were concerned with the point at which the rural and the industrial, the old and the new came together. In the minds of both artists the contrasts had a moral dimension as the sacred and the profane, but they were recognised as bound together. The profane was not to be denied (as it was by Christopher Williams and his generation of national artists) because it sent an undesirable image of Welshness to England. In this respect, the enclosedness of the Welsh language may have been a liberating factor for Gwenallt. Neither was the profane simply profane, nor the godly simply godly. Each partook of the other. There was the humanism of the pit (also emphasised by Archie Griffiths) and, as Evan Walters' friend Caradoc Evans had so acidly demonstrated, the Puritanism and hypocrisy of the countryside:

> Y mae rhychwant y Groes yn llawer mwy
> Na'u Piwritaniaeth a'u Sosialaeth hwy,
> Ac y mae lle i ddwrn Karl Marcs yn Ei Eglwys Ef:

---

19 Gwenallt [David James Jones] *Cerddi Gwenallt. Y Casgliad Cyflawn*, ed. Christine James (Llandysul: Gomer, 2001), 143.

Cydfydd fferm a ffwrnais ar ei ystad,
Dyneiddiaeth y pwll glo, duwioldeb y wlad:
Tawe a Thywi, Canaan a Chymru, daear a nef.[20]

The span of the Cross is wider by far
Than their Puritanism and Socialism,
And there is a place for the fist of Karl Marx in His Church:
Farm and furnace live together in His estate,
The humanism of the pit, the godliness of the countryside:
Tawe and Tywi, Canaan and Wales, earth and heaven.

In conclusion, we return to Lewis Jones. The climax of *We Live* comes in a meeting which has been organised to celebrate the return of men from Cwmardy who have fought in the Spanish Civil War. The visual details of the scene, which takes place in the new Workmen's Hall, may simply have been imagined by Lewis Jones, transferred from an experience elsewhere, or constructed from images seen in the Russian and German films which were screened at some Institutes in the 1930s. On the other hand, he may have observed, or perhaps organised, such a scene in the Rhondda:

> Artists belonging to the Party were commissioned to make large canvas paintings of the men who had left Cwmardy for Spain. When these were completed they were fixed on the red plush curtain that backed the stage. Len's wavy hair and big eyes occupied the centre.[21]

Len is the hero who we first encountered as a child, contemplating paradise lost on the mountain with his father. He is not among the men returned from Spain. His wife, Mary, has read a letter from him, written at the front, and then another letter, from a third party, describing his death in action. She leaps onto the stage:

> In a flash she knew that the people had been told that Len was dead and she turned her head to see his portrait stand out among the others with its drapery of black cloth…
>
> Mary looked again at the painting and fancied she saw the lips form into a smile and the sad eyes soften with encouragement.
>
> She stared at it for some moments and the feeling grew on her that Len was saying: 'Go, Mary. Follow the people, they are your hope and strength'.[22]

---

[20] 'Sir Forgannwg a Sir Gaerfyrddin', *Cerddi Gwenallt*, 152.
[21] Jones, *Cwmardy and We Live*, 871.
[22] Jones, *Cwmardy and We Live*, 879.

Like Evan Walters' pietà, *The Dead Miner*, this is a transferred Christian image, but one presented by a Communist of deep conviction. Lewis Jones employs the imagery of resurrection—of the martyr's injunction from beyond the tomb. Furthermore, it is conveyed through the medium of transferred Christian rhetoric. The transfer is not direct, not even simply biblical, for the resonance of the hymn and the pulpit is also clear, but Jones' choice of Mary as the name of Len's wife suggests the ultimate source. From the empty tomb, it was Mary Magdalene who carried the message that the promise of life after death was fulfilled. The angel said to Mary 'Go quickly and tell his disciples that he is risen from the dead'. Jones says: 'Go Mary ...' The words of Jesus himself, when he found his first disciples, were 'Follow me, and I will make you fishers of men'. Jones says: 'Follow the people ...' In the best Nonconformist tradition, Lewis Jones concludes *We Live* with a hymn:

> Though cowards flinch and traitors sneer
> We'll keep the red flag flying here.

That Golden Decade –
David Jones, Ceri Richards, Merlyn Evans and Josef Herman: the four Gold Medal winners at the Welsh National Eisteddfod in the 1960s

Tony Curtis

I N the 1960s the National Eisteddfod awarded four Gold Medals for Visual Art: none was the subject of open competition, instead each was 'Awarded in Honour'. They were: 1961 at Rhosllannerchrugog to Ceri Richards; 1962 at Llanelli to Josef Herman; 1964 at Swansea to David Jones and in 1966 at Aberavon to Merlyn Evans.

Since its institution at the 1951 Llanrwst Eisteddfod, there had been just six recipients of the medal, Brenda Chamberlain (twice), Charles Burton, D. C. Roberts, John Elwyn, George Chapman and Denys Short. All these had been the reward for submitted work. There was a problem after the first award, however, as the original medal itself was given to Brenda Chamberlain, not the intended replica, and it was not until the Rhyl eisteddfod of 1953 that the local committee secured the return of the original.

The organising principle throughout the 1950s had been that 'artists of standing' of 'high achievement' be invited to exhibit at the National Eisteddfod, with the intention of building on the steady efforts of the nascent Arts Council, CASW, and notable individuals to promote an appreciation of artists born in Wales and presently working in Wales. From the Cardiff exhibition of 1913, through the 1932 National Library 'Artists of Wales' exhibition, to the 1949 'Thirty Welsh Painters of Today', which went on to be shown in London, this impulse to attract both popular and informed critical attention was a significant factor in educating the wider public and encouraging confidence in emerging artists.

The 1960s, however, saw the Eisteddfod, as it were, taking stock and recognising past achievements; but no medal was offered or awarded at Cardiff in 1960, at Llandudno in 1963, at Newtown in 1965 or for another nineteen years after Aberavon and the medal received by Merlyn Evans.

Because the workings of each annual eisteddfod are complicated and involve always a national committee and a strong local input, it is quite difficult to determine what the strategy, if any, and what the specific circumstances might be in the administration and award of the visual arts prize or medal in any given year. Certainly in the 1960s the view was that the Gold Medal should be presented rather in the manner of a lifetime achievement award: all four recipients were established artists with solid British and even international reputations. Ceri Richards was fifty-eight, Josef Herman fifty-one, David Jones was seventy-nine and Merlyn Evans fifty-six. Though the first year of the decade saw no medal offered at Cardiff, there was an off-site exhibition at Sophia Gardens involving Ceri Richards and based on a theme of Music and Poetry, including works inspired by Dylan Thomas and Vernon Watkins.

It seems remarkable that in the 1950s Augustus John had not been so honoured and that, subsequently, Sir Kyffin Williams did not receive such an accolade, nor did Ernest Zobole, Peter Prendergast or Will Roberts. Augustus John died in 1961 and perhaps the Eisteddfod felt that after a decade of the Gold Medal competition some retrospective honouring was more appropriate. During the nineteen years in which no award was presented several very notable artists exhibited and were awarded prizes at eisteddfodau, though none was deemed worthy of the medal. In Cricieth in 1976, for example, Peter Prendergast won first prize, a substantial award of money, but no medal. In some of these medal-less years one reward offered was that the Arts Council supported purchases of selected works, but it could be argued that this fell short of acknowledging parity between the visual arts and the well-established literary Crown and Chair.

It may well be that the decision to establish a more formal award in 1951 was taken as a result of the 1950 Caerphilly Eisteddfod. Charles Burton has recently shared with me some memories of that event in which he participated as a student. The exhibition was organised by Esther Grainger, that visionary and energetic worker in the visual arts who had been involved in the Settlements movement for arts in the community in the Valleys. The Caerphilly exhibition featured the work of many of the leading Welsh painters including Ceri Richards, Alfred Janes, Cedric Morris, Heinz Koppel and Merlyn Evans. Clearly, a taking of stock, a declaration of faith, was being made. There was often an emphasis on those visual artists who were concerned with their *genius loci*, their *bro*, their country and their people. Art was seen as an important contributor to the sense of Wales and the

Welsh as a distinct entity.

However, the Eisteddfod in the 1960s may be seen as focussing on a more internationalist agenda and aesthetic. None of the four recipients in the 1960s was resident in Wales, or had been in residence in Wales for many years. Ceri Richards had left Dunvant for the Royal College and a number of teaching positions, returning to Cardiff in the war to teach at the School of Art and do his fire-watching duties and some tin plate industry war artist work; also to make regular visits to his family and a cottage close to that of Vernon Watkins on the Gower. Josef Herman was resident in Ystradgynlais between 1944 and 1955, eventually succumbing to the cold and damp, as well as personal pressures, and moving on to live in Suffolk and London. David Jones had spent formative years in Capel-y-Ffin with Eric Gill and the lay brotherhood and periods on Caldey Island, but he later became agoraphobic and rarely emerged from his 'bunker' in Harrow, north London in his later years. Merlyn Evans was born in Llandaff, Cardiff in 1910, but his chemist father had moved his family to Glasgow when Merlyn was three years old. After the war he returned from South Africa to a teaching post in London and because of his wife's professional career as a pianist.

In terms of his art and its subject-matter, Richards was, of course, greatly engaged by the work of Dylan Thomas and Vernon Watkins; those poems and the landscape of the Gower were to inform much of his major work. Josef Herman in his work from Ystradgynlais and his presence in that mining community had made a valuable contribution to the recording of an industry and its social context, as well as providing direct stimulus to other artists in Wales, especially his friend Will Roberts. David Jones was the most notable poet-painter since William Blake: his engagement with the idea of Wales, if not the actual country and its people, informed much of his poetry, criticism and painting.

By 1961 Ceri Richards (1903–1971) was well-established as a painter and generally as a figure in the art world in Britain. He would be featured in the Venice Biennale the following year, and win the Einaudi Prize there (see fig. 7). That work would go on to tour to Madrid, Barcelona, Brussels, Munich, Berlin, Delft and Paris. He had been greatly influenced by the work of Dylan Thomas, had decorated the memorial event for Dylan in London in 1954 with his backdrops and had continued to draw inspiration from the poetry. In 1966 the magisterial portfolio of lithographs from the Curwen Press would commemorate Dylan.

In 1960 Richards had been awarded a C.B.E. He had had a solo exhibition in the Sophia Gardens Pavilion that August too. From 1958–65 he acted as a Trustee of the Tate Gallery. He was a member of the Art Committee at the National Museum of Wales from 1958–62 and a member of the Welsh Arts Council from 1952–62. In the same year that he was awarded his Gold Medal, Richards was also awarded an Hon. D.Litt. from the University of Wales and was made an Honorary

Fellow of the Royal College of Art. Honours and acclaim were being bestowed in abundance on an artist whose roots in Wales and commitment to the country were evident; the Gold Medal was, therefore, a safe, unquestionable gesture, both to the artist and from the Eisteddfod as a token of its awareness of contemporary art.

Richards was an artist who worked on themes and concerns in sequence; these were not necessarily linear, though: the Welsh poetry-inspired work began during the war and continued to the last day of his life—from the Dylan Thomas 'Force that through the green fuse' work for *Poetry London* in 1945, published in 1947 to the final lithographs for the Roberto Sanesi's *Viaggio Verso il Nord* portfolio, published posthumously in 1972 and including work in memory of Vernon Watkins. The Sabine theme would occupy him for two years after the war, but would re-appear in the later pianist works and evolve into the Rape of Europa pieces of the late Sixties in his final few years.

And so it was with the influence of music. Richards had been 'put to the piano' as a boy, had grown up in a musical household—his father conducted choirs in Dunvant—and was concerned with music and musical instruments as objects to be painted throughout his life. For nearly thirty years he painted women at the piano, playing the violin—his wife Frances and other family members, idealised feminine figures in a domestic, but artistically-charged context: a woman, flowers, the piano, chairs, carpets, ceramics, wall-paper and Sabine theme paintings in the background (see fig. 8).

In the late Fifties and at the time of his Gold Medal award, Ceri Richards had begun his Cathedral Engloutie series of paintings and constructions. This was to be the major achievement of his mature years. He had honoured Beethoven in the 'Hammerklavier' series of lithographs, St. George's Gallery, 1959, and in paintings such at 'Beethoven and St, Cecilia 1', 1953, now at the National Museum of Wales, and he was to return to that composer with the late Prometheus works; but it was to be Debussy and the Prelude *Cathedrale engloutie* that was to inspire the mature work of great originality and courage (see fig. 9). Exploring this theme took Richards back to the work of three-dimensional construction which he had remarkably produced in the mid-1930s.

At a time when British art was at the cusp of and then tumbling into the trans-Atlantic tide of American Abstract Expressionism, Ceri Richards, apparently intuitively and inexorably explored his own version of that expressive abstraction, though with always one foot firmly planted on the shore of the actual, the world as he knew it. The metaphor of the drowned cathedral and its periodic appearances, the chiming of significance under the surface of things, these were at the centre of so much of what his life as an artist had been about. There is an intriguing correspondence between these works and the important 'Black Apple of Gower' of 1952. In that work the mandela to which Jung had been so drawn is contained and then rises out of the Gower—the home-land Richards shared with Dylan Thomas and Vernon Watkins. The inspiration for these works might have been a French composer and a myth located off the coast of Brittany, but the metaphorical force was one with which Richards, Thomas and Watkins could surely relate.

When the National Eisteddfod honoured Ceri Richards it was in one sense echoing the praise resounding from other institutions, but on the other it was signalling a move into the world of challenging contemporary art. Winifred Coombe Tennant had died some five years before, so we have no idea how she would have reacted to this new work, but some ten years before that formidable supporter of Welsh art, writing to Augustus John in response to the Festival of Britain choices for Wales, had been very critical of contemporary artists:

> The Festival of Britain has commissioned work—one picture—from three 'Welsh' artists out of a number whose names came before their selection committee. They have chosen 1) Ceri Richards! 2) Merlyn Evans (to me his pictures represent men and the visible world in terms of ironmongery!!) 3) A Pole now living in Ystradgynlais...Herman or some such name! And these cranks are to go out into the world as representatives of art in Wales!!!! What has David Bell got to say about this![1]

David Bell would surely have applauded the selection of Ceri Richards, and that of Josef Herman, who was awarded the Gold Medal likewise 'in honour' in the following year, 1962.

The 'Pole now living in Ystradgynlais' had reached the Swansea Valley via Glasgow, occupied France, occupied Belgium and his birth-place in anti-semitic Warsaw. From 1944 to 1955 Josef Herman had lived with his Scottish wife Catriona in Ystradgynlais, but had travelled variously to London, Paris and Italy, after the war. The damp would eventually wear him down, together with the still-birth of a baby and his wife's bad health and he moved to Suffolk and then London, where he lived for over forty years. But on July 21st 1968 he could still write, 'After so many years I still feel Wales is my natural home.'[2]

He brought to Wales a keen eye, tutored by the aesthetics of the Belgian Expressionists, especially Constant Permeke, whom he'd known, an abiding empathy with the life of the labouring peoples and a love of the female form. Herman's influence on his contemporaries in Wales and on successive generations is clear. Together with Heinz Koppel, Arthur Giardelli and Martin Bloch, Herman

---

[1]   Winifred Coombe Tennant to Augustus John, quoted in Peter Lord, *The Democratization of Art* (Cardiff: University of Wales Press, 1998), 239.

[2]   Josef Herman, *The Journals*, ed. Nini Herman (London, Peter Halban, 2003), 70.

was one of those incomers who affected change in the visual arts in Wales to a degree that the Davies sisters of Llandinam had hoped for by their sponsorship of Belgian refugee artists during the 1914–18 war. Herman's friendship with and influence on Will Roberts of Neath was indeed profound. It is possible to trace that influence through to more recent painters—Colin Jones, Jack Crabtree, Mike Davies and James Donovan in particular.

That evening in 1944 when Josef Herman saw the miners coming home from a shift over the bridge at Ystradgynlais has become legendary, a road to Damascus moment which meant that in that universal image of the working men, 'Joe Bach' would see that there was indeed a common humanity, both in labour and suffering and pleasure (see fig. 10):

> John Russell-Taylor once shrewdly observed the miner's cap is for me what the halo was for the medieval artist: a symbol. I want the whole figure to have the same symbolic sense.[3]

It is notoriously difficult to date many of his works—he drew each day from five in the morning until breakfast time, from Wales and Suffolk to London—often returning to his elemental figures—the worker at rest, the labourer in the fields, the fisherman-sailor, the female nude, the elemental tree. Of his Mexican figures he said: 'I am fully aware that the Mexican Indians did not replace my love of painting the miners. The costume differs.'[4]

Herman had admired the political mural painters Orozco, Rivera and Siqueros,[5] and, though he was never an overtly political artist, his commitment to the working classes, the oppressed, the persecuted was clear. It was in 1942 in Glasgow that he learnt from the Red Cross that his entire family, his entire community, had been herded into Nazi gas vans in Poland. He was never to return to the country of his birth. In the early years of the war, in Glasgow, declared unfit for the Polish army in exile, Herman drew and painted his memories of that family and ghettoised community. The Holocaust victims are resurrected in form and spirit by the working figures of his subjects throughout the rest of his long working life. As another visitor to south Wales, Paul Robeson had observed, the lot of the mining communities was akin to that of other oppressed peoples—the American Negro, the ghettoized Jew.

By 1962 Josef Herman had a firm reputation: he had painted a large mural-size

---

3   Ibid., 63–4.
4   Ibid., 61.
5   See Josef Herman, *Related Twilights: Notes from an Artist's Diary* ed. Tony Curtis (Bridgend: Seren, 2002), 129.

work of miners for the Festival of Britain, now in the Glynn Vivian Gallery; he had regular shows with Roland, Browse and Delbanco in London, as well as retrospectives in 1953 and 1954 at Wakefield City Gallery and at the Whitechapel. Work had been shown in Europe and Australia.

After the Holocaust, after the trials of his personal life, it was his art to which he would cling. It was his art's adherence to truth, to life in all its complexity for which he would work:

> Art should be of the same seriousness as religions were in the past and as philosophy has been recently. There can be no humanist art without the recognition of this fact. Yet our humanists and rationalists are frightened of dark images! They still think that a face, for example, lighted up by the sun is truer than a face radiant with human spirit. It is an age-old misunderstanding. Rembrandt was told that he paints figures as though they were in half-lit cellars. They look to comforting signs, those humanists![6]

David Jones (1885–1974) was both artist and poet. His Gold Medal was awarded in 1964. He had received a C.B.E. in 1955. The Welsh Arts Council had already awarded a book prize, in 1960, for *Epoch and Artist* (dedicated to Saunders Lewis, incidentally),[7] and that same year he received an Hon. D.Litt. from the University of Wales. In 1961 he had become a Fellow of the Royal Society of Literature.

In 1964 there were two other events of great importance for David Jones: first, his friend and sponsor Helen Sutherland died, leaving him a considerable sum— £6,000—in her will; second, he moved to Monksdene Residential Hotel in Harrow, an indication that his health, both mental and physical, was still poor. In fact, he would fall six years later and be moved to a nursing home called Calvary. As early as 1934 David Jones had sent work to be shown at the National Eisteddfod: four paintings—*Gunman's Field, Violin and Flowers, Portrait of Prudence* and *King's Cup*. There are watercolours and wood engravings of Caldey Island, as well as a fine memory of his time at Capel-y-Ffin (see fig. 11). Jones's mode of working, though, seems to have been as much dictated by his living circumstances as his subject-matter:

> I've almost forgotten trying to paint in oils. I never did much, as you know, and always preferred doing what I wanted to do in watercolours. But I wish I'd done more oils than I have. But somehow, the other medium has seemed to suit

6　Ibid., p. 33.
7　David Jones, *Epoch and Artist* (London, Faber, 1959).

me and then when I took to writing and also living mainly in one room watercolour...seemed more my thing.[8]

It could be argued that his reputation as an artist has been affected by this lack of oil painting.

Still, we have many magnificent, individualistic watercolours and mixed media works. Consider the 'Capel-y-ffin' image (fig. 11): with its curving, welcoming hills, its symmetry, its ordered trees and horses, it was a clear expression of the healing powers of the Welsh landscape. Jones, war-weary and shocked, needed such a land in which to re-discover and re-invent himself. Jeremy Hooker has described him:

> At Capel, in love
> with the shape of things:
>
> Dai, in his army greatcoat,
> framed in a window, engraving.
> Or walking with his friend
> to unblock the stream
> and free the waters.[9]

Wales in fact, and the Wales of his imagination, was where he located himself: where, like Jeremy Hooker, he was 'a hunter of forms'. Jones characterised himself as a 'carpenter of songs' in the manner of 'the bards of an earlier Wales'.[10] The landscape of Wales was, essentially, the body of the Sleeping Lord himself; a figure the return of whom the Welsh themselves await.

The Swansea National Eisteddfod was recognising the significance of a man who, though he lived and worked in Wales for but a short period, always felt Welsh, and passionately wanted to be recognised as Welsh. Though he was to publish *The Tribune's Visitation* in 1969 and though his art would continue to be exhibited up to and beyond his death, David Jones's best writing and art was already completed by 1964. He said, in 1962, 'I doubt, personally, whether I, myself, shall ever do any half as good as I used to do in the 1930s, as far as painting is concerned.' [11]

---

8   David Jones, in a letter of 1960, quoted in Jonathan Miles and Derek Shiel, *David Jones the Maker Unmade* (Bridgend: Seren Books, 1995).

9   Jeremy Hooker, 'That trees are men walking', *Our Lady of Europe* (1997), collected in *The Cut of the Light: Poems 1965-2005* (London: Enitharmon, 2006), 293.

10 Jones, *Epoch and Artist*, p. 29.

11 David Jones, 1962, quoted in David Alston et al, *A Map of the Artist's Mind* (Cardiff: National Museums and Galleries of Wales, 1995), 46.

Although he later developed calligraphic pieces which wove Welsh, Latin and English words, his works specifically about Wales and its landscape had been achieved in the early twenties when he had joined Eric Gill's community of lay Dominicans at Capel-y-Ffin, and during several periods which he spent with the monks on Caldey Island, where important, formative experiments with seascape painting—movement, perspective and light effects—took place. Having said that, it is clear that both the imagined and remembered Welsh landscape continued to inform his later work. He said as much in his talk for the Welsh Home Service of the BBC in 1954:

> As Sir Ifor Williams tells us, the bards of an earlier Wales referred to themselves as 'carpenters of song'. Carpentry suggests a fitting together and as you know the English word 'artist' means, at root, someone concerned with a fitting of some sort. Well, it would seem to me that round about 1924–26 I was at last understanding something of the nature of the particular 'carpentry' which most sorted with my inclinations and limitations…It was at this propitious time that circumstances occasioned my living in Nant Honddu, there to feel the impact of the strong hill-rhythms and the bright counter-rhythms of the *afonydd dyfroedd* which make so much of Wales such a 'plurabelle' and there was also the rhythm of the Ninth Wave breaking on the *morlan* in Penfro.[12]

Jones delights in using the Welsh place-names and in characterising himself as a maker, a craftsman, in both words and paint. In both mediums he sees his task as that of the skilled tradesman seeking to capture the rhythms of life, the landscape and faith in each medium. His poems and prose-poems are rhythm-ed rather than rhymed; so it is with his art. The paintings shimmer and resonate, their surface seeming to be constantly in motion, quickened by life, unsettled, transitory as his faith instructed him that all life must necessarily be a journey.

The association with Wales, the land of his fathers and grandfathers, was felt in his blood, but also thought through in his mind. He delighted in characterising himself as a bard. The bard, the seer, the poet of his community was a role Jones saw threatened in the twentieth century:

> It is urgently necessary to remember that, in the present phase of our civilization, the 'artist' as such is no longer an integral part of a living culture; he has to swim against the tide. This is a reversal of his natural role. It means at bottom that his activity is as alien to materialistic mass-civilization as is the

---

[12]   David Jones, 'Autobiographical Talk', *Epoch and Artist*, 30.

activity of the ministers of sacramental religion. It is hardly possible to exaggerate the importance of this situation in regard to 'art' today in contrast with the arts of the great cultures.[13]

For David Jones, like the poet Vernon Watkins, whom he knew, the work of the artist was to dissolve the distinctions of the temporal, to work within the vision of a timeless seam of human experience, circular, repeating the essentials: as Eliot said, 'The still point of the turning world'. The London-born Jones's projection of himself as a Welshman was a vital strategy in this world view.

> ...the survival of something which has an unbroken tradition in this island since the end of the sixth century, and which embodies deposits far older still, cannot be regarded as a matter of indifference by any person claiming to care for the things of this island. It is by no means a matter for the Welsh only, but concerns all, because the complex and involved heritage of Britain is a shared inheritance which can, in very devious ways, enrich us all.

He ends that letter 'Welsh Wales', written to *The Times* from his 'dug-out' in Harrow-on-the-Hill in June 1958, by referring to a photograph in that newspaper a few days before: a photograph -

> ...showing the whitening of houses for the coming Eisteddfod in the industrial South, gave one that same sudden range back into lost history; for the early literature so often recalls the gleaming whiteness of the homesteads of tribal Wales, the lime-washed halls of the chief men, the bright-white places of defence, and the glistening white of the little churches. At first glance the photograph of the whitened streets in modern Ebbw Vale seemed prosaic enough; then it became illuminated from this long past. Again, I would thank you.

David Jones, Dai Greatcoat, the man who signed many works and letters 'Dafydd Jones', is living off every available scrap of Welshness; he sustains his identity at every opportunity; he is fighting for his cause by means of letters to *The Times*.

As a young boy growing up in Brockley on the outskirts of London, Jones had drawn 'imaginary Welshmen on hillsides with wolf-hounds'.[14] He learned more about the enforced Anglicisation of his father, the move from Clwyd to London to better oneself, and so David Jones committed himself fully to the task of re-aligning himself with Wales and things Welsh. He enlisted in the London

---

13   Ibid., 'A note on Mr Berenson's Views', 274.
14   See Jonathan Miles, *Eric Gill & David Jones at Capel-y-Ffin* (Bridgend: Seren Books, 1992), 21.

Battalion of the Royal Welsh Fusiliers and was wounded in the assault on Mametz Wood. His remarkable prose-poem *In Parenthesis* weaves together the immediate horrors of the Western Front and historical wars, London voices and Welsh voices. In fact, Jones made *sense* out of those experiences by seeing them as a timeless re-enactment of men in war. As Jeremy Hooker has observed: 'no modern vision of the whole could carry conviction that does not have at its heart, as his does, an experience of maiming and brokenness.'[15]

We now have the useful Seren Books collection of his war-time drawings, poignant and whimsical sketches from the trenches and other deployments in the almost four years he spent on active duty.[16] It was on the Western Front that his epiphany took place. One day he glimpsed through a barn door the candle-lit celebration of the Latin Mass by a priest and a group of soldiers. Framed in the light, that scene had a profound effect on David Jones and it was an image which powered his imagination and directed his spiritual search to the Catholic Church after the war. His move to Wales and the closed community of lay brethren led by Eric Gill was a consequence of that revelation in war-time France, as was his 'desire to uncover a valid sign...Something has to be made by us before it can become for us his sign who made us...No artefacture no Christian religion.'[17]

In 1924 David Jones became engaged to Gill's daughter Petra ('The Bride') and became a Postulant in the Craft Guild of St. Joseph and St. Dominic. He had chosen an identity which was Welsh and Catholic. It was in Wales that Jones developed skills as an artist and carver of wood. It was here that the imagery which would sustain him throughout the rest of his life as an artist and writer would be focussed. But as Eric Gill said, 'Though in one place he may find more inspiration than another, it is not places that concern him. What concerns him is the universal thing showing through the particular thing, and as a painter it is this showing through that he endeavours to capture.'[18] Wales as a place became Wales as an idea, a commitment to a notion of that place and what Jones wished it into being for his particular needs. He characterises himself as a bard:

> For artists depend on the immediate and the contractual and their apperception must have a 'now-ness' about it. But, in our present megalopolitan technocracy the artist must still remain a 'rememberer' (part of the official bardic function in earlier phase of society)...My view is that all artists, whether they know it or

---

[15] Jeremy Hooker, ' "Gathering all in": an essay on the art of David Jones' in *Modern Painters*, (Winter, 1995), 62-4.

[16] See Anthony Hyne ed., *David Jones: a fusilier at the Front* (Bridgend: Seren Books, 1995).

[17] David Jones, 'Preface', *Anathemata* (London: Faber, 1952), 31.

[18] Eric Gill, *Artwork*, 23 (1930), 17.

not, whether they would repudiate the notion or not, are in fact 'showers forth' of things which tend to be impoverished, or misconceived, or altogether lost or wilfully set aside in the preoccupations of our present intense technological phase, but which nonetheless belong to man.[19]

Manawydan's Glass Door, from 1931, owned by Arthur Giardelli, enacts in a south coast house at Portslade, near Brighton, the idea of the Mabinogi myth. If the door is opened then all manner of best forgotten things, events people, will emerge. There is a magic realist quality to this piece. The view is out over the Channel to the French coast and memories of the War Jones had fought in. The warriors in *The Mabinogion* open the door to reveal 'all the evils they had ever sustained…as if all had happened in that very spot…and because of their perturbation they could not rest.' Those things did emerge for Jones, in fact they *merged* for Jones, in the sense that his own experiences as a soldier were those of soldiers all through time; in the sense that he was committed as an artist and as a Catholic to the belief that things signified more than themselves: just as, of course, art did.

> But properly speaking and at the root of the matter, Ars knows only a 'sacred' activity. I believe this must be so once we grant that the notion of 'sign' cannot be separated from this activity of art. Why, granted the sign-making nature of man's art must those signs be 'sacred'? Is sacredness implicit in 'sign'? I think it to be so…[20]

The arts were faith manifested. David Jones was an artist who signified through his art—his belief in the doctrines of his church and his identification of himself as a Welshman. As Jeremy Hooker has said, 'It is a style which aims, by analogy with the action of the Mass, to preserve the identity of being and thing in the act of transubstantiation.'[21]

The Gold Medal in 1964 must have been especially pleasing. However, David Jones was not well enough to attend the ceremony himself, but his friend Vernon Watkins wrote a tribute in the catalogue: 'Wales is today honouring an artist who has already honoured her.' His vision was 'a religious vision projecting a symbolic art, and through this art, whether in literature, painting or drawing, shines his love of man and of all that is precious to him, and a particular love of Wales and these

---

[19] David Jones, *The Dying Gaul and other writings*, ed. Harman Grisewood (London: Faber, 1978), 17

[20] Jones, *Epoch and Artist*, 157.

[21] Hooker, 'Gathering All In', *Modern Painters*, (Winter 1995).

islands drawn from the roots of earliest customs and ways of living.'[22]

Merlyn Oliver Evans (1910–1973), the fourth and final recipient of the eisteddfod medal in the 1960s, is the odd man out, in many respects, and his life and work are far less familiar than those of the other three artists. He was born in Llandaff, Cardiff, to Welsh parents. His father was an analytical chemist who worked for a paper manufacturer. His work took him to Scotland and the family moved to Glasgow when Merlyn was three. He was educated there and went to Glasgow School of Art in 1927. In 1931 he won a Haldane Travelling Scholarship and visited France, Germany, Denmark and Sweden. He witnessed the early activities of the Nazi Party in Berlin and his account of that time reads like a passage from an Isherwood novel. 'Berlin was lecherous and poverty-ridden. Crowds of half starved, ill dressed, ugly women roamed the streets at night. They looked tired, hopeless and aimless.'[23]

That sense of social disintegration, despair and gathering violence was also present in Depression-era Glasgow and Evans said, 'Conventional painting of any kind seemed inappropriate in the world in which I lived.' The 1938 painting *Distressed Area* represents many of Evans's aesthetic ideas and political concerns. He wrote a commentary on it which is explicit in its references and intentions:

An old vulture hovers over the stage and there are flecks of blood issuing from the disintegrating pustules on his bald head. He is the Carrion King. Below him groups of woodpeckers attack the ice-smooth sides of pyramids. The sky burns like a furnace, and in the background the white-hot embers of a dying cactus arrange themselves like a dying Roman gladiator wrapped in the mandibles of a giant crustacean. On the left in a gesture of supplication a ferocious Oedipus turns to the implacable beast of prey. On the right, with a cynical Parody of Lot and his wife, a mining family, in attitudes of incredible depravity, are petrified like remote fossils of lapis and emerald. At their feet are fetishes that fill us with lust and longing. They litter the floor of the stage and beckon with a sinister compulsion.[24]

The painter, clearly, was at pains to communicate his message to the audience. This period was a particularly dark and bleak one for Evans: the social and political ugliness he had observed in Berlin had manifested itself as Fascism; the year before

---

22 Vernon Watkins, quoted in Keith Alldritt, *David Jones Writer and Artist* (London: Constable, 2003), 169.

23 Merlyn Evans quoted in David Fraser Jenkins, 'Background: Merlyn Evans 1956', *The Political Paintings of Merlyn Evans*, (London: Tate Gallery, 1985).

24 Merlyn Evans, *Daily News*, Durban, 15th August, 1938, quoted in *The Political Paintings of Merlyn Evans*.

he had faced the personal grief of the tragic suicide of his mother who'd been suffering from cancer of the mouth. The world was plunging towards another war. He had left England for a teaching post in South Africa, but the war would be a global one, as everyone knew. He would be heavily involved in that war, enlisting in the South African Army in 1942 and fighting in north Africa and Italy. In 1945 he visited Rome and met Georgio di Chirico whose portrait he drew. He also witnessed the hanging of Mussolini from a lamp-post. The artist who'd sought out and visited the studios of Mondrian, Kandinsky, Ernst and Hayter and who had taught with Moholy-Nagy in London, was, with Ceri Richards, the most informed of artists from Wales; he was knowledgeable of, and engaged with, modernist work. In common with Richards, Merlyn Evans was interested in and peripherally engaged with the surrealists in Britain, but, like Richards, he was never fully committed to a surrealist manifesto or agenda. He later wrote: 'I was invited to show at the 1936 Surrealist Exhibition and attended numerous meetings at the home of Roland Penrose, where Herbert Read presided and Humphrey Jennings introduced Courbet and social realism, and read the obiter dicta of Radek the Stalin art dictator...I refused to be implicated politically, and left.'[25]

For Merlyn Evans and the other painters works in three dimensions had a role to play too; in particular, Henry Moore is an important figure in this respect. Moore was known to Richards and Evans: they had exhibited together in the 1936 Surrealist Exhibition. Richards's 1943 'The Sculptor's Landscape (Homage to Henry Moore)' reminds us of that, as does Moore's clearly expressed admiration for the work of Ceri Richards.[26] Merlyn Evans drew portraits of Moore and of Hepworth and Bernard Leach. Richards's wooden constructions of the Thirties were a notable contribution to the Surrealist cause and Evans, too, carved in plaster and alabaster in the 1930s. The international fame of Moore surely legitimised work by his contemporaries. Ceri Richards depicted himself in terms of a career as a sculptor, David Jones painted and carved religious pieces while at Capel-y-Ffin. and Josef Herman, befriended by the elderly Jacob Epstein when he went from Ystradgynlais to London, was encouraged to appreciate and collect carvings from Africa. In the year after his death in 2000 a dedicated Christie's sale of Herman's collection of small carvings, one of the finest in private hands, was held in Amsterdam. Merlyn Evans was a skilled craftsman and if he had lived longer would surely have added to the notable public commissions of his three dimensional

---

25 Ibid., 'Background: Merlyn Evans 1956'.
26 See Henry Moore, *Homage to Ceri Richards 1903–1971* (London: Fischer Fine Art, 1972): 'His drawing is so assured, so full of energy and virility...I have a special liking for Ceri's reliefs—works he did around 1932/3—I find them full of invention, and wit and originality.'

work—a large metal screen at Tower Hamlet Comprehensive School and a brick relief for the Crown Building in Carmarthen. How many of us acknowledge that work?

Evans was committed to the cause of humanity and painfully aware of the suffering of his age; he was no card-carrier, though. He stands as a determined individualistic painter and thinker. He wrote: 'I believe that the artist should be committed to his art only, and should avoid allegiances to groups, isms, politics, religion or science and that he should at least endeavour to be free from external control as fare as the times permit.'[27]

His work often has the staged quality of Dali or Di Chirico and, like them, his stages are peopled by human beings, or 'mechanomorphic' forms, as Evans would describe them.[28] His images address the angst of the mid-twentieth century and, though he was open to influences—from Wyndham Lewis and Ernst to Rothko, Barnett Newman, Robert Motherwell and Ad Reinhart, whom he met in New York in the 1967—he was, essentially, his own man.

The Refugees, a painting from 1946 now in the National Museum of Wales (see fig. 12), was described as 'a uniquely twentieth-century ikon' by Bryan Robertson.[29] Certainly, Merlyn Evans's work represents a counter-balance to the Neo-Romantics of the period. While Piper, Craxton, John Elwyn and Minton celebrated the abiding qualities of the British landscape under the Fascist threat of invasion and bombing, Merlyn Evans was closer to the Michael Ayrton of 'Skull Vision' (1943) and 'The Temptation of St Anthony' (1942–43). He confronts more directly the conflicts and horrors of modern life, as Ceri Richards tried to do in his 'Blossoms' (1940) and 'Falling Forms' (1944) and Paul Nash in 'Totes Meer' (1941). His roots, it may be argued, were in the work of Wyndham Lewis some twenty years before and the Vorticist paintings before and during the First World War—the geometric urban scenes and machine workings of men within that context. His colours, however, were strongly affected by the move to Africa in 1938:

> I arrived in South Africa in the hot season, and settled in Durban in Natal. Violent colour burst on the senses with a harsh, raucous trumpeting. The light was merciless, continuous and blinding. Vermillion and viridian trees and bushes, magenta hedges, a monotonous blue sky that was always the same produced to my eyes hideous dissonances of colour which fascinated me, as in England I would admire the copper glow as the sky would light up in the

---

27 Evans, quoted in Jenkins, *Political Paintings of Merlyn Evans*.

28 Merlyn Evans, quoted in Bryan Robertson, 'The Abstract Images of Merlyn Evans', in *The Graphic Work of Merlyn Evans* (London: Victoria and Albert Museum, 1972).

29 Ibid.

evening with a blast furnace.³⁰

Evans recognised that in order to respond honestly and effectively to the chaotic world around him he would have to take risks, would have to move away from the naturalistic depiction of people and places. The staged, theatrical qualities of much of his painting are those which characterise polemical art, but Evans was simply and directly responding to the dangers and ugliness of the world he lived in—from the slums of Glasgow to the ravaged cities of war-time Europe. The grotesque players in his 'The Chess Players', 1940, were sitting on a board which shaped the destiny of real men and women. The men who worked the machines were becoming machine-like, unfeeling, robotic, destructive. These images still strike us as modern, radical, provocative. The fact is, though, even twenty years after that work the reception such *avant garde* art would receive in the country of the artist's birth could be less than welcoming, as the letter to Augustus John from Winifred Coombe Tennant quoted above indicates.

These four figures—Ceri Richards, Josef Herman, David Jones and Merlyn Evans—are so embedded in our sense of what constitutes the finest in art in Wales that it may now be difficult to appreciate how radical must have appeared their work in the middle decades of the twentieth century. The National Eisteddfod in the 1960s had indeed used the award of the Gold Medal in a radical way, and must be applauded for so doing: the four artists thus honoured were in their different ways producing some of the most radical, challenging art of their time. The signal their win gave to their contemporaries, as well as the new generation of artists in Wales, must have had profound consequences. And we certainly have reason to be grateful for that. From here, it seems that the National Eisteddfod at that time made a serious contribution to the debate concerning contemporary art in Wales.

But what are we to make of that nineteen year hiatus—from Merlyn Evans in 1966 to Alistair Crawford in 1985? Was it caused by a lack of faith in contemporary art? Was it inefficiency? Was it felt that there were simply no artists worthy of honour for nearly two decades? Whatever the cause, from the perspective of this new century, with the visual arts in Wales flourishing, both commercially and in public exhibitions from Artes Mundi to the Venice Biennale, it is clear that the National Eisteddfod in the 1960s marked a significantly high point in the public recognition of art in Wales.

---

30 Evans, quoted in Jenkins, *The Political Paintings of Merlyn Evans.*

'An inorganic life of things': notes on abstraction and nature

Jeff Wallace

I

'T HE idea of nature', wrote Raymond Williams, 'contains, though often unnoticed, an extraordinary amount of human history'.[1] This now-familiar historicization of nature on Williams's part proceeds by identifying the problematic coalescence of two 'singular abstractions': first, 'nature' itself, where the 'multiplicity of things, and of living processes' becomes 'mentally organized around a single essence or principle'; and second, 'the abstraction of Man', as in important ways distinct from nature. Once established, the 'great abstractions of Man and Nature' proceed, as Williams sees it, to obstruct and delimit our ability to think about the complex interactions between the social and the natural. This is all the more significant at a moment in the history of late capitalism when what is at stake may, in effect, be the saving of human life on earth. It would be ironic, Williams observes, if 'one of the last forms of separation between abstracted Man and abstracted Nature is an intellectual separation between economics and ecology'.[2]

This historicization of nature differs, then, from an earlier history of ideas approach as exemplified by R.G. Collingwood's *The Idea of Nature* (1945); it is not, strictly, about cosmology. Rather, in the distinctive manner of his cultural materialism, Williams is only concerned with cosmological world-views insofar as these are expressed in the gradual accretions of linguistic change, a project typified by *Keywords: A vocabulary of culture and society* (1976; revised and expanded, 1983), in which the semantic evolution of concepts is always a social and political as well as

---

[1] Raymond Williams, 'Ideas of Nature', in *Problems in Materialism and Culture* (London: Verso, 1980), p. 67.

[2] Ibid., pp. 68, 75, 83-4.

an intellectual history.

How curious, then, that the word 'abstraction' is absent from *Keywords*. As we have already seen, from this brief glimpse of Williams's discussion of ideas of nature, 'abstraction' is a crucial and recursive term in his estimation of the efficacy of concepts. Moreover, and somewhat ironically in this context, the negative charge carried by 'abstraction' implies the relative *unnaturalness* of a certain kind of intellectual operation, whose effect is to separate us from the complexity and multiplicity of the living. But how much of human history, apparently unnoticed, is contained in this use of the word 'abstraction', and in its assumed antithesis?

In the first part of this essay, I want to begin to sketch out a cultural history of the concept of abstraction. This will not be in the manner of Williams's historical semantics in *Keywords*, but will focus instead on selected instances in modern literary studies and the visual arts. The premise underpinning my exploratory approach in this section is that Williams is far from unusual in an apparent neglect of the crucial mediating role of abstraction in his own critical lexicon. Abstraction, I want to argue, performs a wide range of quasi-invisible, often contradictory tasks in the construction both of aesthetic and of cognitive value. In the second section, I focus attention on abstraction as a principle of non-referentiality in art. My essay is thus a preliminary foray into the questions: what kind of work does abstraction do for us, and why might we want it to do what is does?

Inevitably, we begin with abstraction's negative charge, or with what Peter Osborne has identified in modern philosophical discourse as the 'reproach of abstraction'. The implication is that abstraction, as a withdrawal or disengagement from the concrete, perhaps in the form of a metonymic excision of the part to stand for the whole, or as a generalisation of a state of things, is invariably a *reductive* gesture, implying deficit, inadequacy, a retreat either from the integrity of a totality, or from the vitality of the living. Abstraction tends thus to be accompanied, as Osborne puts it, 'by both a certain *melancholy* (loss of the real object) and a certain *shame* (complicity in the domination of the concept and hence repression of other, more vibrant, more creative aspects of existence)'.[3]

The question then arises of exactly what abstraction's repressed 'other', ghosting the reproach but still, presumably, located in the domain of thought, may look like. What could it mean to retain possession of the real object whilst avoiding the domination of the conceptual? What do we really *want*, in and through the reproach of abstraction? The answer to such questions usually involves recourse to modern aesthetics; to art as a domain of thought, but of a kind at once concrete and extra-conceptual, in the context of a modernity which threatens at

---

[3] Peter Osborne, 'The reproach of abstraction', *Radical Philosophy* 127 (September/October 2004), pp. 21-8; 21.

every turn to instrumentalize rationality. Theodor Adorno saw a principle of autonomy in the 'inherent structure' of art objects rather than in their effects: 'they are knowledge as non-conceptual objects'.[4] Gilles Deleuze and Felix Guattari similarly propose art-objects as 'modes of ideation that, like scientific thought, do not have to pass through concepts' (suggesting a tentative, transversal alliance between art and science just as Pound's Imagist aesthetic endorsed the way of the scientist over the way of the salesman). If the work of art is *a bloc of sensations, that is to say, a compound of percepts and affects*', then it is important for Deleuze and Guattari not to confuse the latter terms with subjective perceptions and feelings: percepts and affects are *'beings'* wrested from those who experience them, so that 'the artist's greatest difficulty is to make it *stand up on its own*'.[5] So Peter de Bolla, in a more recent attempt to forge a new and inclusive language of aesthetic experience, asks of a Barnett Newman canvas 'what this painting might know, or rather what its knowing might be'.[6]

We would not be far wrong in describing all of these attempts at locating cognitive value in the 'thing' (rather than the perceiver) as developments of a familiar modernist aesthetic of impersonality within which, for example, the 'no ideas but in things' of William Carlos Williams echoes Ezra Pound's 'go in fear of abstractions'. D. H. Lawrence remains, above all, the touchstone for a reproach of abstraction in modernist literature, combining it in his case with what looks like a thoroughgoing philosophy of vitalism. Consistently in Lawrence, abstraction is figuratively associated with mechanism, where the machine principle is held to be an antithesis to the fully human or natural. The intellectual homes of machine-abstraction appear to be science and mathematics, while its political expression is the concept of democracy. Instead of examining here the considerable play of 'abstraction' in Lawrence's fiction (it is indicative that the *Shorter Oxford English Dictionary* chooses Lawrence for its fictional illustration of the term: 'White and abstract-looking, he sat and ate his dinner'), let us examine a very concentrated use of the term in the essay 'Democracy' (1919). The subject is Whitman's identification of a universal material entitlement, the 'Law of the Average', as one of the founding principles of modern democracy:

The Law of the Average is well known to us. Upon this law rests all the vague

---

[4] Theodor Adorno, 'Commitment' (1962), quoted in Paul Harrison and Charles Wood eds, *Art in Theory 1900-1990: An Anthology of Changing Ideas* (Oxford: Blackwell, 1995), p. 763.
[5] Gilles Deleuze and Felix Guattari, *What is Philosophy?*, trans. Graham Burchell and Hugh Tomlinson (London: Verso, 1994), pp. 6, 164.
[6] Peter de Bolla, *Art Matters* (Cambridge, Mass., and London: Harvard University Press, 2001), p. 40.

dissertation concerning equality and social perfection. Rights of Man, Equality of Man, Social Perfectibility of Man: all these sweet abstractions, once so inspiring, rest on the fatal little hypothesis of the Average.

What is the Average? As we are well aware, there is no such animal. It is a pure abstraction. It is the reduction of the human being to a mathematical unit. Every human being numbers one, one single unit. That is the grand proposition of the Average.

And, as an alternative proposition:

The actual living quick itself is alone the creative reality. Once you abstract from this, once you generalize and postulate Universals, you have departed from the creative reality, and entered the realm of static fixity, mechanism, materialism.[7]

Elsewhere I have begun to deal with the particularities of Lawrence's critique of abstraction.[8] Here I merely wish to note a discourse of *organicised* dissent set over and against a state of mechanism characterised by highly *organised* and formulaic, abstract intellectual operations. Lawrence's argument draws readily on what Raymond Williams identified as a post-Romantic, 'culture and society' tradition of critique of industrial capitalism. Within such a tradition, democratic *society* can become polarised alongside industrialism as complementary mechanisms at odds with an endangered nature and its cognates ('community', for example). Interestingly, then, Lawrence's 'reproach' of abstraction is echoed in Williams's commentary on the same essay, in his chapter on Lawrence in *Culture and Society 1780-1850* (1958). Despite Williams's wariness of construing Lawrence as 'the familiar romantic figure who "rejects the claims of society"', he argues that Lawrence's conception of present otherness 'removes from the idea of equality that element of mechanical abstraction which has often been felt in it', and sees Lawrence's idea of *spontaneous* selfhood as a counterweight to 'those rigidities of category and abstraction, of which the industrial system was so powerful an embodiment'.[9]

Let us now, however, highlight an alternative construction of abstraction, and this without travelling far from Lawrence, either historically or ideologically—that

---

[7] D.H. Lawrence, 'Democracy', in *Phoenix: The Posthumous Papers, 1936*, ed. Edward D. McDonald (Harmondsworth: Penguin, 1980), pp. 699, 712.

[8] *D.H. Lawrence, Science and the Posthuman* (Basingstoke: Palgrave, 2005), especially 'Postscript: On Abstraction', pp.233-40.

[9] Raymond Williams, *Culture and Society 1780-1950* (London: Chatto and Windus, 1958), pp. 205, 211, 208.

is, from the terms of a critical discourse on industrial capitalism voiced by a modernist outsider-artist at a tangent to bourgeois intellectual culture. In Robert Tressell's early twentieth-century classic of socialist literature, *The Ragged Trousered Philanthropists* (1914), the protagonist Frank Owen continually reflects upon the difficulties he faces in presenting a critique of capital to workmates whose collective habitus seems to militate against thought itself:

> From their infancy they had been trained to distrust their own intelligence, and to leave the management of the affairs of the world—and for that matter of the next world too—to their betters; and now most of them were incapable of thinking of any abstract subject whatsoever.[10]

'Abstract' here signifies, not simply a natural extension of intelligence or thought, but also the ground of thought as *emancipation*. Owen's mates, the philanthropists who donate their lives and labour to their employers, insist on the obvious and the here and now, backed up by the reassuring religious warmth of what Slyme, with an impeccably dropped 'h', calls '"eart knowledge". Owen is satirised for using abstract geometrical shapes such as the 'oblong' to demonstrate ratios such as the distribution of wealth and land in Britain, a strategy invariably seen to be pretentiously indirect and divorced from the concrete ('"I said it was supposed to *represent* England"... "Oh, I see. I thought we'd very soon begin supposin'"' [p.148]). Given that the workers had 'accepted the present system in the same way as they accepted the alternating seasons', Owen's abstractions are presented by contrast as a means of analysing immediate contingencies and of being able to see their structuring conditions, and one's own false consciousness of them, as if for the first time.

Here, however, we see abstraction as an intellectual operation shading into something like the artistic *defamiliarisation* of Russian Formalism, that cherished modernist manoeuvre by which our perceptions are cleansed and renewed through estrangement. Accordingly, Tressell's text is full of graphic illustrations of realia, including lyrics, newspaper extracts, advertisements and posters. Perhaps the most arresting instance is of a blank Rushton and Co. time sheet, awaiting completion by the philanthropist who will thereby sell his labour at a knock-down price ('Each piece of work must be fully described, what it was, and how long it took to do' [393]). From '"eart knowledge', then, to art knowledge; while it is not customary to classify *The Ragged Trousered Philanthropists* as a work of modernism, Tressell's pun (typical of the text's ingenious orthography) underlines a proto-modernist aesthetic

---

[10] Robert Tressell, *The Ragged Trousered Philanthropists* (London: Panther Books, 1985), pp.202-3. Page references hereafter cited in the text.

with its roots in synthetic Cubism and its growing tips reaching towards photomontage and Brechtian alienation effect. Tressell's novel enacts the convergence of *two* models of abstraction as an emancipatory rationality: abstraction as the movement of thought itself, and as 'art knowledge'. Frank Owen's similarly dual commitment is evident in the combination of the lectures on socialism with his own identity as an artist (or a '"bit of a hartist"'), the latter exemplified in the episode in which he takes on the painting of the decorative Moorish frieze for Sweater's drawing room. This is Owen's sacrifice, measured by a considerable outlay of personal time and absence of remuneration, and undertaken as it were in disconnection from his socialist principles: when it comes to the autonomous 'work' of art, even Owen becomes a philanthropist.

In this comparison between Lawrence and Tressell we begin to see something of the range of contradictory work undertaken by the concept of abstraction. It represents the delusory power of the intellect, imprisoning us in concepts when we should be engaging with the real; conversely, it represents intellectual emancipation, freeing us from a false consciousness of the empirical everyday. Nor is it by any means the case that such instances will only be found in polarised form in the work of different thinkers; the contradictions of abstraction are at work *within* particular modernist discourses, as these are engaged in the struggle to shape the intellectual forms required for an analysis of modernity. A rich example of this dialectical play of abstraction is to be found in *Tribute to Freud* (1956), the memoir in which HD (Hilda Doolittle) drew on her experience of psychoanalysis with Sigmund Freud in Vienna between 1933 and 1934. The account builds a symbolic model of the mind of Freud and its understanding of archetypal patterns of human consciousness, uniquely positioned as HD saw it both to heal the psychic damage of the First World War, and, perhaps, to anticipate and ward off that threatened by the Second.

HD describes at length a scene in which Freud shows to her a collection of artefacts drawn from various cultures and carefully arranged on the desk in his study. Freud first presents an Indian ivory figure which HD takes to be a seated Vishnu, and which she also supposes, from its central position in a symmetrical pattern, to be his favourite. HD is therefore anxious about her ambivalent feelings for the figure: while she can appreciate its extreme beauty, with serpent-heads arranged like flower petals over the seated god, she is also repelled by it, and hence attributes her appreciation to an abstract mode of her own vision: 'I was seeing it rather abstractly'.[11] She is therefore subsequently relieved to find that it 'was not his favourite', and can then transfer the reproach of abstraction to the figure itself, 'this

---

[11] HD, *Tribute to Freud* (1956; Oxford: Carcanet Press, 1971), p. 73. Page references hereafter cited in the text.

Oriental, passionate yet cold abstraction' (74). Freud instead declares his preference for a small bronze statue of Pallas Athene, one hand extended but missing something: '"She is perfect", he said, "*only she has lost her spear.*"'

The emphasised phrase is HD's pretext for reflecting upon the nature of the Freudian mind as embodied in the remarkable 'singing quality' of his voice. The beautiful tone of Freud's voice foregrounds and estranges words so that, despite their impeccable English pronunciation, they sound like a foreign language; but the effect is also one of ambivalence, speaking in a 'double sense' or 'two-edged manner' (76, 80). When this occurs, HD tends to see it in terms of a counterbalancing of the function of abstraction. Hence, 'She is perfect' signifies veneration of the statue's perfection as a symbol or 'projection of abstract thought', but also, a perfect material artefact or 'prize' of that period in Greek art in which 'the archaic abstraction became humanized but not yet over-humanized' (75, 76). Similarly, when Freud uses the word 'time', HD notes that it

> seemed to defy the creature, the abstraction; into that one word, he seemed to pack a store of contradictory emotions; there was irony, entreaty, defiance, with a vague, tender pathos. It seemed as if the word was surcharged, an explosive that might, at any minute, go off. (80)

Each is an instance of psychoanalysis as the broader expression, in HD's words, of Freud's 'precise Jewish instinct for the particular in the general, for the personal in the impersonal or universal, for the *material* in the abstract...' (77).

Filtered through an image of the supremely compassionate humanism of Freud's mind, HD is thus able to affirm the beauty and perfection of abstraction whilst advising hesitation about its limits as a mode of vision and the need to temper it with the 'human' defined in terms of singularity, materiality and creatureliness (as in the curious locution 'the creature, the abstraction', between which Freud's word 'time' negotiates a path). Such ambivalence around abstraction is a recurrent pattern. More recently, it emerges in Gayatri Chakravorty Spivak's reflections on the threat of globalization to the multiplicity and singularity of world languages. Socialism, Spivak asserts, provides a vocabulary of 'capital' and the 'social' with which to understand the process, and, as if in affirmation of Tressell's novel, both of these terms 'work by abstraction'. Moreover, the abstract 'is produced by the imagination, for it is not the here and now'; on these terms, while only self-interest can be conceived in the thinking of the immediate present, economic redistribution 'cannot happen without the highly trained sympathetic imagination' required to learn another's language. This association of abstraction with the imagination is of great significance. At the same time, however, Spivak insists that 'the *work* of the abstract requires the wiping out of singularity, the repeatable difference. Most of the workers for globalization do not produce the abstract, but accept it as given, and systematize within it'.[12]

II

In this section I want to turn to a further transmutation in the concept of abstraction in visual art: that is, to abstraction as a non-referential visual language. My starting point is Wilhelm Worringer's *Abstraction and Empathy: A Contribution to the Psychology of Style* (1908), the first coherent attempt to theorise abstraction in modernism, but also and primarily a reading of the burgeoning influence of 'primitive' art on modernism. The object of Worringer's critical scrutiny is the idealisation of natural beauty, co-extensive with the value of the *organic*, in modern European bourgeois aesthetics. This for Worringer is an aesthetic of 'empathy', post-Romantic in its predication of a 'happy pantheistic relationship of confidence between man and the phenomena of the external world', and consolatory in its role as 'objectified self-enjoyment', gratifying a need for 'self-activation' through natural beauty.[13] The critique is of two closely-bound presuppositions: first, that 'nature' is to be defined in terms of the beauty of the organic, and second, that it is the role of art to reproduce this natural beauty. The first is most clearly, for Worringer, an instance of cultural imperialism: the modern aesthetics of beauty leaves us, he argues, ill-equipped or even 'helpless' to comprehend the art of many ages and non-Western cultures. But the second, equally culturally specific, is presented more unequivocally as a fundamental misconception of the status of the work of art in relation to 'nature'. Worringer's founding declaration is that the work of art,

> as an autonomous organism, stands beside nature on equal terms and [is], in its deepest and innermost essence, devoid of any connection with it, in so far as by nature is understood the visible surface of things. Natural beauty is on no account to be regarded as a condition of the work of art, despite the fact that in the course of evolution it seems to have become a valuable element in the work of art, and to some extent indeed positively identical with it (68).

Abstraction thus operates on two levels in Worringer's discussion. It is the inherent condition of art, which is devoid of connection with nature; but it also

---

[12] Gayatri Chakravorty Spivak, 'Remembering Derrida', *Radical Philosophy* 129 (January/February 2005), pp. 19-20.

[13] Wilhelm Worringer, *Abstraction and Empathy: A Contribution to the Psychology of Style* (1908), extract quoted in Harrison and Wood eds, *Art in Theory 1900-1990*, pp. 68-72; 70, 69. Page references hereafter cited in the text.

expresses the 'artistic volition' of 'savage' or 'primitive' and some 'culturally developed Oriental' peoples, for whom 'the urge to abstraction finds its beauty in the life-denying inorganic, in the crystalline or, in general terms, in all abstract law and necessity' (68). Readers today may baulk at some aspects of Worringer's account of the 'primitive', or at least at the contradictions in that account *vis-à-vis* the hierarchies of post-Darwinian racial science. Speculations on the social psychology of the primitive ('empathy cannot possibly have determined artistic volition') appear locked into a narrative of civilizational progress. Abstraction, Worringer argues, was a compensation for, or refuge from, a kind of collective cultural agoraphobia, 'an immense spiritual dread of space' engendered by the bewildered confrontation with the complexity of the physical world, leaving primitive humans 'lost and spiritually helpless' and with 'an immense need for tranquillity' (the heightened rhetoric of 'immense' here emphasising the huge generalisations of world-view undertaken). The disposition towards regularity, 'already present in the germ-cell', became established because 'intellect had not yet dimmed instinct' (70-1).

Yet undoubtedly Worringer primarily sought to unsettle and even invert such hierarchies: abstraction stands not just 'at the beginning of every art' but remains dominant at a level of 'high culture' in certain non-European traditions, and of course then reappears in advanced modernism: 'a causal connection must therefore exist between primitive cultures and the highest, purest regular art forms' (70-71). The scandal of Worringer's challenge to established European aesthetics lay in the insinuation of its pact with, or co-option of, a conception of nature as a value-laden condition of organic life, at once authentic and domesticated. 'Life as such', he noted of the primitive urge to abstraction, 'is felt to be a disturbance of aesthetic enjoyment' (72). We may not be wrong to detect a note of wry humour here; Worringer must have known what it meant to question the pre-eminence of 'natural beauty' as the seamless medium between bourgeois 'life' and Western art. Something of this no doubt informs D. H. Lawrence's portrait of the German modernist sculptor Loerke, who mercilessly excoriates Ursula Brangwen for her anthropomorphic defence of the 'sensitivity' of horses. Loerke accuses Ursula of implying that his bronze statuette might have been '"a picture of a friendly horse to which you give a lump of sugar"'. '"(I)t is part of a work of art"', he intones, '"it has no relation to anything outside that work of art"' and to deny that art and nature are two different planes of existence, to translate one into the other, is '"a darkening of all counsel, a making confusion everywhere"'.[14]

There are, however, instabilities in Worringer's account which open out onto a more complex scenario than the breaking of a pact with nature and the repudiation

[14] D. H. Lawrence, *Women in Love* (1921; Ware: Wordsworth Classics, 1999), p. 376.

of natural beauty. The quality of an abstract work is identified by the 'life-denying inorganic' or 'crystalline', despite the proposition that any work of art is itself an 'autonomous organism'. Abstraction pursues deliverance from 'the seeming arbitrariness of organic existence in general', yet art is devoid of connection with nature only in so far as *by nature is understood the visible surface of things* (my emphasis) (68, 71-2). Beneath Worringer's use of overarching terms such as life and nature, a complex play and exchange of meaning between the *organic* and the *inorganic* takes place. In a familiar sense, abstraction is 'life-denying', seeking for the ideal or absolute form underpinning the messy arbitrariness of the organic. Yet 'nature' does not fully coincide with this messy arbitrariness, provided we are prepared to look below the visible surface of things. There, below, we may find an inorganic or 'life-denying' nature, an indication that nature is not monopolized by the organic. If nature can be inorganic, so the lifeless work of art can be an organism. The fluidity of these boundaries suggests that the relationship between organic and inorganic should be subject to some vigilance.

In his 'Notes on Abstract Art' (1941/48), the English painter Ben Nicholson echoed Worringer in arguing that, while a great deal of contemporary painting and sculpture was concerned with the imitation of nature, colour and form should be used to create *equivalents* to nature—'organisms', perhaps in Worringer's terms. Nevertheless, in constructing an active agenda for the pursuit of abstraction in British cultural life, Nicholson's endorsement was worldlier than anything to be found in Worringer's doctrine of primitivist retreat and tranquillity. Far from representing the withdrawal of the artist from reality, Nicholson saw post-Cubist abstraction as having affected all aspects of everyday design, from architecture to lipstick holders. A yacht designer had noted to him that a 'hair's breadth in design' could equally affect the pace of a vessel or the 'power or lack of power' of an abstract relief. Such questions, Nicholson maintained, matter far more than art-historical musings about the validity of abstraction or why the abstract canvas no longer looks like a Tintoretto:

One can say that the problems dealt with in 'abstract' art are related to the interplay of forces and, therefore, that any solution reached has a bearing on all interplay between forces: it is related to Arsenal *v.* Tottenham Hotspur quite as much as to the stars in their courses. I think the recent liberation of the powerful forces of form and colour is an important event, and when critics announce or foretell the death of abstract art they show the same misunderstanding of the freedom of form and colour as the dictators do of the freedom of the individual...'[15]

Nicholson shares with Herbert Read, another champion of British abstraction in the period, a rather vertiginous estimation of the direct connection between non-referential form and political radicalism: practitioners of abstraction are 'the true revolutionary artists', Read maintained, 'whom every Communist should learn to respect and encourage'.[16] This aside, however, in the vocabulary of *forces*, and the emphasis on the painting of such forces—Arsenal v. Spurs as much as the movement of the stars—Nicholson follows Worringer in articulating a revolutionary break with an organicist aesthetic, but only in order to tie abstraction to an understanding of the deeper vitalism of non-organic nature.

A brief detour into 'organic' and 'inorganic' is necessary here. For, if our discussion concerns the recurrent 'reproach' of abstraction, then we may also reflect upon the relative *irreproachability* of 'organic' in contemporary discourse. It is clear that 'organic' is the primary signifier of an ecological sensibility or politics and a virtual synonym for living or natural processes in general, over and against the artificial manipulation of, for example, food products, either by 'chemicals' and genetic modification or, in the economic sphere, through agri-business and the profit-led control of the market by corporate retailers. In a previous discussion, drawing substantially on the work done (in this case) by Raymond Williams in *Keywords*, I have drawn attention to crucial ambivalences in the development of this complex word.[17] In brief, 'organic' began its life in close if not synonymous association with notions of the mechanical and instrumental, only developing its antithetical meaning during and after industrialism. What we might inherit from this semantic history are associations relating to 'organ', 'organise' and 'organism'. An organ is a part of an animal or plant that performs a particular function, such as digestion or respiration. To organise is therefore to form a structure based around or resembling the function of organs; it is to 'form into a living being or living tissue' where this is predicated on the structured interdependence of organs; it is therefore to 'systematise' as much as to 'give organic structure to' (*Shorter Oxford English Dictionary*). Hence an 'organism', a living body, is an interdependently-structured system or organisation or, as Claire Colebrook puts it, 'a bounded whole with an identity and end'.[18]

---

[15] Ben Nicholson, 'Notes on Abstract Art', extract quoted in Harrison and Wood eds, *Art in Theory 1900-1990*, p. 381.

[16] Herbert Read, 'What is Revolutionary Art?' (1935), extract quoted in eds Vassiliki Kolocotroni, Jane Goldman and Olga Taxidou, *Modernism: An Anthology of Sources and Documents* (Edinburgh: Edinburgh University Press, 1998), p.527.

[17] D. H. Lawrence, *Science and the Posthuman*, pp.207-8.

[18] Claire Colebrook, *Deleuze* (London: Routledge, 2002), p. 56.

All of this suggests how far our adherence to organ(ic)ism contains a hidden human history. It has entailed an investment in ideas of hierarchy (the organs are the key constituents of an organism), unity, systematic totality and teleology. Whilst enshrining a commitment to natural spontaneity, fluidity and unpredictability, over and against the variously unspecified threat of a repressive, administered abstraction, the organic is ghosted—reassuringly?—by its own previous associations with instrumentality and structure. In the domain of concepts, the machine may be a closed system, but so too is the organism.

Why does this conjunction matter? What is at stake in opening out the organism to this process of questioning? Bodies, after all, cannot function without vital organs, without certain anatomical givens, and it seems self-evident that the advances of medical science are predicated upon a concept of the organism whose systematicity, in relation to its various environments, enables reliable knowledge to be formed. The response that I want to explore in conclusion is that there are parallel or adjacent ways of thinking about *inorganic, nonorganic* or *non-organismic* life which increasingly demand our attention. Contemporary science insists on this, but there is a sense in which abstraction has already enabled art and asethetics to have much to say about it.

In her account of the rise of modernist sculpture, Rosalind Krauss distinguishes the work of Marcel Duchamp and Constantin Brancusi from that of a broadly constructivist group of sculptors - Gabo, Lissitsky, Moholy-Nagy and Bill, for example. In the latter group Krauss locates a classical will-to-knowledge which assumes the function of sculpture to be to 'dominate material' and in so doing provide the stationary viewer with a complete perception or understanding of the object through a strategy of 'build(ing) the object out from what appears to be a generative core'. In contrast to this, argues Krauss, Duchamp and Brancusi offer a 'more speculative' approach to the relationship between art and '"knowledge"'. The touchstone for this is the earlier work of Auguste Rodin, in whose reliefs Krauss finds a disruption of narrative time such that it becomes impossible to deduce the essential structure of the figure from its emerging material form. Similarly, Brancusi's *The Newborn* presents a 'cell-like' head detached from the pre-determining structure of the whole body:

> In this isolation of body from figure, in this emphatic rejection of the internal armature and its classical meanings, one hears an echo of Rilke's description of Rodin's *Balzac*, when he spoke of the head as something that seemed to be "living at the summit of the figure like those balls that dance on jets of water". For Rilke was talking about a sculptural perception of the body which does not take for granted that the *meaning* of the body is the same as its anatomical

structure.[19]

Rilke's way of accounting for the implausibility of the *Balzac* head is to invoke forces, 'jets of water' by which the head is precariously sustained, as if in defiance of the logic of anatomy. We could take Krauss's reading of this observation to mean that sculpture is not tied to the mimesis of the body, and that deviations from mimesis are symbolic of selective emphases on the meaning of parts of that body. But the reading intimates something further: we cannot take for granted that an *understanding* of the body should be identical with that which is suggested by its organic structure. Just as it cannot be taken for granted that the organism is the culmination or *telos* of natural processes, so the concept of the organism does not *exhaust* the ways in which we might describe bodies biologically. Alternatively put, there is, as Deleuze finds in Michaelangelo, 'the manner in which the body exceeds the organism or makes it fall apart'.[20]

'The organism is not life', writes Gilles Deleuze, 'it is what imprisons life'.[21] In much contemporary scientific writing orientated towards a general readership, and in related polemics, attempts are being made to refurbish conceptions of nature from the perspectives of inorganic life. In the field of evolutionary molecular biology, since Jacques Monod's *Chance and Necessity* (1970) and Richard Dawkins' *The Selfish Gene* (1989), it has become possible and indeed orthodox to conceive of organisms, including the human, as the chance effects of molecular or genetic forms in their processes of self-perpetuation. This offers a transversal logic by which to conceive of the human in terms of a coalescence of organicism out of the swarming of inorganic matter; as Ansell-Pearson summarises it, 'evolution cannot be restricted to individual organisms, since at the molecular level one is dealing with populations of genetic material whose communication is not governed by fixed or deterministic organismic boundaries'.[22]

While popular science tries to address a clear gap between the scientific understanding of the inorganic and the communication of its importance, polemical debate around the subject tends to resolve itself into a bleak and unproductive impasse: the counsel of enlightened optimism of Dawkins, for whom the non-human origins of human life spell the end of the 'God delusion'; the

---

[19] Rosalind E. Krauss, *Passages in Modern Sculpture* (Cambridge, Mass., and London: The MIT Press, 1981), pp. 67, 96.

[20] Gilles Deleuze, *Francis Bacon: The Logic of Sensation*, trans. Daniel W. Smith (London and New York: Continuum, 2004), p. 130.

[21] Deleuze, *Francis Bacon: The Logic of Sensation*, p. 45.

[22] Keith Ansell-Pearson, 'Bergson and Creative Evolution/Involution: Exposing the Transcendental Illusion of Organismic Life' in ed. John Mullarkey, *The New Bergson* (Manchester: Manchester University Press, 1999), p. 161.

counsel of enlightened despair of John Gray, for whom it is the myths of progress and perfectibility that are exploded. The boldest effort to consider what nature and the human may *look like* from the perspectives of the inorganic remains the philosophy of Deleuze, who sought to bridge advanced science with a highly specific case for the role of abstraction in visual art, and with particular reference to the work of Francis Bacon.

Unequivocally, Deleuze borrowed from abstract modernism a conception of 'forces', such that the 'eternal object' of painting was to paint or to 'capture' forces rather than to figuratively reproduce or invent forms.[23] Specifically, moreover, he revisited Worringer for this analysis, repeatedly invoking the latter's concept of the 'northern line', from *Form in Gothic* (1927). This line exceeds 'organic representation' to produce a 'powerful inorganic life', 'bizarre' and 'intense', 'an abstraction, but an expressionistic abstraction'. Having gone beyond that which can be figured or re-presented in favour of that which can only be presented, Deleuze saw abstraction as the necessary medium of the concept he took up from Artaud as the embodiment of inorganic human life—the body without organs, which is 'opposed less to organs than to that organization of organs we call an organism'.[24]

In the reproachful sense of the term, it seems difficult to imagine, as it were, anything more 'abstract' than a body without organs: the organ(ism)ic body is our here-and-now, the conceptual ground without which we would perish. Equally abstract is the thinking of the body as the site or host of shifting historical populations of genetic or bacterial matter. As Spivak puts it, however, abstraction is the product of the *imaginative* effort necessary to overcome obstacles to thought. The obstacles in our current discussion are the various related concepts of the organic, so thoroughly sequestered in political and aesthetic value that we can no longer see how they limit our ideas of nature. Abstraction in this sense folds back on itself and guarantees *concrete* engagement with inorganic life, beyond the idealisations embedded in the organic. 'Not every organism has a brain, and not all life is organic, but everywhere there are forces that constitute microbrains, or an inorganic life of things'.[25]

We can see abstraction at work thus on Deleuze in his strangely moving readings of what he calls the Figure in Bacon. Bacon, Deleuze claims, never ceased to paint bodies without organs, or bodies in which organs might be seen as temporary or provisional presences, co-existing with but not defining other actualities of the body. Most distinctive in this respect, perhaps, is Deleuze's thesis that Bacon painted heads, not faces, pursuing a project '*to dismantle the face*, to

---

[23] See e.g. *What is Philosophy?*, p.182, or *Francis Bacon: The Logic of Sensation*, p. 56.

[24] Deleuze, *Francis Bacon: The Logic of Sensation*, p. 44.

[25] Deleuze and Guattari, *What is Philosophy?*, p. 213.

rediscover the head or make it emerge from beneath the face'.[26] Faciality in Deleuze constitutes a taking of the human as self-evident, an idealisation of the human in terms of ego psychology; Bacon, however, paints the head as *meat*, 'among the most beautiful of which are those painted in the colours of meat, red and blue' (26). This reorientation towards the human head evokes the 'immense pity' of our condition of flesh, and the sharing of that flesh as a 'zone of indiscernibility' with animals. And this is also, of course a reorientation towards what 'natural beauty' may mean, beyond that set of *données* which are already on the canvas before the painter sets out.

I have tried to suggest in this essay how the traditional antithesis between abstraction and the natural is turned to good effect in modernist and Deleuzian aesthetics, by enabling a re-imagination of theories of life of a kind equally forcefully demanded by contemporary sciences. When Deleuze reconceptualised living systems as 'machinic' rather than either organic or mechanical, defining 'machinic' thus as the open faculty of life to make connections, he drew attention to the constant requirement to reassess and overhaul our theories of life, to be vigilant over the way in which keywords tend to cease to do what we want them to do. Abstraction in intellectual and artistic work promises to continue the task of what Deleuze found in Bacon to be 'one of the most marvelous responses in the history of painting'—that is, to attempt to make invisible forces visible.[27]

---

[26] Deleuze, *Francis Bacon: The Logic of Sensation*, pp. 20-1.
[27] Deleuze, *Francis Bacon: The Logic of Sensation*, p. 58.

V

Literature and Religion

Tony Conran

The Shepherd

To Jeremy Hooker, poet and acknowledger of poets

Y la caballería
A vista de las aguas descendía —
                    San Juan de la Cruz

CAVALRY descending
Within sight of the waters...

They canter to the lakeside.

Tired horses stoop to drink,
Their long legs dallying
In the cold domicile of reeds.

The old shepherd, waking by firelight,
Lips a muttering pipe,
A red twinge in his knuckle.

Daubed on his sleeping flock,
Fire red and red clay mingle.
An owl bleats in the distance.

Gently a stallion neighs —
His rider sweet-talks him softly.
A quick laugh from another.

The lead mare lifts her lips,
Hooves splash, and jingle-jangle
The mounts nudge to dry land.

The shepherd cocks his head,
Smiles, and greets
By name each knight dismounting.

Mimi Khalvati

Northcourt

for Jerry, in lieu of Normandy

i

I HAVE never heard peace—barely a tree
without its rooks in the bluebell and wild garlic
wood—coming into roost be so noisy.
Everything that flies hoots and hums in traffic.

Only the plants are dumb—ferns, hellebores,
primulas, arum lilies by the stream.
Is their beauty a kind of sound then? Or,
because so lovely, is a voice to them

who are so, vulgar, base? Poetry too,
moving the reader to an inarticulate oh!
never spoke more purely than on the page.

Earth, then, is that page. And every crow
that squawks that reader, moved by earth to language.
Who among us is crow? Who, bluebell?

ii

Who among us is crow? Who, bluebell?
Here is a human voice now, calling 'John'
and flat, padding footsteps. Here is Christine
with a bathmat, white and rigid-dry, held

like a baby across her arms. And here is
the moment when she's gone, warmer, fuller.
The garden is a kind of sea—both its surface
and its caves. Bird-fish cross the upper water.

The sea-garden remembers the motions of land:
the northern slopes of The Chalk, the ridged backbone
of the island; the southern slopes of greensand

rolling a frost pocket around Northcourt
where Swinburne swam and rode with Mary to Newport,
reciting 'Atalanta in Calydon'.

iii

Reciting 'Atalanta in Calydon'
over the firm hills and the fleeting sea,
I don't know what is lovelier—to be
atop the world, rocked in the arms of conifer,

a look-out platform snaggled in its branches,
or below, on some nettled path, where acacia
you thought mimosa takes your breath away.
Neither. Comparisons are invidious.

Nothing's lovelier, more worthy of wonder,
than anything else. Instead, on the Wight,
cultivated and wild in equal measure,

spread the Mediterranean, Himalayas,
New Zealand, Australia—micro-climates
for agaves, banana palms, euphorbias.

iv

Agaves, banana palms, euphorbias,
species from all over the world and knowing
the sea is behind your back make you treasure
all the more thistle, buttercup, a hedgerow

on one verge where you sit like an old
pilgrim at the wayside to have a smoke,
a spider disappearing over the fold
of your thigh, sunshine warming your back,

and a field of rape, shoulder-high, on the other.
Traffic is faint and the silence thick as butter
and the sea—or the wind? for the sea's too

far away surely—washing in waves that reach you
through the hawthorns, here, high up in the downs
on a public footpath to Chillerton.

v

On a public footpath to Chillerton
is to feel, as long as you're on the island,
paradoxically more part of the land
for it will always hold you in its basin,

centred, a land animal, homo sapiens
not a crab. How simple to trudge from place
to place: at last, two-leggedness makes sense
and speed's no problem for while you pick up pace

downhill, cows grazing seem to stay stock-still,
sheep on the far ridge pose as cotton plants
and though hawks might see you, how accurately

you see the Red Admiral in your path wing it
at your approach and the greenbottle glinting
as if welding spun glass and sun to metal!

vi

As if welding spun glass and sun to metal,
the Italian garden, lemoning and purpling,
stays out of focus just as dreams dismantle
their shadows and the world comes into colour.

Dawn is about scent and sound and temperature –
sight is on hold till sunrise, is monochrome
and vague. And speech an inadequate stranger,
as it is to grief, when telling your dreams

to someone else. Grief, sorrow, heartbreak:
they too are species eternally submerged.
Bring them up to the light, what do they see, hear?

The mulch of dawn? Leafmould air? Rabbits emerging
now out of, now into, their small brown blurs?
What a tremendous noise the world makes, waking?

vii

What a tremendous noise the world makes waking,
squawking, threatening a multiple birth.
The effort is in the treetops, the crust breaking,
the canopy pressured from underneath –

so many trees and shrubs of varying height,
sometimes the lowest, hunched, being the oldest;
but touch the youngest leaves, despondent in heat,
and they are cold to the palm, almost wet –

till colour comes, pink and rose and lemony,
and the doves quieten, the coot pecks across
the tennis lawn, wheels are heard on the driveway.

Birds alight on turrets. You hear the linen
snap of their wings, like sheets, the pleatedness
of flight, the abrupt silence of arrival.

David Lloyd

Questions about place

for Jeremy Hooker

but the question is, which –
the glassed-in place that might be?

the airy place that was for a moment?
the place that would be if

the right furniture is positioned
with patience? the place obscured

by pinned-up party balloons?
the absent place your father mentioned

when combing your hair?
the nearby place that didn't survive the storm?

the distant place that sometimes seems
a city, sometimes a home?

the place we hide in under the stairwell
in the basement where even children

don't go? or the unstable place
we're forced to leave

when one moment inexplicably
becomes the next?

'At Eternity's Window': Representing Church and Chapel in the Anglophone Literature of Wales

Jane Aaron

IN a seminal essay on Roland Mathias, Jeremy Hooker describes his poem 'Brechfa Chapel' (also discussed in Sam Adams' chapter on Mathias in this volume) as a forceful dramatisation of the 'decay of the Puritan tradition' in Wales.[1] 'What's left of this latish day that began with love' is, in 'Brechfa Chapel', a desolation of gravestones and a 'black half-world' of 'bully unrest'. 'Is the old witness done?' asks Mathias; are the 'strong remembered words' no longer resonant in Wales, or not at least on a communal, congregational level?[2] But though the poem speaks of the loss of a shared intensity of faith, what Hooker finds central to it, and indeed to the work of many of the most eminent Anglophone poets of twentieth-century Wales, is that it draws upon 'religious or spiritual resources that are not available in a mainly secular society'.[3]

It is not my aim in this present chapter to rework that argument which is strongly presented in Hooker's *Imagining Wales: A View of Modern Welsh Writing in English*. Rather I am interested here in the ironic counterpoint to it, that is, in the idea that, both during the high noon of Welsh Nonconformity in the nineteenth century and during the early twentieth-century period of socialist ascendancy which followed it, much of the energy in the literary representation of Welsh religion was devoted not to its celebration but its disparagement. This is true particularly of the English-language prose writers: the desire to administer a death blow to chapel

---

1 Jeremy Hooker, *The Presence of the Past: Essays on Modern British and American Poetry* (Bridgend: Poetry Wales Press, 1987), 150.
2 Roland Mathias, 'Brechfa Chapel', *The Collected Poems of Roland Mathias*, ed. Sam Adams (Cardiff: University of Wales Press, 2002), 223.
3 Jeremy Hooker, *Imagining Wales: A View of Modern Welsh Writing in English* (Cardiff: University of Wales Press, 2001), 200.

culture can be said to be as characteristic and animating a feature of the Anglophone novelists and short-story writers of Wales from, say, 1780 to 1930, as a preoccupation with the loss of that communal religious intensity can be said to pervade the work of Welsh poets in English from, say, 1930 to 1990. In the nineteenth century, just as Welsh-language writing often attacked the Established Church, so English-language literature in Wales often attacked Dissenters and the Nonconformist denominations. In the first decades of the twentieth century, Nonconformity was vigorously attacked by a new breed of Welsh writers in English whose primary loyalties were to the labour movement. But beneath the surface, the literary portrayal of the Christian sects in Wales was always in each epoch more complex than perhaps it initially appeared to be. In the chapter that follows I look firstly at a few representative nineteenth century writers, suspicious of the growing powers of Dissent; and then at literary depictions of the clash of the chapels with socialism in the early decades of the twentieth century, before closing with a brief discussion of the contemporary situation, and of writers who in each epoch were working to build bridges between the religious denominations of Wales.

I

A likely candidate for the title of 'first Welsh novelist' is Anna Maria Bennett (1750–1808); born Anna Maria Evans to a grocer and his wife from Merthyr Tydfil, Bennett was living in London as the mistress of an Admiral of the British Navy when she published her first novel *Anna or Memoirs of a Welch Heiress* (1786). One of this four-volume text's many lively villains is the Reverend John Dalton, a Welsh Methodist preacher, who cheats the orphaned heroine Anna of her inheritance and more importantly, her identity, and so sets her on the long trail of vicissitudes which make up her story. The 'son of a journeyman carpenter, in a large town in South Wales', Dalton 'pleaded a call of the spirit' and declared himself a convert to Methodism purely for gain; though ordained 'he had not the least prospect of even a cure' in the Established Church, but as a Methodist preacher he extorts funds from his Dissenting congregations through his hypocritical sermons. Bennett satirically presents him as typical of his kind: 'to a strong voice, a primitive look, a lank thin person, and a large wig, he added the cunning and cant of an itinerant preacher', she says.[4] That this 1786 novel should be so disparaging of Methodism is of course historically no surprise. The

---

4   Anna Maria Bennett, *Anna: or Memoirs of a Welch Heiress* (London: William Lane, 1786), i, 12, 13 and 15.

Methodist revolutions of the eighteenth century were accompanied by much persecution of the new movement on the part of the supporters of the Established Church. The Welsh historian Theophilus Evans, for example, in his *The History of Modern Enthusiasm* (1752) accuses Methodist preachers of working upon the fears of their congregations until they fling them 'into the greatest agitation and confusion possible'. Methodism, he says, aims 'to alarm the Imagination, and to raise a Ferment in the Passions' rather than to induce sobriety and a true understanding of religion.[5]

Dissenters at this time were characteristically represented by Anglican writers as too excitable, too primitive in their unrestrained enthusiasm; by contrast the Established Church, as seen by the relatively few Anglophone writers of Wales whose sympathies lay with the Nonconformists, is depicted as excessively dispassionate—cold, overly ritualized and incapable of lighting in the heart a religious fire. Jane Cave (1754–1796), for example, born in Talgarth, Breconshire, the daughter of an English exciseman and glover who had been converted to Calvinist Methodism on hearing Howell Harris preach, compares the rituals of the Established Church unfavourably with the enthusiasm of her father's worship. In the poem 'On hearing the Rev. Mr. R—d read the Morning Service...', she criticises Anglican preachers for the lack of zeal in their sermons; they do not convey the passion of the Christian message, or succeed in awakening their audience from its torpor:

> The giddy hearer enters gay and vain,
> And unaffected leaves the Church again.[6]

Her portrayal of Methodist worship in a poem on Howel Harris is considerably more favourable; according to her elegy, Harris's heart glowed 'with pure desire' to save souls as 'Essential truth he faithfully declar'd' in his impassioned sermons.[7]

But in the majority of early and mid-nineteenth-century English-language fictions Welsh Methodism is characteristically depicted as too impassioned by far. Anne Beale's *The Vale of Towey* (1844), for example, later reprinted as *Traits and Stories of the Welsh Peasantry* (1849), portrays many aspects of rural Welsh life with sympathy, but sectarian prejudice appears to have affected her portrayal of its Dissenters. Beale (1815–1900) was an Englishwoman who came to Carmarthenshire

5   Theophilus Evans, *The History of Modern Enthusiasm* (1752), quoted in Geraint Jenkins, 'The New Enthusiasts', in Trevor Herbert and Gareth Elwyn Jones eds *The Remaking of Wales in the Eighteenth Century* (Cardiff: University of Wales Press, 1988), 61 and 62.

6   Jane Cave, *Poems on Various Subjects, Entertaining, Elegiac, and Religious* (Winchester: printed for the author by J. Sadler, 1783), 103.

7   Ibid., 84 and 86.

to work as a governess to a clerical family, but soon developed an independent career as a novelist largely concerned with tales located in Welsh settings. In *The Vale of Towey* her heroine, Rachel, is Anglican, but the Established Church and its few loyal adherents are threatened by the competitiveness, when it comes to the saving of souls, of local Methodists. One of Rachel's neighbours, Pally, seizes her opportunity to attempt a last-minute conversion of Rachel's dying father Jackey at one unlucky moment when Rachel is temporarily not at home to protect him:

> Pally was, like most of her equals amongst her country-people, a Dissenter, and with well-meant religious zeal would fain have made Jackey Bach, and the few who clung to the church, Dissenters too…[S]he contrived to assemble a number of Methodists in Jackey's sick room, for the purpose of holding what is called, in these parts, a prayer-meeting…[T]he stentorian efforts of half-a-dozen illiterate men, without even their minister to head them, accompanied by the groans of twice as many old women, are not the best possible means of leaving good and happy religious impressions upon the mind of a sick or dying man…His well-meaning but injudicious friends, fell upon their knees around him, and shouted by turns for a good two hours…[T]he effect upon the sufferer was anything but beneficial.8

The invalid would have perished in much discomfort, were it not for the fact that 'the kind and good clergyman of the parish, who visited Jackey, by gentle and judicious conversation led his mind to serious thoughts', so that he finally dies calmed and at rest.

Beale's reference to Rachel and her father as amongst 'the few who clung to the church' indicates the extraordinary growth in the numbers of Welsh Nonconformists and Dissenters during the first half of the nineteenth century. By the time of the Religious Census of 1851, only 20% of the Welsh population attended the Church of England; over a quarter of the population were Calvinist Methodists (25.7%) and the rest were Independents (21.8%), Baptists (17.4%), and Wesleyan Methodists (12.4%).9 It would appear that a writer like Beale cannot believe that this growth was arrived at by fair means; she presents her fictional Dissenters as having won such numerous converts through bullying their credulous audiences. Historically a more obvious factor accounting for the Nonconformists' success was their use of the Welsh language. In the 1840s about 70% of the Welsh population—of just over a million people—were Welsh-language speakers, and in the

8 Anne Beale, *The Vale of the Towey; or, Sketches in South Wales* (1844); 2nd edn. *Traits and Stories of the Welsh Peasantry* (London: Routledge, 1849), 249–50, 250–1.
9 See Dot Jones, *Statistical Evidence relating to the Welsh Language 1801–1911* (Cardiff: University of Wales Press, 1998), 425.

most Welsh counties, such as Anglesey and Caernarfon, about 60% had no English.[10] Yet while all the Nonconformist chapels in Welsh-speaking areas used the Welsh language only, the distribution of Welsh-speaking Anglican clergy was erratic; they did not always reach the parishes where they were needed.

This situation is fictionalised in the 1853 novella 'The Welsh Living' by Margaret Charlotte Jones (born circa 1826), the daughter of Sir George Campbell, of Edenwood, Fifeshire, who married David Jones of Pantglas, High Sheriff of the county of Carmarthen, in 1845. The hero of her tale, a well-meaning Englishman called Henry Percy, is initially delighted when he is appointed to a Welsh living:

> When presented to the living…he understood Llandovery to be what is called an English parish; viz, that the church service was performed in the English tongue, and that, with the exception of a few aged persons, invariably worshippers at the meeting-houses, the young and general population had discarded the Attic vernacular, anxious to dissipate that cloud which had so long hovered around their social improvement and foreign intercourse, and had adopted the sister language. Matters soon unfolded themselves in a very different light…[11]

He discovers that the parish is in fact largely Welsh-speaking, and that Church members are leaving to join the Dissenters at a fearsome rate which can only be halted by his rapid acquisition of Welsh. Percy, who is conscientious to a fault, initially rises to the challenge. With 'strict diligence' he applies himself to learn the 'harsh and guttural Cimbrian dialect', fortified by the knowledge that he is 'endowed by nature with an intuitive facility for acquiring languages'.[12] But he has not reckoned with Welsh, which according to Margaret Charlotte Jones is amongst the world's languages 'perhaps the *most* difficult of all to acquire.'[13] To the grave detriment of his health, Percy struggles manfully on, but to no avail. His parishioners commiserate with 'the poor sickly gentleman', but have to confess that 'what with the cough, and the sort of Welsh he has got hold of,'[14] he is of little use to them. In 'The Welsh Living' Welsh is presented as a teasing mumbo-jumbo which can belong only to the primitive Welsh; the vocal apparatus of more civilized races, particularly those of the English, has evolved to so much greater a degree of refinement that they are incapable of uttering its syllables. The struggle

---

[10] Ibid, 212–3.

[11] Margaret Charlotte Jones, 'The Welsh Living' in *Scattered Leaves; or, Twilight Trifles* (London: Routledge, 1853), 18.

[12] Ibid., 22–3.

[13] Ibid., 181.

[14] Ibid., 129.

ends for Percy when, on attempting to give a sermon in Welsh, he faints outright
in the pulpit from the stress and fatigue of his task; half dead, he returns to
England where he quickly recovers. While its author is no advocate for the Welsh
language, the moral of this text is pertinent enough: it attempts to impress upon
the Church the absolute necessity of sending Welsh-speaking clergy to the Welsh-
speaking parishes.

However, by the 1850s when this novel appeared, the Church, and particularly
Church schools, were already heavily implicated from Welsh speakers point of
view, in the English government's attempt to further the teaching of English in
Wales and the concomitant weakening of Welsh. A government-appointed
Commission to investigate the state of education in Wales, when it published its
Report in 1847, found that not only were Welsh schools profoundly inadequate,
particularly when it came to the teaching of English, but that the morality of
Welsh people was also lacking. This immorality was attributed to the barbarity and
primitiveness of Welsh-speaking culture. What was more, the so-called 'giant sin
of Wales', that is, 'the alleged want of chastity in women' was reported to be in
part a direct result of Nonconformist religious practices, in that it was said to be
'much increased by night prayer-meetings, and the intercourse which ensues in
returning home.'[15] Of course, the leaders of Welsh Nonconformist society
protested vehemently against the findings of the *Report*; nevertheless, its
sensationalist account of Welsh immorality was still being reproduced in English-
language fictions located in Wales for decades after the 1840s.

The popular novelist Allen Raine (Anne Adaliza Beynon Puddicombe, 1836–
1908), for example, in her novel *Queen of the Rushes* (1906) links sexual immorality
to Nonconformist night prayer-meetings in a generally disapproving account of the
1904 Welsh religious revival. The daughter of a Castellnewydd Emlyn solicitor,
Allen Raine married an English banker and lived for much of her life near
Croydon. She retained close connections with her native land, however, and chose
Cardiganshire as the setting for her eleven novels and numerous short stories.[16] Yet
her middle-class and English-language upbringing and her subsequent anglicized
allegiances can be said to have coloured her outlook: she often represented the local
practices of her fictional characters, particularly their religious worship, from the
point of view of a disapproving outsider. In *Queen of the Rushes*, Gildas, a
Cardiganshire farmer, becomes worried by his wife Nance's fervent advocacy of the

---

15 *Report of the Commission of Inquiry into the State of Education in Wales…In Three Parts. Part I,
Carmarthen, Glamorgan and Pembroke. Part II, Brecknock, Cardigan, Radnor and Monmouth. Part
III, North Wales* (London, 1847), II, 56
16. For further biographical information, see Sally Roberts Jones, *Allen Raine*, Writers of Wales
series (Cardiff: University of Wales Press, 1979).

revival, which he himself disapproves of. He is right to be worried, for Nance is attending meetings in part in order to meet a young sea-captain with whom she has become enamoured. When Gildas follows her to chapel one night, he is warned of the danger to his marriage by a neighbour, old Fanni, who tells him, 'I am seeing many things; you at home instead of in chapel; mestress, pwr thing, going alone; and—come here, man, let me whisper to you. *Walk home with her yourself over the moor o' nights.*'[17] In other words, the mixed sex and strongly emotional nightly prayer-meetings of Nonconformist Wales are portrayed by Raine in 1906 as incitements to sexual impropriety just as they were in 1847 by the Commissioners of the Government's *Report*.

In fact, however, as part of their attempts to refute such allegations, the leaders of Welsh Nonconformity policed the sexual behaviour of the women of their congregations with a heavy censoriousness during the second half of the nineteenth century. Unwed mothers were excommunicated from chapel membership and publicly shamed, with a repressiveness which became in itself, ironically enough, another factor in the fictional condemnation of Welsh Dissent. Usually presented sympathetically as victim rather than sinner, the fallen woman driven in disgrace from chapel became a familiar trope in popular fiction located in Wales. In another of Allen Raine's novels, *By Berwen Banks* (1899), the animosity between Nonconformists and Anglicans provides the backdrop for a Romeo and Juliet romance with the young lovers separated by the bigotry of their parents. Caradoc Wynne, the vicar's son, and Valmai Powell, the Methodist minister's niece, marry secretly before Caradoc leaves for Australia, but in his absence the pregnant Valmai is excommunicated from her chapel, and driven from her home by her uncle. This does not cause her much personal grief, however, as she has already decided that her own instinct is 'purer and healthier' than her uncle's religion; according to the text, 'her joyous nature could not brook the saddening influences of the Methodist creed.'[18] More typically, the victim of the chapel's scorn is severely traumatised by her public disgrace, as in the well-known scene from Richard Llewellyn's *How Green Was My Valley* in which Meillyn Lewis is bullied by the chapel deacons.[19] The popularity of the Hollywood film of that novel, which lingers over a pitiful enactment of Meillyn's excommunication, helped to make such episodes stereotypically representative of Welsh chapel life. A 1992 novel on the Welsh valleys during the 1930s goes as far as to depict the unfortunate Phyllis Harry as stoned in chapel as part of the ritual of her banishment, the deacons having carried

---

17 Allen Raine, *Queen of the Rushes: A Tale of the Welsh Revival* (1906; Dinas Powys: Honno, 1998), 147.

18 Allen Raine, *By Berwen Banks* (London: Hutchinson, 1899), 28.

19 Richard Llewellyn, *How Green Was My Valley* (1939; London: Penguin, 1951), 104–5.

stones into the chapel for the purpose.[20]

That such scenes for sensationalist reasons exaggerate the degree of communal vilification poured on the miscreant's head is suggested by a very different account of the same practice which came from the pen of one very familiar with the habits of the Welsh Methodists at the close of the nineteenth century: Sara Maria Saunders (1864–1939) was the grand-daughter of one Methodist preacher, the hymn writer David Charles, and the wife of another. The series of linked short stories she published in both Welsh and English characteristically feature village communities whose lives are centred on their chapel, but who can nevertheless resist the propensity of any leading member of the congregation to bully others or apply the double sexual standard too destructively. In her story 'His Majesty of Pentre-Rhedyn', published in the journal *Young Wales* in 1896, the Methodists of Pentre-Rhedyn are in danger of falling under the tyrannical rule of the wealthiest man in the village, Mr Morris, who is also a chapel deacon. But Mr Morris's hold on the congregation is broken by the old preacher Mr Rogers and his wife: when Mr Morris turns Becca, the saddler's pregnant daughter, out of the chapel, telling her that God hates her for what she has done, Mr Rogers intervenes. According to the villager who narrates the tale,

> 'up gets old Mr Rogers, 'is face lookin' (for 'im) very black. "I can't sit still," says 'e, "an' hear the God I loves spoken of like that;" an' he…walks down to where Becca was sittin', an' 'e put 'is 'and on 'er 'ead, an' said:—"Whatever you've done, whatever sin you've been guilty of, remember, God loves you".'[21]

Nevertheless Becca is still excommunicated; her gentle preacher cannot save her from that. But the disgrace she endures is itself turned back against the chapels in the works of later twentieth-century Welsh writers. The repressive measures introduced into chapel organisation post-1847, in order to avoid any repetition of the shame inflicted by the government Commissioners' *Report*, now in themselves become the offences for which they are condemned. Whether damned for inciting uncontrollable passions or for the extreme zeal with which it repressed them, chapel culture is seen as too primitive, too barbaric, in its uncivilised excess, in a manner which accords with Matthew Arnold's 1867 characterisation of the Celts as 'undisciplinable, anarchical and turbulent'.[22] By the close of the nineteenth century, however, quite another type of voice was being raised in the literary attack against

---

20 See Catrin Collier, *Hearts of Gold* (1992; London: Arrow Books, 1993), 144–5.

21 S. M. S. [Sara Maria Saunders], 'His Majesty of Pentre-Rhedyn', *Young Wales*, ii (January, 1896), 6.

22 Matthew Arnold, *On the Study of Celtic Literature* (1867; London: Dent, 1910), 86.

the forces of Welsh Nonconformity.

II

Keir Hardie's election at Merthyr Tydfil in 1900 as Britain's first Independent Labour Party MP testified to the south Wales coalfield's vanguard position in the rise of British socialism; from the first the new movement clashed with a Welsh Nonconformity strongly identified politically with the Liberal party. The Calvinist Methodist denomination, in particular, which included as one of its *Rules* for its members 'that they do not speak evil of dignitaries, but that they conscientiously honour and obey the king, and all that are put in authority under him,'[23] banned from its membership those who 'wore the badge of a benefit society', that is, belonged to the early embryo trade unions.[24] In a historical account which strongly resembles the famous scenes from Daniel Owen's Welsh-language novel *Rhys Lewis* (1885), in which the Methodist mother Mari Lewis pleads with her socialist son Bob to return to the faith, Will Playnter in his autobiography *My Generation* recalls how, in 1921, after his Methodist Sunday School had ejected one of its teachers for becoming a Christian socialist, he renounced his chapel membership, causing his mother 'a great deal of anguish':

> I remember coming home from the pit one afternoon to find the resident minister waiting for me…He tried his best to get me to change my attitude and return to the chapel. Finally he got down on his knees, pulling my mother and me down with him, and prayed for my salvation. Mother started to cry and I became very angry, yanking the minister unceremoniously to his feet, telling him as best I could that I would never respond to such methods. He then told me the story of a similar experience he had had in another mining valley of a lad like me refusing God, and how on the day following his talk with him, while he was walking down the street, the minister saw men carrying a body from the pit. It was this young lad, who, in the minister's words, had 'rejected his eleventh hour chance of salvation'.[25]

Unlike Daniel Owen's Bob, who is indeed killed in a pit accident but not before he

---

23 *Rules and the Design of the Religious Societies among the Welsh Methodists read and agreed upon at their Quarterly Association held at Bala, June 16 and 17, 1801* (Chester: W. C. Jones, 1802), 26–7.
24 E. T. Davies, *Religion in the Industrial Revolution in South Wales* (Cardiff: University of Wales Press, 1965), 54.
25 Will Paynter, *My Generation* (London: George Allen & Unwin, 1972), 27–8. I am grateful to Christopher Meredith for directing me to this reference.

has 'seen the light', Playnter survives, unrepentant, and goes on to become President of the South Wales Miners' Federation and eventually Secretary of the National Union of Mineworkers.

The animosity between chapel and union lodge is effectively dramatised in Merthyr-born J. O. Francis's 1912 play *Change*, which shows a family torn apart by its changing allegiances. The father, John Price, a staunch Methodist, is strongly opposed to the cause of the socialist parliamentary candidate, Pinkerton, who like Keir Hardie himself, is an outsider to Aberpandy, a Glamorgan industrial village. As Price explains,

> I've been in the valley here now for sixty years. I remember Aberpandy before ever the Powell-Griffiths sank the first pit, and the sheep of Pandy Farm were grazing quiet where the Bryndu Pit is now. And I never so much heard talk of this fellow Pinkerton till two or three years ago...D'you ever hear of him so much as darkening the door of a chapel—or even of the Church for a matter of that? Why can't he hold his old meetings on some other day than Sunday?...Who was it built Horeb up there on the hillside, more than forty years ago?...Every day, after coming home from the pit, every day we did a little, tired as we were, for the love of the cause...Stone by stone we built it. With our own hands we built it...And d'you think I'll stand by and see it lost without making a struggle?[26]

However, the consequences of his 'struggle' are the destruction of his family: his sons are alienated from him and even his wife finally pronounces judgement upon him as 'a hard, hard man.'[27]

Another early twentieth-century writer who received much praise from socialist quarters for his radical critique of chapel culture was Caradoc Evans, whose short story collection *My People* when it was published in 1915 was hailed by the Swansea Valley socialist weekly *Labour Voice* as 'by a long way the best book that any Welshman of our day has written'.[28] Evans, the child of a Rhydlewis widow, was brought up in poverty in a rural Cardiganshire dominated by Methodism, believing his mother to be persecuted by the chapel because she had married an Anglican. The deacons and ministers of Welsh Nonconformity are presented in *My People* as corrupt tyrants, who grow fat on the superstitious worship of their bullied congregations. In the tale 'Be this her Memorial', for example, the impoverished

---

[26] J. O. Francis, *Change: A Glamorgan Play* (1912; Cardiff: Educational Publishing Co., 1920), 23 and 30–31.

[27] Ibid., 132.

[28] W. H. Stevenson, reviewing *My People* in *Labour Voice*; quoted in John Harris's 'Introduction' to his edition of *My People* (Bridgend: Seren, 1987), 43.

pensioner Nanni feeds herself on rats in order to save sufficient of her scant funds to buy a Bible as a farewell gift for her minister Bryn-Bevan, about to move to another, richer chapel. Starved and sick, Nanni is not present at the minister's last service when he is handed her gift, only immediately to dispose of it to another member, 'in recognition of his work in the School.'[29] Bryn-Bevan clearly has scant regard for Nanni, but before finally quitting the area, he calls on her in her cottage, only to find her lying on the dirt floor:

> There was no movement from Nanni. Mishtir Bryn-Bevan went on his knees and peered at her. Her hands were clasped tightly together, as though guarding some great treasure. The minister raised himself and prised them apart with the ferrule of his walking-stick. A roasted rat revealed itself. Mishtir Bryn-Bevan stood for several moments spellbound and silent; and in the stillness the rats crept boldly out of their hiding places and resumed their attack on Nanni's face. The minister, startled and horrified, fled from the house of sacrifice.[30]

Such scenes as these, more emotively destructive in their indictment of chapel culture than any outsider criticisms, made the name Caradoc Evans abhorred in Welsh Nonconformist circles. Bryn-Bevan treats his tragically-deluded devotee like vermin: he does not bend to touch her, only pokes at her with his stick, and the way in which he keeps his distance and allows the rats to devour her emphasizes the pointlessness of her sacrifice. But the very concept of 'sacrifice' as a way of life was in itself increasingly becoming challenged, as the majority opinion in industrialised Wales swung behind the socialist principles of fighting for one's rights and no longer acquiescing with exploitation.

Such principles are also implicitly upheld in the first novel of the young Rhys Davies, the son of a grocer from Blaenclydach in the Rhondda. *The Withered Root* (1927) is another fictionalisation of the 1904 revival, this time focussed on the figure of the revivalist himself who rapidly burns himself out in his excessive zeal, much as the historical evangelist Evan Roberts was said to have done. But Rhys Davies's evangelist Reuben Daniels is advised at the outset of his career, as a miner turned preacher, that socialism is the way forward for Wales not a religious revival. His London-educated friend Philip Vaughan, seeing Daniels as typical of his benighted nation, tells him,

> 'You Welsh! A race of mystical poets who have gone awry in some way…To me there seems to be a darkness over your land and a futility in your struggles

---

29 Caradoc Evans, 'Be This Her Memorial', *My People* (1915; Bridgend: Seren Press, 1987), 111.
30 Ibid., 112.

to assert your ancient nationality. Your brilliant children leave you because of the hopeless stagnation of your miserable Nonconformist towns: the religion of your chapels is a blight on the flowering souls of your young…And you, Reuben, with your helpless pity that is instinct with you, pity for the submerged classes I suppose, why don't you work that pity into a burning rage and strive to destroy that which angers you? Instead of worrying over a dead religion.'[31]

His friend's words have little effect on Reuben, who stoutly replies, "That religion is not dead. It is the glory of Wales," but their sentiments are echoed in the work of many other writers of the period.

Idris Davies, the Rhymney poet, for example, rued the fact that, as he saw it, 'In Wales religion is a fungus which spread rapidly after the semi-lunatic Methodist Revival, and which spawned still coarsest after the crudenesses of the 1904–5 Revival.'[32] Like Will Playnter, Davies too had apparently clashed with the deacons in his youth and later left the chapel, involving himself instead during the years in which he worked as a miner with union politics. In *Gwalia Deserta* (1938) he remembers that

> Because I was sceptical in our Sunday School
> And tried to picture Jesus crawling in the local mine,
> The dozen deacons bred on the milk of Spurgeon
> Told me I was dangerous and in danger,
> That I would be roasted and pronged and tossed like a pancake…[33]

But the threat of hellfire appears to have been as ineffective in his case as it was in Playnter's; if anything it but increased such apostates' conviction that chapel culture was repressive and conformist through fear.

In Swansea in the 1930s another young poet similarly disparaged the Welsh Sunday as the day on which the 'Sunday-walkers…put on their black suits, reddest eyes, & meanest expressions' and 'like a river end up in the Sabbath well where the corpses of strangled preachers, promising all their days a heaven they don't believe in to people who won't go there, float and hide truth'. 'I see the rehearsed gestures, the correct smiles, the grey cells revolving around nothing under the godly bowlers,'

---

31 Rhys Davies, *The Withered Root* (London: Robert Holden, 1927), 100–1.

32 Idris Davies, unpublished newspaper correspondence, 3 June 1938, quoted in Islwyn Jenkins, *Idris Davies of Rhymney: A Personal Memoir* (Llandysul: Gomer Press, 1986), 265.

33 Idris Davies, 'Gwalia Deserta', xxiv, *The Complete Poems of Idris Davies*, ed. Dafydd Johnston (Cardiff: University of Wales Press, 1994), 13. Charles Haddon Spurgeon (1834–1892) was a celebrated Baptist preacher.

Dylan Thomas wrote to Pamela Hansford Johnson in 1934, describing the Sabbath scene from his Cwmdonkin window.[34] The enthusiasm and intensity often depicted with so much disapproval in earlier English-language representations of chapel culture is displaced in these examples by a portrayal of Nonconformity as a system of at best stifling respectability and at worst exploitative hypocrisy. To the new twentieth-century communities forged in Wales' industrial areas the chapels often appeared but as agents of reaction and a blight upon the aspirations and political fervour of the young, and their decline was rapid. By the close of the century, only about one sixth of the Welsh population attended a Christian place of worship, and the Church in Wales, disestablished since 1920, was the denomination with the largest membership.[35]

III

But as the chapels emptied, the poets of Wales began to celebrate its very landscape as haunted and numinous, laden with the historical associations of a past spiritual intensity. Or so at least Jeremy Hooker convincingly argues in *Imagining Wales*, which sees the work of such poets as David Jones, Alun Lewis, R. S. Thomas, Roland Mathias, Tony Conran, Gillian Clarke, Hilary Llewellyn-Williams and Anne Cluysenaar as imaginatively engaged with Welsh localities in such a manner as to recreate that 'world within the world' discerned in them by the earlier monks, priests, peripatetic preachers, hymn writers and visionaries who lived and traveled through them.[36] As Hooker has also said of the verse of Rowan Williams, such poetry 'makes room' for the sacred fields of the past within the perception of the derelict modern landscapes which now overlay them.[37] Hooker is here referring to Williams' poem 'Penrhys' which describes 'the worn sub-Gothic infant, hanging awkwardly/ around' its mother amidst the 'broken glass' of this Rhondda Valley council estate, while a footnote reminds us that Penrhys was once 'the site of a medieval shrine of Our Lady'.[38] The Christian associations to which the poet's choice of words give rise insist that the spiritual dimension is not absent although apparently submerged. Hooker sees such double vision as a characteristic

---

34 Dylan Thomas, letter to Pamela Hansford Johnson, 15 April 1934, *The Collected Letters of Dylan Thomas*, ed. Paul Ferris (London: Dent, 1985), 110–11.

35 See John May ed., *Reference Wales* (Cardiff: University of Wales Press, 1994), 99.

36 Jeremy Hooker, *Imagining Wales*, 167; Hooker is here quoting from an essay by Anne Cluysenaar on Henry Vaughan.

37 Jeremy Hooker, 'Interruption and renewal: the new poems of Rowan Williams', *New Welsh Review*, 56 (2001–2), 144.

38 Rowan Williams, *The Poems of Rowan Williams* (Oxford: The Perpetua Press, 2002), 51.

component of Welsh identity, in part because in order to survive as Welsh the imagination has had to rely upon its ability to make the past forever present, once more real, in such a fashion.

The only prose writers included in Hooker's argument in *Imagining Wales* are Emyr Humphreys and John Cowper Powys, but the work of other Welsh novelists and short story writers can also be said to evince similar preoccupations. Arthur Machen, for example, penned some curious tales akin in theme, though sometimes admittedly much cruder in style than the poets' art. In *The Great Return* (1915) the villagers of Llantrisant suddenly experience a communal vision of the Holy Grail which brings them together to celebrate the mass of the Sangraal in their local church. 'The Methodists with their minister and their deacons and all the Nonconformists had returned on this Sunday morning to "the old hive",' says the story's narrator, and the old Calvinist deacons shout '*Gogoniant, gogoniant*—glory! glory!' in ecstasy along with the rest of the congregation.39 Similarly in Machen's later story 'The gift of tongues', the Reverend Thomas Beynon, minister of Bryn Seion Chapel, Treowen, Monmouthshire, while preaching in his pulpit one Christmas morning in the early 1870s, starts suddenly to utter a nobler, more 'awful' chant than his congregation has heard from his lips before. 'Neither Welsh—the language of the chapel—nor English,' his utterance bewilders all, including the Reverend himself who can afterwards give no account of it, for he is not conscious of knowing a third language. All he can say of the experience is that he 'felt that he had been in heaven.' Before the story's close, however, it is suggested that his language might have been Latin: 'Who is to say,' says the narrator, 'that the old preacher had not strayed long before into some Roman Catholic Church at Newport or Cardiff on a Christmas Day, and there heard Mass with exterior horror and interior love?'40 While Machen is no doubt deliberately teasing his Nonconformist readers with these tales of the inerasable influence of 'old Rome', yet their mood is tender, and celebratory of the underlying unity of the denominations and their links with a spiritual Welsh past.

Another fictional work which appears intent upon building bridges between the sects dates from what has historically been considered to be the most intransigent period of church versus chapel bitterness in Wales. In Eleanor Griffiths' *World Worship* (1853), the question of sectarianism is dismissed as entirely insignificant. Far from leading to dangerous excess, 'enthusiasm is the soul's health' in *World*

---

39 Arthur Machen, *The Great Return* (The Faith Press, 1915) collected in *Holy Terrors* (Harmondsworth: Penguin, 1946), 135–6.

40 Arthur Machen, 'The Gift of Tongues' in Peter Haining, ed., *Great Welsh Fantasy Stories* (Llanrwst: Gwasg Carreg Gwalch, 2000), 157–9.

Worship;[41] while adhering too slavishly to the secular mores of a debased and materialist society endangers mental balance. These maxims are spelt out in the novel's plot: the unfortunate Clara Smedley, a middle-class English visitor to Wales, is at the close carried to a madhouse in a state of 'confirmed and hopeless lunacy,'[42] not because she has succumbed to religious enthusiasm but on the contrary because she has resisted it. Caught up in the trammels of 'world worship', Clara denied and betrayed the near-conversion she experienced on a wild Welsh hillside, under the guidance of Welsh evangelist Winfred Egerton. At a crucial moment, when Clara is close to succumbing, Egerton, to encourage her, describes his own conversion, which occurred when, after a period in which he had neglected his religion, he suddenly once again found himself as if by whim entering through 'the doors of a place of religious worship.'

> 'Was it a church or a Dissenting chapel?' asked Clara, with abrupt eagerness.
> 'That is of little moment,' replied Mr Egerton…'It was truth, urged with simple fervour, and with great plainness of speech.'[43]

Nevertheless, the evangelicals in this text are all Anglicans rather than Dissenters. In its insistence on the over-riding importance of the moment of grace which constitutes the conversion experience, and its focus on rural Wales as the 'natural' landscape of true conversion, *World Worship* may read more like an early Welsh Methodist memoir than an English-language novel of the period, yet the author in her preface informs us that its characters were modelled on the Welsh clergy of her acquaintance, along with her Anglican neighbours in Llandeilo Fawr, Carmarthenshire. For these church-goers Welsh hymns have a peculiar importance: Egerton's daughter Margaret is at one point asked to sing 'that wild Welsh hymn that you say you learnt in your childhood.'[44] Egerton by now is dead, and the scene takes place in urban England, where Margaret lives with her guardian. But when she complies and sings the Welsh hymn, she sees again in the mind's eye the wild landscape in which she learned it, and hears 'the piping of the stone-chat' and 'the plashing of the busy rill' which sounded through her childhood. The hymn 'has a voice which stirs the heart to its depths' and 'tones that sweep over the heart's inner temple, and bring to light names and effigies that have been graven there for life.'[45] That is, it has that capacity to evoke a spiritual 'world within the world' which Hooker sees as a characteristic of Welsh poetry generally. The novel

---

41 Eleanor Griffiths, *World Worship* (London: James Nisbet, 1853), 101.
42 Ibid., 369.
43 Ibid., 69
44 Ibid., 277.
45 Ibid, 281.

does not divulge which Welsh hymn Margaret sang, but given the intensity of the characters' concern with religious conversion, the likelihood is that it belonged to the tradition of Methodist hymn writers, with its strong emphasis on the conversion experience, and frequent metaphorical references to the Welsh landscape.

The Welsh-language hymn functions in this 1850s novel, then, much as it does in the work of many twentieth-century Welsh writers, of both languages. In R. S. Thomas's 'Fugue to Ann Griffiths', for example, the hymns of the late eighteenth-century farmer's daughter from Dolwar-fach are similarly represented as having the capacity to reconstruct in their spiritual intensity a 'world within the world' whenever they are sung. Ann 'who had decomposed// is composed again in her hymns,' says the poet. 'In which period/ do you get lost?', he asks his readers. For him 'The roads lead/ under a twentieth century/ sky to the peace of the nineteenth', to Dolwar-fach, and a time when

> Here for a few years
> the spirit sang on a bone bough
> at eternity's window, the flesh trembling
> at the splendour of a forgiveness
> too impossible to believe in, yet believing.[46]

It would appear that for chapel and church men and women alike, and no doubt for many others who continue to find the New Testament 'too impossible to believe in', the hymns of the Welsh Nonconformist tradition still serve to provide an answer to Roland Mathias's question, with which this chapter opened, 'Is the old witness done?' One resource that is yet 'left of this latish day that began with love' is the rich store of Welsh hymnology, particularly those verses dating from the eighteenth-century Methodist revivals. In Anglophone Welsh literature, both the nineteenth-century novelist and twentieth-century poet unite in assuring us that the intensity of feeling captured within these hymns has the capacity to recreate itself as they are sung or heard, and to open a window on a 'road...age-old and never ageing/ a road without a beginning, which is yet new' ('Ffordd...Hen, ac heb heneiddio yw;/ Ffordd heb ddechreu, eto'n newydd').[47]

---

46 R. S. Thomas, 'Fugue for Ann Griffiths', 1987, *Collected Poems* (London: Dent, 1993), 471 and 474.

47 Ann Griffiths, *Gwaith Ann Griffiths*, ed O. M. Edwards (Llanuwchllyn: Ab Owen, n.d. [1905]), 30.

Spires of Grass:
Emily Brontë's Fragment of Eternity

Stevie Davies

G OD had forsaken her. The Father, safe and indifferent in his heaven, surrounded by craven angels in an eternity of sybaritic ease, had turned his back on the mother world. In response, Emily Brontë turned from the Christian God, preferring the natural world from whose suffering he had apparently absconded. Her own mother had died when the child was three: although her mother's remains had been committed to the interior of Haworth Church, Emily experienced the earth as her mother's burial ground and memorial, the site equally of sanctuary and death, play-space and region of loss and reminiscence, inextricably entwined.

> Ah mother, what shall comfort thee
> In all this boundless misery?
> ....…
> Indeed, no dazzling land above
> Can cheat thee of they children's love.
> We all, in life's departing shine,
> Our last dear longings blend with thine;
> And struggle still and strive to trace
> With clouded gaze, thy darling face.
> We would not leave our native home
> For *any* world beyond the Tomb.
> No—rather on thy kindly breast
> Let us be laid in lasting rest;
> Or waken but to share with thee
> A mutual immortality.[1]

---

[1] Emily Brontë, 'I see around me tombstones grey', ll. 29–30, 35–46, in *The Complete Poems of Emily Jane Brontë*, ed. C. W. Hatfield (New York: Columbia University Press, 1941). All further references to Brontë's poems in this chapter are from this edition, silently checked

In this angrily tender poem of 1841, Emily Brontë states her affiliation to the lower world: the totality of animate and sentient life on the mother planet. Such solipsistic bliss as the Bible offered to believers held no attraction for her, being based on an ethic of obedience and a theology at once repugnant and illogical: a concept of love that involved punishment of the sinner by the Absolute was a contradiction in terms. Earth, grounded in affliction and mortality, is the place of solidarity and bonding.

In *Wuthering Heights*, itself a great narrative and dramatic spiritual poem, the seventeen-year-old Cathy Earnshaw narrates a dream that has gone 'through and through' her, 'and altered the colour of my mind'. She dreams she has gone to heaven, where she cannot be happy:

> heaven did not seem to be my home; and I broke my heart with weeping to come back to earth; and the angels were so angry that they flung me out, in the middle of the heath on the top of Wuthering Heights; where I woke sobbing for joy...[2]

Cathy willingly repeats the fall of man, violating and subverting God's fixed law by provoking the angels to violence: those same angels who evicted Lucifer from heaven. She falls from that Miltonic place 'high above all height' to the homely 'top' of Wuthering Heights. A sequence of aspirated 'H's breathes an exhalation of relief as they chart her return journey: *heaven ... home ... heart ... heath*. These—and the word *earth*—are key words of *Wuthering Heights*, recurring throughout the novel but also encoded within the very names of the characters, who share a cryptic ground of identity both with and in one another and with the earth from which they came and to which they are bound in death. The names of Catherine, Heathcliff, Hareton and Earnshaw are nearly anagrammatic, each containing most or all of the words *heath*, *heart*, *hearth* and *earth*. These complex mirrorings at once conceal and intimate, as we read, identity of origin: in the earth. But they also imply the conclusion of the extreme loves of the first generation: in the earth.

Talismanic for Emily Brontë, the word 'earth' often opens and concludes poems:

---

against Janet Gezari's edition, *Emily Jane Brontë, The Complete Poems* (London: Penguin, 1992) and *The Poems of Emily Brontë*, edited by Derek Roper with Edward Chitham (Oxford: Clarendon Press, 1995). I believe Hatfield's text remains more friendly to the reader and very accurate: Gezari's ordering of the poems and the editorial choice by Roper to preserve Emily's bizarre spellings makes these texts less attractive, although Roper's text and introduction are most illuminating for any scholar interested in the manuscripts and in Emily Brontë's conception and composition. Roper's transcriptions of the Gondal records are definitive.

2   Emily Brontë, *Wuthering Heights*, ed. Ian Jack (Oxford and London: Oxford University Press, 1998), pp. 79–80. All further references to Brontë's novel in this chapter are to this edition, abbreviated to WH.

a poem of 1841 opening 'Shall Earth no more inspire thee' (1841) resolves in the penultimate stanza, 'none would ask a Heaven/ More like this Earth than thine'; a lyric of 1843 opens, 'In the earth, the earth thou shalt be laid'; a poem of 1845 begins, 'Cold in the earth and the deep snow piled above thee'. The word *earth* is the ground and foundation of meaning in the mother world. It implies not just the abstract 'world', 'globe' or 'landscape' but peat, clay, fibre and stones, 'the eternal rocks beneath', together with the vegetation this sustains on the surface and the underworld into which life's remains decompose. Jeremy Hooker's and Lee Grandjean's vision of 'the human ground' and 'groundwork' expresses something of Emily Bronté's vision:

> what Lee Grandjean calls 'that ground of elemental energy from which all matter emerges and into which all things are eventually enfolded.' In this latter respect, it is associated with possibility, with loss of ego boundaries in an enlarged sense of being, and with imaginative energy that both makes and breaks images, in an attempt to intimate the power beyond images, on which all life depends.3

Iconoclastic, visionary and yet founded in detailed identification with creaturely life and its habitat, Emily's vision takes its spiritual energy—its Coleridgean 'esemplastic' power—from Romanticism. Grandjean's formulation implies a similar source. Emily Bronte's 'sea of grass', her long view of the moors, expresses the bliss of the 'oceanic feeling' intimated above by Hooker ('loss of ego boundaries in an enlarged sense of being'). In *Wuthering Heights*, Cathy's claim that 'I *am* Heathcliff' (p. 82) brings that boundarylessness into catastrophic and ironic conflict with the finite conditions prevailing on this nether planet. And the self was fatally divided: her great philosophic poems record the strife within: 'three Gods within this little frame/ Are warring night and day' ('The Philosopher', ll. 17–18).

Emily Bronté's conception of the earth, which derives from the Christian concept of the three-tiered universe (heaven, earth, hell), has much in common with the uneasy Greek Eleusinian compact between the overarching upper world of the gods, the surface and the nether world of burial chamber and underworld. Humanity at the centre is menaced from above and below. Emily collapses the distinction between Heaven and Hell: these are complicit realms, fighting what is essentially—as far as her heathen characters are concerned—someone else's battle. It is the homely surface of earth, covered with the vesture of rooted insentient life, composed above a reliquary and vulnerable to the forbidding gods above, that endures at the centre of Emily's vision. Her love was given to the totality of creaturely life with whom she shared air, planet and grave, both predator and prey. Sensing in herself the violence of the carnivore and the softness of the nestling, she was capable of viewing the universe

---

3   Jeremy Hooker, *Adamah* (London: Enitharmon Press, 2002), 107.

(as she wrote in a Brussels essay) as 'created on a principle of destruction'.4 Both *Wuthering Heights* and her poetry teem with animals: hare and deer, wolf and house-dog, merlin, lark, thrush and robin, together with that hunted raptor, man. Nature is a blood-bath: the skeletons of the baby lapwings exposed at the centre of the heath testify to the cost of life on this planet. To all she extended an equal benediction, living as they did under divine curse, in 'earth's storm-troubled sphere' ('No coward soul', l.2).

One of her earliest surviving poems celebrates 'High-waving heather 'neath stormy clouds bending'. The wilderness-world of Emily Brontë's imagination is often alluded to as if heath and heather had magical properties. We roam the moors above Haworth in her footsteps, viewing a world of heather, dark and fibrous, charcoal-black or silver when it has been burnt back, bright with new shoots, purple in August and September. In the heath and rock we intuit Heathcliff and the wild landscape of Emily Brontë's most powerful poetry. Heather is doubtless more poetical than, say, common grass, but on this too she confers something sacramental. Her vision—the light her mind shed on the growing world—is radical. In a dialogue poem of 1843, ('In the earth, the earth'), one voice welcomes the time 'when my sunny hair/ Shall with grass-roots twinèd be' (ll.7–8). In another she visualises the double world, above and underground:

> Upon the earth in sunlight
> Spring grass grows green and fair;
> But beneath the earth is midnight,
> Eternal midnight there.
> ('To A. S., 1830', ll.9–12)

The timeless underworld is the foundation and condition of conscious life in the light and has its own black majesty. The green world, like the 'foliage in the woods' of *Wuthering Heights*, roots down into 'the eternal rocks beneath' (pp. 81–2). The acid peat of moorland soil preserves the dead from fast decay; the dead are mantled in green life.

*

The roots of Emily's sacramental vision of nature go back to her childhood when she played on the moors above her father's church: Charlotte was to call Emily 'a native and nursling of the moors'. Her earliest extant lyrics are dated to July 1836 when she

---

4   Emily Brontë, 'The Butterfly', as translated by Stevie Davies in *Emily Brontë: Heretic* (London: The Women's Press, 1994), 250

was just eighteen years old; the attitudes she held then had long been part of her. Some of these early poems were copied into the two famous notebooks of 1844, 'Gondal Poems' and personal poems; others have come down to us on separate leaves, where Emily had made fair copies in the minuscule writing known as 'Brontë small script'. To imagine these loose manuscripts as formal pages, regularly set out, would be a mistake. They are no more than slips of paper, the smallest measuring about two inches by one, the largest about six and a half by three. In the Brontës' frugal household, paper was scarce, precious and recycled. On one such scrap, known as D12, she copied a series of poems and fragments including one of the most perfect imagist fragments in the language, whose opening phrase I have chosen as the title of this essay. It reads:

> Only some spires of bright green grass
> Transparently in sunshine quivering

No more than that. But these two lines open out a vista to Emily's entire development.

The fragment is one of twelve fair-copied on both sides of a single sheet. The fragments are separated variously by a row of three crosses or a straight line. 'Only some spires' stands as the fourth of six fragments on what is probably the first side: their first lines are as follows:

> 'The battle had passed from the height' (8 lines)
> $+ + +$
> 'How golden bright from earth and heaven' (6 lines)
> $+ + +$
> 'Not a vapour had stained the breezeless blue' (14 lines)
> $+ + +$
> 'Only some spires of bright green grass' (2 lines)
> ⎯⎯⎯⎯
> 'The sun has set, and the long grass now' (8 lines)
> ⎯⎯⎯⎯
> 'Lady, in your Palace Hall' (4 lines)
> ⎯⎯⎯⎯

After the fragment with which I am concerned, Emily has drawn a line, read by some editors as representing the end of the poem. But to my mind, the succeeding fragment, opening 'The sun has set, and the long grass now', constitutes a clear continuation of the meditation pursued in the first four fragments. It may be (and this would be in keeping) that Emily used her own system less than systematically:

lines and crosses might in practice have been interchangeable. This side of the leaf ends with a quatrain, 'Lady, in your Palace Hall', which can less obviously be related to the preceding descriptive and elegiac fragments, though it might well have been composed around the same time and relate to the ongoing story.

That narrative source is the fictional world of Gondal that Emily shared with Anne: a hero has met his end at Lake Elnor. Who, we don't know. And we learn nothing about the battle except that it left many casualties. The poem is unconcerned with these: they contribute only to the irony which lies at the centre of the action, if it can be called action:

> The dead around were sleeping
> On heath and granite grey;
> And the dying their last watch were keeping
> In the closing of the day. (Fragment 1)

The narrative is transferred from the fallen army to the passage of time itself over a landscape: the slow onset of sunset, twilight, evening and moonlight. War yields to the 'golden' sunset which declines 'gloriously' in 'bright rejoicing trees' (Fragment 2). The calm surface of the lake, the safety and rest of the creatures of this landscape, prolong the irony:

> The deer are gathered to their rest
> The wild sheep seek the fold (Fragment 3)

All creatures are bound for home. 'Only some spires' occurs at the threshold of evening, at the liminal moment when a single beam remains to pick out and glorify a patch of grass before evening supervenes. The fifth fragment of the group ('The sun has set') chronicles the scene further into the evening: the long grass has now darkened; the listener in the 'heathy sea' catches only the small sighing of the night wind.

The narrative source in Gondal has been lost. The volumes of prose produced by Emily and Anne over many years, constituting a hinterland to the poems, were destroyed perhaps by Charlotte Brontë after her sister's death or, I think less credibly, by Emily herself when she found herself to be dying.[5] The Gondal saga had been produced in two stages. First Emily and Anne improvised, acted and directed the parts of their numerous *dramatis personae* (both male and female) in the outdoors, when they ran out of the Parsonage to play or on the way to some destination. So the

---

5 The case is set out in Edward Chitham's *A Life of Emily Brontë* (Oxford: Basil Blackwell, 1987), 218.

work that began as childhood play developed into drama. This creative invention left them with broad lines of plot and character development, essentially in a raw form to be adapted at the writing stage. The second part of the process came when, together or (increasingly, as years passed) apart, the sisters committed this to paper, in the form of fiction, fictional histories, lyrics and narrative poetry. Only tantalising threads remain, chiefly in the diary papers: 'The Gondals are discovering the interior of Gaaldine' (1834); 'The Gondalians are at present in a threatening state...' (1841); 'during our Excursion we were Ronald Macalgin, Henry Angora...' (1845).[6] Though it haunts Emily's lyrics, we cannot accurately reconstruct Gondal. In this sense the Gondal poems are all fragments, freed from their narrative matrix like arias from a lost opera, or like ancient Greek poems known only through the survival of partial manuscripts or in quotation.

The two-line poem Emily Brontë saw fit to preserve is therefore a fragment of a fragment. In the Romantic period the poetic fragment had its own high status: a cryptic power of delicate suggestion, a beam of light into eternity. The isolation of fragments from the Greek canon, such as Sappho's lyrics, and the fragmentary ruins of Greece and Rome, stand at the back of these sublime remnants. Sappho's power to shape abandoned longing in a tersely economical form is not lost but further intensified by the arbitrary fragmentariness to which time reduced her poetry, often cutting the remnant suggestively free from grammatical bondings. Emily Brontë used the fragment to express unassuageable desire or inexpressible mystery. Her poetry, which often escaped syntactical precision by eschewing punctuation and suspending its grammar in a present participle, was laconic, sensuous, immediate; like *Wuthering Heights* it addressed itself to a world 'beyond', 'over there', 'beneath', casting the 'anchor of Desire/ Deep in unknown Eternity' ('How beautiful the earth is still'). As a late Romantic poet with profound affinity with German Romanticism, whose influence she was to assimilate on her visit to Europe in the 1842,[7] she appreciated the form of the fragment as embodying the lyricism of lyricism. She was in any case a person of few words, short with others and not always sweet.

Romantic poets and philosophers, especially in Germany, treated the fragment as at once a complete unit (like a crystal) and as a completely open form. Open to multiple construction, the fragment's inconclusiveness and irresolution led on to the

---

6   As transcribed by Roper in *Poems*, 295–6.

7   See *Emily Brontë: Heretic*, chapters 1 and 2, for a fuller account of this debt. Friedrich Schlegel's *Literary Aphorisms* are of the greatest interest in a reading of Emily Brontë's fragment poems: 'Many works of the ancients have become fragments. Many works of the moderns are fragments at the time of their origins' (Aphorism 24); 'Romantic poetry is always becoming and ... can never be complete. It cannot be exhausted by any theory' (Aphorism 116), in *'Dialogue on Poetry' and 'Literary Aphorisms'*, tr. and ed. Ernst Behler and Roman Struc (Philadelphia: Pennsylvania State University, 1968), 134, 141.

domain of Romantic irony. And multivalent irony was close to the sublime, as the mode of expression equating most truly with an infinite and unknowable universe. Emily Brontë, whom I have elsewhere called the sole English novelist with a full understanding of dualistic philosophy,[8] was an ironist of distinction and some ferocity, not—or not only—in the dialectical sense of using the figure of speech we recognise as irony, by which a statement implies its opposite, but in the sense Schlegel would have recognised of a many-valenced field of meaning, Her irony engenders no certainty, only intimations. In Emily Brontë's fiction and poetry, the moorlands themselves are the area of essential and irreducible irony and ambivalence. Her treatment of the uncanny and the unknown moves beyond Gothic to show the familiar universe as *terra incognita*. Her greatest poems have a philosophic dimension and a metaphysical ambition that is not afraid to seem hubristic. But they are rooted—earthed, grounded, I may say—in the mystery of the common world we take for granted.

In the group of poems to which the 'spires of grass' fragment belongs, the focus is on semi-consciousness and imminent return to the earth. The sequence, in its reluctance to develop, implies something of Emily Brontë's custom of composing in a state of reverie, doodling lines on scraps of paper. My guess is that the poems were first drafted in the outdoors, or soon after coming in. However this may be, their development seems to mimic 'real time', solitude in open spaces at the suspenseful close of day. In August, the date that heads the first fragment, sunset falls at mid-evening. Both the Gondal story and the moorlands were equally 'real' to Emily. But in the fragments we are considering, background usurps foreground. Landscape in light—a developing lightscape—becomes the underlying narrative.

'Only some spires' speaks of sublimity in the commonplace: Blake's 'world in a grain of sand' comes to mind. But the poem's experience is not static: it is fully energised, a process of action and reaction—grass and light and wind. In the first line, 'Only some spires of bright green grass', the opening word, 'Only', is both an index of the modest ordinariness of the effect witnessed and its finality. This is all. There is no more light. Nothing but a brief fragment. We have all seen leaves or 'bright' grasses in the low light of the evening sun, a tender and translucent green called out of them. Shape and value are also implied: these are 'spires', not blades or leaves and not many either—'some'. The common grass we tread upon takes on the glow of epiphany. Churches have spires. But everything we know about Emily reveals her as a 'wild, wick slip', a sermon-hating iconoclast: 'An awful Sunday!' exclaims Cathy, exchanging piety for an illicit 'scamper on the moors' *(WH*, pp. 18–20). In *Wuthering Heights* Gimmerton Kirk recrudesces stealthily into the moorland rock from which it was forged: a clearance by wind and weather. Grass, as any ruin teaches us, is

---

8   Ibid, 51.

tougher than stone—and subversive.

The second line, 'Transparently in sunshine quivering' opens with a polysyllable, eloquently placed: the word 'Transparently', literally 'show light through', is from Latin, the present participle of *transparere* (Emily had studied Latin and was conscious of etymologies). The fragment ends with the present participle, 'quivering', followed by no full stop. This punctuation-free writing, characteristic of Emily Brontë's poetry of inspiration, centres the eye not on stasis but in motion, the wind or spirit or breath (these words are cognate in most languages) that, invisibly save in its effects, blows through and invigorates the luminous creation. Where does the viewer stand? One answer would be that she need not stand at all. Lying flat on my stomach and looking up would surely allow me to view this effect most clearly. This is an ironic reversal of eighteenth and early nineteenth century conventions governing the perspectives on picturesque or sublime beauty, where the connoisseur was expected to occupy a position of elevated advantage, to command a vista of fearful grandeur: mountains and valleys, cataracts and cliffs are most favoured. In Emily's poetry, we stoop neither to God, nor to God immanent in the creation, but to the creation itself, and the perceiver's mind as mirrored in that creation.

On a slip of paper, the nineteen-year-old represents a scrap of grass, the casual gleaning of a moment. The modest means of production are apt to the value-system endorsed in Emily's poetic practice. Bring down the mighty. The low is high. My moorland is wiser than your minister. Her private truth was commemorated on oddments of paper, preserved perhaps from a torn-up notebook, waste paper, a bit of mourning stationery, cardboard, grocery wrappings—or, as in *Wuthering Heights*, the defaced margins or end papers of Scripture itself.

※

In a poem of 1846 which has profound affinities with *Wuthering Heights*, Emily vaunted a 'God within my breast':

> No coward soul is mine
> No trembler in the world's storm-troubled sphere
> I see Heaven's glories shine
> And Faith shines equal arming me from Fear
>
> O God within my breast
> Almighty ever-present Deity
> Life, that in me hast rest
> As I Undying Life, have power in thee

> Vain are the thousand creeds
> That move men's heart, unutterably vain,
> Worthless as withered weeds
> Or idlest froth amid the boundless main
>
> To waken doubt in one
> Holding so fast by thy infinity
> So surely anchored on
> The steadfast rock of Immortality
>   ('No coward soul', ll. 1–16)

The 'vain...unutterably vain' creeds of others—presumably the Christian sects Emily despises—are incapable of wakening doubt in this inner deity. While clearly a development of Romanticism and the radical Gospel concept of the believer as the temple of the Holy Spirit, this tenet becomes in her hands an apostate's charter. The imagination of God-in-Emily participates in, asserts 'power in', the action of the spirit that 'Pervades and broods above,/ Changes, sustains, dissolves, creates and rears'. The form of the poem demonstrates this dissolution of boundaries: its almost punctuation-free lines flow like fast wind, annihilating the boundaries of self and other, woman and Creator. Because the author died so young, this hubristic testament has been taken as a final statement. But this is surely fortuitous. For in other poems and in *Wuthering Heights*, she counts the cost of such apostasy: the trinity of 'three Gods' that war night and day in 'this little frame' in 'The Philosopher' make the speaker long for 'the time when I shall sleep/ Without identity'. And *Wuthering Heights* subjects such claims to relentless Romantic irony.

In Emily's later ecstatic response to the world of nature, the membrane between self and other had become for short periods infinitely permeable, thin as air. Spires of grass shaken by the invisible spirit could be through-lit and seen into; they might 'quiver' in the same breeze that made the mind thrill and tremble. In this early fragment, the outside world and mirroring subjective vision were not confused. The mind breathed in a breathing world. But in 'No coward soul', all vision is interiorised as mind-content: if the sun and universe were annihilated, they would still exist in Emily. She has defiantly—and solipsistically—gone the way of the egoism of the more extreme Idealist philosophers: 'Nature is mind made visible and mind is Nature made invisible.'[9] On the psychological level, 'No coward soul' seems to imply implicit breakdown, its vast claims for the self a rhetorical defence against doubt and isolation. The membrane is too thin.

---

9   F. W. J. Schelling, *Ideen zu einer Philosophie der Natur* (1797), Introduction, in *Sämtliche Werke*, Vol. II, ed. Manfred Schröder (Munich: Biederstein, 1946), 20.

Ecstatic visions, under the impulse of the creative spirit, threatened life itself: 'visions rise and change, which kill me with desire' ('Julian M. and A.G. Rochelle', l. 72). Vision leads into a territory of insatiable longing—unappeased spiritual *Heimweh* for another world, always beyond reach. But Emily Brontë could not live without those 'western winds' of vision either: away from the currents of keen air flowing over the exposed moors she shrank into a stifled, needy, silently desperate child. At Roe Head in 1835, Charlotte saw that Emily's 'white face, attenuated form, and failing strength threatened rapid decline';[10] in Brussels in 1842 she lived with her homesick despair as best she might, using her strong will to gather intellectual resources before returning home. Always the need was for the breath of the moorlands, a token of life. In *Wuthering Heights*, the wind sweeping from the high heath reminds the dying Cathy, out of place in her domestic heaven, of her lost home. Wrenching open the window, Cathy admits the cold blast that seems to revive her, prompting Nelly to warn that she will catch her death of cold. And she does.

In the novel's closing moments, Lockwood locates the three graves, the first (Cathy's) half buried in heath; the second (Linton's) partly covered with turf and moss; the third (Heathcliff's) bare. The novel's last word is *earth*:

> I lingered round them, under that benign sky; watched the moths fluttering among the heath, and hare-bells; listened to the soft wind breathing through the grass; and wondered how any one could ever imagine unquiet slumbers for the sleepers in that quiet earth. (*WH*, p. 338)

I lingered ... watched ... listened ... wondered. Like the final pages of Beethoven's late piano sonatas, with their gradual loosening of earthly ties and their entry into the unmeasured stillness of eternity, Emily Brontë's people merge their names, dreams, antagonisms and double-bound desires beneath the counterpane of the vital green world, while in the breeze-blown flora above, echoes still stir and disturb.

---

10   As quoted by Chitham, *A Life*, 89.

R. S. Thomas, Denise Levertov and
the poetry of contemplation

M. Wynn Thomas

IN 1995 the city of Swansea was enabled, by government funding, to hold a year-long festival of writing that featured authors from many nations working across the whole range of 'literary' genres. One of those participating was the noted American-British poet Denise Levertov (conspicuously proud of her Welsh mother and distant forebear Angel Jones of Mold), whose visit coincided with a campaign in Wales to secure R. S. Thomas's nomination for the Nobel Prize for Literature. During my own discussions with Levertov on that occasion her admiration for Thomas's poetry became apparent. I therefore briefly considered attempting to arrange a meeting between the two poets, a possibility that Levertov viewed with a mixture of anticipation and apprehension—she seemed to regard Thomas as a 'grand, grim, passionate old hero' (to quote her own memorable description of Cézanne).[1] Sadly, no such arrangement proved possible, but following her return to Seattle, I received a copy of a letter she, in her capacity as a prominent member of the American Academy of Arts and Letters, had addressed to the Nobel Committee of the Swedish Academy. There, in stating that she would like to nominate Thomas for that year's prize, Levertov not only noted his 'grief for the erosion of Welsh culture', and his 'strong sense of the beauty of mountains and fields, and of individual lives of integrity lived among them', but commented that 'His intimate and often Job-like dialogues with God (God's voice of silence being present by implication) engage both sceptics and believers.'[2]

Since she mentioned *No Truce with the Furies*—the collection published the very year of her letter—it was obvious that Levertov had kept abreast of his writing, and that she

---

1   Denise Levertov, *Tesserae: Memories and Suppositions* (Newcastle: Bloodaxe Books, 1997), 106. Hereafter *T*.

2   I am grateful to my friend and colleague Nigel Jenkins for providing me with a copy of this letter.

herself, as troubled believer and poet, 'engaged' with Thomas's late, religious poetry became apparent to me when, during that same period, she kindly sent me a copy of several of her late collections. There I was startled to find passages such as the following, familiar, I felt, from my acquaintance with Thomas's poetry:

> Lord, not you,
> It is I who am absent.
> At first
> belief was a joy I kept in secret,
> stealing alone
> into sacred places:
> a quick glance, and away—and back,
> circling.
> I have long since uttered your name
> but now
> I elude your presence.3

With its fine capture of the subtle flows and eddies of the meditative impulse, and its sensitivity to the fugitive nature of human relationship to the divine, this seemed almost uncannily similar to Thomas's writing. But reading further, I quickly realised that, while from time to time similarly reminiscent passages intriguingly occurred, they were part of a body of poetry that suggested not so much the influence of Thomas as an unconsciously intimate kinship of concerns between two ageing poets—concerns, occasionally converging but mostly proceeding in parallel, to evolve a poetic discourse authentically answerable to the spiritual crises of late twentieth-century civilization. I noted, for future reference, that a comparison of late Thomas and late Levertov might therefore prove fruitful, and this would seem to be an appropriate occasion to attempt such a study, in grateful homage to Jeremy Hooker, who has made such a distinguished contribution to our understanding of the distinctive spiritual idioms of twentieth-century art and artists, in the process paying particularly fine attention to R. S. Thomas. There is also a connection of sorts with Levertov, in that Jeremy Hooker shares with her an indebtedness to the American Objectivists, he being one of the few important British poets to have profited richly from their practice.

How to relate God to the universe, the natural world, human beings and historical events?—these were profound perplexities common to both poets, reluctant heirs as they were to Darwinian science and appalled witnesses to the cataclysmic social and political events of their century (Levertov's father was a 'Jewish Christian' and her

---

3 'Flickering Mind', in Denise Levertov, *A Door in the Hive/ The Evening Train* (Newcastle: Bloodaxe Books, 1993), 68. Hereafter *DHET*.

parents had been active during the thirties in assisting refugees from Hitler's Germany). Both struggled with the temptation to hold God culpable for His implacable silence and His incorrigible absence, although Levertov did so only occasionally whereas for Thomas it was a piercing obsession. Her poem 'Psalm Fragments (Schnittke String Trio)' begins by railing against a 'Tyrant God./ Cruel God./ Heartless God.// God who permits/ the endless outrage we call History', but concludes by acknowledging the beneficent all-sustaining Lord who 'provide[s]'.4 Even in that opening litany of indictments, the childishly absolute tone suggest this is a premature, petulant, intemperate, unconsidered response. It is the irrepressible benedictions of life that are Levertov's constant impulsive theme, and when she places herself 'Again before your altar, silent Lord', the sound of rushing waters and crooning doves bespeak for her 'your hospitable silence' (*SW*, 136).

Not so Thomas, a chronically bereft soul who, while sometimes ready, like Levertov, to blame God's invisibility on his own spiritual inadequacy, was habitually altogether more intransigent in his accusatory pursuit of an inaccessible deity. Much of the writing of his last thirty years took the form of poetic strategies for addressing (but never resolving) this moral and metaphysical conundrum. Their range and resourcefulness are already apparent in the pivotal volume, *H'm* (1972), which contains the celebrated 'Via Negativa', its classic formulation of the existential consequences of a godhead apparent only as 'that great absence/ In our lives' prefaced by an impatient dismissal ('Why no! I never thought other...') in advance of the poem's subsequent moving affirmations ('He keeps the interstices/ In our knowledge').5 Elsewhere the volume offers a Gnostic vision of the monstrous god of creation and a believer's chilling experience of the alterity of the natural world : 'And the dogfish, spotted like God's face,/ Looks at him, and the seal's eye-/Ball is cold.' (*CP*, 224) That second line-break, effectively reducing 'eye' to 'ball', brilliantly underlines the unnerving absence of human reciprocity in the creaturely world—what he called 'this blank indifference... the neutrality of [nature's] answers' (*CP*, 206). His description of the seal parallels Emily Dickinson's description of a bird's eyes as 'frightened beads'.6 Most piercing of all is the title poem 'H'm', with its disturbingly grotesque account of the way a preacher's attempt to speak of God turns into a would-be gesture of all-inclusive love that is appallingly thwarted by the inability of starving children, rendered helplessly weak by hunger, to stagger to the sanctuary of his arms. Not the least

---

4   'Psalm Fragments (Schnittke String Trio)', in Denise Levertov, *Sands of the Well* (New York: New Directions, 1996), 117–118. Hereafter *SW*.

5   'Via Negativa', in R. S. Thomas, *Collected Poems* (London: Macmillan, 1993), 220. Hereafter *CP*.

6   'A Bird Came Down the Walk', in Thomas H. Johnson, ed., *The Complete Poems of Emily Dickinson* (London: Faber, 1977), 156.

disturbing aspect of this, surely one of the most powerful poems Thomas ever wrote, is its punning reference to Christ's famous injunction 'Suffer the little children to come unto me': rarely could the word 'suffer' in that celebrated biblical passage have been tortured (by human anguish) into such a terrifying parody of its intended meaning. But to such bleak, black disavowals of divine concern Thomas, paradoxical as ever, juxtaposes extraordinary affirmations. 'The Coming' offers one of those comparatively rare instances of his focussing on the crucifixion, in this case read in terms of the incomprehensibly selfless act of a Father and Son moved by the scene of human sufferings to the ultimate sacrifice. And in 'The River' Thomas produced another relative rarity, a love poem to God's nature, magical as a Chagall painting, in which fish, 'speckled like thrushes', are seen as 'Silently singing among the weed's/ Branches' (*CP*, 226). In this case, with the line break we turn the corner into a world of wonder.

Chagall was a very important painter for Denise Levertov. In *Tesserae*, the marvellous memoir she constructed out of shards of memory to capture 'the wraiths and shifts of time-sense',[7] she associates Chagall with her Russian-Jewish father. And in her early poetry, her sense of spiritual immanence in the natural world is sometimes mediated through the mystical Hassidic Jewish theology that was her patrimony. The result is Chagall-like moments, such as when, in 'A Happening' (*SP*, 27), birds metamorphose into people, or, in 'Come into Animal Presence', 'The lonely white/ rabbit on the roof is a star/ twitching its ears at the rain.' (*SP*, 35)

Around the time of her conversion to Catholicism (c.1992) Levertov became enthralled by the work of Catholic thinkers such as Maritain, and began to draw on Christian orthodoxy for her language of immanence. But throughout her life the crux of her spiritual poetic was an insistence that the transcendent had to be mediated through what Blake termed the 'minute particulars' of mundane, concrete experience: it was her distinctive version of her mentor William Carlos Williams's celebrated maxim, 'no ideas but in things.' Her signature poem 'The Jacob's Ladder' (1961) is her most complete and memorable establishing of this cornerstone of her faith and her poetry. In it she insists that the stairway is 'not/ a thing of gleaming strands/ a radiant evanescence' but rather full of 'sharp/angles' (the line-break turning the text itself into such) on which 'a man climbing/ must scrape his knees' (*SP*, 40). And her early poetry, in particular, is full of wonderfully sharp-angled observations, surprising the reader with its unexpected perceptions, mixed registers and lexicons, such as when, exhorting us to 'taste and see' (*SP*, 55), she urges 'the imagination's tongue' to savour 'grief, mercy, language,/ tangerine, weather'. She convinces us of the authenticity of her relish by that succulent insertion of a humble citrus fruit into exalted abstract company. In the best of the poetry of these early decades her poetry goes 'much as that dog goes, intently

---

7 'Olga Poems, vi', in Denise Levertov, *Selected Poems* (Newcastle: Bloodaxe Books, 1994), 73. Hereafter *SP*.

haphazard/... dancing/ edgeways, there's nothing/ the dog disdains on his way' (*SP*, 19). In her late decades, her poetry lost some of that vivacity of perception and of language. Thus the late poem corresponding to the early 'The Jacob's Ladder' is 'On Belief in the Physical Resurrection of Christ', a poem that, characterising her new baptised poetic, unintentionally signifies her settling (at some cost to her poetry) for a calmer, more muted rapture. It accepts that 'people so tuned/ to the humdrum laws' can't accept a symbol 'unless convinced of its ground,/ its roots/ in bone and blood.' Hence the significance of the meal at Emmaus, where the bread was broken by 'warm hands' (*SW*, 115–116).

All her life Levertov was a believer in what Hopkins called 'inscape' (the indwelling spiritual-material form that gives a thing its quiddity) and 'instress' (human imaginative perception of that informing *telos*).[8] Indeed several of her brief late praise-poems to the universe of sense resemble the rapid notations of such perceptions found in Hopkins' notebooks:

> Pearlblossom bright white
> against green young leaves that frame
> each tuft, black
> pinewoods, graybrown buildings (*SW*, 32)

This typical, painterly, viewing of a scene in terms of juxtapositions of colour and texture reminds one not only that the young Levertov went on a pilgrimage to visit Cézanne but also of her account, in *Tesserae*, of her period of training, as a youngster, to be a painter. What she was primarily taught was to see 'the complex interaction of three-dimensional objects in space, and their transmutation into compositions; forms and colors on a flat surface.' (*T*, 79) In passages such as the above her poetry performs an analogous miracle, and in the process conveys her sense of the intricate interdependence of otherwise highly individualised phenomena, making material 'the indivisible/ shared out in endless abundance.' (*SW*, 37) She characteristically glosses Hopkins's concept of 'inscape' as involving 'intrinsic form, the pattern of essential characteristics both in single objects and (what is more interesting) in objects in a state of relation to each other' (*PW*, 7).

Accordingly, Levertov particularly prized poetry born of what she termed 'the ecstasy of attention' (*PW*, 97), no doubt, given the interest in etymology evident in her prose writings, being fully aware that the root meaning of the word is 'to stand outside of oneself.' In one of the finest of her later poems, 'Looking, Walking, Being', she hymns the heightening of the faculty of sight: 'I look and look./ Looking's a way of

---

8   This is discussed in Levertov's important early essay 'Some Notes on Organic Form', collected in *The Poet in the World* (New York: New Directions, 1973), 7–13. Hereafter *PW*.

being' (*SW*, 91). Elaborating on the actively investigative power of the excited eye, she appropriates to it the powers of several of the other senses, as if it were a synthesis of them all:

> The eyes
> Dig and burrow into the world.
> They touch
> Fanfare, howl, madrigal, clamor. (91)

Even in her late poetry she remained capable of such powers of perception, albeit in relatively muted form. Treasuring throughout her life Albert Schweitzer's doctrine of 'Reverence for Life', she insisted it involved 'the recognition of oneself as *life that wants to live* among other *forms of life that want to live*. This recognition is indissoluble, reciprocal, and dual' (*PW*, 53), and her poetry is usually a loving acknowledgement of those 'other forms of life'.

Of course, on a few memorable occasions, R. S. Thomas did match Levertov's excited awareness of 'a beauty not to be denied' (*SW*, 35), but he always seemed chary of presenting them as anything but rarities to be circumspectly cherished. Contrasted to the prodigality of natural epiphanies in Levertov, it is not only the parsimony but the conditionality of revelation in Thomas that strikes one. Although 'The Bright Field' is routinely instanced as one example of radiant immanence, few have noted the spiritual self-misgiving that so characteristically lies at the very heart of the poem. He may well briefly have glimpsed 'the pearl/ of great price, the one field that had/ the treasure in it', but viewing this ephemeral wonder as he does through the lens of Biblical phrasing, Thomas knows full well 'that I must give all that I have/ to possess it.' (*CP*, 302) That's the rub. He is honestly human enough implicitly to admit that he is not Moses enough to turn aside 'to the miracle/ of the lit bush'. He is really of the company of those farmers in 'Hill Christmas' (*CP*, 290) who attended the festival's communion service, 'felt it sharp/ on their tongue, shivered as at a sin/ remembered, and heard love cry/ momentarily in their hearts' manger' only to go back to 'their poor/ holdings, naked in the bleak light/ of December.' To Levertov's 'The Jacob's Ladder', Thomas tartly retorts with a question—'Are there angels or only/ the Furies?'9—and, in the face of European history, sceptically enquires 'Where is/ the ladder or that heavenly/ traffic that electrified Jacob?'

In such instances, the blame may be said to reside with humans, but there were also many occasions when Thomas, typically, viewed nature's joyous revelations as 'God's roguery' (*NTWF*, 45), a divine jape to detract attention from the evil that is naturally inherent in the divinely created world. A neat—perhaps over-neat—way of

---

9   R. S. Thomas, *No Truce with the Furies* (Newcastle: Bloodaxe, 1995), 64. Hereafter *NTWF*.

distinguishing his vision in this regard from that of Levertov is to compare their respective treatments of the owl. Her belief in the fundamental 'innocence' of all creatures apart from the human encompasses acceptance that they kill, because they do so only to satisfy 'natural' needs such as hunger. Accordingly, she can capture with equanimity the dual aspect of an owl that, while 'the terror of those he must hunt' (the innocence is in that 'must'—an imperative of nature), sounds his 'mournful notes [in] tones much like the dove's.' (*SW*, 13) For Thomas, though,

> The owl has a clock's
> face, but there is no time
> on it. No raptor ever
> is half-past its prey. (*NTWF*, 68)

In the same volume, God Himself becomes the supreme raptor, 'brushing me sometimes/ with his wing so the blood/ in my veins freezes':

> I have heard
> him scream, too, fastening
> his talons in his great
> adversary, or in some lesser
> denizen, maybe, like you or me. (*NTWF*, 52)

Decades earlier, and his vision had been equally steady, equally uncompromising. In *The Way of It* (1977), he noted that the barn owl 'happens/ like white frost as/ cruel and as silent'; over the 'bleached bones' of is victims echoes its 'night-strangled cry'. (*CP*, 319) For Thomas, it is the fact that God-made nature lives, moves and has its being in a process to which pain and cruelty are endemic that is perennially disturbing. As he repeatedly insisted, the painful question was not 'Is there a God' but rather 'what sort of a God *is* He?' given the accusatory witness not only of human history but also of the history of creation itself. 'Stoats, weasels, ferrets/ have evil reputations, and are indeed/ without mercy', Levertov too admits, but goes on imperturbably to note as a fact of nature that only human beings, for all their cruelty, have the potential of mercy for a species other than their own. She ends up charmed by a tame ferret that nuzzles up to her as if 'willing to try out/ the Peaceable Kingdom' (*SW*, 47). It is a moment indicative of the conciliatory character of her own vision of nature: not for her Thomas's anguished sense of a natural world at once unbearably beautiful and unbearably ferocious, 'a self-regulating machine/ of blood and faeces' (*CP*, 286). She is inclined to see nature as existing in the sunlight of God's constant love: he, on the other hand, is at best conscious only of a sky 'shot/ with the rainbow of [God's] coming and going.' (*CP*, 280)

Where both are, however, in full agreement, is in passionately protesting human assault not only on other human beings but also on the environment. Thomas and Levertov were indefatigable campaigners and protesters. Her activism was a strong family trait, characteristic not only of her parents but also of her wayward older sister, Olga, whose lifelong devotion to radical causes led to 'years of humiliation,/ of paranoia and blackmail and near-starvation' (*SP*, 73), as well as alienation from all who loved her, culminating in her death at fifty. As for Levertov herself, she came to prominence in the US, her adopted country, during the sixties and early seventies, as one of the leading poets publicly protesting against the Vietnam War. Later conflicts such as the Gulf War similarly provoked her to desperate, impassioned public statement:

> The choice: to speak
> or not to speak.
> We spoke.
>
> Those of whom we spoke
> had not that choice.
>
> At every epicentre, beneath
> roar and tumult,
>
> enforced:
> their silence. (*DHET*, 173)

Every stanza in this poem consists of two lines, with the exception of the one which starkly states 'We spoke': the form itself thus enacts the act of stepping out, of exposing and isolating oneself, that was the price, and challenge, involved in the unpopular act of voicing outrage. As a 'speaker' against social evils, Levertov was an indefatigable as she was impassioned, always insistent that 'the days of separating war, and racism, and pollution of natural resources, and social injustice, and male chauvinism, into neat little compartments are over.' (*PW*, 122) Thomas would have been sympathetic to such a radically holistic approach. An objector to the Second World War, he went on to protest against the military's appropriation of Welsh land, the building of nuclear power stations, the violent degrading of the environment (particularly in his local Llŷn), and, of course, the colonisation of Wales, and the undermining of the Welsh language and culture. Of these causes, it was these last only that were addressed explicitly in his poetry, whereas Levertov was an incomparably more politicised, producing works that attempted (mostly unsuccessfully) to translate her outrage at a range of US imperialistic military adventures into poems.

As her late poetry makes clear, such an imperative as she felt to speak on such issues was, for her, mandated by God: '*The earth is the Lord's,* we gabbled,/ *and the fullness thereof*—/ while we looted and pillaged, claiming indemnity'. (*DHET,* 168) For her, man is a travesty of his original Adamic self, created as he was 'to have been/ earth's mind, mirror, reflective source./... to be those cells of earth's body that could/ perceive and imagine'. (*DHET,* 168) Whereas Thomas might have balked at phrasing it exactly in these terms, his poetry, too, engages with the fall of man, insofar as that has increasingly taken the form of falling for 'the Machine'. The image became, for him, a convenient shorthand for what F. R. Leavis used to call a 'technologico-Benthamite' civilization, one dominated by the doctrine of functionality. For both, this meant a nexus of evil, involving the arrogant and violent subjugation of the natural world to the service of gross, demanding human needs: human reason was (ab)used to turn scientific discoveries into technological tools for exploiting the environment. This was the apotheosis of knowledge as power. Very conscious of being the heir to the great English Romantic tradition, from the time of Blake to that of Lawrence, critiquing such a malign philosophy of life, Thomas repeatedly made 'the Machine' the subject of his most acid poetry in his later years. This Urizenic monster is born of the temptation Thomas clearly identified in *H'm* as the human temptation to take the material world as its own invention. For him, then, the fall happened when 'the mind climbed up into the tree/ of knowledge, ... and began vaunting its frustration/ in spurious metals, in the cold acts of the machine.' (*CP,* 287) Ubiquitous in Thomas's volumes for three decades, the indestructible Machine epitomised everything he feared, hated and despised about a modern world forcibly maintained by destruction: 'The machine appeared/ In the distance, singing to itself/ Of money. Its song was the web/ They were caught in, men and women/ together.' (*CP,* 235)

For Levertov it is the poet who now performs the duty God originally envisaged the whole of mankind as performing, the Adamic duty of 'perceiving and imagining' the earth, of serving as the consciousness of the created world. In the process, the poet also brings mankind to full, spiritually awakened consciousness—Levertov was haunted by a phrase from one of Rilke's letters, where he referred to 'the unlived life of which one can die' (e.g. *PW,* 20): she understood it to refer to the unfulfilled potential of a largely secularised human existence. One of the strongest sections of her last collection, *Sands of the Well,* was devoted to reflections on poetry, and it included a poem on the loss of one of the branches that had given a tree the shape of a lyre. She ends with a prayer to be blessed with the power to hymn the tree's 'unlived life':

> O Orpheus,
> Lead me power to sing
> The unheard music of that vanished lyre. (*SW,* 93)

The head of the Orpheus whom she addresses had itself, of course, continued to sing even after it had been torn from its trunk by the voracious Maenads (referred to in *PW*, 68), and Levertov was vividly conscious of herself as an Orphic poet.

In that same section of *Sands of the Well* she is also tormented by the futility of continuing to write in old age, when all that seems possible is a repetition of earlier achievements. She is comforted in part by memories of the old Cézanne, 'doggedly *sur le motif*', persisting in painting and repainting Mont Sainte Victoire, 'his mountain/ a tireless noonday angel he grappled like Jacob,/ demanding reluctant blessing.' (*SW*, 96) But a more urgent and therefore compelling motive for persisting is the need to register wonders that would otherwise go unnoticed, their lives, so to speak, 'unlived':

> it's the way
> radiant epiphanies recur, recur,
> consuming, pristine, unrecognized—
> until remembrance dismays you. And then, look,
> some inflection of light, some wing of shadow
> is other, unvoiced. You can, you must
> proceed. (*SW*, 96)

Levertov passionately believed that the arts were precious 'expanders of consciousness', a revolutionary medium whose implicit message was always that which Rilke seemed to hear when viewing the 'Torso of an Archaic Apollo': 'You must change your life.' She cherished Wallace Stevens's maxim that a poem 'stimulates the sense of living of being alive.' (*PW*, 101)

Thomas was less exercised by the issue of language's relation to the created world than by its relation to the divine, and although he produced innumerable poems sceptically pondering this relationship, he also persisted in affirming that only through the arts could man imaginatively apprehend ultimate spiritual realities. In his last collection he was still epigrammatically asserting that 'Not electricity/ but the brush's piety/ affords divinity.' (*NTFW*, 85) And the very last poem in that last collection was 'Anybody's Alphabet', at once a gamesome bagatelle, a linguistic tour de force, and a final homage to the inexhaustible human but also spiritual potential of the poet's medium, language. It is also a witty meditation on the profound implications of the primary human need to play—throughout his career, Thomas retained a sense that the relation between man and God was inescapably ludic, and that poetry was the best game for apprehending it. This—a central aspect of his writing that tends to pass unremarked—finds no real echo in Levertov's work. It stems directly from his deep fascination with the 'mysterious way' of God. 'I'm fascinated by that mystery', he penetratingly observed in a revealing late interview, 'and I've tried to write out of that experience of God, the fantastic side of God, the quarrel between the conception of

God as a person, as having a human side, and the conception of God as being so extraordinary.'[10]

Where Thomas and Levertov do agree is that poetry is the redemption of language—that 'normal' human language is defaced and debased by the diminishing, degrading, and sometimes evil, uses to which it is routinely put. 'There is an aggression of fact', wrote Thomas in 'After Jericho', 'to be resisted successfully/ only in verse, that fights language with its own tools.' (*CP*, 56) He therefore exhorts the poet to smile 'among the ruins of a vocabulary/ you blew your trumpet against.' 'It is the poet', wrote Levertov, 'who has language in his care, the poet who more than others recognizes language also as a *form* of life and a common resource to be cherished and served as we should serve and cherish earth and its waters, animal and vegetable life, and each other.' (*PW*, 53)

Levertov's late poem 'Mysterious Disappearance of May's Past Perfect' ponders the disappearance of the verb form 'might' from common vocabulary, beginning with the example of a report about an oil spillage from a tanker at sea. She speculates first that fear—of facing the fact that 'causes do / produce effects'—might account for this, but then widens her field of explanation into an indictment of modern discourse with particular reference to political discourse:

> Or, in these years
> when from our mother-tongue some words
> were carelessly tossed away, while others hastily
> were being invented—chiefly among them, *overkill*—
> has the other meaning, swollen as never before,
> of *might* thrust out of memory its minor
> homonym, so apt for the precise
> nuance of elegy, for the hint of judgement,
> reproachful clarities of tense and sense? (*DHET*, 167)

The passage is both a reflection on, and an instance of, the nature of a poet's social responsibilities.

Given the high value both Levertov and Thomas place on the role of poetry (and the other arts) as an unique form of human understanding, a medium for exploring man's spiritual being, it is not surprising that when, in old age, they attempted an audit of the mystery of their own lives (Glyn Jones's valediction to his life, 'Goodbye, what were you?' would have appealed to them both)[11] they produced spiritual

---

10 Molly Price-Owen, 'R. S. Thomas in Conversation', *The David Jones Journal*, R. S. Thomas Special issue (Summer/ Autumn, 2001), 97.

11 Glyn Jones, *Goodbye, What Were You?: Selected Writings* (Llandysul: Gomer Press, 1994).

autobiographies that, as such, inevitably traced in each of their cases the distinctive growth of a poet's life. *Tesserae* is a remarkable volume, a self-portrait in a crazy mirror. The daughter of a scholarly Russian Jewish father who became an Anglican priest, and an ebulliently imaginative Welsh mother who relished the adventure of living, Levertov could scarcely fail to regard her life as a maze of conjunctions as vividly amazing as her own parents' unlikely first meeting in Constantinople. In *Tesserae* she writes as the oracle of her own past, producing her own Sibylline leaves as memory multiplies its enigmas. The strange coincidences seem to represent what, in *The Jacob's Ladder*, she called 'profound/ unanswer, sustained/ echo of our unknowing.' The book is about our profound unknowing of ourselves, the hidden interconnections between people, the secret collusion between fact and fiction, the inalienable mystery of origins—and of signs.

She is also aware of herself as one whose native language is art quite as much as 'nature'—there is for her the important example of Magritte, a master of 'magic transformation, *entre chien et loup*.' It is not the fierce political campaigner for civil rights, and against the bomb and the USA's sinister involvement in Latin America, who appears in this portrait, but that different self which dwells with ambivalence and which trusts to metamorphoses. In *Tesserae* personal recollection hovers between 'memories and suppositions'. As for the poet in her, its memories are of ambivalent status in a further way. 'I have remembered it always', Levertov writes of thrilling to a nun's spectrally sensuous voice rising high, in an 'intensity of beauty', out of a hidden choir, 'or have remembered at least what words and images might have described it.'(*T*,101) In registering experience, words also displace it. Transfiguring or disfiguring, either way they perhaps distort. Whenever Levertov submits to an audit of memory—when she checks her recollections against those of others—she is invariably entranced by the disparities that emerge. This is a feature of an artist's imagination she highlights in 'The Heron', a poem from her last collection. Noting of a poet friend that 'the Great Blue Heron' 'turned white in your mind,/ conflated with regrets', she notes that this is how symbols form. They are thus the product of

> experience feeding
> the mind's vision, that moves
>
> with beating wings
> into and over
> the page, the parable. (*SW*, 101)

Tesserae is both a collection of a poet's involuntary parables (born of vision's intercourse with experience) and a reflection on her life as a process of parable-making.

But for her such parables are not arbitrary, nor are they merely of personal, psychological provenance and significance. Rather, they are means of revelation—of revealing the otherwise hidden spiritual contours of mundane existence. They are the divining rods that map the subterranean forces and energies of the spirit, just as, in her signature poem 'A Map of the Western Part of the County of Essex', she wrote as cartographer of her native region that was also her special imagined place (*SP*, 34–35). No wonder that in *Tesserae* she mourns the loss of a childhood treasure, the torn copy of Peter Heylyn's 1665 'Cosmography in four books. Containing the choreography and history of the whole world, and all the principal kingdoms, provinces, seas and isles thereof.' (*T*,III) Her poetry was, in a way, the creation of her own special substitute cosmography, her own wonders of the invisible world, her own record of her adventures in the realm of the spirit.

Although he wrote two valuable prose memoirs, one of them particularly idiosyncratic, the 'writing of self' by R. S. Thomas that most interestingly corresponds to *Tesserae* is *The Echoes Return Slow*. One of the very finest books published by Thomas, it is also noteworthy for its combination of prose and of poetry—the former on one side of the page, the latter on the page facing—a twin-track approach that is as thought-provoking as it is singular. As the following extract illustrates the 'prose' is, in fact, something far more crafted and refined than anything that normally passes for such:

> Minerva's bird. Athene noctua, too small for wisdom, yet unlike its tawnier cousin active by day, too, its cat's eyes bitterer than the gorse petals. [12]

This is not ordinary workaday prose, rather it is prose concentrate, prose compressed into what might surely not inaccurately be described as prose poetry. The question is why? What is going on here? One way to think of it would be consider it as a demonstration of the way in which a poet's memory selects and shapes experience in a fashion that turns it into rich soil for poetry. 'The creative mind', it is observed in *The Echoes Return Slow*, 'judges, weighs and selects, as well as discarding, in the act of composing.' (*ERS*, 60) A useful comparison might be made with Jeremy Hooker's practice in his *Welsh Journal*. There he punctuates his journal entry with poems that seem to arise out of, and obliquely to illuminate, the experiences being recorded. As he notes in his Foreword, 'Instead of an exact temporal "placing" [i.e. the exact allocation of poems to a supposedly specific time and place of origin] my aim has been to relate poems to the imaginative and experiential grounding—the life—from which they evolved.'[13] The same, after a somewhat different fashion, seems to be true of Thomas's practice in *The Echoes Return Slow*. He is, of course, writing retrospectively, and knows

---

12 R. S. Thomas, *The Echoes Return Slow* (London: Macmillan, 1988), 78. Hereafter *ERS*.
13 Jeremy Hooker, *Welsh Journal* (Bridgend: Seren, 2001), 5.

that recollection is also palimpsest—the overwriting of the past by subsequent experience, so that the result is a richly layered deposit, a multi-faceted and creatively stimulating imaginative construct. The crafted 'prose' passages in *The Echoes Return Slow* foreground the fact that what we are being given is not the unmediated past, but the past as mediated by the present, a present in which a memory that is specifically that of a poet is at work carving out materials suitable for present purpose. And, for a poet, that 'purpose' is poetry—a poetry that, in turn (or so the *Echoes Return Slow* implies), is the best instrument for accessing, grasping, comprehending and articulating the otherwise hidden spiritual *gestalt* of an individual life. Poetry reaches the parts of a life that prose, however beautifully crafted, can never fully reach.

So what is the poem towards which the prose poem quoted above may be said to 'aspire', or of which it may be said to be the forerunner and enabler? It opens as follows:

> There are nights that are so still
> that I can hear the small owl calling
> far off, and a fox barking
> miles away. It is then that I lie
> in the lean hours awake, listening
> to the swell born somewhere in the Atlantic
> rising and falling, rising and falling
> wave on wave on the long shore
> by the village, that is without light
> and companionless. (*ERS*, 79)

In being so evidently a different order of writing from the prose, embryonically 'poetic' though that may be, this is also a manifestation of the multi-dimensionality of human existence. It underscores Thomas's belief, not only founded in his faith but also grounded on his familiarity with Kierkegaard's writing, that every individual is a mysterious composite of different *categories:* the temporal and the spiritual. As *The Echoes Return Slow* repeatedly makes clear (and as Thomas many times stated in his prose writings and interviews) for him poetry was the language of the spirit, a language of image and of symbol—appropriately enough, for his was the belief succinctly voiced by (I think) Yeats that 'the truth cannot be known, it can only be symbolised.' It therefore made sense for Thomas bluntly to state (with characteristic tactlessness) that 'Jesus was a poet' (*ERS*, 89). Elsewhere, he remarks that 'against the deciduousness of man there stand art, music, poetry. The Church was the great patron of such.' (*ERS*, 78) What is more, Thomas once suggested that the New Testament itself was a work of poetry, so scandalising the faithful who did not understand what he meant by the phrase. This explains why he so witheringly objects in *Echoes* to the replacing of the majestic King

James Bible by the new revised version. 'What committee', he enquires with reference to the latter, 'ever composed a poem?' (*ERS*, 96) It is as if, in some of the prose-poems in *Echoes*, he were consoling himself for this desolating loss by composing his own alternative spiritual meditations—rather as Henry Vaughan famously composed *Silex Scintillans* when the victorious Puritan reformers and iconoclasts had effectively closed the doors to him on the ancient festivals, rituals, sacraments and symbols of the Established Church.

Even in *The Echoes Return Slow*, R. S. Thomas includes poems that address 'the deafness of space' (*ERS*, 117), that speak of the one 'who has not come' (*ERS*, 89), that pursue the endlessly recessive 'being' 'who is called God' (*ERS*, 61). 'I lift my face', he poignantly records, 'to a face, its features dissolving/ in the radiation out of a black hole.' (*ERS*, 39) There is no real equivalent in Levertov's writing to Thomas's poetry of the *Deus Absconditus*. The nearest to it is the sequence of late poems reflecting on the way a mountain distantly visible from her Seattle home varies greatly in clarity depending on light and weather: 'The mountain comes and goes/ on the horizon' (*DHET*, 112). What she comes to accept is the mountain's otherness, that its power 'lies in the open secret of its remote/ apparition' (*DHET*, 122), and even when it is shrouded in mist she knows that it is always solidly there, 'obdurate, unconcerned' (*DHET*, 114). It is an image of her faith, which is never remotely rooted, like Thomas's, in anguished uncertainties. We equate, she writes,

> God with these absences—
> Deus absconditus.
> But God
>
> is imaged
> as well or better
> in the white stillness
>
> resting everywhere,
>
> giving to all things
> an hour of Sabbath[.] (*DHET*, 113)

The constancy of God's presence, whether manifest or not, was itself a solid constant of Levertov's faith in the world, whatever form experience might take. That is what made her a sacramental poet—somewhat unorthodoxly so in the decades of her youth and maturity, but orthodox in expression in her late, final years after her conversion. One of the poems in the same section of *The Evening Train* as the mountain sequence begins with a vivid registering of the quiddity of bird life:

> A gull far-off
> rises and falls, arc of a breath,
> two sparrows pause on the telephone wire,
> chirp a brief interchange, fly back to the ground (*DHET*, 121)

All is prelude, though, to the poem's conclusion; '*This is the day that the Lord hath made,/ let us rejoice and be glad in it.*' (*DHET*, 121)

The religious poetry of Denise Levertov and R. S. Thomas does, however, have one feature in common: they are both contemplative poets, in the sense of the term suggestively outlined by Levertov herself. She is discussing the origin of 'this demand: the poem':

> The beginning of the fulfilment of this demand is to contemplate, to meditate; words which connote a state in which the heat of feeling warms the intellect. To contemplate comes from '*templum*, temple, a place, a space for observation, marked out by the augur.' It means not simply to observe, to regard, but to do these things in the presence of a god. And to meditate is 'to keep the mind in a state of contemplation'; its synonym is 'to muse', and to muse comes from a word meaning 'to stand with open mouth'—not so comical if we think of 'inspiration'—to breathe in. (*PW*, 8)

How this translates into the movement and form of a poem on the page is what she makes clear in an interview entitled 'Line-breaks, Stanza-spaces, and the Inner Voice', and what she has to say also affords valuable insight into the way that a late, religious poem by R. S. Thomas also works—a lesson of which many contemporary critics seem in urgent need. For Levertov, form, rhythm, spacing, line-breaks are all means of transcribing the 'inner voice' onto the page. She thinks of the end of a line as equivalent to 'half a comma'; in other words, she uses it as a subtle way of punctuating her text, so that it seems to capture and convey the very breath and pulse of her contemplating intelligence. And for her the 'inner voice' is the poet 'talking to himself, inside of himself, constantly approximating and evaluating and trying to grasp his experience in words… The written poem is then a record of that inner song.' (*PW*, 24).

A good example of such 'inner song' is provided by 'What One Receives from Living Close to a Lake', a poem that concludes with the following passage:

> a clearing amid the entangled
> forest of forms and voices,
> anxious intentions, urgent
> memories, a deep, clear

> breath to fill
> the soul, an internal
> gesture, arms
> flung wide to echo
> that mute generous outstretching
> we call *lake*. (*SW*, 108)

The layout maps the movement of mind, the line-breaks repeatedly suggesting the brief searching for the right noun to follow the qualifying adjective ('entangled/ forest', 'urgent/ memories', 'clear/ breath', 'internal/gesture'), for the precise verb for its purpose ('arms/flung wide), for the object that exactly complements the verb ('to fill/ the soul'). The result is the conveying not of thoughts but rather of the act of concentrated thinking—in other words, of 'contemplation' sufficiently sustained so as to become 'meditation'. It is a fine example of what Wallace Stevens famously called 'the poem of the act of the mind'.

And there are exact counterparts aplenty to such a passage to be found in the later poetry of R. S. Thomas. A notable instance is provided by that exceptionally fine poem 'Sea-watching':

> Nothing
> but that continuous waving
>   that is without meaning
> occurred.
>   Ah, but a rare bird is
> rare. It is when one is not looking
> at times one is not there
>   that it comes.
> You must wear your eyes out,
> as others their knees. (*CP*, 306)

All the line breaks are potent conveyors of the process of focussing both the outer and the inner eye. It highlights the pun in 'waving', the chiming of that word with 'no meaning' so that the perfect, trite, rhyme establishes the bland pointlessness of the sea's incessant motions. The deliberate repetition of the word 'rare' brings out the tautology in the statement; the stating of the self-evident that dramatises the mind's arrival at a dead end; the implicit confession that a miracle is a miracle is a miracle. And the holding back of the second use of the word reinforces this by suggesting that the mind's labours of intensive thought, allowed for in the timing that's recorded in the spacing, lead only back into repetition and not forward into revelation.

The late poetry of both Levertov and Thomas affords a powerful example of what might be called the poetics of contemplation and of meditation. No wonder that Thomas was fascinated by poets such as Herbert, Wordsworth and Edward Thomas, all of whom were masters of this particular art. But in the end, as has been indicated in this essay, the American poet and the Welsh were naturally and spiritually inclined to practise this poetics to rather different ends. Levertov entitled the penultimate poem she ever wrote 'Thinking about Paul Celan'. Recalling that genius's suicide, brought on in part by his appalling experience of the Nazis' death camps, Levertov prays for his forgiveness of those, such as herself, who 'flourish/…exceed/ our allotted days':

> Saint Celan,
> Pray for us
> that we receive
>
> at least a bruise,
> blue, blue, unfading,
> we who accept survival.[14]

She herself certainly exhibits such bruises in her poetry, most notably when she engages with the obscenities and atrocities of war. But unlike Thomas she did not suffer from a chronic 'hernia/ of the spirit' (*ERS*, 97). All his greatest poetry may perhaps have derived from that. Not so hers. She once recalled that her father, when on his deathbed, got up and danced an ecstatic Hassidic dance in celebration of life. Levertov was herself, to the very end, her father's daughter. In her poem 'Joy' she recalled Rilke's dying words 'Never forget,/ dear one, life is magnificent!'. 'I looked up "Joy"' in a dictionary, she goes on:

> and came to
>
> 'Jubilation' that goes back
> to 'a cry of joy or woe' or to 'echoic
> *iu* of wonder.' (*SP*, 65)

Her greatest poetry is the record of that echo.

---

14 Denise Levertov, *This Great Unknowing* (Tarset: Bloodaxe, 2001), 58.

Bibliography of Jeremy Hooker

Poetry Collections

The Elements (Llandybïe: Christopher Davies, 1972).
Soliloquies of a Chalk Giant (London: Enitharmon Press, 1974).
Landscape of the Daylight Moon (London: Enitharmon Press, 1978).
Solent Shore (Manchester: Carcanet Press, 1978).
Englishman's Road (Manchester: Carcanet Press, 1980).
A View from the Source (Manchester: Carcanet Press, 1982).
Master of the Leaping Figures (Petersfield: Enitharmon Press, 1987).
With Lee Grandjean, *Their Silence a Language* (London: Enitharmon Press, 1993).
Our Lady of Europe (London: Enitharmon Press, 1997).
With Lee Grandjean, *Groundwork* (Nottingham: Djanogly Art Gallery, 1998).
Adamah (London: Enitharmon Press, 2002).
The Cut of the Light: Poems 1965–2005 (London: Enitharmon Press, 2006).

Prose Journals

Welsh Journal (Bridgend: Seren, 2001).
Upstate: A North American Journal (Exeter: Shearsman Books, 2007).

Critical Studies

John Cowper Powys, Writers of Wales series (Cardiff: University of Wales Press, 1973).
David Jones: An Exploratory Study of the Writings (London: Enitharmon Press, 1975).
John Cowper Powys and David Jones: A Comparative Study (London: Enitharmon Press, 1979).

Poetry of Place: Essays and Reviews 1970–1981 (Manchester: Carcanet Press, 1982).

The Presence of the Past: Essays on Modern British and American Poetry (Bridgend: Poetry Wales Press, 1987).

Writers in a Landscape (Cardiff: University of Wales Press, 1996).

Imagining Wales: A View of Modern Welsh Writing in English (Cardiff: University of Wales Press, 2001).

Editions

Poems '71 (Llandysul: Gwasg Gomer, 1971).

With Arthur Neal, *Edward Thomas: A Centenary Celebration* (London: Eric and Joan Stevens, 1978).

With Gweno Lewis, *Selected Poems of Alun Lewis* (London: Allen & Unwin, 1981).

Frances Bellerby, *Selected Stories* (London: Enitharmon Press, 1986).

Uncollected Writing and Tributes Written for Les Arnold (Bath: Plain Sailing Press, 1995).

Inwards Where All The Battle Is: A Selection of Alun Lewis's Writing from India (Newtown, Powys: Gregynog Press, 1997).

At Home on the Earth: A New Selection of the Later Writings of Richard Jefferies (Totnes: Green Books, 2001).

Edward Thomas, *The Ship of Swallows* (London: Enitharmon Press, 2005).

Mapping Golgotha: Letters and Poems of Wilfred Owen (Newtown, Powys: Gregynog Press, 2007).

Pamphlets

Dragon in the Snow (London: Erica and Joan Stevens [1979]).

With Norman Ackroyd, *Itchen Water* (Winchester: Winchester School of Art Press, 1982).

Three Poems (Leamington Spa: Other Branch Readings, 1983).

With Mansel Thomas, *Earth-borne: song* (Magor: Mansel Trust, 1986).

With Tony Nesbit, *In Praise of Windmills* (London: Circle Press, 1990).

Arnolds Wood (Pilton: Flarestack, 2005).

'Reflections on *ground* and Seventeen Poems', *Free Poetry*, 1/i (2005).

Contributions to Books

'Brut's Albion', in *David Jones: Eight Essays on His Work as Writer and Artist*, ed., Roland Mathias (Llandysul: Gwasg Gomer, 1976), pp. 123–38.

'Poet of an uncommon reality', in *The Poetry of Dannie Abse: Critical Essays and Reminiscences*, ed. Joseph Cohen (London: Robson, 1983), pp. 57–66.

'For the unfallen: a sounding', in *Geoffrey Hill: Essays on His Work*, ed. Peter Robinson (Milton Keynes: Open UP, 1985), pp. 20–30.

'Seeing the world: the poetry of George Oppen', in *Not Comforts But Vision: Essays on the Poetry of George Oppen*, ed. John Freeman (Budley Salterton: Interim Press, 1985), pp. 26–41.

'From graven image to speech', in *The Art of Edward Thomas*, ed., Jonathan Barker, (Bridgend: Poetry Wales Press, 1987), pp. 85–100.

'In the labyrinth: an exploration of *The Anathemata*', in *David Jones: Man and Poet*, ed John Matthias (Orono, ME.: National Poetry Foundation, 1988), pp. 263–84.

'Foreword' in Rutger Kopland, *A World Beyond Myself: Selected Poems*, trans. James Brockway (London : Enitharmon, 1991).

'Seeing place', in *In Black and Gold: Contiguous Traditions in Post-War British and Irish Poetry*, ed. C. C. Barfoot, DQR Studies in Literature, 13 (Amsterdam: Rodopi, 1994), pp. 27–44.

' "The centre cannot hold": place in modern English poetry', in *Poetry in the British Isles: Non-Metropolitan Perspectives*, eds Hans-Werner Ludwig, Lothar Fietz, and Christopher Harvie (Cardiff: University of Wales Press, 1995), pp. 73–96.

'Conran's brag', in *Thirteen ways of looking at Tony Conran*, ed. Nigel Jenkins (Cardiff: Welsh Union of Writers, 1995), pp. 217–26.

'John Matthias's England', in *Word Play Place: Essays on the Poetry of John Matthias*, ed. Robert Archambeau (Athens, OH: Swallow, 1998), pp. 104–114.

'David Jones and the matter of Wales', in *David Jones: Diversity in Unity*, eds. Belinda Humfrey and Anne Price-Owen (Cardiff: University of Wales Press, 2000), pp. 1–10.

'Geoffrey Grigson—English writer', in *'My Rebellious and Imperfect Eye': Observing Geoffrey Grigson* eds C. C. Barfoot, R. M. Healey and Tom Paulin, (Amsterdam: Rodopi, 2002), 17–32.

'Anne Stevenson's Welsh affinities', in *The Way You Say the World: A celebration for Anne Stevenson*, eds John Lucas and Matt Simpson (Nottingham: Shoestring Press, 2003), pp 67–75.

'Poetic lands and borderlands: Henry Vaughan to Robert Frost', in *Beyond the*

Difference: Welsh Literature in Comparative Context, eds Alyce Von Rothkirch and Daniel Williams (Cardiff: University of Wales Press, 2004), pp. 206–222.

Journal Articles

'The writings of Edward Thomas I', *Anglo-Welsh Review*, 18:41 (1969), 20–28.
'Image and argument: a review article of *The Lilting House*', *Anglo-Welsh Review*, 18:42 (1970), 65–76.
'The writings of Edward Thomas II: the sad passion', *Anglo-Welsh Review*, 19:43 (1970), 63–78.
'The poetry of Roland Mathias', *Poetry Wales*, 7:1 (1971), 6–13.
'Land of the Living', *Planet*, 8 (1971), 68–72.
'H'm', *Poetry Wales*, R. S. Thomas special no., 7:4 (1972), 82–93.
'Ends and New Beginnings', *Poetry Wales*, David Jones special no., 8:3 (1972), 22–31.
'On *The Anathemata*', *Anglo-Welsh Review*, 22:50 (1973), 31–43.
'The accessible song: a study of John Ormond's recent poetry', *Anglo-Welsh Review*, 23:51 (1974), 5–12.
'The poetry of Anthony Conran', *Anglo-Welsh Review*, 25:54 (1975), 172–82.
'A seeing belief: a study of Emyr Humphreys' *Outside the House of Baal*', *Planet*, 39 (1977), 35–43.
'T. F. Powys, "The Bass Note" ', *Powys Review*, 4 (1978–9), 35–43.
'Honouring Ivor Gurney', *PN Review*, 17 (1980), 16–19.
'A dream of a country: the Raymond Williams trilogy', *Planet*, 49/50 (1980), 53–61.
'Frances Bellerby in place', *PN Review*, 20 (1981), 32–4.
'Poem and place', *PN Review*, 25 (1981), 27–31.
'Seeing the world: the poetry of George Oppen', *PN Review*, 41 (1984), 17–22.
'Mary Casey: the poetry of aloneness', *Agenda*, 22:3–4 (1984–1985), 134–43.
' "The boundaries of our distances": George Oppen's "Of Being Numerous", *Ironwood*, 13:2 [26], 'George Oppen: A Special Issue' (1985), 81–103.
'Jeffrey Wainwright', *PN Review*, 46 (1985), 53–5.
'Roland Mathias: "the strong remembered words" ', *Poetry Wales* 21/1 (1985), 94–103.
'Crossings and turns: the poetry of John Matthias', *Poetry Wales*, 20/4 (1985), 48–58.
' "A big sea running in a shell": the poetry of Gillian Clarke', *PN Review*, 50 (1986), 18–20.

'Resistant voices: five young Anglo-Welsh poets', *Poetry Wales* 22/3 (1987), 69–94.

'The new iconoclasm', *Planet*, 72 (1988–9), 65–70.

'Profile: Roland Mathias', *New Welsh Review* 1/4 (1989), 17–21.

'The naked shingles of the world: modern poetry and the crisis of religious language', *New Welsh Review* 2/3 (1989/90), 46–53.

'Questions of identity', *Planet*, 87 (1991), 59–65.

'Their silence a language', *Modern Painters*, iv/2 (1991), 54–8.

'Doubly subversive: an interview with Bobi Jones', *Planet*, 94 (1992), 48–53.

'The sun centred in darkness: the poetry of Gerard Casey', *Planet*, 95 (1992), 83–9.

'Versions of freedom: Nicolas Berdyaev and John Cowper Powys', *Powys Journal* 2 (1992), 65–79.

'Donald Davie's *Poems about the Sacred*, *PN Review*, 19:2 [88] (1992), 33–5.

'Thomas Hardy, John Cowper Powys and Wessex', *Powys Review*, 27/28 (1992/93), 23–32.

'A story of a poem and a sculpture', *Planet*, 99 (1993), 78–85.

'Romancing at the cave-fire: the unabridged *Porius*', *Powys Journal*, 4 (1994), 216–31.

'Les Arnold: poet and teacher', *PN Review*, 95 (1994), 6–7.

'Natives and strangers: a view of Anglo-Welsh literature in the twentieth century', in *Writing Region and Nation: Proceedings of the Fourth International Conference on the Literature of Region and Nation*, Special No. of the *Swansea Review*, eds James A. Davies and Glyn Pursglove, 14 (1994), 23–42.

' "Gathering all in": an essay on the art of David Jones', *Modern Painters*, viii/4 (1995), 62–4.

'Ceridwen's daughters: Welsh women poets and the uses of tradition', *Welsh Writing in English; A Yearbook of Critical Essays*, 1 (1995), 128–44.

'Henry Vaughan', *Swansea Review*, 15 (1995), 22–32.

With Raymond Garlick and Sally Roberts Jones, 'Roland Mathias: three birthday greetings", *New Welsh Review* 8/3 (1995–96), 28–31.

'Roy Fisher, magician of the common place', *PN Review*, 22:3 [107] (1996), 28–30.

'To fit a late time: a reading of five American poets', *PN Review*, 22:5 [109] (1996), 37–41.

'Christopher Middleton: the poem as act of wonder', *PN Review*, 23:4 [114] (1997), 38–41.

'One is trying to make shape', *David Jones Journal*, 1:2 (1998), 6–19.

'Quickness', *Scintilla*, 2 (1998), 141–52.

'A note on the *Groundwork* poems', *Scintilla*, 2 (1998), 156–7.

'Ditch vision', *Powys Journal*, 9 (1999), 14–29.

'Richard Jefferies: a personal discovery', *Richard Jefferies Society Journal*, 9 (2000), 3–17.

'What is sacred poetry?', *Scintilla*, 4 (2000), 7–21.

'Interruption and renewal: the new poems of Rowan Williams', *New Welsh Review*, 56, (2001–2), 143–7.

'Elizabeth Bewick: recovering greenness', *South*, 28 (October 2003), 2–4.

'Poets, language and land: reflections on English-language poetry since the Second World War', *Welsh Writing in English: A Yearbook of Critical Essays*, 8, (2003), 141–56.

' "Calling the female into presence": the poetry of Wendy Mulford', *Swansea Review*, 22 (2003), 134–48.

'From *Upstate: a North American journal*', *Scintilla*, 8 (2004), 77–85.

'Habitation for a spirit: the art of Christopher Middleton', *Chicago Review* 51:1–2 (2005), 60–70.

'Nostalgia and the kiss of life', *Scintilla*, 9 (2005), 9–24.

' "Adventurers in living fact": the poetry of Dick Davis, Robert Wells, and Clive Wilmer', *London Magazine* (December/January 2007), 68–75.

'Metaphysical presence', *Scintilla* 11 (2007), 9–25.

Published Interviews and Audio Publication

'Interview with Jeremy Hooker' in David T. Lloyd, ed., *The Urgency of Identity: Contemporary English-Language Poetry from Wales* (Evanston, Illinois: Triquarterly Books, Northwestern University Press, 1994), pp. 68–77; rptd. as 'Interview with Jeremy Hooker (I)' with 'Interview with Jeremy Hooker (II)' in David T. Lloyd, *Writing on the Edge: Interviews with Writers and Editors of Wales*, Coserus New Series 112 (Amsterdam-Atlanta, GA: Rodopi, 1997), pp. 41–56.

'Silence under all: Jeremy Hooker interviewed by Jacqueline Gabbitas', *Planet*, 177 (2006), 57–64.

'Mystery at the heart of things: an interview with Jeremy Hooker', conducted by Fiona Owen, *Green Letters*, 8 (2007), 3–12.

Jeremy Hooker [sound recording of poems read by the author] (Bournemouth: Canto, 1984).

Jeremy Hooker Reading from his Poems, CD (London: The Poetry Archive, 2005).

Note: Jeremy Hooker has also published a large number of short reviews and poems in journals and anthologies. Such publications are not listed here.

List of Subscribers

Jane Aaron, Prifysgol Morgannwg
Linda Adams, Cowbridge
Sam Adams, Caerleon
Donald Allchin, Upper Bangor
Sandra Anstey & Robert Harding, Llantrisant
Ann & Adrian Arnold, London
John Barnie, Aberystwyth
Reverend Stephen Batty, Vicar of St. Aldhelm's Church, Branksome, Poole
Sheila Beskine & Richard Leigh, London
Ruth Bidgood, Llanwrtyd Wells
William Blissett, Toronto, Canada
Kirsti Bohata, Swansea University
Dr John Bollard, Florence, Massachusetts
Tilla Brading
Richard Bright, Frome
Tony Brown, Bangor University
Herbie Butterfield, Colchester
Gillian Clarke, Llandysul
Anne Cluysenaar, Llantrisant
Tony & Lesley Conran, Bangor
Tony Curtis, University of Glamorgan
Dr Peter Davies, Abergavenny
Stevie Davies, Swansea University
Walford & Hazel Davies, Aberystwyth
Kevin and Gail Dean, Blackburn
Tom Durham, Dorset
Roger Ebbatson, Loughborough University
Colin Edwards, Bath Spa University
Gavin Edwards, University of Glamorgan
Anne England, Prifysgol Morgannwg

Alice Entwistle, University of Glamorgan
Peter Faulkner, Exeter
Claire Flay, Cwm Ogwr
Matthew Francis, Aberystwyth University
Tony Frazer, Exeter
Francis Freeman, Menston, Ilkley
Katie Gramich, Cardiff University
Lee Grandjean, Royal College of Art, London.
Philip Gross, University of Glamorgan
Tessa Hadley, Bath Spa University
Dr. Elizabeth Haines, Clunderwen
Greg Hill, Coleg Ceredigion
Colin Hughes, Gerrards Cross
Emyr Humphreys, Llanfairpwll
Jennifer Hunt, MA, Weymouth
Jim Insole, 'old friend with mandolin'
Nigel Jenkins, Swansea University
Ceinwen & Tom Jones, Pontypridd
Cyril Jones, Glyntaf, Pontypridd
Professor Emeritus W. J. Keith, University College, University of Toronto
Richard Kerridge, Bath Spa University
Mimi Khalvati, The Poetry School
Professor Stephen Knight, Cardiff University
John T. Koch, Canolfan Uwchefrydiau Cymreig a Cheltaidd
Richard Leigh, London
Gweno Lewis, Aberystwyth
David Lloyd, Le Moyne College, Syracuse
Dr Margaret Lloyd, Springfield College, Massachusetts
Peter Lord, Cwm Rheidol
Ruth McElroy and Martin Willis, University of Glamorgan
Rachel McNaughton, Cardiff
Maggy McNorton, University of Glamorgan
Carl Major, Southampton
Ursula Masson, University of Glamorgan
Glyn & Ann Mathias, Aberhonddu
Kevin Mills, University of Glamorgan
Dr Charles Mintern
Wendy Mulford, Saxmundham
Fiona Owen, Tŷ Croes, Ynys Môn
Helen Phillips, Cardiff University

John Pikoulis, Dinas Powys
Dr Anne Price-Owen, Swansea Institute
Dr Barbara Prys-Williams, Swansea
Sheenagh Pugh, University of Glamorgan
Johan Schimanski, Universitetet i Tromsø
Norman Schwenk, Cardiff
Emeritus Professor Meic Stephens & Mrs Ruth Stephens, Caerdydd
Seán Street, The Media School, Bournemouth University
Professor Ian Stuart-Hamilton, University of Glamorgan
Stephen Stuart-Smith, London
Kim Taplin, Oxford
Val & George Thatcher, Lauragh, South Kerry
Dr Ceri Thomas, University of Glamorgan
Professor M. Wynn Thomas, CREW, Swansea University
Ned Thomas & Ceridwen Lloyd-Morgan, Aberystwyth
Jeffrey Wainwright, Manchester
Diana Wallace, University of Glamorgan
Jeff Wallace, University of Glamorgan
June Walsh, University of Glamorgan
John Powell Ward, Dartford
Daniel & Sioned Williams, Abertawe
Gareth Williams, Prifysgol Morgannwg
Archbishop Rowan Williams, Lambeth Palace
John & Pauline Young, Cardiff

Institutions
Yr Academi Gymreig/ The Welsh Academy
The David Jones Society
Enitharmon Press
The Learning Resources Centre, University of Glamorgan
The Library, Glasgow University
Seren Books

CELTIC STUDIES PUBLICATIONS
series editor: John T. Koch

CELTIC STUDIES PUBLICATIONS I

The Celtic Heroic Age: Literary Sources for Ancient Celtic Europe and Early Ireland and Wales, ed. John T. Koch with John Carey (Fourth Edition, revised and expanded, 2003) Pp. x + 440

ISBN 1–891271–09–1

CELTIC STUDIES PUBLICATIONS II

A Celtic Florilegium: Studies in Memory of Brendan O Hehir, ed. Kathryn Klar, Eve Sweetser, and †Claire Thomas (1996) Pp. xxxvi + 227

ISBN hc 0–9642446–3–2 pb 0–9642446–6–7

CELTIC STUDIES PUBLICATIONS III

A Single Ray of the Sun: Religious Speculation in Early Ireland—three essays by John Carey (Second Edition, revised 2004) Pp. viii + 123

ISBN 1–891271–12–1

CELTIC STUDIES PUBLICATIONS IV

Ildánach Ildírech. A Festschrift for Proinsias Mac Cana, ed. John Carey, John T. Koch, and Pierre-Yves Lambert (1999) Pp. xvii + 312

ISBN 1–891271–01–6

CELTIC STUDIES PUBLICATIONS V

The Inscriptions of Early Medieval Brittany/Les inscriptions de la Bretagne du Haut Moyen Âge, Wendy Davies, James Graham-Campbell, Mark Handley, Paul Kershaw, John T. Koch, Gwenaël Le Duc, Kris Lockyear (2000) Pp. xviii + 340

ISBN 1–891271–05–9

CELTIC STUDIES PUBLICATIONS VII

Yr Hen Iaith: Studies in early Welsh, ed. Paul Russell (2003) Pp. viii + 224

ISBN 1–891271–10–5

CELTIC STUDIES PUBLICATIONS VIII

Landscape Perception in Early Celtic Literature, Francesco Benozzo (2004) Pp. xvi + 272

ISBN 1–891271–11–3

CELTIC STUDIES PUBLICATIONS IX

Cín Chille Cúile—Texts, Saints and Places: Essays in Honour of Pádraig Ó Riain, ed. John Carey, Máire Herbert, and Kevin Murray (2004) Pp. xxiv + 405

ISBN 1–891271–13–X

CELTIC STUDIES PUBLICATIONS X

Archæologia Britannica: Texts and Translations, Edward Lhwyd, ed. Dewi W. Evans and Brynley F. Roberts (2007)

ISBN 978–1–891271–14–4

CELTIC STUDIES PUBLICATIONS XI

Ireland and the Grail, John Carey (2007) Pp. xxii + 421

ISBN 978–1–891271–15–1

CELTIC STUDIES PUBLICATIONS XII

An Atlas for Celtic Studies: Archaeology and Names in Ancient Europe and Early Medieval Ireland, Britain, and Brittany, John T. Koch with Raimund Karl, Antone Minard, and Simon Ó Faoláin (2007) Pp. viii + 216

ISBN 978–1–84217–309–1

CELTIC STUDIES PUBLICATIONS XIV

Moment of Earth: Poems & Essays in Honour of Jeremy Hooker, ed. Christopher Meredith (2007) Pp. xvi + 313

ISBN 978–1–891271–16–8